International Crises

INTERNATIONAL CRISES: Insights from Behavioral Research

Edited by
Charles F. Hermann

Fp The Free Press, New York
Collier-Macmillan Limited, London

THE FREE PRESS
A DIVISION OF THE MACMILLAN COMPANY
866 THIRD AVENUE, NEW YORK, NEW YORK 10022

COLLIER-MACMILLAN CANADA LTD., TORONTO, ONTARIO

Library of Congress Catalog Card Number: 74–165102

printing number
1 2 3 4 5 6 7 8 9 10

to Robert C. North

CONTENTS

Part Four: Games and Simulations of Crisis

Part Five: Coping with Crisis

Part Six: Conclusions

PREFACE

On April 7-8, 1967, a group of scholars engaged in path-breaking research on international crises participated in a symposium sponsored by Princeton University's Center for International Studies. This volume stems from papers prepared as a result of those sessions. I am grateful for the support extended by Klaus Knorr, then director of the Center, and by Cyril Black, who followed him in that post.

In addition to the contributors to this book, several other people participated directly or indirectly in the development of ideas considered at the symposium. Oran Young, who has written several major books on crisis, offered me helpful suggestions in preparing for the conference, although other commitments prevented him from attending. During the symposium, we benefited from informal discussions with two individuals who provided expertise in quite different fields, both relevant to the examination of crisis. Over an extended luncheon, Carl Hempel joined with us in considering crisis as an illustration of concept formation. He brought to our deliberations his knowledge of the scientific development of concepts through his extensive exploration of the subject as a philosopher of science. The first evening of the symposium was spent in conversation with Charles Yost, whose distinguished diplomatic career was subsequently to be expanded by his appointment as United States Ambassador to the United Nations. He shared with us the insights he had garnered from his involvement in international crises and answered numerous questions of concern to his interlocutors. Acknowledgment also should be given to Anthony Wiener of the Hudson Institute whose active participation in the symposium regrettably did not result in a chapter for this volume, but did enrich the contributions of the rest of us. The several excerpts from the transcript of the symposium that appear in this book are possible because of the technical assistance of Stephen Salmore, who subsequently aided me by reading and commenting on several chapters.

I received an International Affairs Fellowship from the Council on Foreign Relations that led to my spending a year as a staff member for the National Security Council. That opportunity delayed the editing of papers for this book which were not completed before I went to Washington. Work on the chapters that already had been finished, however, began during the first six weeks of the fellowship while arrangements for the staff appointment were being completed. Therefore, I gratefully acknowledge the Council on Foreign Relations for their support of this effort for a brief period, as well as the contributors for their patience and forbearance with an editor who temporarily disappeared in the bureaucracies of the federal government.

As with any book, the final preparation benefits from the labor of many valued associates. Robert Cantor checked references and made helpful editorial suggestions. Kay Neves typed and retyped various portions of the manuscript and maintained her cool under my insistence that "this must be done today —or tonight." My colleague and friend, James Rosenau, brought me together with the Free Press and nurtured that association. The custom of acknowledging one's spouse may mislead the reader in this instance as my wife's contribution has been far more than the usual passive support. Margaret Hermann read the entire manuscript with her professional eye and made numerous vital suggestions. As a social psychologist, who has conducted experiments on stress behavior, her ideas on that subject had considerable influence on the construction of the individual stress model presented in the concluding chapter.

As editor, I count myself fortunate to have a talented group as contributors, including individuals such as Charles McClelland and James Robinson, who were early leaders in the systematic identification and quantitative study of crises as critical phenomena in international politics. Another distinguished scholar in this category is represented indirectly by Ole Holsti and Dina Zinnes who worked closely with him at earlier points in their careers. This quiet, unassuming, intellectual powerhouse has influenced numerous students and professional colleagues, including my wife and myself, who spent a rewarding summer with his project during the first year of our graduate education. He continuously conducts a penetrating investigation of international conflict and crisis in an effort to generate the knowledge that will increase the ability of mankind to live in peace. These tireless efforts offer a model that is an inspiration to many of us. For these reasons, this book is dedicated to Robert C. North.

Charles F. Hermann
Columbus, Ohio

International Crises

part one

AN OVERVIEW OF CRISIS RESEARCH

chapter one

SOME ISSUES IN THE STUDY OF INTERNATIONAL CRISIS

Charles F. Hermann

References to crises pervade observations on the contemporary world. On the first two pages of a Sunday edition of the *New York Times*, six of the thirteen news stories mentioned crises.[1] In his memoirs, Dwight Eisenhower related that "since July 25th of 1956, when Nasser announced the nationalization of the Suez, I cannot remember a day that has not brought its major or minor crisis."[2] Former Secretary of State Dean Rusk told a Senate subcommittee that the world experienced forty-seven international political crises in the five and one half years between January 1961 and the middle of 1966.[3] A research biophysicist recently wrote in a scientific journal that the rate of change in the world is creating "a storm of crisis problems from every direction" and that in order for life as we know it to continue we must order these crises in terms of their overall impact on mankind to make certain that adequate resources are mobilized to address the most severe of these dangers.[4]

Although one could readily argue that the word *crisis* has been overused, included in the array of situations to which the term supposedly applies are events with enormous and often shattering consequences for those persons and groups experiencing them. In international politics crises most often involve governments, but in the present age a governmental crisis can quickly engulf whole societies or possibly the entire planet with the capacity to transform or destroy those involved. Given the far-reaching implications of some international crises for the future, it is not surprising that many individuals have expended considerable effort to investigate such events.

PROBLEMS IN ACCUMULATING KNOWLEDGE ABOUT CRISES

Policy makers, journalists, and academics all have undertaken descriptions and analyses of international crises. But one remarkable quality about most studies of crises has been their failure to provide cumulative knowledge about the class of events they investigate. Recollections of crises in the autobiographies of statesmen or reconstructions of events by reporters and scholars provide a more or less satisfactory interpretation of a particular crisis, but these analyses prove of limited value in understanding subsequent crises. As a given crisis recedes into

1. *New York Times*, December 8, 1968, pp. 1–2.

2. Dwight D. Eisenhower, *The White House Years*, vol. 2, *Waging Peace*, 1956–1961 (New York: Doubleday, 1965), p. 226.

3. Statement of Dean Rusk at Hearing before the Preparedness Investigating Subcommittee of the Committee on Armed Services, United States Senate, 89th Congress, 2nd sess., August 25, 1966.

4. John Platt, "What We Must Do," *Science*, 166 (November 28, 1969), 115.

history, critical attention shifts to the new, current crises. Because the accounts of former crises lack relevance for the most recent situations, new studies are prepared and substituted for the previous ones only to be replaced themselves by accounts of still other events that draw nothing from those already compiled.

At least three reasons can be offered for this state of affairs in the study of crisis. First, the prevailing mode of analysis has been the detailed case history of a single crisis. Despite the satisfaction gained by reading a thorough and well-written case study, this method of analysis makes it unnecessary for the writer to consider how the crisis under examination compares with other situations.[5] Not only is the development of empirically verifiable generalizations by the original author hampered, but the absence of parallel constructions between case studies makes it difficult for the reader of several studies to abstract hypotheses.

A second restriction limiting much of the research is that many individuals who write about crisis seem to believe in the uniqueness of every situation. At least, they find unique the combination of properties necessary to provide a satisfactory explanation of a specific event. For example, in discussing some implications of economic theory for international relations, Aron observes: "It has not yet been proven that 'crisis situations' are all alike. It is possible that each crisis is unique or, if you prefer, has its own particular story."[6] If we foster the conviction that each crisis is totally distinct from those encountered in the past and to be encountered in the future, then it is not surprising that we have little accumulated knowledge about crises.

Finally, only the vaguest common meaning appears attached to the concept of crisis. Since many analysts fail to define crisis at all, the reader is left to infer from the context that the situation concerns some "critical" or "urgent" problem. In the attempt to call attention to every important issue, we suffer from the indiscriminate use of the term *crisis*.

These inhibitions in the study of crises must be overcome if we are to develop any knowledge about crises as a class of events. The kind of knowledge that both policy makers and scholars might reasonably be expected to want about international crises includes the answer to such questions as the following: When do crises lead to war or otherwise drastically alter the system in which they occur? As compared to noncrises do participants in a crisis behave more or less rationally—that is, behave so as to maximize their likelihood of obtaining desired goals? How can crises be averted? Can potential crises be detected in advance? Once a crisis occurs, how can it be managed? When can crises be used as opportunities to gain political, military, or economic advantage? Under what conditions can a crisis be settled peacefully? When, and with what degree of certainty, is one crisis likely to manifest the same features as some previous one? Can the concept of crisis be usefully incorporated into theories accounting for a broad range of human behavior?

5. Insightful statements concerning the problems of case studies can be found in Glenn D. Paige, *The Korean Decision* (New York: The Free Press, 1968), chap. 1; and James N. Rosenau, "Moral Fervor, Systematic Analysis, and Scientific Consciousness in Foreign Policy Research," in Austin Ranney, ed., *Political Science and Public Policy* (Chicago: Markham, 1968), chap. 9.

6. Raymond Aron, "What Is a Theory of International Relations?" *Journal of International Affairs*, 21, no. 2 (1967), 188.

Despite the weaknesses that limit the ability of many crisis studies to provide the beginnings of answers to such questions, there has been a small but growing body of research applying the methods of scientific inquiry to the investigation of international crises. This research involves such activities as delimiting and operationalizing the variables to be examined, identifying empirically testable hypotheses, using various techniques to obtain reproducible evidence that supports or refutes the hypotheses, and searching for more general theories to which specific hypotheses might be fitted. Among those social and behavioral scientists who employ scientific methods in their research and who actively engage in the study of international politics, crisis has received considerable attention. The total number of individuals engaged in the scientific study of crisis, however, remains relatively small and for the most part they have worked in isolation from one another. The Princeton Symposium on International Crises, which ultimately led to this volume, was called to bring some of these scholars—but by no means all of them—together to discuss each other's work and to assess the general state of research and knowledge on crisis.

The discussions at the symposium and the papers that resulted from it have definite implications for the three problems in the study of crisis mentioned earlier. For example, the authors of several chapters address the problem of the isolated case study of crisis. Comparative studies of two or more crises—which oblige the authors to consider the similarities and the differences between different situations—replace single case analyses. Moreover, in chapter after chapter the authors derive explicit hypotheses from their case studies that can be applied to other crises, thus contributing to the accumulation of knowledge.

Although none of the following chapters deals explicitly with the argument that each crisis can be understood only if treated as a unique phenomenon, their common emphasis on the discovery of more general patterns applicable to various crises permits us to infer their position. The authors appear to reject the contention that the only meaningful statements about crisis are those tailored exclusively to one and only one specific situation.

Every situation is novel when all its properties are considered. Even two simple situations—one a carefully executed replication of the other—differ in numerous ways. Between these occurrences, time will have elapsed. The earth and solar system will have moved. Human actors will be older and will have had intervening experiences. Given the novelty of simple, controlled situations, it is clear that countless differences exist between two complex international events such as the Berlin blockade of 1948 and Khrushchev's ultimatum on Berlin in 1958. Man would be unable to cope with his daily existence, however, if he did not treat most new situations as comparable to some situations he has met or learned about in the past. For purposes of evaluation and action, all humans categorize events according to a limited number of properties and ignore the rest. The adequacy of a response to a situation will depend, in part, upon the quality of the classifying categories and our ability to correctly recognize the situation as a member of a class of events. Having established how the present circumstances are related to some already experienced, man can bring the success or failure of past responses to bear on his present action. Of course, explanation and action are not the same; nor are the simple situations of daily living similar to the complex ones of international events. Nevertheless, if we correctly recognize a few critical properties of an international situation which identify it as a member of a general set of situations, we may establish numerous things about it even without examining many other qualities that make it unique.[7]

DEFINITIONS OF CRISIS

The utility of considering crises as a class of phenomena with some shared properties that have implications for other aspects of those situations depends upon how the concept is defined. Definition brings us to the third problem in the study of crisis mentioned earlier. As the following chapters reveal, the symposium members reached no complete consensus on this issue although they wrestled with it from the first moments of the meeting. The participants recognized that the definition of crisis was intertwined with a number of issues, including the general theoretical perspective and kinds of questions with which any research is concerned. At the first session of the symposium, during the discussion of an earlier version of James Robinson's paper (now Chapter 2), the issue of definition quickly surfaced. The reader will find much of interest in the exchanges on this issue as the participants in their first encounter with one another struggled to describe and clarify positions. For this reason a major portion is reproduced below with minimal editorial correction (and without any subsequent modifications by the participants themselves who may now hold different views or might wish to state them differently). The reproduced section of the extemporaneous dialogue begins with Charles McClelland speaking about the absence of a systemic perspective in the Robinson paper.

> CHARLES A. MCCLELLAND: *What I find missing here, of course, is my own preoccupation, that is, a view of crisis as an unusual manifestation of the interflow of activity between the participants. In other words, there is, I believe, a very specific perspective or point of view, that looks at the whole interplay as if it were traffic, which I do. The general idea I want to get over is that at least there are two, if not ten, basic perspectives* [*on crisis*]. *One is the viewpoint toward the participant—what he does, how he feels, how he responds to messages, and all that sort of thing. There is another which looks on the whole configuration of parties participating back and forth.*
>
> JAMES A. ROBINSON: *I think your point is well taken, and I do recognize the important distinction between confining oneself to the perceptions of members of the intra-national unit as contrasted with objective and system considerations. I wonder if we should discuss what differences there are in these approaches to crisis and what implications these differences have for theorizing about crisis.*
>
> MCCLELLAND: *Well, I think first of all, the difference is the difference in the conceptualization of the subject matter. And this is a great big difference. If you think of the work on Korea by* [*Glenn*] *Paige concerning the decisions by American policy makers during those days in June 1950, the first question*

7. Of course, policy makers can get into serious trouble by the misclassification of events. See Arthur M. Schlesinger, Jr.'s *The Bitter Heritage* (Boston: Houghton Mifflin, 1967). The problem of situation recognition and classification is somewhat different for the art of policy making than it is for the development of a science of politics. In the latter case new situations provide an opportunity for hypothesis testing and refinement of categories, whereas in the former an unfamiliar situation introduces the risk of a policy misfortune.

is: Is that the entire crisis? And that question introduces at least issues of definitions, preconceptions, and original starting points for the study of crisis. Depending upon your answers, you just simply get different kinds of material involved, it seems to me.

HOWARD H. LENTNER: *There would not be a crisis for the decision-making unit if there weren't something out there. And so, there must be some relationship between the two* [*approaches*]. *I would also suggest that there is, perhaps, even another kind of focus which links the two. That additional perspective has to do with the bargaining process in the crisis. In one sense bargaining brings in decision making and also this systemic business.*

MCCLELLAND: *Conceptually, it seems to me that* [*crisis*] *interaction is likely to be in terms of* [*effects on the*] *stability or equilibrium of the system, or disturbance of the normal run of business conducted between actors. It is quite clear that this systemic-level activity becomes the external input to the decisional group and the link between the approaches is obviously there. But it is a difference, I should think—a very big difference—as to how both ideas and data get organized in the systemic and decision-making approaches to crisis.*

GLENN H. SNYDER: *I was just going to quote Charles McClelland himself where he makes the point that interaction analysis provides the answer to the "what", if you will; whereas, when you are in a decision-making mode of analysis it provides the "why"—why the actors move as they did on specific occasions.*

MCCLELLAND: *Well, that's from* [*Richard C.*] *Snyder; where he got it, I don't know. I think a lot of "why" questions might well be answered in other than decision-making terms. When you say, for example, "Why won't my car work?" Well, there are all sorts of approximations to the answer of why my car won't work. Some of these tend to be internal and some of them tend to be external.*

DAVID C. SCHWARTZ: *It seems to me that consideration of the difference between the McClelland approach, as I read it, and some of the decision-making studies does not call for defensive statements that seek to establish the legitimacy of each approach but rather for questions about where do we go from here. Specifically, we should be asking which of those interactions that constitute an operational definition of crisis in McClelland's terms gets perceived by decision makers and with what effect. Similarly, which of these systemic factors act as constraints irrespective of what the decision maker sees?*

ROBINSON: *Howard's* [*Lentner*] *paper is relevant here. It seems to me we have these two situations to investigate. One is what difference does it make if the decision makers call it a crisis or don't call it a crisis. It may be that recognizing it—or labeling it as such—affects their behavior; in which case, of course, it's important to know how they use the term. If they don't use the term, what are the functional substitutes for it? On the other hand—and this is where I plug into Charles'* [*McClelland*] *work, and why I think that it's valuable—if you take a functional definition, it doesn't make any difference what they call it at all. What you are concerned about is whether certain characteristics inhere in the situation. If those characteristics are present, then you consider their effect on some dependent variables.*

Thus it would be interesting to me to take the quantitative material that McClelland turns out and say: Here is a situation having a high information loading, changes in traffic volume, or whatever properties you use to identify a crisis. And then ask of these high-load situations: What are the implications of these properties for decision processes or whatever other variables might be of interest? It does seem to me, his [Charles McClelland's] conception of crisis has the merit of avoiding having to know what was in the decision maker's mind. You just take it for granted that you've got a crisis if you meet McClelland's operational definition.

OLE R. HOLSTI: *What criteria would you want to use for identifying the kinds of situations you want to include as crises? That is, presumably there are some events that you would put your bets on right now as the kind of situations you'd want to look at. How would you, in a preliminary way, define these?*

MCCLELLAND: *I think the ideal way would be to have for an extended period of time—say, for two centuries—a complete running record of the traffic or interactions between nations. And then, you see, it would be merely a matter of watching the flows and deciding that the sharp fluctuations were crises.*

CHARLES F. HERMANN: *Let me build on that by calling your attention to the definition of crisis by Oran Young, an absent colleague, who takes the systemic perspective in addition to McClelland and others. Young states that "crisis refers to situations which have important implications for the stability for some pattern of interaction, system, or subsystem. Crises are in no sense limited to situations which actively jeopardize the stability of the international system, but they do raise certain considerations concerning stability. To begin with, stability refers here to the ability of a system or pattern of interactions to undergo a disruptive sequence of events without breaking down or suffering qualitative changes of nature."*[8] *It seems to me that in addition to asking how does crisis affect decision making, or what are its consequences for individuals or groups of policy makers, the question can be asked: What are the consequences for the international system? And maybe we haven't been properly attentive to this.*

ANTHONY J. WIENER: *I'm really very surprised at the suggestion that we focus on the international system, just as I am surprised that Chuck [Hermann] calls our attention to Oran Young's definition. It seems to me we really practically never talk about crisis in the international system, as such. We don't really talk about international crises. We talk about crises in national subsystems of the international system which are brought on by inputs from the international system. And then, once we are talking about a national crisis stemming from international relations, we may talk about the two linked subsystems and their communication. Are we really in a position to discuss the international system, which several times during the last two centuries changed its configuration very radically, and to talk in general terms about crises in that context, or are we really talking primarily about the U.S. national crises and sometimes some other nation?*

LENTNER: *Of course, 1914 is an international crisis system.*

8. This definition of crisis by Oran R. Young appeared in an unpublished working paper. He subsequently revised and expanded his definition in his *The Politics of Force* (Princeton: Princeton University Press, 1968), pp. 6–15.

WIENER: *We know something about the balance-of-power system and the breakdown of that system, but that is almost a special case. Is it comparable to the others?*

HOLSTI: *The question you are really raising is that if you use this kind of definition, then you only pick presumably those situations which have a visible impact on the configuration of the system. And maybe you are excluding an awful lot.*

WIENER: *And you would exclude most of the cases we have.*

HERMANN: *Well, I gather that what Tony* [*Wiener*] *is arguing is that the difference* [*between systemic and foreign policy crisis definitions*] *is maybe not as great as definitions like Oran's* [*Young*] *suggest. In other words, maybe there is more of a commonality in concerns than if you really were interested in asking what are the consequences for the international system. McClelland is still interested in asking essentially questions about the impact on national actors. But looking at this through interaction data. He's not asking, as I read it, as many questions about the consequences for the international system qua system.*

HOLSTI: [addressing McClelland] *You have a far less restricted definition of crisis because you are presumably interested in situations other than those that have a sharp impact on the system. Right?*

MCCLELLAND: *A crisis can exist for certain relationships within an international system at a given time involving a sharp confrontation, a short, violent interaction—but still not destroy a particular set of relationships existing at a given time. You don't have to insist on an upset in the system every time you have a crisis.*

SCHWARTZ: *If you are concerned with system change, I would suggest that you would be very badly advised to define crises so restrictively as only to look at those cases in which an international crisis, however defined, changes the system, for two reasons. One, you would obviate the possibility of making observations about those changes which are incremental, which occur for nonpolitical reasons over great lengths of time.*

WIENER: *But would they be crises, though?*

SCHWARTZ: *No, but if you are interested in explaining system change, they would be system changes. Second, it would be inappropriate to restrictively define crises because you would be unable to compare such system-changing crises with crises which somehow did not result in major transformations of the rules by which nations interact with one another. And what would be exciting, really, is to know the difference* [*between system-changing and non-system-changing crises*]. *We should search for a "transition rule" to distinguish a crisis which profoundly affects nations as against a crisis which does not change the nations' interactions.*

SYSTEMIC AND DECISION-MAKING PERSPECTIVES[9]

The preceding excerpt touched upon a number of important issues—distinctions between crisis defined in terms of the policy makers' perceptions as opposed to

9. Some of the following material is reproduced with the permission of The Free Press from my article, "International Crisis as a Situational Variable" which appeared in James N. Rosenau, ed., *International Politics and Foreign Policy*, rev. ed. (New York: The Free Press, 1969), pp. 411–416.

indicators used by independent observers, possible distinctions between the decision-making and systemic definitions of crisis (e.g., the kinds of questions asked and data collected), possible linkages between the two approaches to crisis (e.g., through bargaining or the use of systemic crisis data as inputs for decision makers' crises), whether any analyses are performed on crises affecting the entire international system, and whether such crises must transform the system. The discussions at the symposium led the editor to reflect further on the implications for crisis studies of the systemic and decision-making approaches. Because the distinction runs through this book like a thread, further consideration of some implications of these two perspectives seems appropriate.

We shall stipulate that a system is a set of actors (e.g., nations, international organizations, and so on) interacting with one another in established patterns and through designated structures. In any given international political system, critical variables must be maintained within certain limits or the instability of the system will be greatly increased—perhaps to the point where a new system will be formed. A crisis is a situation which disrupts the system or some part of the system (i.e., a subsystem such as an alliance or an individual actor). More specifically, a crisis is a situation that creates an abrupt or sudden change in one or more of the basic systemic variables.

In the present international system, the existing military relationships depend in part on the relative superiority of the strategic weapon systems of the two superpowers and their deterrence capabilities with respect to each other. A sudden change in one of the superpowers' ability to deter the other would constitute a crisis for the system. The deterrence crisis might not transform the system or the subsystem comprised of the Soviet Union and the United States, but it has the potential to do so.

The characterization of crisis from the systemic approach suggests the relationship of the concept to such terms as *change* and *conflict*. Because crises engage one or more of the critical variables necessary to maintain the existing pattern of relationships between actors, they necessarily can effect significant changes in the international system. Whether or not a crisis actually produces significant change depends on a number of factors such as the nature of the modified variables, the existing destabilizing factors, and the available techniques for crisis management. Thus, in the editor's view, the suggestion that systemic crises must involve transformation of the system is misleading. What is required is that the crisis have the potential of system change. Just as not all crises lead to important changes, not all significant changes are crises. A gradual shift in the rate of exchange between nations could ultimately have a profound effect on the system, despite only small increments of change at any given point in time. The association of crisis with abrupt change also bears on its relationship to conflict. A conflict between parties that continues at a relatively constant level of intensity would not constitute a crisis, but a sudden shift in the level of hostilities—most notably from peace to war—would be a crisis at least for the subsystem comprised of the combatants.

Although the proposed systemic definition of crisis has been an arbitrary one, it is consistent with much of the writing about crisis from a systemic perspective. Thus crisis has been described as "intensive inputs to the international system . . . unbalancing stabilities,"[10] or as "some kind of boundary or

10. Jan F. Triska and David D. Finley, *Soviet Foreign Policy* (New York: The Macmillan Company, 1968), p. 317.

turning point,"[11] or as "involving significant actual or potential international conflict in either a novel form or at an abruptly changing level."[12] One of the more complete systemic definitions of crisis is offered by Young: "An international crisis, then, is a set of rapidly unfolding events which raises the impact of destabilizing forces in the general international system or any of its subsystems substantially above 'normal' (i.e., average) levels and increases the likelihood of violence occurring in the system."[13] An abrupt increase in the likelihood of international violence or war is the most common systemic definition of crisis in the remainder of this volume.

If a class of crisis situations can be operationally defined from the guidelines discussed above, what contribution might this variable make to the analysis of international political systems? The structures and processes that maintain an international system may be more or less subject to the sudden stresses imposed by crisis. The question then arises as to what structures and processes are most "sensitive" to crisis situations. Sensitivity can vary in several ways, including the tendency for some parts of the system to be more frequently exposed to crises. For example, interactions between actors who seek alterations in their international status are more prone to crises than interactions between actors who have accepted their status positions. Sensitivity also develops because some elements of a system can vary less than others without exceeding critical thresholds. For example, a system may be able to withstand considerably greater variation in the degree of conflict between smaller states than it can between major states. Essentially, these questions concern the effect of crisis on system stability and transformation.

Because international systems differ, the impact of crisis can be expected to vary according to the type of system. This observation leads to such research questions as: Does the nature of the international system influence the frequency with which crises occur? Are certain systems better structured to allow policy makers to cope with crises without destroying the system? According to Waltz, one "distinguishing factor in the bipolar balance, as we thus far know it, is the nearly constant presence of pressure and the recurrence of crises."[14] In addition to finding crises more frequent in a bipolar system than in a multipolar system, Waltz also contends that in a multipolar world a nation's policy makers can create a crisis to further their objectives with the hope that opponents of the change will not coalesce in opposition. In a bipolar system the permanency of opposing polar powers greatly increases the probability that any move to initiate a crisis will be countered.[15] Thus two relevant hypotheses from the Waltz study are that the type of international system influences (1) the rate with which

11. Kenneth E. Boulding, *Conflict and Defense* (New York: Harper & Row, 1963), Torchbook edition, p. 250.

12. Anthony J. Wiener and Herman Kahn, eds., *Crisis and Arms Control*, Hudson Institute, Advanced Research Projects Agency Contract no. SD-105, October 9, 1962, p. 12.

13. Oran R. Young, *The Intermediaries: Third Parties in International Crisis* (Princeton: Princeton University Press, 1967), p. 10.

14. Kenneth N. Waltz, "The Stability of a Bipolar World," *Daedalus*, 93, no. 3 (1964), p. 883.

15. It is interesting to note in this context that one of the polar powers in the present system, the United States, was directly or indirectly involved in one-third of the forty-eight crises mentioned by Secretary Rusk. See footnote 3.

crises occur, and (2) the probability of direct confrontations between actors when any actor attempts to abruptly change significant systemic variables.

Conflicting hypotheses exist concerning the systemic consequences of numerous crises. Wright contends that the probability of war in a given period of time increases with the frequency of crises.[16] McClelland and Waltz make the counter-hypothesis although they use different arguments.[17] The nature of a given international system may be introduced as a mediating variable to resolve this apparent contradiction. In some inherently unstable systems the appearance of a single crisis might trigger war. In other systems with effective regulatory mechanisms, crises might be repeatedly managed without resort to war. The availability to both the Soviet Union and the United States of a tremendous destructive capability that can be applied even after absorbing an initial nuclear attack may serve as such a regulator of crisis effects in the present international system.

These questions and hypotheses are only a few that might be examined using crisis as a systemic variable. As the symposium discussion suggested, however, few empirical studies have been designed to investigate issues of this type which concern the entire international system. Authors with commitment to the systemic framework tend to examine the interaction of a subsystem in a single crisis.[18] The inspection of subsystem interaction or even a single national actor, treated as a system component, undoubtedly can yield important insights into the nature of crisis. But the effect of crisis on the relations within an alliance or between two adversaries may be quite different from the effect of that same crisis on the overall system. A specific crisis may drastically alter a subsystem without having any destabilizing consequences for the total international system.

An alternative perspective to the systems approach for conceptualizing crisis is decision making. As the name suggests, central to the decision-making approach is the process by which decisions are made on questions of policy. Also basic to this organizing framework are the persons who, as individuals or in some collective form, constitute the authoritative decision makers. The decision makers behave according to their interpretation of the situation, not according to its "objective" character as viewed by some theoretical omnipotent

16. Quincy Wright, *A Study of War*, 2nd ed. (Chicago: University of Chicago Press, 1965), p. 1272.

17. Charles McClelland proposes that experience is gained with the management of each crisis; therefore, policy makers cope more successfully with subsequent crises. See his "The Acute International Crisis," *World Politics*, 14, no. 1 (1961), 187–188. Kenneth Waltz suggests that if continuing hostility exists between two parties, crises may become a substitute for war ("Stability of Bipolar World," p. 884). Raymond Aron notes a "trend toward the diminution of the force used" in direct crises between the Soviet Union and the United States, but he does not speculate that this pattern could be generalized to all parties experiencing repeated crises. See his *Peace and War*, translated by R. Howard and A. B. Fox (Garden City, N.Y.: Doubleday, 1966), p. 565.

18. Examples of subsystem crisis studies are William P. Davison, *The Berlin Blockade* (Princeton: Princeton University Press, 1958); Charles A. McClelland, "Decisional Opportunity and Political Controversy: The Quemoy Case," *Journal of Conflict Resolution*, 6, no. 3 (1962), 201–213. Albert Wohlstetter and Roberta Wohlstetter, *Controlling the Risks in Cuba*, Adelphi Paper no. 17, Institute for Strategic Studies (London), April 1965.

observer.[19] Therefore, in attempting to explain how different kinds of situations influence the type of choice that is made, the analyst must interpret the situation as it is perceived by the decision makers.

The use of crisis as a situational variable which increases the likelihood of a certain kind of decision by the policy makers is not unlike the stimulus-response model familiar to psychologists. Crisis acts as a stimulus; the decision represents a response. In the usual experimental application of this model, the researcher varies an event or condition which is used to account for any observed variation in the respondent's behavior. Applying this model to the interaction between policy makers of two nation-states, several political scientists expanded the paradigm to include (1) the stimulus or actual policy of the initiating state, (2) the perception of that stimulus by the decision makers in the recipient state, (3) the response or actual reply of the recipient state, and (4) the perception of that response by the decision makers in the initiating state.[20] As in this modification of the stimulus-response model, the definition of crisis required by the decision-making approach must take into account the screening processes of human perceptions.

Those analysts who have studied crisis using the decision-making framework display no more agreement regarding the definition of crisis than do their counterparts who have applied the systemic approach. As before, we stipulate a definition which delimits a class of situations and contains some of the properties frequently associated with crisis. Specifically, a crisis is a situation that (1) threatens high-priority goals of the decision-making unit, (2) restricts the amount of time available for response before the decision is transformed, and (3) surprises the members of the decision-making unit by its occurrence. Threat, time, and surprise all have been cited as traits of crisis,[21] although until recently all three properties have not been combined. Underlying the proposed definition is the hypothesis that if all three traits are present then the decision process will be substantially different than if only one or two of the characteristics appear. Contained in the set of events specified by this definition are many that observers commonly refer to as crises for American policy makers—for example, the 1950 decision to defend South Korea, the 1962 Cuban missile episode, and the 1965 decision to send marines to the Dominican Republic. But other situations would not be considered crises for policy makers in the United States—the 1958 ultimatum on Berlin, the extended Greek–Turkish–Cypriot dispute, and the mission in 1964 to rescue Europeans in Stanleyville (Congo) are illustrative in this regard. The exclusion of these and other situations that do not contain at least one of the three traits does not deny the importance of these situations or the significant consequences of the resulting decisions. The classification of them as noncrises simply indicates that these situations may be different with respect to the decision process in some systematic ways from those included in the crisis set.

19. Harold and Margaret Sprout are among those who have carefully explicated this point. See their *The Ecological Perspective on Human Affairs* (Princeton: Princeton University Press, 1965), especially pp. 28–30.

20. Ole R. Holsti, Richard A. Brody, and Robert C. North, "Affect and Action in International Reaction Models," *Journal of Peace Research*, no. 3–4 (1964), 170–190.

21. See the review of these traits in Charles F. Hermann, "Some Consequences of Crisis Which Limit the Viability of Organizations," *Administrative Science Quarterly*, 8, no. 1 (1963), 61–82, and Charles F. Hermann, *Crises in Foreign Policy: A Simulation Analysis* (Indianapolis: Bobbs-Merrill, 1969).

Because situations differ in their degree of threat, in their duration through time, and in their amount of surprise, each of the three traits that define a crisis can be conceived as one extreme on a dimension with scale positions for every possible quantity of each property. When taken together at right angles, these

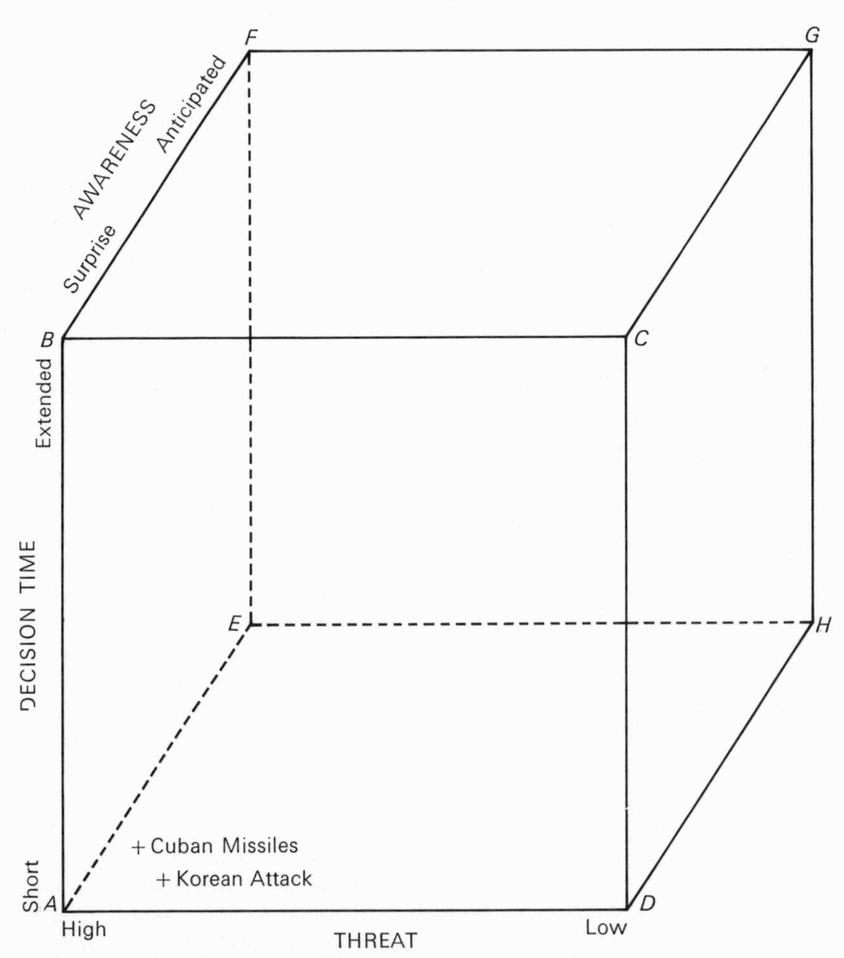

FIGURE 1. A situational cube representing the three dimensions of threat, decision time, and awareness with illustrative situations from the perspective of American decision makers. (*Note*: The representation of a three-dimensional space in a two-dimensional diagram makes it difficult to interpret the locations of the situations; their positions should not be considered exact in any case.)

A. Crisis Situation
High Threat/Short Time/Surprise
B. Innovative Situation
High Threat/Extended Time/Surprise
C. Inertial Situation
Low Threat/Extended Time/Surprise
D. Circumstantial Situation
Low Threat/Short Time/Surprise
E. Reflexive Situation
High Threat/Short Time/Anticipated
F. Deliberative Situation
High Threat/Extended Time/Anticipated
G. Routinized Situation
Low Threat/Extended Time/Anticipated
H. Administrative Situation
Low Threat/Short Time /Anticipated

three scales form a three-dimensional space in which all situations can be located according to their degree of threat, time, and awareness (surprise).[22] In Figure 1 this space has been closed to form a cube, the eight corners of which represent all possible combinations of the extreme values of the three dimensions. Thus the corners of the cube represent ideal types of situations with respect to threat, time, and awareness. Few, if any, actual situations can be considered to correspond to these ideal types, but as the location in the cube of a specific situation approaches one of the corners, that situation can be treated as influencing decision making in a manner similar to the ideal type.

To illustrate the location of a situation along a dimension, consider the element of decision time in both the Korean crisis of 1950 and the Cuban crisis of 1962. As the South Korean army crumbled before the North Korean advance, the initial optimism of American decision makers changed to a realization that unless the United States intervened quickly the invaders would control the entire peninsula. The first meeting with the President to discuss the Korean situation occurred on Sunday evening, June 25. After a series of steps taken in the next several days to support the faltering South Korean army, President Truman decided early Friday morning, June 30, to commit American ground forces. Although Truman and his advisers considered the time available to them to be extremely short, other situations such as the response to be made upon detection of a launched ballistic missile attack could offer even less time for decision. Thus on the time dimension the Korean decision would be located near the short time end of the scale, but not at the most extreme point. The Cuban missile crisis also presented short decision time because, as the American policy makers observed, once the missiles were operational they would be extremely difficult to remove without the possibility that some of them would be launched in retaliation. With missiles prepared for firing, the situation facing the leaders of the United States would be drastically altered. The first presidential session on that crisis occurred on the morning of Tuesday, October 26; the following Tuesday, President Kennedy issued the "Proclamation of the Interdiction of Offensive Weapons" ordering the blockade to begin the next morning. In actual time the decision in the missile crisis was more extended than that in the Korean crisis. If the decision makers' perceptions of available time are used, some evidence indicates that the Korean crisis as compared to the Cuban crisis involved even less time than estimates based on clock or calendar. Despite these differences, the perceived time for both decisions puts them near the extreme of short time and both decision processes could be expected to bear resemblance to ideal type situations involving short decision time.

The effects of a crisis on decision making can be compared with the hypothesized consequences of situations that approach the ideal types represented by the other seven corners of the cube in Figure 1. Examples of the eight kinds of situations—crisis, innovative, inertial, circumstantial, reflexive, deliberative, routinized, and administrative situations—have been presented elsewhere together with propositions about the implications of each situation for the decision

22. We shall use surprise as one extreme on an awareness dimension in order to permit a construction parallel to that for threat and time. Thus the complete absence of awareness is surprise; the other extreme is anticipation. Because awareness refers to a condition of the decision maker (i.e., his perception), the term is less satisfactory when one deals with the observers' estimation of the properties present in the situation.

process.[23] Other aspects of the decision-making perspective as it applies to crisis are examined by James Robinson in Chapter 2.

THE NATURE OF THIS BOOK

This book continues the examination of the issues originally considered at the symposium. Here, as at the Princeton symposium, the purpose is to bring together in one place representatives of the advanced research on the study of international crisis disposed to the application of the methods of science. We looked for shared problems, areas in need of further inquiry, implications for our own work that may exist in what others have done, and an assessment of the present status of knowledge on international crisis that may be of use to others. Some chapters in this volume restate and extend previously reported inquiries of the authors; others represent totally new undertakings. The editor felt that all were necessary to present an overview of current research.

Admittedly, the scientific analysis of crisis has only begun, as the authors of this book would readily admit. More attention is paid to concept formation, simple empirical mapping, and hypothesis generation than to hypothesis testing and theory development. Methodologically, the techniques employed in this volume reflect considerable variation both in terms of the extent to which the methods have been developed and the length of experience of the author with the technique he applies. Taken as a whole, the state of the methodological advance found in crisis research, such as reported here, depends on one's perspective. Looking back, it appears that we have come some considerable way; looking ahead, it is evident that a long road remains ahead of us in increasing our methodological skills and in improving the fit between methodologies and substance.

In reading through the chapters in this volume, one discovers certain recurrent issues or themes—sometimes stated or approached in different ways that may momentarily hide the underlying commonality of concern. Among these issues is the question of the definition of crisis which we have already discussed. Another issue, related to the question of definition, is the differentiation of crisis from noncrisis. How can you detect a crisis? How does it differ from other situations? An extension of that concern manifests itself in the effort to differentiate stages or phases of a crisis. For example, one might discover that there are periods when escalation is most rapid or when bargaining meets with more likelihood of success. Various authors examine the relationship of crisis to other international phenomena such as war, conflict, and threat. Others seek to explore the linkage between crisis and concepts—such as individual stress—for which considerable data exists in other fields. The conditions precipitating crises and the consequences that follow from them occupy attention in a number of chapters. As Robinson notes at the end of Chapter 2, one form of the debate on the consequences of crisis is whether they promote pathological or beneficial effects. Among the beneficial effects of crisis that have been noted are its tendency to serve as a substitute for war, to promote innovation and collaboration, to foster decision, to increase group cohesion, and to attract the attention and interest of the most able actors to previously ignored problems. The other side of the coin sees crisis as increasing the probability of war, making conservative

23. See Charles F. Hermann, "International Crisis as a Situational Variable."

behavior more likely, producing system disorder and instability, and increasing nonrational and affective behavior that reduces the ability of men to make wise decisions.

This book is organized into six parts. This chapter, together with the following one, provides an introduction and an overview to the contemporary study of international crises. In the second section, three chapters report comparative case studies of selected crises. Part III contains two chapters that consider crisis from the perspective of the policy makers—one of the issues we have touched upon in this introduction. The authors of Chapters 8 and 9 in Part IV apply a widely used technique for studying crises—games and simulations. In Part V the authors deal with means of coping with crises and thus provide chapters that may be of particular interest to those who face such situations. In the concluding section of the book (Part VI), we abstract hypotheses from all the preceding chapters and attempt to suggest some models of crisis into which the propositions may be fitted. Of course, a number of alternative ways of organizing this book are possible which would give emphasis to other similarities or differences between the contributions. In an effort to highlight some of these other features and to underscore the distinctive contribution of each chapter to the larger mosaic, the editor has written an introduction to each subsequent chapter other than the concluding one.

chapter two

EDITOR'S INTRODUCTION

As readers of the previous chapter know, an earlier version of Robinson's review of the crisis literature stirred a lively discussion at the Symposium that led to this volume. The exchange in Chapter 1 concerned the emphasis Robinson places in the present chapter on the decision-making approach for the study of crisis. The author's commitment appears in his assessment of alternative formulations of the concept of crisis and in his preference for the definition he developed jointly with the editor. (See Chapter 9 for an empirical investigation of some effects of this definition.) Although that definition—which lends itself to a decision-making perspective—proved compatible with the research interests of some contributors, others found that it neglected what they regarded as salient qualities of any crisis. In any event this chapter highlights the necessity of assigning specific meaning to the concept of crisis and illustrates the implications of one such definition.

The essay also raises fundamental questions about the utility of the concept of crisis in international politics—or any other area—unless it is an integral part of a theory. As Robinson makes clear in the present chapter, he found little evidence that crisis plays a significant part in any existing formal theory. The conferees discussed this topic extensively. Some points in contention can be grasped by examining excerpts of an exchange between Robinson and Dina Zinnes in which the role of crisis in the theory of games was used to illustrate the broader issue.

> DINA A. ZINNES: *I would like to say one thing on this notion of game theory not contributing much to the notion of crisis. That's sort of like saying content analysis or Markov chains haven't done much for the notion of crisis. . . . Really, what you are questioning is that the studies that have been done thus far have not utilized this technique* [*game theory*] *to explore crisis. But it could very easily be done.*
>
> JAMES A. ROBINSON: *If you start out saying you are going to review the concept of crisis in decision making . . . it seems to me you have to look at the major decision theories, so to speak, and say: Do they use the concept? If they do, what do they have to say about it? When I did this* [*paper*] *I had just spent a good deal of time looking at some decision theories, like the theory of games. I was struck by the absence of it* [*crisis*].
>
> ZINNES: *But you don't mean the theory of games, do you? You mean the* [*absence of*] *studies utilizing game theory. . . . You don't mean Von Neumann and Morgenstern?* [*John Von Neumann and Oskar Morgenstern, the authors of* Theory of Games and Economic Behavior]
>
> ROBINSON: *I mean Von Neumann and Morgenstern do not make a place for crisis.*
>
> ZINNES: *Well, that doesn't make sense in my terminology.*
>
> ROBINSON: *If someone can derive it* [*crisis*], *fine. It hasn't been done yet.*
>
> ZINNES: *But these things are in different dimensions altogether. To say that they haven't made room for crisis and . . . .*

ROBINSON: *It's not a criticism, it's just saying if you want to study crisis decision making, don't look at the theory of games.*

ZINNES: *Well, it's just that these are techniques, or shall I call them "substance-free" or something of the sort. They are branches of mathematics. I think it's really a terminological problem, and I don't think there is any basic disagreement. I think the difficulty is that you are using a term, game theory, in a way which I would prefer you not use it. It would be as if you said, "Algebra doesn't hold much for understanding crises." That's neither here nor there. If one had a hypothesis, one might be able to use algebra, or might be able to use game theory, or might be able to use certain concepts of these techniques.*

ROBINSON: *Maybe so, but let me just explain autobiographically how I came to this point. What political scientists mean by decision-making theory is different from what other social scientists mean by decision theory. Agreed? So, when I read that other literature to see what I could find that would be of use to people interested in crisis (as of whatever day I terminated my review of the literature), I just didn't find it there. Now I should be sure that it* [*the present chapter*] *doesn't say crisis can't be derived, or a creative mind using decision theory can't find a place for crisis.*

In addition to highlighting the issues about the definition of crisis and its theoretical relevance, Robinson challenges the widely held assertion that crises are almost totally bad. Hypotheses that indicate what are usually regarded as undesirable consequences of crises are scattered throughout subsequent chapters in this book. It may be that the positive functions of crisis have less often been recognized. The general problem of the value of crises receives further evaluation in Thomas Milburn's chapter on crisis management (Chapter 11). In brief, the reader will find in this chapter not merely a descriptive review of the crisis literature, but a selective examination and critical evaluation of certain basic problems that must be addressed by anyone who wishes to use crisis as a concept with both theoretical and empirical import.

James A. Robinson is well qualified to undertake the difficult task of reviewing research on crisis. Through his study of decision making, Robinson became interested in crises as "occasions for decision."[1] After preparing an article entitled "The Concept of Crisis in Decision Making,"[2] he received a contract from the U.S. Navy for the study of crisis through simulation.[3] The author has reviewed the research on crisis on several occasions as he mentions in the chapter's initial footnote. At the time the article was prepared, James A. Robinson was Director of the Mershon Center for Education in National Security at the Ohio State University. Later as Provost and Academic Vice President of Ohio State he had occasion to apply his theorizing about crises to the academic turmoils of Spring, 1970. He is now President of Macalester College.

1. For development of this formulation see his article with Richard C. Snyder, "Decision-Making in International Politics," in Herbert C. Kelman, ed., *International Behavior* (New York: Holt, Rinehart & Winston, 1965), especially pages 440–443.

2. The article appeared in *Series Studies in Social and Economic Sciences*, no. 11 (Washington, D.C.: National Institute of Social and Behavioral Science, 1962).

3. Part of the resulting research is reported in James A. Robinson, Charles F. Hermann, and Margaret G. Hermann, "Search Under Crisis in Political Gaming and Simulation," in Dean G. Pruitt and Richard C. Snyder, eds., *Theory and Research on the Causes of War* (Englewood Cliffs, N.J.: Prentice-Hall, 1969), pp. 80–94.

chapter two

CRISIS: AN APPRAISAL OF CONCEPTS AND THEORIES*

James A. Robinson

The ordinary use of the term *crisis* usually implies an important situation or a violent or potentially violent one. The tendency to extend the meaning of the term to embrace a wide range of situations is understandable in informal or in exploratory analysis. It is not, however, especially helpful in building systematic knowledge about social phenomena. Terms whose use covers almost any situation or event are not helpful in analyzing variables and the relations among variables. If many different kinds of events are labeled crises, then the factor becomes a constant, variations of which do not exist and cannot, therefore, be related to variations in other aspects of social processes. Consequently, we favor careful definitions of crisis and efforts to convert the concept into a variable that may be related to other variables in hypotheses and theories.

Uses of the term crisis may be broadly classified as *substantive* and *procedural*. Substantive conceptions of crisis identify the content of a particular policy, problem, or situation. Procedural definitions emphasize generic characteristics of crises without regard to their subject or substance; for example, without regard to whether a crisis is international or local, political or economic, individual or group.

A substantive definition of crisis is Kahn's enumeration of forty-four distinguishable steps on the ladder of escalation, from a minor provocation to full-scale nuclear holocaust.[1] This refined delineation of the large number of possible subtle increases in the level of crisis is a helpful instrument of "crisis management." It suggests that decision makers have available several stages through which to increase pressure on an adversary without necessarily precipitating a hastened escalation into full-scale war.

Kahn's forty-four steps are less helpful for predicting behavior and for building a theory of crisis than for crisis management. The typology is limited to nuclear or potential nuclear crises. It is not comprehensive enough to be applicable to other kinds of crises. Not only is Kahn's typology overly refined, but the state of theories about crisis, or the state of theories in which crisis plays a role, is not sufficiently complex to use a variable that takes forty-four —or even, say, twenty-one—values. Imagine a bivariate table with crisis as one dimension; forty-four cells would be on one axis and only two or three on the other. The possibility of filling many of the cells with data is most unlikely.

* This paper draws from a report originally prepared for Project Michelson, United States Navy, under Contract N60530-10338. Parts of it appear in the *International Encyclopedia of the Social Sciences.* A more extensive version appears in *Political Science Annual*, vol. 2 (Indianapolis: Bobbs-Merrill, 1970), pp. 111–148. R. Roger Majak assisted in reviewing research.

1. Herman Kahn, *On Escalation* (New York: Praeger, 1965).

Another substantive conception of crisis is provided by Triska's inquiry into the conditions under which the Soviet Union takes risks and the ways in which these conditions relate to variations in the extent and level of risk taking in Soviet foreign policy.[2] Triska identified seven kinds of crisis situations in which Soviet foreign policy makers choose the risk they will take. These situations are distinguished according to the participants and the initiator of situations. The first kind is one in which the Soviet Union is involved with a contiguous non-Communist nation. The second is a civil war in a non-Communist country contiguous to a Communist party state. A third is a Western initiative against the Soviet Union. A fourth is an independent Communist party state's reaction to a move by the Soviet Union. A fifth involves China and a non-Communist state. A sixth is a confrontation between the major East and West powers. And the seventh is an armed intervention by the West. Triska's analysis includes cases of each of these seven kinds of crises and shows that Soviet foreign policies vary in the extent of risk taking with different occasions.

Like Kahn's conception, Triska's is policy specific. Unlike Kahn's, it contains the germ of a comprehensive classification of crises, including such factors as participants, initiators, and levels of intensity of violence. Also, unlike Kahn's, the values that Triska's conception of crisis can take are relatively few in number—seven.

Such substantive definitions of crisis are likely to be more helpful to policy makers, to managers of conflict and crisis, than procedural definitions. If limited in theoretical implications, they have an immediate relevance and policy applicability that commends them as examples of analyses that might be applied to a number of nations.

Procedural characteristics identify elements that inhere in any crisis. Two reviews of scholarly and scientific work relating to crisis summarize a variety of elements or characteristics that have been used to define crisis according to procedures or processes. Wiener and Kahn[3] enumerate twelve generic dimensions: (1) Crisis is often a turning point in an unfolding sequence of events and actions. (2) Crisis is a situation in which the requirement for action is high in the minds and planning of participants. (3) Crisis is a threat to the goals and objectives of those involved. (4) Crisis is followed by an important outcome whose consequences and effects will shape the future of the parties to the crisis. (5) Crisis is a convergence of events whose combination produces a new set of circumstances. (6) Crisis is a period in which uncertainties about the assessment of the situation and alternatives for dealing with it increase. (7) Crisis is a period or situation in which control over events and their effects decreases. (8) Crisis is characterized by a sense of urgency, which often produces stress and anxiety among the actors. (9) Crisis is a circumstance or set of circumstances in which information available to participants is unusually inadequate. (10) Crisis is characterized by increased time pressures for those involved. (11) Crisis is marked by changes in the relations

2. Jan F. Triska et al., *Pattern and Level of Risk in Soviet Foreign Policy Making: 1945–1963*, Studies of the Communist System, Stanford University, dittoed report to Project Michelson, September 10, 1964; and Jan F. Triska and David D. Finley, *Soviet Foreign Policy* (New York: The Macmillan Company, 1968), especially chap. 9, pp. 310–349.

3. Anthony J. Wiener and Herman Kahn, *Crisis and Arms Control* (Harmon-on-Hudson, N.Y.: Hudson Institute, 1962). Compare with Alistair Buchan, *Crisis Management* (Boulogne-sur-Seine, France: Atlantic Institute, 1966), pp. 20–21.

among participants. And (12) crisis increases tensions among the actors, especially in political crises involving nations.

Obviously, several of these characteristics, which are derived from historical, psychological, and sociological studies, are redundant. For example, the concept of crisis as a turning point (1) is similar to the concept of crisis as an event involving an important outcome likely to reshape the future (4). Similarly, the characteristic that action is required (2) resembles the characteristic of urgency culminating in stress and anxiety (8). The element of increasing uncertainty (6) is very much like that of increasingly inadequate information (9).

Miller and Iscoe[4] also have reviewed several traits of crisis used in psychological and sociological research: (1) Crisis is acute rather than chronic, although the length of the crisis is usually unspecified. (2) Crisis produces changes in behavior that are frequently "pathological," such as inefficiency, frustration, and scapegoating. (3) Crisis is characterized by threat to the goals of the persons involved. (4) Crisis is relative in that what is a crisis for one party or participant may not be for another. And (5) crisis produces tension in the organism, including physical tension and anxiety.

It is apparent that Miller and Iscoe have identified some of the same traits of crisis as Wiener and Kahn. For example, both lists enumerate threat to goals and such pathological effects as frustration and anxiety.

The Stanford Studies in Conflict and Integration (including Robert North, Ole Holsti, Dina Zinnes, and Richard Brody) have undertaken extensive studies of the crises eventuating in World War I as well as of more recent Sino-Soviet and Soviet-American conflicts, including the Cuban crisis of 1962. The Stanford associates adhere to a classical definition of crisis that can be traced to the original Greek meaning, one that persists to this day in the medical view of the term.[5] This definition identifies crisis as a "turning point" in the development or evolution of an event or organism. Crisis is the "critical point" that determines the favorable or unfavorable outcome of the evolution—life or death, violence or nonviolence, resolution or protracted conflict. The difficulty with this conception is the obverse of the one we attributed to Kahn's. Whereas Kahn's refined forty-four stages of crisis are too numerous for theory-building, the concept of crisis as a turning point alone seems too restricted. An event is either a crisis or it is not, it is either a turning point or it is not, it has either a favorable outcome or it has an unfavorable outcome. These dichotomies are insufficiently subtle.

A similar and unrestricted meaning is taken by Triska, who holds that crisis connotes "an extraordinary, non-routine, abnormal situation . . . result of new input . . . accelerating paces, increasing tensions, quickening responses, disbalancing stabilities, and containing elements of danger of war."[6] Once more we have a broad definition, but now one that encompasses a number of dimensions—nonroutine, abnormality, new inputs, acceleration of activity, increased tension, quickened responses, instability, and threat of war.

These elements, traits, or characteristics reveal a continuing problem of crisis investigations. Definitions are either extraordinarily specific and hence not widely applicable to a variety of situations, organizations, and subjects; or

4. Kent Miller and Ira Iscoe, "The Concept of Crisis," *Human Organization*, 22 (Fall 1963), 195–201.

5. Robert C. North, Ole R. Holsti, M. George Zaninovich, and Dina A. Zinnes, *Content Analysis* (Evanston, Ill.: Northwestern University Press, 1963), p. 4.

6. Triska et al., *Pattern and Level of Risk*, p. 8.

they are so broadly inclusive as to blur distinctions between crises and noncrises. Either so many values are given to the variable that it cannot conveniently be hypothetically related to variations in the values of other factors, or it is categorized as crisis or noncrisis with the effect that analyses are gross and indiscriminate. The strategy for overcoming this difficulty is contained in an adage that I believe has been attributed to Paul Lazarsfeld: the more things are the same, study the differences; the more things are different, study the similarities.

In pursuing this line, I once proposed a threefold concept of crisis based on a number of case studies.[7] This preliminary characterization of crisis included identification of the origin of the event (whether external or internal for decision makers); time available for response (short, intermediate, or long); and relative importance to participants of the values at stake (low or high). The origin of the situation was provisionally selected because of the apparent differences between such crises as the Korean invasion of 1950, which came as a surprise to American foreign policy makers, and the Bay of Pigs crisis of 1961, which was precipitated by the American government. This dimension recognized what other studies had found important—that is, that a crisis for one party may not be a crisis for another, and that elements of the crisis may differ depending upon whether one precipitates the crisis or is confronted by it.

Response time was thought important because of some of its apparent consequences for the content of decisions or reactions. For example, Snyder and Paige reported that after the Korean invasion alternatives available to the American government were few in number and were quickly reduced to one.[8] On the other hand, the development of the Marshall Plan over a fifteen-week period in 1947, in response to rapidly deteriorating economic and political stability in Western Europe, offered a somewhat longer period to search for ways to deal with a problem.[9] Different from both the Korean response and the Marshall Plan was the settlement of the Japanese Peace Treaty, which was reached during a number of years and which permitted extensive search for alternatives and exploration of the acceptability of alternative treaty formulations.[10]

The third element in this concept, relative importance of the values at stake, was selected for the obvious reason that crises have potential consequences of high salience and profound importance. In international affairs the stakes may be violent or nonviolent and, among violent outcomes, they may involve conventional or nuclear war in varying degrees. In crises other than international political ones, the stakes may be varying degrees of economic stability or instability, organizational growth or decline, or personal well-being or misfortune.

Working initially with this typology, Charles Hermann reviewed organizational studies and constructed a partial model of some consequences of crisis for

7. James A. Robinson, "The Concept of Crisis in Decision-Making," *Series Studies in Social and Economic Sciences*, no. 11 (Washington, D.C.: National Institute of Social and Behavioral Science, 1962).

8. Richard C. Snyder and Glenn D. Paige, "The United States Decision to Resist Aggression in Korea," *Administrative Science Quarterly*, 3 (December 1958), 341–378.

9. Joseph M. Jones, *The Fifteen Weeks* (New York: Viking, 1955).

10. Bernard C. Cohen, *The Political Process and Foreign Policy: The Making of the Japanese Peace Settlement* (Princeton: Princeton University Press, 1957).

organizational viability.[11] In formulating an inductively derived theory of effects of crisis on organizations, Hermann also had in mind the eventual simulation of foreign policy organizations to test implications of his theorizing. While moving between the original typology based on foreign policy making and more abstract organizational theory, and considering implications for the simulation of organizations, Hermann concluded that a modified version of this three-dimensional definition was desirable.

For purposes of simulating foreign policy crises through Inter-Nation Simulation, Hermann categorized occasions for decisions as either anticipated or unanticipated, as involving short or long response time, and as involving low, medium, or high threat to the goals or objectives of the decision-making unit.[12] His research arbitrarily dichotomized both anticipation and response time and trichotomized threat. Obviously, these three dimensions could be scaled in a more refined fashion, but they appropriately yielded twelve occasions for decision, a number expected to be reasonably practicable for analysis. Later, however, the "research design" proved insufficiently complex to deal with twelve different values, and it was necessary to compromise by comparing most crisis-like with least crisis-like situations.

Subsequent consideration of this threefold conception of crisis disclosed serious difficulties with the element of response time. Duration is relative.[13] What is a short time for one problem may be more than ample for another. The complexity of tasks for decision units confronting crises may require more time for problem identification, alternative search and selection, and implementation than other occasions.

Response time should not be equated with clock time for at least two reasons. The first is that time has different meanings and effects for different decision makers. Owing to variations in cognitive capacity or in decision-making style, one individual needs a small amount of time to work on a task for which another requires a comparatively long time period. Obviously, some decision makers take time to reflect, while others move quickly to evaluate a situation. The same decision outcome may be proposed by the reflective and the decisive, but their personal procedures for deciding differ. This conceptual problem can be transferred to another set of variables that interact with situation in the total decision-making process—that is, such individual or personal characteristics as mental agility, intelligence, creativity, and decision style may be treated as psychological variables. One can think of research designs in which personality variables are related to crisis variables and, in doing so, the problem-solving or decision-making characteristics of the individual participants can be treated elsewhere than in the conception of crisis.

The second difficulty with duration cannot be so easily disposed of or transferred conceptually. We refer again to task complexity as an element of

11. Charles F. Hermann, "Some Consequences of Crisis Which Limit the Viability of Organizations," *Administrative Science Quarterly*, 8 (June 1963), 61–82.

12. Charles F. Hermann, *Crises in Foreign Policy* (Indianapolis: Bobbs-Merrill, 1969).

13. James A. Robinson and Richard C. Snyder, "Decision-Making in International Politics," in Herbert Kelman, ed., *International Behavior* (New York: Holt, Rinehart & Winston, 1965), pp. 440–442. For a summary of current thinking about subjective time, see John Cohen, "Psychological Time," *Scientific American*, 211 (November 1964), 116–124.

response time. Even when duration is long, the situation is so complicated that many tasks need to be performed in formulating a policy. A notable case that illustrates this is Britain's first attempts to secure membership in the Common Market. Between 1960 and 1962 the British Foreign Office confronted a wide range of detailed tasks in an effort to negotiate entry into the European Economic Community (EEC).[14] Britain enjoyed a relatively lengthy period, by calendrical measurement, in which to gather information, formulate alternative courses of action, and implement them in negotiation. If, on the other hand, one takes into account the immense technicality and complexity of the details, the effort to secure membership in the Common Market did not seem of long duration to the participants. And, while dealing with the obtuse EEC problem, Britain was simultaneously confronted with other critical occasions for foreign policy decisions. This was the period of the 1960 Summit Conference, of a reappraisal of defense policy and weapons strategy, and of troubles with the former colonies in Africa. The competition of other problems further reduced the time and effort available to top-level foreign office officials for work on the already complicated matters of economic union.

To these difficulties, complexities, and other issues were added the rather large number of interests involved in the Common Market negotiations. Not only were talks in progress between Britain and the six members of the EEC, but Britain also had to consider the interests of its Commonwealth members, of the six northern European members of the Free Trade Association, and of several politically important domestic interest groups.

In brief, while the calendar for negotiation was nearly three years long, it was crowded by demands and competition. Duration, therefore, should hardly be treated as an absolute. It varies with the intricacies of the task at hand. I am unaware, however, of research that takes into account the relationship between task complexity and duration. Given the difficulties to be encountered in devising such a study, this is not surprising.

Any appraisal of the concept crisis would be incomplete without reference to the related terms *stress*, *conflict*, *tension*, *panic*, *catastrophe*, and *disaster*. We have seen that the enumerations of meanings and consequences associated with crisis include stress, tension, and anxiety. Hermann has reported that the term crisis is used less frequently than are these sister terms.[15]

These terms, like crisis, have many meanings, as Horvath showed with respect to stress.[16] The most common usage of stress is that of thwarting or potentially thwarting some motive state, resulting in affective arousal. Margaret

14. Roland Young and James A. Robinson, "Parliamentary Decision-Making in Great Britain: The Case of the Common Market." Paper delivered at the annual meeting of the American Political Science Association, Washington, D.C., September 1962. For another example of the relativity of time see Roberta Wohlstetter, "Cuba and Pearl Harbor," *Foreign Affairs*, 43 (July 1965), 696.

Charles McClelland's chapter in this volume also notes that the life of crises, such as those over Berlin and Taiwan, may be months or even years. I may add, incidentally, that I have not otherwise referred to McClelland's unusual analyses of crisis because their distinctive contributions are to measuring crisis. This chapter, as the reader has by now observed, is limited to conceptual and theoretical problems and foregoes concern for operational ones.

15. Charles F. Hermann, *Crises in Foreign Policy*, p. 26.

16. Fred E. Horvath, "Psychological Stress: A Review of Definitions and Experimental Research," *General Systems Yearbook*, 4 (1959), 203–230.

Hermann used the concept in an Inter-Nation Simulation.[17] Her definition was "... in stress an individual perceives that a situation (stimulus) threatens to obstruct or actually obstructs a goal which he is motivated to achieve." A negative affect is a frequent consequence of stress and constitutes a collective term for anxiety, fear, frustration, hostility, and tension. The difficulties with using stress and crisis synonymously center upon the unidimensional character of stress. As a block or a threat to goals, stress is only one of the major characteristics of crisis, as we propose to use the term.

Similar problems arise with respect to such related concepts as conflict. Conflict is commonly regarded as an incompatibility between parties with respect to an object or a goal.[18] Here, again, we confront the dimension of threat to an objective, one of the three major characteristics of our concept of crisis.

Tension is obviously related to crisis. It is, however, a consequence of one of the dimensions of crisis and is not itself a characteristic of crisis. It seems useful to exclude from the concept of crisis its effects or outcomes. Moreover, tension refers to a psychological response, and problems arise in compounding psychological and organizational (sociological) variables.

A further difficulty with many of the related concepts and with stress especially is that, with only a few exceptions, they have been investigated in problem-solving rather than in decision-making research.[19] Although it is not uncommon to use the terms *decision making* and *problem solving* interchangeably, serious difficulties occur if one is not alert to their technical differences. Typically, problem-solving experiments present subjects with problems for which alternatives are given and for which there is a determinate and "best" solution. It does not demean these experiments or their value to underscore what is readily apparent—namely, that decision making differs considerably from problem solving. Current models of decision do not concentrate on the selection among alternatives; rather, they emphasize that the search for alternatives and the formulation and negotiation of alternatives is an integral part of the decision process. Moreover, as Simon has suggested, these stages of the total decision process consume a much larger share of the total time for making a decision than does the selection among alternatives.[20]

Alternatives are not given in most decision situations—certainly not in such important ones as crises—and the search for alternatives constitutes a substantial portion of decision-making time. Further, decisions are not subject to determinate and best solutions. To be sure, routine or recurring decisions may be subjected to linear programming or other computational operations that result in near-determinate solutions. The kinds of situations that crisis ordinarily connotes, however, are of a different order. Accordingly, the relevance of many

17. Margaret G. Hermann, "Testing a Model of Psychological Stress," *Journal of Personality*, 34 (September 1966), 381–396.

18. Kenneth Boulding, *Conflict and Defense* (New York: Harper & Row, 1962); Robert C. North, Howard E. Koch, Jr., and Dina A. Zinnes, "The Integrative Functions of Conflict," *Journal of Conflict Resolution*, 4 (September 1960), 355–374.

19. One exception is Margaret G. Hermann, *Stress, Self-Esteem, and Defensiveness in an Inter-Nation Simulation* (Unpublished Ph.D. Dissertation, Northwestern University, 1965).

20. Herbert A. Simon, "Political Research," in David Easton, ed., *Varieties of Political Theory* (Englewood Cliffs, N.J.: Prentice-Hall, 1966), p. 19.

of the problem-solving experiments on stress to crisis decision making is diminished. Dahl and Wood have warned against applying findings and implications of findings from non-decision-making experiments (such as problem solving) to arenas in which policies and decisions are taken.[21]

In addition to these limitations on stress as a synonym for crisis, other limitations apply to panic, catastrophe, and disaster research. Typically, these studies have not been decision-making investigations but have been concerned with mass behavior and other responses dissimilar to decision-making processes.[22] Panic, catastrophe, and disaster, although subject to study in important social contexts, are less technical in meaning. Rarely have they been the subject of investigation in organizational contexts.[23]

THEORIZING ABOUT CRISIS

So far we have considered crisis and related terms apart from theories for which they provide foundation stones. We may open the discussion of theories by stating flatly that there is no such thing as a theory of crisis or even theories of crisis. We have, however, the beginnings of theorizing about the phenomenon. Notable theorizing has been undertaken by Charles Hermann, who inductively reviewed hypotheses and placed them in a chain of independent, intervening, and dependent variables. In addition, Hermann advanced ad hoc predictions about some of the relations between crisis and other variables. In some cases, however, the ad hoc predictions were arbitrary, and contradictory theories or reasons could be given for opposite predictions. However innovative this is for formulating testable hypotheses, it indicates the lack of a rich deductive theory involving crisis.[24]

Not only is crisis theory barren, but other social theories rarely accommodate crisis. Consider first theories about decision making. For example, the theory of games, which deals with decision making under certain conditions, does not include the concept.[25] The critical aspects of decision with which game theory deals are conflicts between parties under conditions of uncertainty. In a theory about crisis, conflict is only one dimension (threat to values), and it must be a variable rather than a constant. Uncertainty is also a variable in crises; that is, the amount of uncertainty in a situation or occasion for decision may vary, and

21. Robert A. Dahl, *Who Governs?* (New Haven: Yale University Press, 1961), p. 98; Robert C. Wood, *1400 Governments* (Cambridge: Harvard University Press, 1961), p. 17.

22. Neil J. Smelser, *Theory of Collective Behavior* (New York: The Free Press, 1963); William N. McPhee, *Formal Theories of Mass Behavior* (New York: The Free Press, 1963).

23. An exception is Thomas E. Drabeck, *Laboratory Simulation of a Police Communication System Under Stress* (Unpublished Ph.D. Dissertation, Ohio State University, 1965).

24. Charles F. Hermann, *Crises in Foreign Policy.*

25. References to crisis are not found in John Von Neumann and Oskar Morgenstern, *Theory of Games and Economic Behavior* (Princeton: Princeton University Press, 1944); Duncan Luce and Howard Raiffa, *Games and Decisions* (New York: Wiley, 1957); or Anatol Rapoport, *Strategy and Conscience* (New York: Harper & Row, 1964). However, theories of deterrence have been strikingly influenced by game theory, and nuclear strategists such as Thomas Schelling have distinguished between the use of nuclear threats in crisis and in noncrisis.

all crisis decisions will involve some elements of uncertainty. Because the theory of games treats conflict and uncertainty as constants, it is difficult to make obvious or strongly tenable connections between game theory and crisis.

Recent extensions of the theory of dissonance to decision making also fail to incorporate crisis.[26] Moreover, except for the original field study in which Festinger and associates investigated dissonance,[27] most studies have been problem-solving experiments and, therefore, subject to strictures already mentioned.

Economic models of decision making also have omitted crisis, as in a certain logical sense they must. Classic economic models assume that all alternatives are known, that the consequences of all alternatives are predictable, and that preferences among these are available and ordered. As we have indicated, an important part of decision making is the search for alternatives in the face of uncertainties; hence classic economic models are not free to deal with the kinds of problems associated with crisis.

If game theory, dissonance theory, and economic theory are barren of crisis, so also are the more recent efforts to construct decision models around the concepts of "satisficing" and "incrementalism." However, as we shall point out later in discussing some of the positive consequences of crisis for an organization, the satisficing and incremental models have implications for crisis, though their application to date in decision-making studies and experiments has not been related to crisis.

If no crisis theory exists and if no well-developed theories of decision making explicitly incorporate crisis, what of nondecision theories? Have they, and if so, how have they included crisis? Certain theories of psychotherapy, including those of Erikson and Dobrowski, have regarded crisis as inevitable in the development of the identity of the individual.[28] The relevance of this for abstract crisis theorizing is contained in its suggestion of the positive character of crisis for the development and evolution of the personality.

In certain theorizing about negotiation, as in labor-management bargaining, crisis has been identified as an inevitable and positive occurrence that precedes any resolution or settlement.[29]

Communication theories concerned with the processing of information and with the possibilities of overloading networks of messages have implicit relation to crisis.[30] If we consider one dimension of crisis, that of anticipation or lack of it, we can readily see that the processing of information within an organization may make a difference for whether certain warnings about impend-

26. Leon Festinger, Vernon Allen et al., *Conflict, Decision and Dissonance* (Stanford: Stanford University Press, 1964). An exception appears in Charles F. Hermann, *Crises in Foreign Policy*, chap. 7, pp. 151–194.

27. Leon Festinger, Henry W. Riecken, and Stanley Schachter, *When Prophecy Fails* (Minneapolis: University of Minnesota Press, 1956).

28. Erik H. Erikson, *Identity and the Life Cycle* (New York: International Universities Press, 1959), pp. 50–100; Karl W. Dobrowski, *Positive Disintegration* (Boston: Little, Brown, 1964).

29. Ann Douglas, *Industrial Peace-Making* (New York: Columbia University Press, 1962).

30. For example, Karl W. Deutsch, *The Nerves of Government* (New York: The Free Press, 1963); Richard L. Meier, "Information Input Overload: Features of Growth in Communications-Oriented Institutions," *Libri*, 13, no. 1 (1963), 1–44.

ing events reach top-level decision makers. For example, prior to the outbreak of the Korean War, an anticipatory warning of possible Soviet penetration of the Western defense perimeter in the Pacific apparently circulated in the higher echelons of the American government, but it did not reach the President or his closest advisers.

With respect to nondecision theories, we may say that any theory in which situation is a variable is one to which crisis would be relevant.[31] Perhaps we should make more explicit than we have that our concept of crisis is situational. We regard crisis as an occasion for decision.[32] That is, crisis is a situation or an event that confronts decision makers with an opportunity for response, either action or inaction.

This summary of theories is intended to highlight the difficulties of extending crisis as a concept if it does not play a part in theoretical formulation. Just as a fact has no meaning apart from a hypothesis, so a concept can hardly have meaning or productivity if it does not relate to other variables in the hypotheses of a theory. This theoretical deficiency imposes an important restraint on any effort to inventory propositions and hypotheses concerning crisis. As criticisms of other propositional inventories have indicated (for example, those of Berelson and Steiner's *Human Behavior*), hypotheses stripped of their theoretical context are virtually uninterpretable.[33] The reason is that the multifaceted relations of a given hypothesis to other hypotheses are missing and, were the hypothesis put in its richer context, the relations among variables might be altered. Hence, in reviewing research, we shall want to adopt some analytic framework or outline for incorporating hypotheses.

Propositions and hypotheses about crises can be organized into two parts. The first considers the units of analysis and the levels of analysis used in crisis investigations. The second reviews and illustrates hypotheses about the consequences of crisis for foreign policy organizations. Special reference will be given to positive effects of crisis, with a view to considering the relevance of crisis as a technique in influencing an adversary.

Units and Levels of Analysis

A unit of analysis refers to the object of one's investigation—whether an individual, an organization, or a society. A level of analysis refers to the explanation used in understanding, explaining, and predicting the behavior and actions of a unit under crisis. Types of analysis levels may correspond to types of units—that is, individual, organizational, and societal. As we will see, however, a unit of analysis may be analyzed by a different kind of level. For example, an organization may be taken as a unit of analysis, but the level of explanation for its actions and behavior may be individual—that is, psychological.

31. Dean G. Pruitt, "Definition of the Situation as a Determinant of International Action," in Kelman, ed., *International Behavior*, pp. 391–432.

32. Chester I. Barnard, *The Functions of the Executive* (Cambridge: Harvard University Press, 1938), pp. 189–192; Richard C. Snyder, H. W. Bruck, and Burton Sapin, eds., *Foreign Policy Decision-Making* (New York: The Free Press, 1962), pp. 80–81.

33. Kenneth Janda, "Keyword Indexes for the Behavioral Sciences," *American Behavioral Scientist*, 7 (June 1964), 55–58; Kenneth Janda, *Data Processing* (Evanston, Ill.: Northwestern University Press, 1965).

Many crisis studies, as we have noted, have a psychological focus. At least three crisis investigations reflect this emphasis. The first was the study of the circumstances leading to the outbreak of World War I conducted by the Stanford Studies in Conflict and Integration. Through content analysis, North and his colleagues attempted to reconstruct the perceptions of the individual decision makers. The decision makers as individuals were the object of their analysis. Although North et al., along with other investigators, nominally refer to the state, they carefully define the state as the individual decision makers who are authorized to speak on behalf of the country and the government.[34] Individuals are emphasized to the exclusion of any roles or relationships among them, such as would characterize the examination of the foreign policy organization that made the decisions for the adversaries in the 1914 events.

Margaret Hermann carried out a simulation of stress as part of a larger study on crisis.[35] She was concerned about the relationship between stress and self-esteem, on the one hand, and affect and coping behaviors on the other. Her unit of analysis comprised the individuals who participated in the simulation which, in the fashion of Inter-Nation Simulation, consisted of four or five decision makers in each of six countries. Decision makers were tested prior to their participation in the simulation and were to some extent selected on the basis of their scores on tests for variations in self-esteem.

More recently, Pool and associates have undertaken a computer simulation of crisis with special reference to the processing of information and communications.[36] Their simulation consists of two players, one representing the head of government of the United States. The computer model is based on several propositions about the selective perception of human decision makers. Pool and Kessler have enumerated five basic assumptions of their model:

1. People pay more attention to news that deals with them.
2. People pay less attention to facts that contradict their previous views.
3. People pay more attention to news from trusted, liked sources.
4. People pay more attention to facts that they will have to act upon or discuss because of attention by others.
5. People pay more attention to facts bearing on actions they are already involved in—that is, action creates commitment.

The evidence for these assumptions consists of basic experiments in social psychology, studies of communication by journalists, and the television audiences' reception of information. Plans for complicating the model remain primarily psychological. Additional decision makers may be added, but the object being simulated remains processes of individual selective perception and distortion. In addition to developing the basic model, a trial simulation has already been undertaken using materials developed by the Stanford study of World War I. Two decision makers, the Kaiser and the Tsar, were represented in the model.

Studies that take an organization as a unit of analysis include Triska's work.[37] His principal finding is that the Soviets are relatively low risk takers in

34. North, Holsti, Zaninovich, and Zinnes, *Content Analysis*, pp. 39–40.

35. Margaret G. Hermann, *Stress, Self-Esteem, and Defensiveness*.

36. Ithiel de Sola Pool and Allan Kessler, "The Kaiser, the Tsar, and the Computer," *American Behavioral Scientist*, 8 (1965), 31–38.

37. Triska et al., *Pattern and Level of Risk*.

foreign policy making, that they are conservative, cautious, deliberate, and unwilling to engage in actions that they think will cause them to lose. He argues that they act on capabilities rather than on attitudes. Variation in their risk taking is observed depending upon differences in whether they must respond to a given event or have themselves initiated it. Likewise, depending upon whether the situation is one of direct interest to the Soviet Union and the relative strength of the parties, Soviet foreign office officials vary in the extent to which they will take risks. Triska does not treat the decision makers individually but, rather, looks at the collective responses of the Soviet foreign policy apparatus in more than twenty cases.

Charles Hermann, in an Inter-Nation Simulation of crisis foreign policy making, adopted a four-man organization as the unit of analysis.[38] He then compared responses of different organizations to variations in the level of crisis. Hermann's operational definition of organization averaged individual perceptions of the four members of each organizational team; he acknowledged not only the problems of averaging perceptions as a way of representing an organization but also the difficulties of developing typical organizational characteristics in a unit of no more than four members. Size is not necessarily a condition of organization; rather, such characteristics as mediated communications, specialization of roles, and authority structure are fundamental to an organization. Inter-Nation Simulation has not yet fully mastered the development of a rich organizational context, but clearly it presents something more than a small group and surely something more—or the possibility of something more—than individual action.

Snyder and Paige carried out an extensive historical reconstruction of events surrounding the American decision to join the Korean War in the summer of 1950, emphasizing the organizational setting in which this decision was taken.[39] An ad hoc group of fourteen men participated in the crucial decision made in the company of the President. Snyder and Paige derived an extensive number of ad hoc propositions from their case, including such variables as values, information, relations among participants, and search for alternatives.

I analyzed studies of twenty-two foreign policies of the United States in a thirty-year period, comparing the role of Congress and that of the executive in making these decisions. Congress was viewed as a highly decentralized, relatively nonbureaucratic organization in contrast to the more typically bureaucratic character of the executive.[40] Not only was the bureaucratic variable related to the capacity of the organization to respond in a short time but, in contrast to observations of Lippmann[41] and others, Congress was found less likely to favor violent responses than was the executive.

Studies taking the society as a unit of analysis are less numerous than the types discussed above, although classic political and economic theories frequently examine what might be regarded as social crises—for instance, revolutions. Marx developed a theory of social change that depended heavily upon arousing crises. Naroll has engaged in studies of culture stress, but the

38. Charles F. Hermann, *Crises in Foreign Policy*.

39. Snyder and Paige, "Decision to Resist Aggression," pp. 341–378.

40. James A. Robinson, *Congress and Foreign Policy-Making*, rev. ed. (Homewood, Ill.: Dorsey, 1967).

41. Walter Lippmann, *Essays in the Public Philosophy* (Boston: Little, Brown, 1955).

immediate relevance of these to foreign policy decision making is not obvious.[42] Similarly, although Coblentz has examined ten cultural crises in the history of civilization, great stretches of imagination are required to combine such sweeping historical and anthropological inquiries with individual units and organizational units in theorizing about crisis.[43]

Levels of analysis, as we have noted, refer to the kinds of theories that are invoked to explain the unit of analysis under study. Both Pool and Kessler's computer simulation and the Hermanns' runs of the Inter-Nation Simulation rely on individual-level or psychological explanations. We have listed some of the basic operating assumptions of the Pool and Kessler model. Charles Hermann's analysis of organizations follows the theoretical style of March and Simon's analysis of organizations.[44] The satisficing model of organizational decision making, in which individual decision makers with limited cognitive capacity operate under conditions of "bounded rationality," is emphasized by Hermann's simulation of foreign policy organizations. Margaret Hermann, in her study of stress, explains actions of individuals according to variations in their self-esteem.[45]

North has analyzed English, German, and Russian foreign policy makers in the pre-1914 period in terms of the selective perception and distortion of individual decision makers. One of the most striking phenomena observed by North and his colleagues is the conflict spiral, in which the first party misperceives the intent of the second party, which then acts upon the misperception that further confirms the original misperception of the first party. Thus conflict continues to spiral until it culminates in violence.

Among organizational levels of analysis as applied to crises is a comparison of bureaucratic and legislative response to crisis.[46] The executive has not only constitutional advantage in the conduct of foreign policy, but also bureaucratic expertise and organization that permit it to process and coordinate information more effectively than legislative organizations are able to do.

As an example of the societal level of analysis, we refer again to Triska's study. His explanation of Soviet foreign policy organization transcends the particular organizational norms or operating rules. For example, Triska says that "all successive Soviet decision makers, believing in the ideological inevitability of the victory of socialism in the world, have tended to prefer low over high risks."[47] The explanation has to do neither with the skills of the individual decision makers nor with the roles and relationships among them. Rather, it depends principally on socialist ideology of the Marxist–Leninist variety, which transcends the individual occupants of roles and the relationships among them. It is a characteristic of the state or society to which the individuals belong and whom the organization represents.

42. Raoul Naroll, *Data Quality Control* (New York: The Free Press, 1962).

43. S. A. Coblentz, *Ten Crises in Civilization* (New York: Follet, 1965).

44. James G. March and Herbert A. Simon, with Harold Guetzkow, *Organizations* (New York: Wiley, 1958).

45. Margaret G. Hermann, *Stress, Self-Esteem, and Defensiveness.*

46. Robinson, *Congress and Foreign Policy-Making.*

47. Triska et al., *Pattern and Level of Risk.*

Consequences of Crisis

We have already indicated that conventional formulations of crisis regard it as pathological, as something to be avoided. Miller and Iscoe report that crises typically produce such undesirable behavioral manifestations as inefficiency, frustration, and scapegoating.[48] Other investigators emphasize the dangerous potential of crisis, including increases in the likelihood of violence in global politics.

Crisis alters organizational plans and objectives by disrupting the regular schedule of activities. As a result of crisis, or in order to handle crisis, personnel assignments are reallocated and top-level decision makers focus their attention exclusively on the crisis, postponing action on other matters that may originally have had a higher priority on their scale of values. The Cuban crisis of October 1962 provides a notable example. President Kennedy instructed top-level officials to put aside all other problems for the thirteen-day period in which the decision was taken in response to the presence of the Soviet missiles.[49]

For the participants involved in crisis, personal exhaustion and physical risks increase. Even officials known for working twelve-hour days put in unusually long hours. During the Cuban missile crisis, Sorensen worked several days without a hot meal.[50] And an Assistant Secretary of State was reportedly involved in an automobile accident at four o'clock in the morning while driving home after several exhausting days of around-the-clock work on the Cuban crisis.

In addition to these reasonably obvious effects of crisis, those that affect the decision-making process have been identified by Hermann, Snyder and Paige, and Holsti. Hermann reports that fewer alternatives are likely to be considered in crisis than in noncrisis.[51] Snyder and Paige have emphasized that decision makers tend to have less information than usual on which to operate and that they must, therefore, follow value premises more heavily than is customarily the case in top-level decision making.[52] This effect is, of course, especially critical in crises involving the possibility of nuclear war. Decision makers, whatever their previous experience at making critical decisions, have virtually no personal experience in deciding on moves that may escalate into nuclear war.[53] Politicians are especially gifted in making judgments on the basis of relatively little information combined with explicit value orientations. In crises, however, experience and judgment may be less helpful than in other decision situations because of their nonroutine, virtually unique character. Holsti's hypotheses, derived from related psychological findings, suggest that crisis may affect decision makers' perceptions, particularly those regarding the intentions and range of alternatives open to their adversaries.[54]

48. Miller and Iscoe, "Concept of Crisis."

49. Theodore C. Sorensen, *Kennedy* (New York: Harper & Row, 1965), p. 675.

50. *Ibid.*, p. 693. Many similar examples are recorded by John Bartlow Martin from his experience in a series of crises as ambassador to the Dominican Republic. See his *Overtaken By Events* (Garden City, N.Y.: Doubleday, 1966).

51. Charles F. Hermann, *Crises in Foreign Policy.*

52. Snyder and Paige, "Decision to Resist Aggression." Roberta Wohlstetter notes, however, that in some crises information is abundant, not scarce, and the critical problems pertain to interpretation. "Cuba and Pearl Harbor," pp. 691–707.

53. Richard Neustadt, *Presidential Power* (New York: Mentor, 1964), p. 188.

54. Ole R. Holsti, "The 1914 Case," *American Political Science Review*, 59 (June

Finally, if the judgments, experience, and perceptions of one's own decision makers are constrained in crisis, the adversary may be expected to labor under similar difficulties. Thus the predictability of an adversary's response may be reduced by crisis. It is to overcome this dire consequence that such studies as Triska's are especially valuable. They have the great merit of reviewing the response of an adversary in a large number of crises.

If crises are sometimes pathological, have they no positive or functional consequences? In certain psychoanalytic theories, crisis is regarded as functional for the development of the individual personality. Erikson refers to "beneficial clinical crisis," and Dobrowski emphasizes the values of "positive disintegration."[55] Hare reviews the familiar inverse U-curve regarding stress and reports that moderate stress leads to creativity, whereas mild and severe stress reduce the probability of creative problem solving.[56] Although these findings are exceedingly remote from foreign policy making, they underscore the importance of looking for the paradoxically positive consequences of a phenomenon ordinarily thought to be unfortunate.[57]

As for organizations, Triska has noted on the basis of his examination of a number of Soviet crises that, despite the crisis level, Soviet foreign policy makers are able to maintain and continue low-risk policies.

Both classic economic theories of organizations and modern amendments in the form of satisficing and incrementalizing theories indicate certain positive characteristics of crisis for organizational decision making. If an individual or an organization is limited in its cognitive capacity, then it is well advised to use crisis as a means of determining its agenda. If an agenda is determined solely according to one's value of priorities, politicians may discover that interests, both domestic and international, do not hold similar priorities. This being the case, the limited political resources of the politician will soon be expended on objectives that are difficult to accomplish. If, on the other hand, organization allows the external environment to determine salience, politicians may then invest their resources in dealing with problems that are more or less tractable.

Thus the costs of crisis, however great they may be in physical exhaustion and surprise, may be economical for setting agendas and accomplishing tasks. Moreover, because a crisis tends to bring a problem or an issue to the top of an organization's hierarchy, it permits bypassing much of the bureaucratic lethargy that often characterizes foreign offices. A crisis decision will be taken by officials near the top and, given the demands of time, they can afford to bypass many customary procedures in making decisions.

In inter-organizational conflict and crisis, such as negotiation, crisis may be effective for resolving conflicts. Douglas uses the phrase "crisis into settlement" to characterize one of the inevitable and positive functions of negotiation

---

1965), 365–378, and his essay in this volume. On the other hand, Albert and Roberta Wohlstetter describe U.S. and Soviet decision makers as calculated, controlled, and rational rather than emotional and irrational in the Cuban crisis. See their "Controlling the Risks in Cuba," *Adelphi Paper 17* (London: Institute for Strategic Studies, 1965).

55. Erikson, *Identity*; Dobrowski, *Positive Disintegration.*

56. Paul Hare, *A Handbook of Small Group Research* (New York: The Free Press, 1962), p. 265.

57. Lewis Coser has done this research with respect to conflict. *The Functions of Social Conflict* (New York: The Free Press, 1956).

conflict.[58] Analogous to this is the apparent improvement of U.S.–Soviet relations as a result of the Cuban crisis.

At the societal level, North et al. argued that integration among sub-units is more likely to be increased as a result of conflict and crisis.[59] They stress the positive functions of crisis for the integration of alliances and nations.

To date, as this review is meant to reveal, students of crisis have relied heavily on ad hoc theorizing and few have placed their investigations in any fundamentally theoretical context. Until efforts are launched toward systematizing and integrating theories, knowledge will remain relatively superficial and anecdotal and not, in principle, more adequate than the personal judgment and experience of people who have lived through crises or observed them firsthand. Perhaps it is not too much to hope that this volume constitutes a meaningful contribution to that necessary integration.

58. Douglas, *Industrial Peace-Making.*
59. North, Koch, and Zinnes, "Integrative Functions of Conflict."

part two

COMPARATIVE CASE STUDIES OF CRISIS

chapter three

EDITOR'S INTRODUCTION

On any list of major crises in international politics certain situations are extremely likely to appear. In enumerating crises in America's foreign relations in the period since World War II, the Korean War, the Taiwan Straits, the various confrontations over Berlin, and the Cuban missile crisis would comprise prominent entries. If the list were expanded to include all major crises during the twentieth century, the outbreak of World War I would certainly be another entry. The authors of the next three chapters make comparisons between various combinations of these six widely recognized crises. Each chapter represents a variation on what probably is the most widely used method for the examination of a crisis, the case study—that is, the detailed examination of the events seen as important in the development of some problem, policy, or international episode.

Because the case study has contributed much of our knowledge about crises, we should examine it as a research technique. The author of the present chapter, Glenn Paige, has given considerable attention to the case study as a means of scientific inquiry. Elsewhere, he has summarized the strengths and weaknesses of the *single* case study as follows:

> *Among the possible theoretical uses of single-case research might be included:* (1) *the assembling of an empirical basis from which theoretical propositions may be induced with or without an explicit* a priori *frame of reference;* (2) *the provision of an empirical test of preexisting propositions—possibly a crucial test where propositions of universal validity have been asserted;* (3) *the demonstration of the empirically possible;* (4) *the establishment of an empirical basis for creating a conceptual framework or typology;* (5) *the testing of the empirical relevance of a preexisting analytical scheme;* (6) *the provision of sufficient empirical detail to permit the exploration of alternative explanatory hypotheses; and* (7) *the provision of an empirical data base so rich in detail as to permit the reintegration of fragmented disciplinary insights into a unified body of knowledge. . . .*
>
> *In constructing and in interpreting a single case there are several persistent problems which the analyst must solve or at least appreciate. These include questions about* (1) *the boundaries of the case—what is to be included or excluded;* (2) *the level of case comparability to be sought—the extent to which the case method employed will permit replication and comparison;* (3) *the representativeness of the case—the universe of behaviors to which the case findings are hypothesized to apply; and* (4) *the adequacy of explanation—questions concerning the relative merits of competing explanatory hypotheses, including choices among internally induced and externally introduced explanations.*[1]

The last two difficulties mentioned by Paige are sometimes stated as a rule: You cannot generalize from a single case. The corollary of the rule is that

1. *The Korean Decision* (New York: The Free Press, 1968), pp. 10–11. Reprinted by permission of The Free Press.

a case study cannot be used for a scientific test of a hypothesis unless stated in universal terms (i.e., "in every case"). These difficulties can be reduced by comparing the same features of multiple crises. This comparative use of cases represents a hallmark of the next three chapters. The question remains how the comparisons of crises are to be made. On this point the three authors differ. In Chapter 3, Paige uses his remarkable skill in developing propositions from narrative accounts. Thus empirically verifiable hypotheses constitute the method of comparison, and the presence or absence of support in one crisis for a hypothesis generated by the case study of another provides the means of establishing similarity.

As noted above, many individuals contend that a case study is so completely grounded in the details of a particular situation that it provides no basis for the development of higher level abstractions. Thus we may learn something about a given crisis but we learn almost nothing about crises as general phenomena. For example, Rosecrance, who refers to a case study as "detailed empirical analysis," states that it "plunges deeply into the subject matter, but produces few common threads of analysis. To use a somewhat exaggerated metaphor, detailed empirical analysis tends to miss the forest for overconcentration on the trees."[2] Though this criticism may be true of many case studies, the development in this chapter of hypotheses testable in other crises should challenge the myth that case studies cannot be used in theory-building.

Unfortunately, one myth which this chapter will not expose is that the decision-making approach, which Paige employs, can only be investigated through case studies. As Robinson implied in the previous chapter—and this is confirmed by any bibliography of decision-making studies in the social sciences[3]—most of the research outside of political science on decision making involves techniques other than the case method for both crisis and noncrisis studies.

In a completely unintended way, Paige may be partially responsible for the association of case studies of crises with the decision-making approach. The reason is that the article on the U.S. decision to enter the Korean War, which he jointly authored with Richard C. Snyder, offered one of the first political science applications of Snyder's decision-making framework.[4] Paige followed that article with his book, *The Korean Decision*, which, perhaps, cemented for many readers the association of decision making with crisis case studies. Currently a Professor of Political Science at the University of Hawaii, Glenn D. Paige is concentrating upon the study of public leadership.

2. Richard N. Rosecrance, *Action and Reaction in World Politics* (Boston: Little, Brown, 1963), p. 4. Without stating that case studies must necessarily prevent the development of hypotheses, James N. Rosenau contends that most authors of such works in political science fail to develop them. He reviews seven recent case studies in his "Moral Fervor, Systematic Analysis and Scientific Consciousness in Foreign Policy Research" in Austin Ranney, ed., *Political Science and Public Policy* (Chicago: Markham, 1968), pp. 226–236.

3. For example, see Paul Wasserman with Fred S. Silander, *Decision Making: An Annotated Bibliography* (Ithaca, N.Y.: Graduate School of Business and Public Administration, Cornell University, 1958) and their supplement published in 1964.

4. Richard C. Snyder and Glenn D. Paige, "The United States Decision to Resist Aggression in Korea: The Application of an Analytical Scheme," *Administrative Science Quarterly*, 3 (December 1958), 341–378. The original framework appears in Richard C. Snyder, H. W. Bruck, and Burton Sapin, eds., *Foreign Policy Decision Making* (New York: The Free Press, 1962).

chapter three

COMPARATIVE CASE ANALYSIS OF CRISIS DECISIONS: KOREA AND CUBA

Glenn D. Paige

The methodology of theory-oriented case studies of foreign policy decision making is still in its infancy. Although a fruitful conceptual framework for the study of foreign policy making has been suggested by Snyder, Bruck, and Sapin,[1] and although an application of this framework has been attempted in a single case,[2] much work remains to be done before the method becomes a reliable intellectual tool and before greater degrees of confidence are warranted in the propositions produced by this kind of analysis.

The principal task of the present chapter is to attempt to contribute to the symposium's goals of clarifying concepts, methods, and findings in the study of international crises by means of a comparative case analysis of the Korean and Cuban decisions. At the same time it represents an effort to explore the usefulness of the Snyder, Bruck, and Sapin decision-making framework in comparative inquiry.

The empirical bases of the comparison are narrative reconstructions of the Korean decision (June 24–30, 1950)[3] and of the Cuban decision (October 15–28, 1962).[4] For purposes of this inquiry the period of decision in each case is taken as the interval between initial receipt of information about the precipitating event and the first public announcement by the President of military measures to be taken in response to it. For the Korean decision this includes the 64-hour period from 8:00 P.M., Saturday, June 24, 1950, to 12:00 noon, Tuesday, June 27. In the Cuban decision this is a period of seven days (168 hours) between 7:00 P.M., Monday, October 15, and 7:00 P.M., Monday, October 22, 1962. Although some reference will be made to antecedent and consequent events, the main focus of attention will be on these periods. It will be noted that this analytical choice means that the period of the Cuban decision was a little over two and a half times that of the Korean decision.

Four preexisting elements were combined to produce the present analysis: the Snyder, Bruck, and Sapin conceptual framework for the study of foreign policy decisions;[5] a narrative reconstruction of the Korean decision based on that framework;[6] a set of propositions induced from the Korean decision;[7] and

1. Richard C. Snyder, H. W. Bruck, and Burton Sapin, *Foreign Policy Decision Making* (New York: The Free Press, 1962).

2. Richard C. Snyder and Glenn D. Paige, "The United States Decision to Resist Aggression in Korea," *Administrative Science Quarterly*, 3 (December 1958), 341–378; and Glenn D. Paige, *The Korean Decision* (New York: The Free Press, 1968).

3. *Ibid.*, chaps. 4–11.

4. Theodore C. Sorensen, *Kennedy* (New York: Bantam Books, 1966), chap. 24; and Elie Abel, *The Missile Crisis* (New York: Bantam Books, 1966).

5. Snyder, Bruck, and Sapin, *Foreign Policy*, pp. 14–185.

6. Paige, *Korean Decision*, chaps. 4–11.

7. *Ibid.*, chap. 12.

reconstructions of the Cuban decision prepared without reference to the decision-making framework.[8] The sequence of investigation was as follows. First, the Cuban case materials were studied in the light of the decision-making frame of reference but there was no explicit attempt to "test" or to relate to this decision the propositions derived from the Korean decision. In this way it was hoped to maximize the probability of appreciating new features and relationships among variables. Thus the Cuban case materials were first studied with the following general questions in mind: What relationships among organizational, informational, and normative variables does this case suggest? What similarities and differences are suggested through general comparison with the Korean decision? A second step was to review a list of about fifty propositions based on the Korean decision for the purpose of identifying those that seemed supported, contradicted, or needful of modification on the basis of the Cuban materials. This review of the emerging inventory of decision-making propositions for relevance to the Cuban case was done intuitively. It might better have been accomplished by a panel of judges employing explicit criteria of relevance. Third, the implications of the comparison for the Hermann crisis variables were examined. Finally, an attempt was made to reflect more broadly upon the significance of the comparison for understanding crisis decisions in international politics and for the further development of decision-making analysis.

Before presenting some of the results of this inquiry, it will be helpful to recall the principal event structure of the two decisions under study. Both decisions seem to meet the three criteria for a "crisis decision" that have been suggested by Hermann: short decision time, high perceived threat to values, and surprise.[9]

THE KOREAN DECISION

On Saturday, June 24, 1950 (Washington time), the North Korean People's Army invaded the Republic of Korea without warning. The news reached Washington at 8:00 P.M. against a background of vigorous domestic political criticism of the Administration's China policies, but with relatively little attention devoted to Korea. That night the President, who was then home in Missouri, approved the recommendation of the Secretary of State and a small working group at the State Department that the United States bring the matter before the United Nations Security Council. This was done on the afternoon of Sunday, June 25, when a resolution was obtained calling for a cease-fire and a North Korean withdrawal. The President returned to Washington as the Security Council met. En route to the capital the President asked the Secretary of State to assemble a group of advisers to confer with him upon arrival at Blair House. Subsequently, a core group of thirteen advisers met with the President in two major conferences held on the evenings of June 25 and June 26. The group included eight officials from the Department of Defense (the Secretary of Defense, the Service Secretaries, and the Joint Chiefs of Staff) and five officials from the Department of State (the Secretary of State, the Under Secretary of State, the Assistant Secretary of State for United Nations Affairs, the Assistant Secretary of State for Far Eastern Affairs, and an Ambassador-at-Large). As

8. Sorensen, *Kennedy*; and Abel, *Missile Crisis*.

9. Charles F. Hermann, *Crises in Foreign Policy* (Indianapolis: Bobbs-Merrill, 1969).

the North Koreans rapidly advanced, it became clear that only direct military assistance would save the Republic of Korea. The decision makers were unanimous in their belief that acceptance of a successful North Korean Communist invasion of the Republic would constitute intolerable "appeasement" that would surely lead to World War III, just as unopposed aggressions of the 1930s had led to World War II. They hoped by positive action—affirmation of the principle of "collective security against aggression"—to help strengthen the newly established United Nations. They calculated that neither Soviet nor Chinese Communist counter-intervention was probable and that the United States held a margin of military superiority over its principal potential opponent—the Soviet Union. The Secretary of State took the lead in proposing courses of action for approval by the President. There was no division among the President's advisers over competing alternatives. Thus, on the evening of June 26, the President decided to commit American air and naval forces to combat in the area south of the Thirty-eighth Parallel, to deter an anticipated Chinese Communist invasion of Taiwan by committing the Seventh Fleet to its defense, and to increase military assistance to the Philippines and to Indochina. These decisions were announced on June 27. By June 30 the President had authorized air and naval operations into North Korea and had approved the commitment of two infantry divisions to combat. Thus the United States became engaged in a war that lasted for three years—measured in terms of casualties this became the fifth most costly war in American history.

THE CUBAN DECISION

On Monday, October 15, 1962, at about 7:00 P.M., it was reported to the higher levels of the Kennedy Administration that photoanalysts of the Defense Intelligence Agency had discovered preparations for the emplacement of Soviet medium-range ballistic missiles in Cuba. This report came against a background of American warnings against the emplacement of offensive nuclear weapons in Cuba, of Soviet denials that they intended to deploy them there, and of vociferous Republican charges that the Russians already had done so. The President was informed of the results of the photographic interpretation on the morning of October 16. He immediately requested that a group of fifteen advisers meet with him to consider the situation. This group consisted of five close associates of the President (three presidential assistants, the Attorney General, and the Secretary of the Treasury), four officials from the Department of State (the Secretary and Under Secretary of State, the Assistant Secretary for Inter American Affairs, and an ambassadorial specialist on Soviet affairs), four officials from the Department of Defense (the Secretary and Deputy Secretary of Defense, the Assistant Secretary for International Security Affairs, and the Chairman of the Joint Chiefs of Staff), the Vice President, and the Deputy Director of the Central Intelligence Agency (later, the Director). This group of "fourteen or fifteen men,"[10] with slight changes and supplemented by the President's consultations with three respected private citizens (a former Secretary of State, a former Secretary of Defense, and a former High Commissioner to Germany), served as the core decision-making body throughout the period of choice. Only on October 22, nearly a week after its formation, was the group formally designated as the Executive Committee of the National Security Council. In deciding upon

10. Sorensen, *Kennedy*, p. 760.

an appropriate response to the Soviet military action, the President and his advisers considered at least six alternatives: to do nothing; to lodge a complaint with the United Nations; to establish a military embargo and naval blockade of Cuba; to destroy the missile sites by precision bombing; and to invade Cuba with ground forces. In a prolonged evaluation of these alternatives, extending over the week preceding the public announcement of intended action, the President's advisers divided in favor of two responses: a naval blockade or "quarantine" and an air attack. There was some disagreement over the degree of increased military threat to the United States posed by the missiles in Cuba, but there was a strong immediate consensus that their presence was an intolerable threat to the principles of the Monroe Doctrine. No dominant analogy with the past was perceived; the Soviet action in stationing nuclear weapons outside its own territory was unprecedented except at sea.

On occasion, the President deliberately absented himself from the discussions of his advisers. His brother, the Attorney General, tended to emerge as the informal discussion leader, eliciting alternatives and challenging proponents to defend them. After an initial inclination to follow a preexisting plan of direct military action against Cuba,[11] the President finally decided upon a naval blockade that seemed to be favored by a majority of his advisers. But he assured those advisers who had argued strongly for an air attack that their proposal would be made a part of contingency planning. The President's decision was announced on October 22. At that time he estimated the probability of aggressive Soviet counteraction to be "somewhere between one out of three and even."[12] On October 28 the Soviet Union agreed to remove the objectionable weapons from Cuba on the condition that the United States would agree not to invade Cuba.

Some major similarities and differences. Crisis decisions, like personalities, can be compared either as a whole or in part. A general comparison reveals many similarities and differences. Some salient ones are the following.

The Korean and Cuban decisions were similar in that the precipitating event came to the decision makers by surprise even though there had been unconfirmed reports that it would indeed happen. In both cases the event seems to have been the product of mutual miscalculation; neither side apparently foresaw accurately what the other side would do. Both precipitating events were perceived as threatening deeply held values: no appeasement of aggression in the Korean case; the inviolability of the Monroe Doctrine in the Cuban decision. There was a strong sense of foreshortened time imposed by the rapidly changing objective situation: the Republic of Korea would be overrun within hours; the Soviet missiles in Cuba would be operational within one week. At the time of the crises both American administrations were under strong domestic political attack for failure to take more resolute counteractions against the extension of Communist power and influence. In each case the initial inclination of the President was to adopt a firm posture of resistance against the threat; this sense of resolve was shared by his advisers. In both cases the President decided to act without obtaining prior Congressional authorization and without engaging

11. The President is quoted as saying, "We'll have to do something quickly. . . . I suppose the alternatives are to go in by air and wipe them out, or to take other steps to render the weapons inoperable." Sorensen, *Kennedy*, p. 36.

12. *Ibid.*, p. 795.

members of the Congress in the decision-making process. In both cases efforts were made to keep contemplated responses secret, to avoid alarming the American public, to obtain international organizational legitimation for actions taken, and to inform preferentially key domestic and international political figures of contemplated action prior to public announcement. In each case the President legitimated a consensus, or at least a majority opinion, reached by his advisers. In each case the decision makers seemed ready to engage their opponents in expanded conflict if their initial effort to remove the perceived threat failed. In both cases the decision makers initially attempted to provide an opportunity for voluntary opponent withdrawal.

There were also many marked differences. Cuba was at the forefront of domestic American political debate when the precipitating event occurred; Korean policy was not a major domestic issue when the North Korean attack took place. In the Cuban crisis the precipitating event was secret; in Korea it was generally known throughout the world. For coping with a Soviet military threat from Cuba there was a preexisting plan for direct military counteraction; in Korea there was nothing except a standard plan for the evacuation of citizens in the event of an outbreak of hostilities. In the Cuban decision the United States was directly confronted by Soviet military power, vastly increased over 1950 by the addition of nuclear weapons; in the Korean case the United States, favored by a near monopoly of atomic weapons, faced the Soviet Union indirectly in the actions of a close Soviet ally. American military security was a much more salient value in the Cuban decision than in the Korean case. In the Cuban decision there was sharp conflict among the President's advisers who advocated two different courses of action; in the Korean decision there was group consensus around a single action proposal. The Korean decision did not contain contingency plans; the Cuban decision envisaged escalating application of military measures. In the Korean case legitimating international support preceded, but in the Cuban case followed, the American military action. In the Korean decision the United States obtained the support of a "universal" international organization (the United Nations); the Cuban action was supported by a regional international organization (the Organization of American States).

COMPARISON AND DECISION-MAKING ANALYSIS

If we narrow attention to specific analytical aspects of foreign policy decisions and compare the two cases in terms of decision-making variables and propositions derived from the Korean decision, the following principal findings are suggested.

Organizational variables. Investigation of the Cuban case reveals strong support for the Korea-derived hypothesis that *crisis decisions tend to be made by small, ad hoc decisional units*. It will be recalled that the decisional unit in the Korean case numbered fourteen officials; in the Cuban case, about sixteen. That this size group may be optimum for high-level decisions under existing psychological and technological conditions is further suggested by the fact that the contemporary ruling Presidium of the Communist Party of the Soviet Union now numbers thirteen officials. An especially important point to note is that these crisis decisional units are of an ad hoc nature. Neither the formal National

Security Council nor the Cabinet was used in either case. It is to be noted also that the units vary in their ad hoc qualities. Some official roles were constant across the two cases—that is, the President, the Secretaries of State and Defense, and the Chairman of the Joint Chiefs of Staff (four roles). Even if the roles of regional Assistant Secretary of State and of experienced Ambassador are considered as functional equivalents in the two cases, still less than half the members of the decisional units occupy the same roles in the two decisions (a total of six roles). This suggests that the ad hoc properties of crisis decisional units are well worth close attention. So also does a report from Moscow that during all-night deliberations connected with the Israeli–Arab crisis of June 1967, the Soviet Presidium was joined by at least one nonregular member—Foreign Minister Andrei Gromyko.[13]

A comparison of the composition of the Korean and Cuban decisional units reveals a majority of military-related roles in the former and a plurality of special presidential advisers in the latter. The full-scale representation of the top leaders of the military establishment in 1950 may have been correlated with the newness of the Department of Defense; their absence in 1962 may have been related to the Department's strength and to the President's confidence in its leadership. The absence and presence of the head of the Central Intelligence Agency may be related to similar considerations. But, in any event, the President has been seen in two instances to have exercised wide latitude in deciding who should participate in determining the nation's response to crisis. By comparison, the Korean unit seems much more formal and hierarchical; the Cuban unit seems more diverse and reflective of different presidential needs.

Evidence to support another proposition derived from the Korean decision also seemed to be found in the Cuban case; that is, *the greater the crisis, the more the leader solicitation of subordinate advice*. This was originally suggested by President Truman's practice in the Blair House conferences of asking each of his advisers, in turn, what he thought of the situation. President Kennedy went beyond this in 1962. Not only did he withdraw from deliberations among his advisers so that they might freely express their views without distortions occasioned by his presence (it was found, for example, that departmental subordinates were less inclined to challenge the views of their own superiors in the President's presence),[14] but he sought the advice of experienced officials then outside government. At a late stage of decision, on October 21, he even sounded out the views of the British Ambassador, a long-time friend.[15] If the Cuban crisis is regarded as of greater magnitude than that in Korea, the differential search for advice might then be explained on the basis of objective characteristics of the situation. On the other hand, perhaps the somewhat different pattern of advice-seeking can be explained on grounds of different presidential personalities. One of the tasks of the further development of decision-making analysis will be to devise means for separating such factors and arriving at judgments about their relative importance.

A third proposition suggested by the Korean–Cuban comparison was one not originally entertained: *the greater the crisis, the greater is the clarity of differentiation between task leadership and emotional affect leadership roles.* In both decisions one official, who regarded himself and was recognized by others

13. *New York Times*, June 9, 1967, p. 8.
14. Sorensen, *Kennedy*, pp. 765–766.
15. Abel, *Missile Crisis*, p. 89.

as having especially close affective ties with the President, seemed to emerge into a salient position as the adviser who contributed most to clarifying a recommended course of action to lay before the President for decision. In the Korean decision the task of presenting courses of action for decision by the President was performed by the Secretary of State; in the Cuban decision it was performed outstandingly, but not exclusively, by the President's brother, the Attorney General. In both cases it was true, of course, that the President himself ultimately had to decide—to think through and to be ultimately responsible for the measures proposed for the task of crisis management. But at the same time his emotional affect role (or perhaps, better, his authoritative decision or legitimating role) was perhaps even more salient. "He pulled us all together" was the way one participant of the Blair House conferences explained President Truman's role. And it may well be imagined that President Kennedy's reassurance to the air strike advocates that their course of action was not completely out of the question did much to preserve the cooperative behavior and satisfaction with group performance among his advisers after hours of conflict among advocates of different alternatives. If such enhanced role differentiation proves characteristic of crisis decisions in international politics, then an important link can be made with analogous findings of small group research in social psychology with interesting mutual implications.

Informational variables. Two propositions from the Korean decision pertaining to information and communication variables were also seen reflected with some modification and with deepened appreciation of their significance as a result of comparison with the Cuban decision. These were that *crisis tends to be accompanied by increased search behaviors for new information about the threatening event* and *the greater the crisis, the more information about it tends to be elevated to the top of the organizational hierarchy*. These two propositions describe a pattern of search and centralization of new information in organizational behavior under crisis conditions. They were suggested by persistent requests for new information from Korea after the first press report of the invasion, by President Truman's orders to all American missions throughout the world to provide him with any new information about possible Soviet moves, and by the speed and directness with which essential information was brought to his attention (including delivery of a report from General MacArthur at 5:00 A.M. on June 30). The same pattern of intensified search for new information was observed in the Cuban decision where the President immediately authorized more aerial reconnaissance missions to verify the findings of early photographic analysis. Although such flights involved risk, the President was willing to take it for the needed information.

Both the Korean and Cuban decisions saw temporary exceptions to the second proposition cited above: the sleeping General MacArthur in Tokyo was not informed of initial reports of the North Korean invasion during the early morning hours of June 25 until his aides had confirmed that the news was really serious; President Kennedy was not informed of the initial discovery of the Cuban missile sites on the evening of October 15 until the next morning because an adviser wished to protect his health by allowing him a good night's sleep after arduous travel to prepare for the difficult days ahead.

Both of these stoppages on the upward path of information were temporary and in these cases did not have a significant effect upon the decisions taken.

However, the attention given to them, especially the latter, underscores the widely appreciated necessity for relevant information to reach speedily the highest decisional levels under crisis conditions. This pattern of behavior, if it proves general, has very important implications for crisis management; for it means that decision makers under crisis are not to be viewed as impervious to new informational inputs but are, on the contrary, to be seen as actively seeking news of relevance. This means that knowledge of criteria of relevance and channels of communication would permit placing information from outside sources into the search and centralization pattern of the organization responding to crisis.

Another proposition based on the Korean case held that *the greater the crisis, the greater is the propensity to supplement information about the objective state of affairs with information drawn from past experience.* This was suggested by the fact that decision makers in 1950 tended to view the North Korean invasion as having the same significance as the German, Japanese, and Italian aggressions of the pre-World War II period. The Cuban decision was different; the Russians had never done what they were found to be doing in Cuba—never before had they stationed nuclear weapons on foreign soil. Somehow, no historical analogy came readily to mind. But one Leninist maxim, identical to one cited in the course of the Korean decision, was recalled out of the past: the advice that "if you strike steel, pull back, if you strike mush, keep going."[16] This maxim was introduced into the deliberations of the President's advisers, as it was in the Korean decision, in the absence of more direct knowledge as information bearing upon Soviet motivations and probable responses to American actions. Comparative analysis thus aids appreciation of the kinds of information that can be added from past experience: historical analogy and asserted codes of behavior. Where one is not readily available, the other may be invoked.

A new proposition suggested by the Cuban case is that *the more the flow of past unconfirmed warnings that the crisis-precipitating event will occur, and the more the face-to-face assurances by an opponent that the action is not contemplated, the greater is the emotional shock when the event takes place.* This proposition combines two elements: frequency of unconfirmed prior reports and mode of communicating denial of intended action. In both the Korean and Cuban cases there were rumors and reports that what did happen would happen. But only in the Cuban case were there explicit denials by Soviet spokesmen to the President and to other high American officials that the Soviet Union did not intend to deploy offensive nuclear weapons in Cuba. When the undeniable evidence finally emerged, the President and his advisers seemed especially "angry" at Soviet duplicity; there was a sense of betrayal.[17] In the Korean decision there were no such direct Soviet assurances of nonthreatening behavior; the President and his advisers seemed to react with less emotion to the surprise attack. One suspects, however, that most crisis situations will be characterized by a rather strong emotional tone and that prior warnings and direct reassurances are intensifying rather than prerequisite conditions for emotional arousal. In the Korean decision, for example, Soviet leaders seem to have been shaken by the American action even though the two factors noted above were not present from the Soviet point of view. As Andrei Vyshinsky said to a Korean decision participant just prior to the former Soviet diplomat's

16. Sorensen, *Kennedy*, p. 763.

17. *Ibid.*, p. 759.

death, "We can't believe anything you Americans say. You led us to believe that you wouldn't do anything in Korea and then you did."

Normative variables. A basic proposition concerning values from the Korean decision that seems supported in the Cuban case is that *crisis tends to evoke a dominant goal-means value complex that persists as an explicit or implicit guide to subsequent responses.* In the Korean decision this proposition was suggested by the immediate response of the American officials to try to secure their goal of a cessation of North Korean aggression through collective action within the framework of the United Nations. Their first thought was not of direct military counteraction and there was no prepared plan for it. In the Cuban decision the first response of American officials was that the United States would have to take some kind of military action to attain the goal of withdrawal of Soviet missiles from Cuba;[18] there were, in fact, plans ready for military action against the island.[19] Although there is no information about the President's initial reaction to the reported presence of the missiles, an authoritative account of the first conference measures involving air, naval, or ground action were salient in the discussions of his advisers from the outset. And one of the first directives given by the President as a result of this conference was that the armed forces should prepare for military action against Cuba within a week. Thus in Korea the initial American response was a diplomatic one with military overtones; while in Cuba it was a military move with diplomatic correlates. Both cases suggest the importance of the initial frame of normative reference (desired goals and preferred means of achieving them) that emerges in a crisis situation.

A proposition suggested by the Cuban case enables new appreciation of related behaviors in the Korean decision. This is that *moral persuasion can lead to changes in preferred courses of action by at least some officials.* In the Cuban decision, following an eloquent argument by the Attorney General that a surprise attack was not in the American tradition, the Secretary of the Treasury changed his preference from air attack to naval blockade.[20] On the other hand, the same moral appeal was rejected as irrelevant by former Secretary of State Acheson who continued to favor the air attack alternative. Nevertheless, the potency of moral suasion in at least one case suggests a new appreciation of President Truman's moral commitment to the United Nations revealed at the very outset of the Korean decision. Movingly, before the first formal deliberations began, the President was heard to say, "We can't let the U.N. down." Although there was no record of conflict over alternatives or changes of preference associated with values in the Korean case, the shared desire to avoid world war by strengthening the United Nations takes on new importance as an explanation for the strong consensus behind military resistance in Korea in 1950.

Interestingly, the Korean–Cuban comparison suggests the proposition that *in international crisis decision making there is a taboo against explicit general discussion of the domestic political implications of the event or of intended action*—at least in the American case. An intriguing finding of the Korean case was that there was no discussion of domestic politics in the two Blair House conferences. When the Under Secretary of State tried to begin such a discussion at the end of the first conference, he apparently so annoyed the President that he was

18. Abel, *Missile Crisis*, p. 36.
19. *Ibid.*, p. 21.
20. *Ibid.*, p. 67.

excluded from the second meeting. In the Cuban decision the only record of consideration of such matters was a note passed surreptitiously to presidential assistant Theodore Sorensen by a Republican air strike proponent who warned that unless effective action were taken to remove the missiles a Republican House of Representatives would be elected in the impending mid-term elections. The private transmittal of this note seems to underscore the sensed impermissibility of open discussion of such issues. The derivation of this proposition illustrates how a fact perceived in one case comes to be perceived as part of a possibly significant general pattern only on the basis of inquiry into other cases. The qualification that this may apply only to American experience has been added; crossnational studies of foreign policy crisis decisions will be required before this proposition will merit more general confidence.

Organizational process, intellectual process, and decisional outcome. The primary tasks of decision-making analysis are to describe and to explain decision-making processes and outcomes. In pursuing these tasks, two main processes can be separated analytically: an organizational process and an intellectual process. It is further assumed that these two processes are in a relationship of mutual influence. In the first process organizational roles are mobilized for decision; information is received, gathered, and recalled; and relevant values are given, identified, or newly thrust upon the decision makers. In the second kind of process the main elements of decision are identified, evaluated, combined, and selected in group activity. The outcomes—the chosen alternatives, the plans for implementation, and the contingency plans—are thought of as being the product of the interaction of the organizational and intellectual processes.

The comparison of the Korean and Cuban decisions permits a somewhat clearer understanding of the importance of organizational and intellectual processes for decisional outcomes than was possible on the basis of the Korean decision alone. One factor—intellectual task leadership—seems to stand out with greater importance as a key element in explaining the nature of decisions taken in response to crisis. The Korean and Cuban decisions differ in their antecedent conditions, organizational processes, intellectual processes, and decisions taken. In the Korean decision there was no *a priori* contingency plan for military action; yet a decision was taken to engage in military combat. In the Cuban case plans for a military attack on Cuba were in existence, but a limited blockade short of direct attack was chosen. Compared with the Cuban decision, the organizational roles engaged in the Korean decision were less heterogeneous, there was more formality in organizational structure, the information available to the decision makers was less comprehensive and accurate, and the values perceived to be threatened were less complex. In terms of intellectual process, the Korean decision was characterized by commentary upon a single proposed course of action; the Cuban decision was marked by contention over preferred alternatives. The Korean decisional outcome was limited in the scope of its anticipation of subsequent events. It was not a composite of the various courses of action proposed—a composite that envisioned increasingly costly commitments to action, as was represented by the Cuban decision where possible Soviet counter moves had been hypothesized. The Korean decision was undertaken with less perceived risk of Soviet counteraction than was the Cuban decision. Both decisions were similar, however, in the strong initial agreement among the officials that the course of events perceived as taking place in the international environment had by some means to be reversed. What remained at issue was how and when.

Now no single factor explanation will be sufficient to account for these similarities and differences in process and outcome; indeed, a basic assumption of decision-making analysis is that appreciation of the *interaction* of the multiple variables to which attention is called by the framework is a more adequate approach to understanding. Yet, as empirical research proceeds in the case study of decisions, undoubtedly some factors will come to be perceived as more directly and importantly contributive to outcomes than others. On the basis of the Korean–Cuban comparison the exceptional importance of the President's style of leadership can be seen. His choice of who should advise him in the crisis is a vitally important element of organizational process. Furthermore, his choice —either explicitly made or implicitly accepted—of the process by which alternative courses of action are to be identified, evaluated, and presented to him is an element of high importance for the intellectual process of decision. In the Korean decision the President supported the intellectual leadership of the Secretary of State and the latter fulfilled his responsibility according to his own definition: an adviser should present to the President a set of considered recommendations that are the product of staff work involving interdepartmental coordination. The tone of the two Blair House conferences was not one of group creativity in identifying and evaluating proposed courses of action; in fact, some participants and close observers noted the lack of exploration in depth of the implications of the decision. This is not to say that the President inhibited the free expression of views; he did not. In fact he called for them. But the relationship between the President and the Secretary of State was so intimate, the intellectual style of the Secretary was of such a nature, and relationships with the Secretary of Defense were so avoidant, that no truly wide-ranging exploration of the issues raised by the attack was made. Thus a decision to fight was taken without explicit plans for possible ground intervention or for measures to be taken in response to Soviet counterintervention if it should occur. By contrast, President Kennedy chose his advisers in part in terms of intellectual intimacy. He encouraged creative group problem-solving processes. No one adviser was his "first minister," but he allowed his brother to lead intellectually an extended exploration of alternatives in nearly a week of questioning. The product was a decision that foresaw a great many contingencies and was prepared for multiple courses of action. The difference in time available for the two decisions, of course, was a variable of high importance, but the significance of both organizational and intellectual task leadership seems striking when the two decisions are compared.

COMPARISON AND THE CONCEPT OF CRISIS

Another approach to the comparative analysis of the two decisions is to examine their implications for the three components of crisis that have been suggested by Hermann and to explore their implications for crisis management.

Time as an independent variable. The Cuban decision took place over a longer period of time than did the Korean decision. Thus it may be possible to identify some of the more important correlates of long versus short decision time by comparing the two decisions. It may be argued that it is tautologically or at least trivially true to say that "the longer the time, the longer the something" because "something" in this case can mean "anything." And yet out of the infinite universe of anything that might happen during the longer time of the Cuban decision as compared with the Korean decision, only some things thrust themselves before our attention as potentially significant. It is these that we will note briefly here, ordering them in terms of categories of the decision-making framework. Thus our comparison suggests for *organization* that the longer the decision time, the greater the conflict within decisional units and the greater the investment of emotional affect in policy and personal differences; the greater the needs for affective leadership within decisional units; the greater the achievement of decisional unit consensus through processes of changes in individual positions and withdrawal of dissenters; the greater the efforts to secure decisional reversals by proponents of different courses of action; the greater the consultation with persons outside the core decisional unit; the greater the proliferation of functionally specific subordinate organizations designed to provide the decision makers with premises for choice; and the greater the probability that the dominant leader will seek confirmation of the soundness of his choices from trusted friends before public commitment. For *information*, extended decision time implies greater inputs of written versus oral information and interpretation; and greater probability of information disclosures that may facilitate unfavorable opponent counteraction. In *normative* matters, it is to be expected that long decision time will be accompanied by shifts in the value bases designed to legitimate the crisis responses—for example, in the Cuban decision it was decided to legitimate American action under Articles 6 and 8 of the Rio Treaty rather than under the United Nations Charter as first contemplated. In relationships with the *external* and *internal settings*, longer decision time implies greater efforts to communicate with allies on a face-to-face basis (e.g., Mr. Acheson's mission to Europe to inform NATO allies of the American position), and greater frequency of public deception to conceal information about the way in which the crisis is perceived and about the probable costs of coping with it. In terms of *intellectual process* it is to be expected that the longer the decision time, the more the alternative courses of action considered.

Aside from the above hypothesized empirical correlates of longer decision time, comparison of the two cases suggests some strategies for manipulating the variable of time in producing crisis conditions. At least three techniques are possible: creating short decision time by ultimatum; pursuing rapid deprivational action; and overloading the problem-solving capacities of the decision makers so that they can devote but little attention to the problem at hand. Conversely, to provide more extended time for crisis decision deliberations one would avoid issuance of an ultimatum, act slowly in relation to opponent values, and minimize other problems thrust upon his attention.

Threat to values as an independent variable. Comparison of the Korean and Cuban decisions suggests that it may be fruitful to begin to create a typology of the kinds of values perceived as threatened in crisis situations. Both crises suggest that there is a tendency to perceive one central value as severely threatened and then to distinguish many other important values related to it. In the Korean case the main value seemed to be that of protecting the United Nations as an instrument of peace by successfully carrying out a collective security response to aggression; thus world war would be averted. Related values were the confidence of allies in American assurances of support and the security of Japan. The North Korean invasion was not perceived as an immediate threat to the military security of the United States. By contrast, in the Cuban decision the military security of the United States was the central value. The viability of the principles of the Monroe Doctrine and the confidence of American allies in Latin America and elsewhere were related values.

Thus, building upon the kinds of values seen threatened in the two decisions, a typology might be suggested that includes at least: threats to military security (immediate and long-range), threats to asserted universal principles of international order, threats to regional stability and integrity (proximate and distant), and threatened loss of international political support.

In terms of crisis management the Korean–Cuban comparison suggests that the sense of increased threat to values can be manipulated by targeting on values of high priority in the opponent's normative hierarchy, by threatening many values simultaneously, by evoking past threats to values (as the North Korean invasion unwittingly did), and by acting close in psychological space (as the Russians did in Cuba). Lesser threat to values can be achieved by avoiding such behaviors.

Surprise as an independent variable. Comparison of the two decisions reveals a different quality of surprise in each case that may well be worth considering further in studies of crisis. The type of surprise represented in the Korean case can be defined as AGUS surprise (*A*nticipated *G*enerally but *U*nanticipated *S*pecifically). In the spring of 1950, American intelligence analysts had anticipated that something unusual of a military nature was about to happen along the Soviet periphery but they were unable to pinpoint the exact location. Korea was generally discounted as their analysis focused upon the Middle East and Europe. They also expected a Chinese Communist invasion of Taiwan in the summer of 1950, but they did not expect correlated Korean action. Thus the Korean attack occurred within a context of expected military action somewhere along the periphery of the Communist countries. The surprising thing was that it came in Korea.

The kind of surprise involved in the Cuban decision was somewhat different. It might be termed BATO surprise (*B*etrayed *A*ssurances *t*o the *O*pposite). In this kind of surprise the event is anticipated, even specifically, but the opponent gives explicit reassurances that the action will not be taken. In fact, the prelude to the Cuban decision presents a classic paradigm for this kind of surprise: The actor warns the opponent not to do it. The opponent says he has not done it. The opponent says he will not do it. The opponent has actually never done it in the past. The opponent says that he can gain his goals in other ways. The actor agrees that the opponent can achieve his goals in other ways. The opponent offers plausible explanations of facts that might suggest he will do it. There are numerous unconfirmed reports that the opponent has done or is doing it. The opponent does it. Surprise!

The principal difference in the effect of AGUS versus BATO surprise is that the latter seems to produce a much stronger emotional reaction. Americans will recall that national indignation over the attack on Pearl Harbor was much greater because Japanese diplomats were "talking peace" in Washington at the time it occurred, something that wartime commentators almost never failed to emphasize. Whether higher degrees of emotionality in crisis responses will lead to perceptual distortions or to greater propensity for risk taking is something that will have to be explored in further studies of crisis decision making. A seeming difference in the emotional quality of surprise in the two decisions studied can only be mentioned here.[21]

With respect to crisis management, the above paradigm might be followed to produce an emotional quality of surprise in adversaries—or might be avoided to diminish that quality.

CONCLUSIONS: DEVELOPING CASE STUDIES OF CRISIS DECISIONS

The analysis presented above by no means exhausts the potentialities for comparative analysis of the Korean and Cuban decisions. Since there is a hypothetically infinite variety of analytical aspects that can be created to describe a concrete social object, much more extended inquiry into the two cases is warranted both within the decision-making framework and from other perspectives.

But, in addition to further analytical efforts employing existing frameworks for case studies on available materials, several other lines of development for decision-making case analysis have been suggested by the present inquiry. The first is greater refinement of single case and comparative case study methods. The case study method is well known for its diagnostic usefulness in probing complex relationships among variables, in identifying important variables that may be overlooked in less deep immersion in events, and in achieving comprehension of the unity and integration of political action. But can it also become a reliable tool for cumulative development of theory through comparative analysis?

A second important need is to raise the question through comparative analysis as to whether capacities for coping with foreign policy crises at the national level improve over time. Such a study would raise issues similar to those studies in the fields of political and administrative development. It would benefit enormously from advances in the study of organizational learning. An important early task would be to develop criteria for effective crisis coping and then to compare at least two decisions made within the same national context on these dimensions over time. External theory and research could be introduced to suggest desirable directions for developing crisis-coping capacities.

A third essential study will be to reconstruct "normal" decisions and to compare them with crisis decisions. A suggestion of methodological perspective for such studies may be taken from the findings of the study of personality development through research on letters written by the individual to various correspondents. It has been found that a much more adequate understanding of the individual has been obtained by studying the letters written to a stable set of correspondents over a long period of time than by analysis of a series of letters to the same individual or fragmentary letters to various correspondents, either concentrated or scattered in time.[22] This suggests that a much better understanding of crisis decisions and of foreign policy decision making in general will be achieved when the behavior of the decision makers can be viewed in the

21. A third type of surprise situation is also worth investigating—NEATA surprise (*N*ot *E*xpected *At* *A*ll).

22. Hedda Bolgar, "The Case Study Method," in Benjamin B. Wolman, ed., *Handbook of Clinical Psychology* (New York: McGraw-Hill, 1965), pp. 33ff.

context of normal activities of directing the national or international organizational course in international politics.

A fourth essential task, very high in terms of priority, will be to introduce into the analysis of case study materials interpretive hypotheses derived from the other behavioral science disciplines. The very nature of the decision-making framework encourages this kind of approach to understanding since it calls for data bearing upon theories of organizational behavior, information theory, and theories of motivation in individual and group psychology. Strategies may well be devised for relating theories of learning, change, conflict, control, creativity, and other social science perspectives. Except for the pioneering work of de Rivera,[23] this has not been seriously attempted for case studies and remains a worthy challenge.

A continuing task will be to relate the findings of crisis case studies to those obtained by laboratory simulations, experiments, documentary studies, mathematical analyses, and attitude surveys. Somehow, the scattered resources of more or less reliable propositions about crisis decision making will have to be inventoried and subjected to a constant process of integration-evaluation-selection-reintegration in the pursuit of deeper understanding. Comparative case studies of crisis decisions offer only one approach—but a challenging one—toward that end.

23. Joseph H. de Rivera, *The Psychological Dimension of Foreign Policy* (Columbus: Merrill, 1968).

chapter four

EDITOR'S INTRODUCTION

The contrasts may dominate one's initial considerations in comparing the European crisis in the summer of 1914 with that resulting from the Soviet placement of missiles in Cuba during October 1962. The Cuban crisis constituted a bilateral confrontation between the leaders of a world that militarily was characterized by bipolarity. Despite the opposition of the Dual Alliance and the states more loosely associated in the Triple Entente, the 1914 crisis was multilateral in a militarily multipolar world. The Soviet Union and the United States faced one another in 1962 as nuclear powers with access to the products of military technologies that would have been fathomless to Poincaré, William II, Grey, Nicholas II, Franz Joseph, and their contemporaries. Furthermore, one crisis resulted in war; the other did not. Given the many disparities between these two crises, Holsti's attempt to confirm hypotheses in both situations provides a significant test of the assumption that there exists a class of phenomena called crises, and that members of this class involve certain relationships regardless of how different they are in numerous particulars.

In the present chapter Holsti first reviews some of his previous statistical analysis of hypotheses using data from the 1914 crisis. Then he expands on this prior research by a more impressionistic examination of the Cuban missile crisis to determine if the relationships found in the earlier situation can be sustained. Whereas Paige, in the previous chapter, used case studies to generate hypotheses, Holsti uses them to test hypotheses. By using a hypothesis-testing strategy, the author treats case study material in a different way. He need not comb the detailed narrative of a crisis first one way and then another to construct the richest possible propositional inventory. Instead, he approaches accounts of the crisis having already established the relationships for which he is looking. On first examination of the data, a social scientist might be satisfied with the identification of illustrative behavior in the crisis that appears to confirm or refute the hypothesized relationship (as Holsti does with the Cuban missile crisis). Eventually, however, the scientist will want to devise operational measures for the variables in the hypotheses and abstract data that will permit a more rigorous test (as Holsti does with the 1914 crisis).

Similar to Paige in the previous chapter, Holsti adopts predominantly a decision-making perspective. His hypotheses about perceptions of available alternatives, perceptions of the time available for action, and the pattern and volume of communications all treat variables regarded as basic in any examination of choice processes. However, his last hypothesis concerns the relative frequency of intra-coalition communication as opposed to inter-coalition communication. With that proposition the author moves beyond the confines of decision making and into consideration of the interaction between parties to the crisis, thus providing a link to the following chapter by McClelland and the later one on bargaining by Snyder (Chapter 10).

Two further introductory observations should be brought to the reader's attention. First, most of Holsti's hypotheses concern changes in the level of stress experienced by policy makers during the crisis. He thereby introduces the question of the relationship between the concepts of stress and crisis. Although the author does not explicitly differentiate between the terms, his usage seems consistent with that suggested by Milburn (Chapter 11). For Milburn a crisis is a situation or stimulus that produces certain psychological states in the decision makers—one of which is stress. Holsti divides the 1914 and Cuban crises into two periods distinguished by differences in the level of stress. A recurrent issue throughout this volume concerns the possible existence of empirically identifiable and theoretically useful stages in any crisis. Whereas Holsti uses the level of stress as a partitioning variable, Schwartz (Chapter 8) and Snyder (Chapter 10) use changes in the type of activities involved to mark the boundaries of stages in a crisis.

Finally, all three chapters in this section involve the comparison of two crises. The present chapter, however, also introduces comparison of different nations and alliances in the same crisis (1914). Given the restricted access of scholars to the working materials of contemporary policy makers in their own country—to say nothing of materials from other governments—Holsti demonstrates the value of examining crises sufficiently removed from the present to permit examination of opened diplomatic archives. This strategy offers one solution to the dilemma faced by those who wish to consider the behaviors within governments during a crisis. Of course, a problem arises if one attempts to extrapolate findings from such historical events to present or future crises without accounting for the critical variables that may have changed during the intervening time. Holsti attempts to identify such variables for his two crises, widely separated in time, in his concluding remarks.

Ole R. Holsti is a Professor of Political Science at the University of British Columbia. Before accepting his present post, Holsti was affiliated with the Conflict and Integration Project at Stanford University where he and his colleagues performed extensive and varied analyses of the outbreak of World War I.[1] In addition to his work on crisis behavior, Holsti has conducted research on the images and perceptions that individual policy makers have of others.[2] Closely related to both of these substantive interests has been his work on the application and extension of content analysis—particularly computer content analysis—to international documents.[3] Together with two associates, Holsti is currently writing a volume reporting empirical research on alliance behavior.

1. In addition to "The 1914 Case" from which material is drawn for the present chapter (see asterisked footnote, Chapter 4), Holsti's work on crisis includes Ole R. Holsti, Richard A. Brody, and Robert C. North, "Measuring Affect and Action in International Reaction Models: Empirical Materials from the 1962 Cuban Crisis," *Peace Research Society Papers*, 2 (1965), 170–190; Ole R. Holsti, "Perceptions of Hostility and Economic Variables," in Richard Merritt and Stein Rokkan, eds., *Comparing Nations* (New Haven: Yale University Press, 1966), pp. 169–190; Ole R. Holsti, Richard A. Brody, and Robert C. North, "Perception and Action in the 1914 Crisis," in J. David Singer, ed., *Quantitative International Politics* (New York: The Free Press, 1968), pp. 123–158; and Ole R. Holsti, *Crisis Escalation War* (Montreal: McGill-Queen's University Press, 1972).

2. Examples are Ole R. Holsti, "The Belief System and National Images," *Journal of Conflict Resolution*, 6 (September 1962), 244–252; and David J. Finlay, Ole R. Holsti, and Richard R. Fagen, *Enemies in Politics* (Chicago: Rand McNally, 1967).

3. See Ole R. Holsti, "An Adaptation of the 'General Inquirer' for the Systematic Analysis of Political Documents," *Behavioral Science*, 9 (1964), 382–388; Ole R. Holsti, "Content Analysis," in Gardner Lindzey and Elliot Aronson, eds., *The Handbook of Social Psychology*, 2nd ed. (Reading, Mass.: Addison-Wesley, 1968), pp. 596–692; and Ole R. Holsti, *Content Analysis for the Social Sciences and Humanities* (Reading, Mass.: Addison-Wesley, 1969).

chapter four

TIME, ALTERNATIVES, AND COMMUNICATIONS: THE 1914 AND CUBAN MISSILE CRISES*

Ole R. Holsti

This chapter compares two of the most dramatic and significant international crises of the twentieth century—that leading up to World War I in 1914 and the Soviet-American confrontation in October 1962 over the emplacement of offensive missiles in Cuba. For the 1914 crisis we will be concerned with the six weeks between the assassination of Archduke Franz Ferdinand and the British declaration of war on Germany at midnight, August 4. In the case of the Cuban crisis, we will examine aspects of decision making during the week (October 15–22) of secret deliberations between the small group of American leaders who knew of the presence of Soviet missile sites in Cuba, as well as during the subsequent week (October 22–28), in which a rapidly escalating crisis was brought to a peaceful resolution.[1]

The conception of crisis used in this chapter is borrowed from Hermann; that is, a *crisis* is defined as an unanticipated situation of severe threat and short decision time.[2] The 1914 and Cuban situations both conform to this definition. The assassination of Archduke Franz Ferdinand was clearly unanticipated, as was the rapid escalation of a local incident to a world war; perceived pressures of time dictated many of the most important decisions during the climactic stages of the crisis; and, increasingly, leaders in all of the nations involved perceived their national interests—or even their national existence—threatened by the actions of their adversaries.

It is equally clear that the discovery of Soviet missiles in Cuba precipitated a crisis and that it was regarded as such by those formulating a response to the Soviet move. Despite widespread rumors of Soviet missile installations in Cuba, photographic evidence of their presence was a surprise to virtually all officials in

* The sections of this chapter dealing with the 1914 crisis are drawn from my article, "The 1914 Case," with the kind permission of *The American Political Science Review*.

1. Limitations of space do not permit even a brief narrative of events during these crisis periods. An authoritative account of the 1914 crisis may be found in Sidney B. Fay, *The Origins of the World War* (New York: The Macmillan Company, 1928). The Cuban missile crisis has been described in Elie Abel, *The Missile Crisis* (Philadelphia: J.B. Lippincott, 1966); Robert F. Kennedy, *Thirteen Days* (New York: Norton, 1969); as well as other recent memoirs of the Kennedy Administration.

2. See Charles F. Hermann, *Crises in Foreign Policy* (Indianapolis: Bobbs-Merrill, 1969), pp. 29–36. Although Hermann's definition is taken as a starting point, there will also be an attempt to shed light on its usefulness; for example, the impressionistic judgment that time pressure is an attribute of situations that clearly qualify as crises is tested quantitatively in the 1914 crisis and more qualitatively in the Cuba situation.

Washington; the rate of construction on the missile sites made it clear that any decision to prevent their completion could not be long delayed; and almost all who joined the American decision group interpreted the Soviet move as a serious threat to national security.[3] As one participant in these discussions put it: "Everyone round the table recognized that we were in a major crisis. We didn't know, that day, if the country would come through it with Washington intact."[4]

The 1914 and Cuban situations are similar in a number of respects and differ in others. For our purposes the similarity of primary interest is that both situations conform to the previously cited definition of crisis. The most significant difference is that the events in 1914 led to a world war whereas the Cuban confrontation was resolved without recourse to war. Stated somewhat differently, the inputs to decision makers in the two crises shared a number of attributes (surprise, threat, short decision time), but the outputs were significantly different (world war versus nonviolent resolution).

Naturally, the question then arises: How can we account for the different outcomes? In an attempt to explore this question, this chapter examines and compares three aspects of the decision-making process in these crises: time pressure, the search for and definition of alternative courses of action, and the patterns of communication.

The comparisons to be drawn here are necessarily less rigorous than might be desired. The 1914 data are relatively complete, thereby permitting systematic quantitative analyses of several hypotheses. On the other hand, primary documentation for the Cuban crisis is limited to the formal communications between Soviet and American leaders during the week following President Kennedy's disclosure of the presence of missiles in Cuba. Notably lacking are documents from the week of October 15–22, during which the decision to undertake a naval blockade of Cuba was made. Hence for this crucial period we are forced to rely on the numerous memoirs and journalistic accounts of these deliberations. Moreover, whereas the 1914 data reveal something of the decision processes in all the major capitals of Europe, we are lacking even anecdotal information on Soviet decision making during the Cuban crisis.[5] Owing to these limitations, only some of the hypotheses supported with 1914 data can be retested in the Cuban crisis, and then impressionistically rather than exhaustively.

PERCEPTIONS OF TIME

1914

Data for the 1914 crisis were derived by content analyses of all documents written between June 27 and August 4 by British, French, Russian, German, and Austro-Hungarian decision makers filling the roles of head of state, head of government, foreign minister, under secretary of foreign affairs, and minister of

3. The one notable exception appears to have been Secretary of Defense Robert McNamara, whose initial reaction was that "a missile is a missile. It makes no great difference whether you are killed by a missile fired from the Soviet Union or from Cuba." Quoted in Abel, *Missile Crisis*, p. 51.

4. Douglas Dillon, quoted in Abel, *Missile Crisis*, p. 48.

5. There have, however, been efforts to analyze Soviet motives and strategies in the Cuban crisis. See, for example, Arnold L. Horelick, "The Cuban Missile Crisis," *World Politics*, 16 (1964), 363–389.

war or chief of the general staff. While these documents do not include all messages initiated by the designated leaders—notably lacking are oral communications—they do represent a substantial sample (albeit of unknown representativeness) of all messages. The 1914 documents yielded nearly five thousand thematic units or "perceptions" upon which the present analysis is based.[6]

The entire set of 5,078 perceptions derived from the decision makers' documents was coded to test two hypotheses relating crisis to perceptions of time. Every statement in which there was reference to time as a factor in decision making was extracted. The 167 time perceptions were classified according to date[7] and stated reason for the relevance of time. As shown in Table 1, most of the time perceptions in these data fall into four major categories which correspond to the development of events within the crisis. (In Table 1 the four substantive categories are designated *A–D* and the residual category is *E*.) The shifts in the prevalent reasons given for the concern with time divide the crisis into four periods: June 27–July 20, July 21–29, July 30–August 2, and August 3–4.

TABLE 1. FREQUENCY AND TYPE OF PERCEPTIONS OF TIME AS A FACTOR IN DECISION MAKING: TOTALS FOR AUSTRIA-HUNGARY, GERMANY, FRANCE, RUSSIA, AND GREAT BRITAIN

Period	Total Perceptions	*Type of Time Perception*					
		A	*B*	*C*	*D*	*E*	*Total*
June 27–July 20	1,031	15	1	0	2	4	22
July 21–29	1,658	11	29	10	2	1	53
July 30–August 2	1,910	1	8	29	16	9	63
August 3–4	479	0	0	2	22	5	29
Total	5,078	27	38	41	42	19	167

NOTE: *A*—Time as a factor in Austro-Hungarian action towards Serbia.
B—Time as a factor in localizing conflict.
C—Time as a factor in mobilization.
D—Time as a factor in political commitments.
E—Others.

Through July 20, references to time focus on the prospects of early Austro-Hungarian actions against Serbia. Count Alexander Hoyos, for example, wrote on July 7 that "from a military standpoint . . . it would be much more favorable to start the war now than later since the balance of power would weigh against us in the future." Hoyos' fear that "through a policy of delay and weakness, we at a later moment, endanger this unflinching support of the German

6. For a description of the units of analysis and coding rules, see Robert C. North, Ole R. Holsti, M. George Zaninovich, and Dina A. Zinnes, *Content Analysis* (Evanston, Ill.: Northwestern University Press, 1963), and Ole R. Holsti, Robert C. North, and Richard A. Brody, "Perception and Action in the 1914 Crisis," in J. David Singer, ed., *Quantitative International Politics* (New York: The Free Press, 1968).

7. In other studies of the 1914 crisis, the content analysis data were divided into twelve periods of approximately equal volume of documentation, as in Table 1. Thus time periods early in the crisis are longer than those in the days immediately preceding the outbreak of war. The overall intercoder reliability for the content analysis performed for this study was 0.87.

Empire,"[8] was not wholly without foundation. Germany was exerting considerable pressure on its ally not to postpone a showdown until a less clearly defined future. Gottlieb von Jagow, German Foreign Minister, wrote on July 15: "We are concerned at present with the preeminent political question, perhaps the last opportunity of giving the Greater-Serbia menace its death blow under comparatively favorable circumstances."[9]

Once the content of the Austrian ultimatum became known, the forty-eight-hour deadline given the Serbian government to draft a reply became an immediate subject of concern. The time perceptions from July 21 to July 29 focus predominantly on the necessity of delaying the course of events in the Balkans in the hope of averting war, or at least containing it within a local area.

By July 30 it was apparent that war between Austria-Hungary and Serbia could not be prevented. At the same time it was increasingly evident that a chain reaction was in danger of being set off. As late as August 1 many European decision makers asserted that if time permitted reconvening the concert powers, general war might be avoided. The British Foreign Minister wrote: "I still believe that if only a little respite in time can be gained before any Great Power begins war it might be possible to secure peace."[10] By this time, however, the major concern for many decision makers was that one's nation not be caught militarily unprepared in case of war.

The dilemma was obvious. Time was required to avert a general European war; above all, a moratorium on military operations was necessary. On August 1, King George wrote of his efforts "to find some solution which permits in any case the adjournment of active military operations and the granting of time to the powers to discuss among themselves calmly."[11] But, increasingly, this consideration was overshadowed by the fear that a potential adversary might gain a head start in mobilizing its military power. Although no official mobilization orders except those of Austria-Hungary and Serbia were issued until July 29, there were increasing rumors and suspicions of secret preparations.

In the early hours of the morning of July 30, the Kaiser wrote on the margin of a message from the Czar, ". . . I can not agree to any more mediation, since the Czar who requested it has at the same time secretly mobilized behind my back. It is only a maneuver, in order to hold us back and to increase the start they have already got. My work is at an end!"[12] Later, the Kaiser added, "In view of the colossal war preparations of Russia now discovered, this is all too late, I fear. Begin! Now!"[13]

8. Austro-Hungarian Monarchy, Ministerium des k. and k. Hauses und des Äusseren, *Österreich-Ungarns Aussenpolitik von der bosnischen Krise 1908 bis zum Kriegsausbruch 1914; Diplomatische Aktenstücke des Österreich-Ungarischen Ministeriums des Äussern*, Ludwig Bittner and Alfred Pribram, Heinrich Srbik and Hans Uebersberger, eds., vol. 8 (Vienna and Leipzig, 1930), no. 10118. In this chapter references in documentary collections are made by document number rather than by page number.

9. Max Montgelas and Walther Schücking, eds., *Outbreak of the World War, German Documents Collected by Karl Kautsky* (New York: Oxford University Press, 1924), no. 48.

10. Great Britain, Foreign Office, *British Documents on the Origins of the War, 1898–1914*, vol. 11, G. P. Gooch and Harold Temperley, eds. (London, 1926), no. 411.

11. France, Commission for the Publication of Documents Relative to the War of 1914, *Documents Diplomatiques Française (1871–1914)*, 3rd series, vols. 10 and 11 (Paris, 1936), no. 550.

12. Montgelas and Schücking, *Outbreak*, no. 390.

13. *Ibid.*, no. 433.

The previous day Russia had ordered—and then cancelled—a general mobilization. Later, it was decided in St. Petersburg that the mobilization of the four southern military districts would deter an Austro-Hungarian attack on Serbia without alarming Berlin. But technical difficulties caused the Russians to reverse their decision once again on July 30 in favor of general mobilization—German warnings notwithstanding.

In response to what was perceived as a mounting threat against its eastern frontiers, the German Empire proclaimed a "state of threatening danger of war" on July 31 and dispatched a twelve-hour ultimatum to Russia demanding a cessation of military preparations. Berlin then ordered mobilization on August 1. The reason for the German decision was, that ". . . we could not sit back quietly and wait to see whether a more commonsense view would gain the upper hand at Petersburg, while at the same time the Russian mobilization was proceeding at such speed, that, if the worst came, we should be left completely outstripped in a military sense."[14] A general mobilization was simultaneously ordered in Paris. The French General Staff stated that ". . . any delay of twenty-four hours applied to the calling up of reserves and to the sending the telegram ordering covering troops will result in a backward movement of our troops, that is to say an initial abandonment of a part of our territory, either 15 or 20 kilometers every day of delay."[15] Although official British mobilization was delayed until August 2, many had advocated such action considerably earlier. On July 31, Arthur Nicolson had urged immediate military preparations: "It seems to me most essential, whatever our future course may be in regard to intervention, that we should at once give orders for mobilization of the army."[16]

During the final two days of the crisis period, when only the question of Britain's entry into the war remained to be decided, attention turned to time as a factor in political commitments. Almost 80 percent of the statements during August 3–4 referred to the desire among various leaders in major European capitals for alliance partners (e.g., Italy, at least a nominal ally of Germany and Austria-Hungary) and smaller European nations to commit themselves as soon as possible to the war effort.

Ten days after the small-scale mobilizations by Serbia and Austria-Hungary on July 25, each of the major European nations had ordered a general mobilization; the armies totaling less than four hundred thousand men called to fight a limited war had grown to nearly twelve million men. As each mobilization was ordered it was described as a necessary defensive reaction—made more urgent by the pressure of time—to a previous decision within the other alliance, although in 1914 such an act was commonly regarded as tantamount to a declaration of war. Thus each mobilization acted as a stimulus that elicited an almost reflex-like response.

Although the cataloguing of the data according to the policy makers' concern with time was undertaken as a preliminary to the testing of several hypotheses, the results in Table 1 are noteworthy for other reasons. In 1914—and perhaps in other crises as well—it is possible to identify distinctive stages based on the changing reasons the policy makers had for being interested in time. If decision makers are more receptive to new information when it pertains to their immediate concerns, then the stages found in the time perception data suggest

14. Montgelas and Schūster, *Outbreak*, no. 529.

15. France, *Documents*, no. 401.

16. Great Britain, *British Documents*, no. 368.

that some communications about time will more likely be attended to at one period of a crisis than at another.

The 1914 data were used to test two hypotheses relating the stress of crisis to perceptions of time; the first states:

> As stress increases in a crisis situation, time will be perceived as an increasingly salient factor in decision making.[17]

In order to perform a valid test of the hypothesis, the frequency of time references for each of the twelve periods (Table 1) was adjusted as follows:

$$\frac{\textit{Time Perceptions} \times 100}{\textit{Total Perceptions}}$$

The resulting scores were then aggregated into the two periods, divided by the outbreak of war between Austria-Hungary and Serbia on July 28.

A Mann-Whitney U test of the direction and magnitude of differences between the two periods was used on the data for each coalition. The hypothesis is strongly supported by the data for the Triple Entente (France, Russia, and England), whose leaders perceived time as a factor in decision making significantly more frequently during the culminating stages (July 29–August 4) of the crisis than during the earlier period (June 27–July 28) ($U = 3, p = .009$). The data for the Dual Alliance (Germany, Austria-Hungary) reveal that differences between the early and late periods of the crisis are in the predicted direction, but that the difference is not statistically significant ($U = 11.5, p = .19$).[18]

According to the second hypothesis:

> As stress increases in a crisis situation, decision makers will become increasingly concerned with the immediate rather than the distant future.

Of the total of 167 statements in which time was perceived to be a factor in decision making, only eight revealed a concern for the more distant future. All

17. The literature from which these hypotheses have been derived is reviewed in my "Perceptions of Time, Perceptions of Alternatives, and Patterns of Communication as Factors in Crisis Decision-Making," *Peace Research Society, Papers*, 3 (1965), 79–86.

Stress is used here as a consequence of one of the defining attributes of crisis—threat to important values. Eight of the hypotheses tested with the 1914 data postulate changes derived from increasing crisis-induced stress. The outbreak of war between Serbia and Austria-Hungary will be used as the dividing point between the period of *lower* (June 27–July 28) and *higher* (July 29–August 4) stress. The intuitive expectation that European decision makers were under greater stress during the latter period is supported by measures of both attitudes and actions. The 1914 documents contained 882 *perceptions of hostility* directed against the perceivers' nations, which were scaled by the Q-sort method. The results indicate significantly higher intensity during the July 29–August 4 period for each alliance ($Z = 10.81$ and 3.88; both are significant at the .0001 level). A scaling of the *actions* taken by members of each alliance also reveals a significantly higher level of violence or potential violence during the last week prior to the outbreak of general war ($Z = 2.24$ and 5.58, significant at the .025 and .0001 levels respectively). Thus the two periods meet the requirements necessary to test the hypotheses.

18. These and other data are analyzed by nation and on a day-to-day basis in the author's *Crisis Escalation War* (Montreal: McGill-Queen's University Press, 1972). For this hypothesis the correlation (Goodman-Kruskal *gamma*) between perceptions of increasing hostility and time perceptions is: Austria-Hungary, .16; Germany, .33; Britain, .61; France, .68; and Russia, .82.

perceptions of the distant future occur during the June 27–July 28 period and none are found in the last week of the crisis, a distribution which is statistically significant (Fisher exact test, $p = .002$).

Cuban Missile Crisis

The photographic evidence of construction activities in Cuba presented to President Kennedy on October 15 indicated that the Soviet missile sites in Cuba would be operational within a week to ten days. This expectation placed American leaders under considerable time pressure. There was no imperative for a reflex response—at least as the situation was defined by the President. This is not to deny, however, that decision time was short. American officials were fully aware that their task would become immeasurably more difficult once construction on the launching sites was completed: "For all of us knew that, once the missile sites under construction became operational, and capable of responding to any apparent threat or command with a nuclear volley, the President's options would be dramatically changed."[19] Moreover, deadlines other than that established by the rate of construction on the missile sites also weighed heavily upon those responsible for formulating American policy. According to Theodore Sorensen:

> *The knowledge that time was running out dominated our discussions and kept us meeting late into the night. The stepped up U-2 flights had apparently not alerted the Soviets to our discovery. But we had to formulate and declare our position, said the President, before they knew we knew, before the matter leaked out to the public and before the missiles became operational.*[20]

Finally, as James Robinson points out elsewhere in this book, decision time must be considered in relation to the task at hand, not merely against calendar time. In view of the awesome implications of the situation, it is hardly surprising that all accounts of decision making during the Cuban crisis—especially that of Robert F. Kennedy—are replete with indications of time pressure.

Despite the sense of urgency created by these deadlines, the President and his advisers sought to reduce the probability that either side would respond by a "spasm reaction." Hence efforts were made to delay taking overt actions as long as the situation permitted, and to select those responses which would lengthen rather than reduce the time available for considering other options. Equally important, there was a sensitivity for the time pressures under which the adversary was operating. There was a concern that Premier Khrushchev not be rushed into an irrevocable decision; it was agreed among members of the decision group that "we should slow down the escalation of the crisis to give Khrushchev time to consider his next move."[21] An interesting example of a tactic designed to increase the adversary's decision time emerges from the President's management of the naval quarantine. He ordered American ships to delay intercepting Soviet vessels until the last possible moment, *and had the order transmitted in the clear*.[22]

19. Theodore C. Sorensen, *Decision-Making in the White House* (New York: Columbia University Press, 1963), p. 31.
20. Theodore C. Sorensen, *Kennedy* (New York: Harper & Row, 1965), p. 680.
21. Elie Abel in television program of the National Broadcasting Company, "Cuba: The Missile Crisis" (February 9, 1964), mimeograph transcript, p. 19.
22. Roger Hilsman, "The Cuban Crisis," *Look*, August 25, 1964, p. 19.

The Soviets, who were certain to intercept the message, would at least know that they had time in which to decide how to react to the blockade. Similarly, the Soviet decision, on October 25, to slow down the westward progress of their ships in mid-Atlantic can be interpreted as an effort to lengthen decision time.

A content analysis of the messages exchanged between Moscow and Washington during the crisis indicates the relationship between perceived developments during the week of October 22–28 (Figure 1). Soviet and American

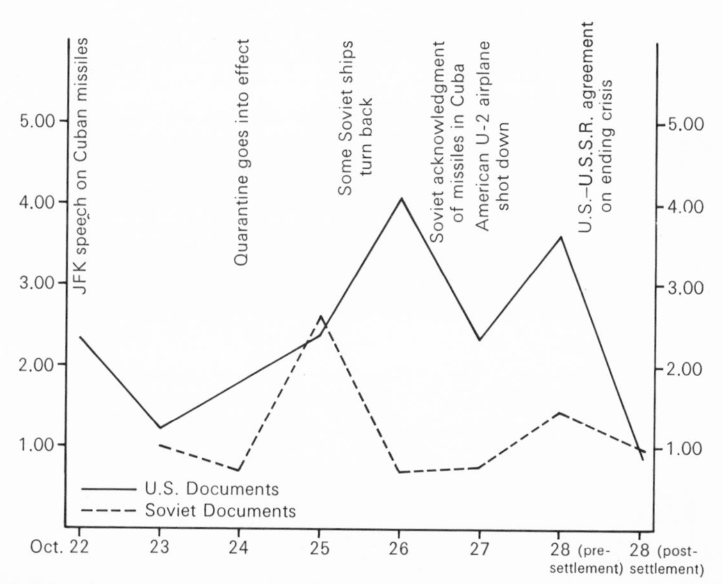

FIGURE 1. A graph depicting the relative frequency of references to time in Soviet and American documents between October 22 and October 28, 1962. The frequency of time references has been adjusted according to the following formula:

$$\frac{\text{References to Time}}{\text{Total Words in Document}} \times 100.$$

documents indicate that concern with time reached a peak at about the time that the Russian ships heading for Cuba turned back, thereby reducing the probability of a naval war in the Atlantic. That this was true slightly earlier for the Soviet Union than for the United States is perhaps explained by the fact that Soviet leaders were aware of their decision not to challenge the blockade before this was apparent in Washington. References to time pressure arose again on October 28 as it became increasingly clear that steps beyond a blockade might be taken by the United States to insure removal of the missiles. After the agreement to dismantle and remove the missile sites in exchange for a pledge against invading Cuba, references to time pressures declined in both Soviet and American documents.

A comparison of these two crises again confirms the "Thomas Theorem": "If men define situations as real, they are real in their consequences."[23] An

23. Quoted in Robert Merton, *Social Theory and Social Structure*, rev. ed. (New York: The Free Press, 1957), p. 421.

analysis of military technology and doctrines reveals that "objectively" time was of incalculably greater importance in 1962 than in 1914; that is, the period between a decision to use force and the execution of military acts is far shorter in an age of intercontinental ballistic missiles capable of reaching any target on earth in a matter of minutes. In contrast to the Soviet and American ability to strike at each other within minutes, estimates of the time required for Austria-Hungary to field a full army ranged from three to four weeks. The necessities of harvesting the summer's crops were an important factor in military timetables. Russia's inability to mount a rapid offensive against Germany could be discounted; this assumption, in fact, was the basis of the Schlieffen plan. Yet the "reality" as defined by European leaders in 1914 was quite different. They perceived that any delay might be fatal—and they acted on that assumption. During the culminating phases of the crisis, they increasingly perceived potential enemies as able to deliver a sudden punishing blow. As a result the penalties for delaying immediate military action were perceived to be increasingly high. Or, to use the language of deterrence theory, the nations of each coalition perceived those of the other alliance as able and willing to launch a decisive first strike and thus they hastened their own preparations. Hence the entire European concert system—which was assumed to act as an equilibrating mechanism—became instead a "runaway system."

Similarly, decision makers in the Cuban crisis were aware of the pressure of time and of the potential costs of delaying action. But they also perceived the dangers of acting in haste, and they were successful in mitigating the most severe dangers attending such pressures. They resisted the pressures for premature decisions and, perhaps even more important, they avoided putting their adversaries in a position of having to act in haste. Such efforts to prolong decision time within the limits established by the situation were instrumental in the ultimate resolution of the crisis by means short of war. President Kennedy himself later acknowledged that the ability to delay a decision after receipt of the photographic evidence of missile sites was crucial to the *content* of American policy: "If we had had to act on Wednesday [October 17], in the first 24 hours, I don't think probably we would have chosen as prudently as we finally did, the quarantine against the use of offensive weapons."[24]

PERCEPTIONS OF ALTERNATIVES

1914

The entire set of 5,078 themes in the 1914 documents was recoded, yielding 505 statements classified as perceptions of "choice," "necessity," or "closed" alternatives. The *choice* category includes all statements in which more than one course of action is perceived. The *necessity* category includes all statements indicating that the author sees only one possible course of action. The *closed* classification includes all statements indicating that some course of action is not possible.

24. Columbia Broadcasting System, "A Conversation with President Kennedy" (December 17, 1962), mimeograph transcript, pp. 2–3. This point is made even more forcefully in Robert F. Kennedy, *Thirteen Days*, p. 170.

The initial hypothesis to be tested with these data is as follows:

> In a crisis situation, decision makers will tend to perceive their own range of alternatives to be more restricted than those of their adversaries; that is, they will perceive their own decision making to be characterized by *necessity* and *closed* options, whereas those of the adversary are characterized by *open* choices.

TABLE 2. PERCEPTIONS OF ALTERNATIVES: FREQUENCY OF "CHOICE", "NECESSITY", AND "CLOSED" ALTERNATIVES FOR OWN NATION AND ENEMIES

Germany

	Choice	*Necessity*		*Choice*	*Closed*
Self	10	110	Self	10	20
Enemies	25	2	Enemies	25	0
$X^2 = 85.8$, $p < .001$			$X^2 = 26.2$, $p < .001$		

Austria-Hungary

	Choice	*Necessity*		*Choice*	*Closed*
Self	13	80	Self	13	7
Enemies	1	1	Enemies	1	0
Fisher exact $p =$ n.s.*			Fisher exact $p =$ n.s.*		

Russia

	Choice	*Necessity*		*Choice*	*Closed*
Self	7	20	Self	7	7
Enemies	6	2	Enemies	6	0
Fisher exact $p = .02$			Fisher exact $p = .04$		

France

	Choice	*Necessity*		*Choice*	*Closed*
Self	1	13	Self	1	5
Enemies	12	2	Enemies	12	2
$X^2 = 17.8$, $p < .001$			Fisher exact $p = .008$		

Great Britain

	Choice	*Necessity*		*Choice*	*Closed*
Self	7	20	Self	7	23
Enemies	21	2	Enemies	21	0
$X^2 = 21.6$, $p < .001$			$X^2 = 29.3$, $p < .001$		

* n.s. means nonsignificant or $p > .05$.

Table 2 reveals that British, French, Russian, and German decision makers perceived significantly fewer options open to themselves than to their adversaries.[25]

25. There may, of course, be political and strategic reasons for such assertions, quite aside from the way in which the situation is actually perceived. This is particularly likely in documents which are intended for wide public circulation. On the other hand, the most "private" documents—intended only for circulation within the various decision groups—do not differ materially from the entire set of documents in respect to the findings reported here. See, for example, the Kaiser's marginal annotations, or the various minutes of Sir Eyre Crowe, Assistant Under-Secretary of State in the British Foreign Office.

Austro-Hungarian decision makers also perceived themselves to be acting out of necessity and closed options rather than choice, but there are only three Austro-Hungarian statements regarding the options of the enemies and none are perceptions of choice. This finding is not surprising, for the policy of punishing Serbia was pursued in Vienna with a single-mindedness not evident in the British policy of seeking a mediated solution; nor in the German policy of trying to preserve the "dignity and honor" of her ally while averting a general war which many Germans perceived would end disastrously; nor in the Russian policy which, like that of Germany, sought to support the prestige of a weak ally without a world war.

Leaders of the Triple Entente nations perceived few acceptable alternatives open to themselves in regard to the Balkan crisis. Sir Edward Grey wrote on July 24 that "we can do nothing for moderation unless Germany is prepared *pari passu* to do the same."[26] Almost to the end leaders in Berlin opposed mediation. According to Bethmann-Hollweg, "We cannot mediate in the conflict between Austria and Serbia but possibly later between Austria and Russia."[27] Nor were the Russians inclined to mediation because, in the words of Sazonov, "We have assumed from the beginning a posture which we cannot change."[28] Yet the same leaders tended to perceive more freedom of action for members of the other alliance.

The tendency to perceive one's own alternatives as more restricted than those of the adversary is also evident in the reaction to the events leading up to general war. On July 28, Nicholas II had warned that "I foresee that I will succumb very soon to the pressure put upon me and will be compelled to take extreme measures which will lead to war."[29] Three days later—in the course of his desperate last-minute correspondence with the Kaiser—the Czar asserted, "It is technically impossible to stop our military preparations which were obligatory owing to Austria's mobilization."[30]

The reaction of German decision makers to the series of events leading up to mobilization and war was almost identical to that of the Czar. On the one hand, they repeatedly asserted that they had no choice but to take vigorous military measures against the threat from the East. These assertions were, on the other hand, interspersed with statements that only Russia was free to act to prevent war. And Wilhelm, like the Czar, finally asserted that he had lost control of his own military and that only the actions of the adversary could stop further escalation.[31]

The same theme of a single option open to one's self, coupled with

26. Great Britain, *British Documents*, no. 103.

27. Montgelas and Schücking, *Outbreak*, no. 247.

28. Russia, Komissiia po izdaiiu dokumentov spokhi imperializ imperializma: *Mezhdunarodnye otnosheniia v ipokhu imperializma*; dokumenty iz arkhivov tsarkogo i vremennogo pravitel 'stv 1878–1915 gg., seriia 3, toma 4 and 5 (Moskva-Leningrad, 1931 and 1934), no. 118.

29. *Ibid.*, no. 170.

30. Montgelas and Schücking, *Outbreak*, no. 487.

31. To students of strategy the assertions of the Kaiser and the Czar may appear to be a "real life" application of the tactics of "commitment: a device to leave the last clear chance to decide the outcome with the other party, in a manner that he fully appreciates; it is to relinquish further initiative, having rigged the incentives so that the other party must choose in one's favour." See Thomas C. Schelling, *The Strategy of Conflict* (New York: Oxford University Press, 1960), p. 37.

perceptions that the initiative for peace rested with the enemy, is evident in the French and Austrian statements regarding their own mobilizations. During the last week only the British consistently stated that they were able to act with some degree of freedom. Owing in part to a badly divided Cabinet, to estimates of public apathy, and to pressure from the business community for neutrality, Grey asserted that British "hands were free."[32]

According to the second hypothesis relating stress to perceptions of alternatives:

> In a crisis situation, decision makers will tend to perceive their allies' range of alternatives to be more restricted than those of their adversaries.

European leaders perceived fewer alternatives open to themselves than to their adversaries; they regarded their allies to be in a similar position. On the one hand, German documents are replete with explanations that Austria was pursuing the *only* policy open to her, thus preventing Germany from playing a moderating role in Vienna. On the other hand, the Kaiser was apparently convinced that England could perform the very function which he felt was impossible for Germany—restraint of the most belligerent member of the coalition. The assumption of British freedom, coupled with restrictions on German policy, is nowhere as clear as in one of the Kaiser's marginal notes:

> *He* [*Grey*] *knows perfectly well, that if he were to say one single serious sharp and warning word at Paris and Petersburg, and were to warn them to remain neutral, both would become quiet at once. But he takes care not to speak the word, and threatens us instead! Common Cur! England* alone *bears the responsibility for peace and war, and not we any longer!*[33]

The behaviour of military leaders in St. Petersburg and Berlin proved, however, that neither monarch was merely bluffing. After Sazonov and General Tatishev had browbeaten the vacillating Nicholas into ordering general mobilization, the former called General Ianuschkevitch and said: "Now you can smash the telephone. Give your orders, General, and then—disappear for the rest of the day."

In Berlin, General Moltke effectively undermined belated German efforts to restrain Austria-Hungary by wiring: "Stand firm to Russian mobilization. Austria-Hungary must be preserved. Mobilize at once against Russia. Germany will mobilize."

In Vienna, Conrad von Hötzendorf insured himself against any second thoughts Franz Joseph might have had by ordering mobilization one day ahead of schedule.

One factor which contributed to the perceptions of a single alternative was the rigidity of the various mobilization plans. The Russian attempt to mobilize against only Austria was anathema to the Russian generals because no such plan had been drawn up. According to General Dobrorolski, "The whole plan of mobilization is worked out ahead to its final conclusion and in all its detail. . . . Once the moment is chosen, everything is settled; there is no going back; it determines mechanically the beginning of war." See Virginia Cowles, *The Kaiser* (New York: Harper & Row, 1964), pp. 343–346.

Similarly, the Kaiser's last-minute attempt to reverse the Schlieffen plan—to attack only in the East—shattered Moltke, who replied: "That is impossible, Your Majesty. An army of a million cannot be improvised. It would be nothing but a rabble of undisciplined armed men, without a commissariat. . . . It is utterly impossible to advance except according to a plan; strong in the west, weak in the east." See Moltke, *Erinnerungen*, quoted in *ibid.*, pp. 348–349

32. Great Britain, *British Documents*, no. 447.

33. Montgelas and Schücking, *Outbreak*, no. 368.

This approach to the problems of allies was not confined to Berlin. Nicolson wrote on July 29 : "I do not think that Berlin quite understands that Russia cannot and will not stand quietly by while Austria administers a severe chastisement to Serbia."[34] Grey assessed the requirements of his French ally in similar terms. At the same time, however, he believed that Germany could constrain her southern ally. Only when mobilizations and other actions had gone too far to be stopped were some futile attempts made to restrain the militant members of each alliance. For example, at the last minute Bethmann-Hollweg tried to hold Austria in check, but he was effectively countermanded by Moltke's wire to Vienna urging immediate general mobilization.

Because there are relatively few perceptions of allies' alternatives, the data for the second hypothesis have been aggregated by alliance rather than by nation (Table 3). For both the Triple Entente and the Dual Alliance there is a significant ($p<.02$) difference between the choice and necessity perceptions for allies and enemies. The difference between perceptions of choice and those of closed alternatives is significant for the Dual Alliance and is in the predicted direction for the Triple Entente, but in the region of doubt.

TABLE 3. PERCEPTIONS OF ALTERNATIVES: FREQUENCY OF "CHOICE", "NECESSITY", AND "CLOSED" ALTERNATIVES FOR ALLIES AND ENEMIES

DUAL ALLIANCE

	Choice	*Necessity*
Allies	13	20
Enemies	26	3

$X^2=17.6, p<.001$

	Choice	*Closed*
Allies	13	3
Enemies	26	0

Fisher exact $p=.05$

TRIPLE ENTENTE

	Choice	*Necessity*
Allies	30	17
Enemies	39	6

$X^2=6.4, p=.02$

	Choice	*Closed*
Allies	30	7
Enemies	39	2

$X^2=3.75, .10>p>.05$

The next hypothesis states:

As stress increases, decision makers will perceive the range of alternatives open to themselves to become narrower.

A valid test of the hypothesis, free from the effects of message volume, required a prior adjustment that consisted of dividing the frequency of perceptions of "necessity" by the total number of all perceptions. A similar adjustment was made for "closed" perceptions. The resulting figures were again divided into two periods: June 27–July 28 and July 29–August 4. A Mann-Whitney U test reveals that the difference for each coalition is in the predicted direction and is statistically significant ($U=7, p=.05$).

According to the final hypothesis relating crisis-induced tension to perceived alternatives:

As stress increases, decision makers will perceive the range of alternatives open to adversaries or potential adversaries to expand.

To test the hypothesis, frequency of perception was again adjusted for message volume and the data were divided into the periods of lower (June 27–July 28)

34. Great Britain, *British Documents*, no. 264.

and higher (July 29–August 4) stress. A Mann-Whitney U test lends only partial support to the hypothesis. For both alliances differences between the early and late periods are in the predicted direction—the "choice" alternatives open to members of the opposing coalition were perceived to be increasing as the crisis deepened. In the case of the Dual Alliance, the increase in perceptions of open alternatives for adversaries is significant ($U=5$, $p=.02$); for the Triple Entente, however, the difference does not reach the .05 significance level ($U=10$, $p=.13$).

Cuban Missile Crisis

During the Cuban missile crisis the search for alternatives was intimately related to time pressures; in the words of Arthur Schlesinger, "the deadline defined the strategy."[35] Pressures of time notwithstanding, American policy makers made efforts to prevent premature foreclosure of options. Despite widely circulated rumors that offensive missiles were being deployed in Cuba, the Kennedy Administration had resisted taking action until photographic evidence of launching sites became available on October 15. As late as October 18 a series of alternatives was being considered pending more accurate information; and, while the decision to institute a blockade was being hammered out, open discussion of the alternatives was encouraged. The President recalled that "though at the beginning there was a much sharper division . . . this was very valuable, because the people involved had particular responsibilities of their own."[36] Another participant in the crisis decision group asserted that President Kennedy, aware that discussion of alternatives in the National Security Council would be more frank in his absence, encouraged the group to hold preliminary meetings without him.[37] Thus the eventual decision was reached by relatively open and frank discussion.

Six alternative responses emerged from the initial discussions between the President's advisers. The United States could: do nothing; rely on diplomatic pressure against the Soviet Union; attempt to split Castro from the Soviets; initiate a blockade of Cuba; undertake an air strike against military targets in Cuba; or launch an invasion to overthrow the Castro government.[38] The choice soon narrowed down to the blockade and the air strike.

Initially, the option of a sudden air strike against the missile sites had strong support among most of the conferees, including that of the President.[39] But after numerous discussions and much shifting of positions the blockade emerged with a majority in the decision group. The decision to impose a naval quarantine was based on the reasoning that this strategy offered a reasonable prospect for inducing Soviet withdrawal of the offensive missiles while minimizing the probability of provoking a violent Soviet response. The desire to avoid killing Soviet troops weighed heavily against an air strike on Cuba, and the blockade shifted the immediate burden of decision concerning the use of violence to Premier Khrushchev. And, should the blockade have proved unsuccessful, it did not preclude later employment of "a much more massive

35. Arthur M. Schlesinger, *A Thousand Days* (New York: Houghton Mifflin, 1965), p. 804.
36. Columbia Broadcasting System, "Conversation," p. 4.
37. Sorensen, *Decision-Making*, p. 60.
38. Sorensen, *Kennedy*, p. 682.
39. *Ibid.*, pp. 883–884.

action."[40] By this step no irrevocable decisions had been made, and multiple options remained for possible future actions by the United States.

American decision makers also displayed a sensitivity for the position and perspective of the adversary, trying to insure that a number of options other than total war or total surrender were available to Soviet leaders.[41] A further advantage of the blockade over other strategies was that it appeared to avoid placing Soviet leaders in that situation. An air strike on the missile bases or invasion of the island would have left Soviet leaders only the alternatives of capitulating to the United States or of counterattacking. In that case the latter might have seemed the less distasteful course. A blockade, on the other hand, would give the Soviet government a choice between turning back the weapons-bearing ships or running the blockade. Even the latter course would have left the United States with an option other than sinking the Soviet ships—disabling their rudders.[42] Thus Soviet leaders were afforded both the time and the opportunity to reassess their position.

The blockade of Cuba, which went into effect on October 24, did not end consideration of alternative American strategies. By October 26 it seemed clear that, Khrushchev's earlier threats notwithstanding, Soviet ships would not challenge the blockade. But, despite the advent of negotiations, the situation was still dangerous. After an American U-2 reconnaissance plane had been shot down over Cuba and several other planes had been fired upon, the Defense Department warned that measures would be taken to "insure that such missions are effective and protected."[43] At the same time it announced that twenty-four troop-carrier squadrons—fourteen thousand men—were being recalled to active duty.

It was, moreover, far from certain that the Soviet missiles would be removed from Cuba; indeed, there was ample evidence of an accelerated pace of construction on the launching sites in Cuba which, it was then believed, would be completed by October 30. Again, the question of increasing the pressure on the Soviets was considered in case the blockade proved insufficient to force withdrawal of all offensive missiles. Among the options considered were tightening the blockade to include all commodities other than food and medicine, increased low-level flights over Cuba for purposes of reconnaissance and harassment, action within Cuba, an air strike, and an invasion.[44] These were the alternatives which, had the crisis not been settled by the Kennedy-Khrushchev agreement of October 28, were to have been considered at what would have been "the most serious meeting ever to take place at the White House."[45] Just before that meeting was to have started, Premier Khrushchev agreed to withdraw all offensive missiles from Cuba in exchange for President Kennedy's pledge not to invade Cuba.

40. John F. Kennedy, in Columbia Broadcasting System, "Conversation," p. 4.

41. This was not, however, true of the President's military advisers. Throughout the crisis—and even after the Soviet agreement to withdraw the missiles—the Joint Chiefs of Staff continued to press for a military attack on the grounds that the Soviet Union would do nothing in response. One member of the JCS even suggested a *nuclear* attack because the Soviets would use such weapons if they were attacking the United States! See Robert F. Kennedy, *Thirteen Days*, pp. 9, 149, 172.

42. National Broadcasting Company, "Cuba," p. 27; Ben H. Bagdikian, "Press Independence and the Cuban Crisis," *Columbia Journalism Review*, 4 (Winter 1965), 6.

43. *New York Times*, October 28, 1962.

44. Sorensen, *Kennedy*, p. 711.

45. Statement made by Theodore C. Sorensen in telecast by National Broadcasting Company, "Cuba," mimeographed transcript, p. 42.

PATTERNS OF COMMUNICATION

1914

To test hypotheses relating to communication in crisis, all 5,269 documents in the Austro-Hungarian, British, French, German, and Russian collections, rather than those authored by selected decision makers, were counted and classified into four categories.

1. Documents from officials abroad (ambassadors, ministers, attachés, consuls, etc) to their central decision makers.
2. Documents from central decision makers to their officials abroad.
3. Documents circulated within a central decision-making unit.
4. Documents from the central decision makers of one nation to those of another nation.

The initial communication hypothesis to be tested is as follows:

The higher the stress in a crisis situation, the heavier the load of channels of communication.[46]

Message volume for all five nations reveals sharp increases in daily average message volume during the latter stages of the crisis. During late June and early July, for example, the average frequency of messages from a nation's diplomats abroad was approximately four per day. By July 30 this figure had risen over ten-fold.

For purposes of testing the hypothesis, the data have again been divided into two periods: June 27–July 28 and July 29–August 4 (Table 4). A Mann-Whitney *U* test for the direction and magnitude of differences between the two periods was applied to the message volume of each nation and for each type of communication.

The increase in message volume appears to depend upon the nation's degree of involvement in the early stages of the crisis and the channel of communication. Austria-Hungary was most deeply involved in the crisis during the early period, and increases in Austro-Hungarian message volume from the early to the later period of the crisis are generally lower than for Germany. Among members of the Triple Entente, Russia was the first to be involved in the Balkan crisis and the increase in Russian message volume is less significant than that for either France or England. Thus the less dramatic increase in message volume for Austria and Russia during the most intense period of crisis adds support to the hypothesis.

The change in message volume also appears to depend on the source and destination of the documents. The rate of increase was highest for messages from ambassadors and other officials abroad to the various capitals of Europe. This finding is generally consistent with the thesis that the decision makers in 1914 were "snowed under by the blizzard of information" [information input] and that "decisions [information output] tended to lag behind events."[47] The

46. Whether the increased load in communications constitutes a communication "overload" is discussed, but not resolved, in my "The 1914 Case," *The American Political Science Review*, 59 (June 1965), 365–378.

47. Edmund Taylor, *The Fall of the Dynasties* (Garden City, N.Y.: Doubleday, 1963), pp. 220–221.

TABLE 4. DAILY AVERAGE MESSAGE VOLUME FOR AUSTRIA-HUNGARY, GERMANY, FRANCE, RUSSIA, AND GREAT BRITAIN COMBINED BY TYPE OF DOCUMENT (PART I) AND DATE (PART II)

PART I

Type of Document	*Daily Average Number of Documents*											
	June 27 –July 2	*July 3–16*	*July 17–20*	*July 21–25*	*July 26*	*July 27*	*July 28*	*July 29*	*July 30*	*July 31*	*Aug. 1–2**	*Aug. 3–4**
Documents from Officials Abroad to Central Decision Makers	21.6	27.8	35.2	82.8	134.0	181.0	166.0	197.0	236.0	213.0	154.0	152.0
Documents from Central Decision Makers to Officials Abroad	4.6	12.1	19.5	75.4	83.0	120.0	145.0	136.0	127.0	161.0	98.0	88.0
Documents within Central Decision-making Units	5.2	8.2	9.1	25.2	27.0	37.0	42.0	38.0	36.0	49.0	34.0	27.0
Documents from Central Decision Makers of One Nation to Those of Another	1.2	1.4	1.0	3.4	4.0	6.0	17.0	12.0	15.0	29.0	18.0	12.0

PART II

Differences in Message Volume Between Early (June 27–July 28) and Late (July 29–August 4) Periods of the 1914 Crisis (Mann-Whitney U Test)

	Messages from Officials Abroad to Central Decision Makers		*Messages from Central Decision Makers to Officials Abroad*		*Messages within Central Decision-making Unit*		*Documents from Central Decision Makers of One Nation to Those of Another*	
	U	*p*†	*U*	*p*†	*U*	*p*†	*U*	*p*†
Austria-Hungary	0	.008	5	.133	15	>.583	3	.058
Germany	2	.005	3	.009	3	.009	0	.001
England	1	.003	5	.024	8	.074	5	.024
France	3	.009	5	.024	7	.035	6	.037
Russia	2	.005	9	.101	14	.319	4	.015

* Germany, France, Russia, and Great Britain only.
† $n_1=7$ $n_2=5$, except for Austria-Hungary, $n_1=7$, $n_2=3$.

differences in message volume within the central decision-making unit between the early and late period of the crisis are in the predicted direction, but rather marginal. This probably results, in large part, from increased reliance upon oral communication during the final days prior to war.

Prior to World War I, the normal and most important channel of communications between two nations was the diplomatic corps. When leaders in London wished to communicate with their counterparts in Berlin, the message was sent to the British Ambassador to Germany, who would then convey its contents to the proper German decision makers. Direct communication between top-level leaders was clearly the exception to normal procedures. According to the second hypothesis relating stress to communications:

> The higher the stress in a crisis situation, the greater the tendency to rely upon extraordinary or improvised channels of communication.

Of the 2,780 inter-state messages, 1,530 occurred from June 27 to July 28; of this total, only 74 (4.8%) were direct communications between central decision makers. During the last seven days of the crisis, on the other hand, 116 out of 1,250 (9.3%) messages were sent directly to another state's decision makers, bypassing the ambassadors. The difference between the two periods is statistically significant ($X^2 = 21.3$, $p < .001$).

As crisis deepens, the need for clear and unimpeded communication between potential adversaries is likely to become both more urgent and more difficult. It is unlikely that similar difficulties in communication will arise between members of the same coalition. Hence the hypothesis:

> The higher the stress in a crisis situation, the higher the proportion of intra-coalition—as against inter-coalition—communication.

When inter-nation messages are classified according to date and divided into inter-coalition and intra-coalition communications, the results support the hypothesis. During the first month after the assassination, 830 out of 1,530 (54.3%) inter-nation messages were exchanged between members of opposing coalitions. During the week prior to the outbreak of general war, on the other hand, inter-coalition messages account for only 580 out of 1,250 (46.4%) messages. The difference between the two periods in regard to communications within and between alliances is significant ($X^2 = 17.3$, $p < .001$).

Cuban Missile Crisis

Limited access to Soviet and American documents during the missile crisis precludes a complete analysis of patterns of communication. Nevertheless, some comparisons are possible. Perhaps the most striking similarity between the 1914 and Cuban crises was the use of improvised channels of communication. Before the discovery of the missiles was made public on October 22, President Kennedy relied on a special emissary, Dean Acheson, rather than on the normal diplomatic channels to inform General de Gaulle and NATO of the situation in Cuba.

More important to the ultimate resolution of the crisis was the use of ad hoc methods of communicating American intentions to the Soviets during the week of October 22–28. As the President himself noted after the crisis had passed, normal channels of communication with the Kremlin were "very poor."[48]

48. Columbia Broadcasting System, "Conversation," p. 21.

Some extraordinary means were devised in an effort to overcome this problem. Reference has already been made to an important message affirming American desires to slow down escalation of the crisis which was sent to patrolling ships in the clear, rather than in code. Upon intercepting the message, the Soviets would presumably attach greater credence to its contents than had direct channels of communication been used. Similarly, Premier Khrushchev's acceptance of President Kennedy's formula for settlement of the crisis was broadcast in the clear via public media in order to bypass the four hours required to encode, transmit, and decode messages through the normal diplomatic channels. John Scali, an American Broadcasting Company correspondent, and Aleksandr S. Fomin, a counselor at the Soviet Embassy, were used as a major channel of negotiation during the crisis, another example of the tendency to seek extraordinary means of communication. According to Scali, Fomin suggested: "In order to benefit from this near disaster from now on Secretary Rusk should meet three times a day with the Russian Ambassador so that they could avoid future crises and what he called future misunderstandings."[49] The important role played by both the Kennedy-Khrushchev and Scali-Fomin negotiations in the resolution of the crisis led directly to establishment of the White House–Kremlin "hot line." The first use during crisis of this channel of communication came in the Arab-Israeli war of 1967 to prevent any misunderstanding between Moscow and Washington which might have led to a direct Soviet-American confrontation in the Middle East. Thus one means to escape the limits of ordinary channels of communication in crisis has been institutionalized.

Although there were certain similarities in methods of communication during the 1914 and 1962 crises, responses to information about adversaries—whether in the form of written communications or physical actions—differed rather sharply during the two situations.[50] In 1914 the leaders of the Dual Alliance (Germany and Austria-Hungary) at almost every stage of the crisis pursued policies with a higher level of violence or potential violence than did members of the Triple Entente (England, France, and Russia). Over the crisis period as a whole, the actions of the Dual Alliance nations were significantly more violent (Table 5). A further analysis of the data disclosed that German and Austro-Hungarian leaders perceived themselves as the targets of consistently increasing hostility directed at them from England, France, and Russia. This was true even when the actions of the Triple Entente nations were relatively conciliatory, as was the case during the first month after the assassination of Franz Ferdinand.

In contrast, up to a few days before they were drawn into war, leaders in London and Paris were somewhat complacent about the broader implications of the dispute between Austria-Hungary and Serbia. During the final week of July the British House of Commons was the scene of a bitter exchange on the Irish question, but the European crisis was not debated until August 3, the day before England declared war on Germany. During the same period much French attention was directed to the sensational trial of Mme. Caillaux, wife of the

49. American Broadcasting Company, "John Scali, A.B.C. News" (August 13, 1964), mimeograph transcript, p. 9.

50. Quantitative content analysis data supporting the comparisons of the 1914 and 1962 crises in the following paragraphs may be found in Ole R. Holsti, Richard A. Brody, and Robert C. North, "Measuring Affect and Action in International Reaction Models," *Journal of Peace Research*, 3–4 (1964), 170–190.

TABLE 5. PERCEPTION OF OPPONENTS' HOSTILITY IN 1914 AND CUBAN MISSILE CRISES

1914 Crisis	*Triple Entente*			*Dual Alliance*		
Time Period	*Level of Other Actor's Violent Behavior*	*Perception of Other Actor's Hostility: Self as Target*	*Level of Own Violent Behavior*	*Level of Other Actor's Violent Behavior*	*Perception of Other Actor's Hostility: Self as Target*	*Level of Own Violent Behavior*
June 27–July 2	4.25*†	2.67†	4.38†	4.38*†	3.98†	4.25†
July 3–16	4.25	0.00	2.58	4.38	3.93	3.00
July 17–20	3.00	0.00	2.62	2.58	4.08	2.83
July 21–25	2.83	0.00	4.28	2.62	4.45	5.38
July 26	5.38	6.00	3.68	4.28	4.87	5.37
July 27	5.37	0.00	4.95	3.68	4.10	5.87
July 28	5.87	0.00	4.68	4.95	5.16	6.06
July 29	6.06	5.33	5.07	4.68	4.89	4.64
July 30	4.64	5.33	4.60	5.07	6.62	5.10
July 31	5.10	6.43	5.50	4.60	5.48	6.30
Aug. 1–2	6.30	6.19	5.90	5.50	7.00	5.88
Aug. 3–4	5.88	6.98	6.03	5.90	6.50	6.08

1962 Crisis	*United States*				*USSR*			
		Positive Evaluation of the U.S.S.R.	*Negative Evaluation of the U.S.S.R.*			*Positive Evaluation of the U.S.A.*	*Negative Evaluation of the U.S.A.*	
Oct. 22	3‡	1.3§	33.5§	2‡	2‡			3‡
Oct. 23	1	0.3	30.3	3	3	2.4§	27.2§	1
Oct. 24	2			1	1	5.9	19.6	2
Oct. 25	5	17.8	15.6	4	4	0.0	16.7	5
Oct. 26	6	13.5	8.1	5	5	0.0	29.7	6
Oct. 27	4	10.7	16.1	6	6	15.9	12.9	4
Oct. 28	7	25.3	13.4	7	7	12.6	16.6	7
Oct. 29	8			9	9			8
Oct. 30	9			10	10			9
Oct. 31	10			8	8			10

* The level of the other actor's violent behavior is equivalent to the level of the actor's own violent behavior during the previous time period.
† These figures indicate the average intensity level, arrived at by scaling action and perceptual data by Q-Sorting.
‡ These figures are rank-order figures, with the U.S.A. and U.S.S.R. ranked separately. Thus they do not indicate magnitude.
§ These values are percentages of the total loading of the documents whose content was analyzed.

Finance Minister, who had killed Gaston Calmette for publishing defamatory materials about her husband. The lower level of concern is revealed in the almost complete absence of perceptions of hostility, until July 29, in messages written by leaders of the Triple Entente nations, even though war between Austria-Hungary and Serbia had broken out by that time.

In the Cuban crisis, however, both sides tended to perceive rather accurately the nature of the adversary's actions and then proceeded to act at an "appropriate" level (Table 5). As the level of violence or potential violence in Soviet or American actions diminished, the adversary's perceptions of those actions increased in positive affect and decreased in negative affect, and the level of violence in the resulting policies also decreased. There was a marked tendency to perceive conciliatory actions by the adversary as genuine efforts to delay or reverse escalation—rather than as tricks. Thus, unlike the situation in 1914, efforts by either party to delay or reverse the escalation were generally perceived as such and responded to in a like manner.

CONCLUSION

Time pressure, the search for alternatives, and patterns of communication are usually treated as core variables in decision making. Data from the 1914 crisis reveal that these factors did, in fact, vary as crisis-induced stress increased, and these changes apparently had a dysfunctional effect on critical policy decisions. A more impressionistic analysis of these variables during the Cuban confrontation suggests that the ability of American decision makers to mitigate some of the adverse consequences of crisis contributed to its eventual peaceful resolution. In many respects President Kennedy's behavior during the Cuban crisis appeared consciously designed to avert repetition of the 1914 disaster. Indeed, he frequently referred to the decision processes leading up to World War I as a negative model of mistakes which must be avoided during crises in the nuclear age.[51] Yet the ability of American and Soviet leaders to avoid a nuclear Armageddon is not assurance that even great skill in crisis management will always yield a peaceful solution. As President Kennedy said some months later, referring to the missile crisis, "You can't have too many of those."

Comparison of these crises sheds some light on the behavioral consequences of crisis, but some interesting questions remain unanswered. This research has considered the nature of the situation (i.e., crisis) as the independent variable which appears to explain some aspects of decision making. But to this point we have not considered how the consequences of crisis may be affected by organizational, personal, or other intervening factors.[52] Several possible further observations might be made, although our data clearly permit only speculation rather than any definitive answers.

From a *systemic* perspective we can point to several plausible explanations.

51. For example, when discussing the Cuban missile crisis some weeks later, he asserted: "Well now, if you look at the history of the century where World War I really came through a series of misjudgments of the intentions of others . . . it's very difficult to always make judgments here about what the effect will be of our decisions on other countries." Columbia Broadcasting System, "Conversation," p. 3.

52. See, for example, Charles F. Hermann, *Crises in Foreign Policy*, and Margaret G. Hermann, *Stress, Self-Esteem, and Defensiveness in an Inter–Nation Simulation* (China Lake, Calif.: Project Michelson, 1965).

Perhaps nuclear capabilities, and the recognition in both Washington and Moscow that their use would entail destruction without parallel in history, served as a constraint against undue provocation of the adversary. But we should perhaps not draw unduly optimistic conclusions from this for other situations. Although we have now been able to avoid nuclear war for a quarter of a century, only the most optimistic would assert that nuclear terror is a perfect guarantee for peaceful solution of crises.[53] The availability of the United Nations as a systemic institution for communication and negotiation may also have been a factor, although the public evidence to date suggests that the most important channels of communication were those outside the United Nations. In 1914, on the other hand, the so-called "Concert System" was in fact a series of ad hoc conferences, and efforts to convene it at the height of the crisis were wholly unsuccessful.

A second possible explanation for the different outcomes in 1914 and 1962 can perhaps be found in the *crisis-management experiences* of the leaders involved. By 1914 Balkan crises had come and gone for a generation without leading to general war. On the surface, at least, it seemed to many that European leaders were able to cope with such recurring crises—at least to the point of limiting the use of violence to local areas. There is some evidence, admittedly anecdotal, of confidence that this, too, was a crisis which could be settled peacefully by reasonable men. Even such a political "realist"—or, in more contemporary terminology, a "superhawk"—as Winston Churchill, British First Lord of the Admiralty, wrote less than three days before the outbreak of war: "I went to bed with a feeling that things might blow over . . . we were still a long way, as it seemed, from any danger of war."[54]

In contrast, American leaders in 1962, less than two years earlier, had experienced an almost classic case of how not to handle a crisis. Whatever sense of overconfidence about the management of foreign affairs the Kennedy Administration may have possessed upon coming into office in early 1961 must surely have been diminished by the disastrous events surrounding the abortive Bay of Pigs invasion. The bitter lessons of 1961 may well have contributed to the skill with which the President and his advisers managed the much more dangerous situation eighteen months later.

A third possible explanation is that *situational factors* in 1914 and 1962 were different in one critical respect: perhaps the Cuban situation did not reach a stage that was as stressful as that in the latter days of the 1914 crisis. The evidence on this point is at best mixed, and interpreting it is virtually impossible.

53. Some analysts (e.g., Thomas Schelling, *Arms and Influence* [New Haven: Yale University Press, 1966]) have suggested that, one way or another, Soviet and American leaders would certainly have found a way to avoid war over the missiles in Cuba. Robert Kennedy's revelations about the recommendations of the Joint Chiefs of Staff—one of whom was a Vice-Presidential candidate in 1968—should go a long way toward dispelling any overoptimism. It takes no great act of imagination to conceive of another President facing the same situation who would be willing to rely very heavily upon the advice of his military commanders. In such circumstances it is difficult to believe that Russian leaders would have shown the restraint necessary to avoid a Soviet-American war. More generally, it would be a potentially tragic misreading of history to assume, on the basis of the Cuban missile crisis, that a "way out" will always be found.

54. Winston S. Churchill, *The World Crisis, 1911–1914* (New York: Scribner's, 1928), p. 208.

Most accounts of the decision-making process in Washington indicate no evidence of the type of personal breakdown under duress that the Kaiser apparently suffered in late July 1914. Nevertheless, as Robert F. Kennedy's memoir of the crisis makes clear, tensions during some days of the crisis reached an almost unbearable intensity and "some [American decision makers], because of the pressure of events, even appeared to lose their judgment and stability."[55] On the Soviet side, there is considerable controversy surrounding Premier Khrushchev's message to President Kennedy on the evening of October 26 (the only message from either Washington or Moscow that has never been made public). Of the few that have seen it, some have asserted that it reveals the incoherence of a person on the verge of a total collapse; others have interpreted it as the message of a concerned, but nevertheless, wholly coherent individual.

The latter point suggests at least the possibility that whether the level of stress in the two situations was different is perhaps less important than possible differences in tolerance for stress among decision makers. For example, it seems clear that time pressure weighed heavily on American leaders during the Cuban crisis. But reactions to short decision time were far from uniform. President Kennedy took a number of steps to reduce its potentially adverse effects on both American and Soviet decisions. In contrast, when Senators Richard Russell and William Fulbright were informed of the situation in Cuba, they argued that a blockade could not be effective in the short time remaining before the launching sites in Cuba became operational. Their plea for an invasion to remove the Soviet missiles, if heeded, would clearly have altered the outcome of the crisis. Did their reactions stem from the fact that their roles differed from that of the President? From different information about the situation? From personality or other idiosyncratic differences? Would Kaiser Wilhelm and Czar Nicholas (or Richard Nixon and Alexei Kosygin, or Lyndon Johnson and Leonid Brezhnev) have reacted differently to the Cuban missile crisis than did Kennedy and Khrushchev? These are, of course, unanswerable questions. The value of asking them in this context is to raise the possibility that behavioral consequences of crisis may also vary according to personality factors.

55. Robert F. Kennedy, *Thirteen Days*, p. 8.

chapter five

EDITOR'S INTRODUCTION

The author of this chapter, Charles A. McClelland, views international crises as transitional periods between peace and war. By definition, then, all crises have the potential of escalating into war, but in fact most of them subside without massive inter-nation violence. From this characterization of crises come two questions that provide the core of McClelland's research: What distinguishes a crisis that culminates in war from one that does not? How can the beginning and end of a crisis be differentiated from noncrisis times? To address these questions, the author selects two regions of conflict that have been the source of repeated crises but that have abated short of war—Berlin from 1948 to 1963 and the contest from 1950 to 1964 over various islands lying off the coast of China.

McClelland's definition of crisis as a situation that might rapidly expand into war is quite similar to that offered by Schwartz (Chapter 8) and Snyder (Chapter 10) as well as by Schelling and Young in their writing elsewhere.[1] This definition of crisis contrasts with that proposed by Robinson (Chapter 2) and Hermann (Chapter 9) which is also used by some other contributors to this volume. The reader interested in the sharpest comparison of these alternative definitions and their use in empirical research may wish to read this chapter in conjunction with Chapter 9. As noted in the Introduction to this volume, the difference in definition frequently is associated with alternative theoretical perspectives. McClelland and others who emphasize crisis as a critical stage in an evolving conflict situation tend to be interested in interactions or in systemic issues, whereas those who define crisis in terms of threat, time, and surprise are inclined to deal with internal decision processes within one party to a crisis. Furthermore, crisis as a condition of potential war is a definition more clearly tailored to the phenomena of international politics whereas the other definition tends to be nonsubstantive. (See Robinson's discussion in Chapter 2 for the development of this point.)

In this third chapter in the section on comparative case studies, McClelland offers a different approach to comparative analysis than either of the previous authors. Both Paige (Chapter 3) and Holsti (Chapter 4) establish comparability between their crises by means of empirically testable hypotheses. Paige searched imaginatively for the identification of the same hypothesis in both cases; Holsti emphasized both statistical and impressionistic testing of hypotheses identified before examination of the crises. For McClelland the method of comparison is the pattern of behavior in the crises. He constructs profiles of the frequency with which various types of activity occur in both conflict arenas and then compares the distributions between the two regions and between crisis and noncrisis intervals in the same region.

Given the way in which McClelland examines crises, one may question the decision to locate his contribution in a section on comparative case studies. The reader will look in vain in his chapter for a detailed verbal account of the events involved in the crises analyzed. Yet McClelland is very much concerned

1. See Thomas C. Schelling, *Arms and Influence* (New Haven: Yale University Press, 1966), pp. 96–97; and Oran R. Young, *The Intermediaries* (Princeton: Princeton University Press, 1967), p. 10.

with the sequence of events initiated and received by the parties to the crises. He uses descriptive statistics to portray the ebb and flow of crisis activity. Certainly, as we pass from Paige to Holsti to McClelland, we move progressively further away from the usual notion of case studies, but all the authors share a concern with setting forth and comparing what each regards as essential features of the crises under examination.

McClelland's concern with patterns of behavior and interaction sequences leads him to an examination of the types of activities in which states engage during crises. It is remarkable that, with the exception of the war–no war distinction, relatively little empirical research has been devoted to the study of the actions, behaviors, and policies undertaken by governments in crisis.[2] This is not to say that case studies of crises have not described in detail specific actions by governments in a given crisis—for example, the landing of American troops during the Lebanon crisis in July 1958 or during the Dominican Republic crisis in April 1965. But only minor attention has been given to ways of constructing more general categories for classifying types of crisis behavior. Such neglect parallels the underdevelopment of typologies of policy in the general study of foreign affairs. Under these circumstances the McClelland categorization should be of particular interest.

Charles A. McClelland, a Professor of International Relations at the University of Southern California, has been one of the pioneers in the scientific study of crisis. Like another early and major contributor—Robert C. North, who has conducted extensive investigations into the outbreak of World War I—McClelland has devoted considerable energy to the detailed examination of several crisis areas (including Taiwan and Berlin). He has written important theoretical articles based primarily upon his research into these crises.[3] His writing on systemic analysis is related to his research on crisis because the latter is treated as a major concept in his systemic theoretical framework.[4] The present chapter provides an indication of the direction of his present research which builds upon his classification and collection of interactive event data.[5]

2. There are a few exceptions such as Herman Kahn's efforts to describe escalatory steps in a crisis in his *On Escalation* (New York: Praeger, 1965). The chapters in this volume by Zinnes, Zinnes, and McClure (Chap. 7) and Schwartz (Chap. 8) seek to describe crisis behavior in terms of the degree of hostility, which is certainly one important dimension of crisis activity.

3. Illustrative of McClelland's work on crisis are "The Acute International Crisis," *World Politics*, 14 (October 1961), 182–204; "Decisional Opportunity and Political Controversy: The Quemoy Case," *Journal of Conflict Resolution*, 6 (September 1962), 201–213; and "Access to Berlin: The Quantity and Variety of Events, 1948–1963," in J. David Singer, ed., *Quantitative International Politics* (New York: The Free Press, 1968), pp. 159–186.

4. Representative of McClelland's work on systems theory are "Systems Theory and Human Conflict," in Elton B. McNeil, ed., *The Nature of Human Conflict* (Englewood Cliffs, N.J.: Prentice-Hall, 1965), pp. 250–273; and *Theory and the International System* (New York: The Macmillan Company, 1966).

5. See also Charles A. McClelland and Gary D. Hoggard, "Conflict Patterns in the Interactions Among Nations," in James N. Rosenau, ed., *International Politics and Foreign Policy*, rev. ed. (New York: The Free Press, 1969), pp. 711–724.

chapter five

THE BEGINNING, DURATION, AND ABATEMENT OF INTERNATIONAL CRISES: COMPARISONS IN TWO CONFLICT ARENAS

Charles A. McClelland

CRISIS BETWEEN PEACE AND WAR

In the relations between sovereign nations there is no more visible and important development than the transition from peace to war. When a series of events having the potential of this transition is recognized, national governments give close attention to all utterances and occurrences that appear to relate to the prospect of a change to war. Also, public interest becomes focused on the train of events leading along "the road to war." With gratifying frequency, the anticipated transition does not run its full course. It turns out to be a false prelude; the involved parties somehow find escape routes to avert a showdown and hence the shift from peace to war does not occur. Over the past century the concept of *international crisis* has come into use in international politics to identify this transition. A crisis refers to both a real prelude to war and an averted approach toward war. Crises are most commonly thought of as interpositions between the prolongation of peace and the outbreak of war.

Twentieth-century crises that have led to great wars have been examined after the fact in great detail by historians and social scientists. A narrative and a leading interpretation have become attached to each crisis sequence. Thus a generation of diplomatic historians examined the 1914 crisis arising from the assassination of the Austrian archduke to locate the "immediate" causes of World War I and they also explored international history from 1870 to 1914 to identify the "underlying" causes. The dominating interpretation fifty years after the event is that a "needless" war may have taken place mainly because the major participants failed to understand and control the dynamics of the immediate crisis.

The narrative and interpretation of the prelude to war between 1933 and 1939 have taken a different direction. The Axis powers prepared for war and, in due course, actively sought to promote an international struggle. An ascending series of international crises punctuated this progress to World War II and the dominant interpretation has been that the only real chance to stop the outbreak of war lay in early intervention to eliminate the threat from Germany. This lesson of history has been taken very much to heart in the post–World War II era. References to Munich and advice against appeasement policies have arisen during almost every international crisis episode since 1945.

The basic contrast in the interpretations of the two world wars is that in the first conflict the transition from peace to war had the potential of being reversible almost to the last moment before war started, whereas in the second the crisis became virtually irreversible after an early critical time. The foregoing historical interpretations have not risen above challenge; competing explanations of the causes and the preludes of the two global wars have been set forth and, no doubt, will continue to be presented. In fact, the perennial difficulty in linking an overall interpretation of international historical events with the shift from peace to war is only one of the problems in the analysis of international crises.

The part played by crises in the international politics of peace and war remains only vaguely understood. Although the notion of a clear transition from peace to war seems sound, the historical circumstances, especially in recent decades, challenge the realism of the idea. In many post–World War II conflicts, a kind of quasi-peace has alternated with a kind of quasi-war. Indian-Pakistani relations and Arab-Israeli relations during the past twenty years provide precise examples. In some places and at some times the international politics of the Soviet Union and the United States have had these part-war, part-peace characteristics. There are other instances to be found as well. Under these circumstances a question that intrudes and remains unanswered is whether or not international crises have the same functions and are interposed in the same way in these quasi-peace situations as in the preceding periods of international history when the demarcation between peace and war appears to have been much more definite. Further, there is neither a logical nor a psychological reason to expect that a crisis will (or must) precede the onslaught of something called a "war" under circumstances which have already included many armed attacks and sporadic outbursts of military violence across national boundaries—often over a period of years.

The relations between hostile and contending nations may become exacerbated at times so that observers characterize the resulting interchanges as evidence that a crisis exists. These instances may be only fluctuations in the amount or type of confrontation and should not properly be called crises. On the other hand, it is possible that a serious and important sequence of exchanges between the parties to a long-standing international conflict will occur as a final exploration of positions before the "ultimate" step of concerted warfare is undertaken. There is, in other words, a problem in knowing how to distinguish between a crisis and a pseudo-crisis.

Especially when this distinction remains shadowy, a party to a conflict may try to manipulate its opponent (and other parties, as well) into believing that what is really meant to be only a pseudo-crisis is the genuine article. Thus, in an international situation that is chronically close to the balance point of peace and war, any of the antagonists may commence a line of action which looks like a prelude of war-to-the-hilt and yet have no intention of pressing the case that far. This party will provoke some change in international relations resembling crisis action. The resulting interplay produces a pseudo-crisis. The other possibility is that the resulting interplay, despite the initial intentions of one or more parties, may get out of hand or otherwise go in unanticipated directions. What was meant to be only a tactical move for advantage in international politics may develop into a full-blown and entirely genuine crisis, according to the common definition of a crisis as a transition from peace to war.

The analyst who undertakes a close examination of international crisis phenomena, in general, faces the fundamental problem of accounting for the differences which would explain why many crises are begun and then abated while some lead on into war. The contemporary blurring of the line between peace and war adds a serious complication to an already difficult problem of analysis. As noted above, the complexity of the analytical problem, particularly when current international conditions are taken into account, is increased further by at least the following possibilities:

1. Fluctuations in the political and military exchanges between hostile and contending nations over a conflict issue may be mistaken for a crisis.
2. A real crisis may occur because one or more hostile and contending nations become determined to put an end to a chronic conflict issue and are willing to undertake any action necessary for the realization of that end. A real crisis may arise from other circumstances: for example, from a seemingly random conjunction of crisis-inducing events or from the irrationality or inefficiency of a government's leaders or groups.
3. A real crisis may be abated by actions taken by one or more of the crisis participants or by intervening efforts made by other parties.
4. One or more hostile and contending parties may induce a pseudo-crisis by taking actions typical of crisis behavior but without the purpose of pursuing this course to the full extent.
5. A pseudo-crisis may be abated by its participants or by other parties.
6. Through any of a number of transitional processes, a pseudo-crisis may turn into a real crisis and subsequently may be abated or not.

Research on international crises would be fruitful if it succeeded in establishing when these various effects and outcomes occur in international politics. Perhaps the results would contribute to the theory of change in international systems and have practical consequences as well. For example, when a nation that is a participant in a chronic conflict situation induces a pseudo-crisis and is then apparently dissuaded by the intervening efforts of outside parties, it seems likely that the latter serve as unwitting allies and encourage the offending party to try even bolder forms of brinksmanship. Research and analysis, able to identify past cases of such political maneuvering, would tend to diminish third-party support for these practices.

THE SYSTEMIC APPROACH TO THE STUDY OF CRISES

Different research approaches need to be called into play to deal with different aspects of crisis problems and with the several distinctions noted above. For some questions about crises the most direct approach is in the study of the foreign policies of the participants. Given the relevant records of the decision makers of governments involved in a crisis, the study of the intentions, the perceptions, the incoming information, and the decisions of the participants would tell most of the story of how the crisis happened and what role, if any, it played in a transition between peace and war. Although important parts of the data having to do with policy processes, perceptions, information, intentions, and alternative courses of action are usually guarded from the public view, research on crisis decision making has been going forward with considerable success. Many of the studies reported in this volume have been done from the decision-making or "actor" point of view. Another approach is to develop analyses from the standpoint of "system" phenomena.

The main characteristic of the systemic approach to crisis is its preoccupation with the exchanges of words and deeds occurring in the arena of conflict.

It is the "external behaviors" of the parties in the conflict that are given full attention. Those who concentrate on crisis decision-making problems deal mainly with *intra-unit* situations and processes whereas the students of international systems primarily investigate *inter-unit* phenomena. Of course, both intra-unit and inter-unit analyses should eventually be joined and synthesized, but at present there is an advantage in having different approaches to discover as much as possible according to these different perspectives. A division of labor is justified. Some problems are handled more effectively by one basic approach and some are more easily studied according to the other orientation. Different combinations of data are made and different organizing concepts are utilized. A practical reason for developing at least two kinds of attacks on the research problems of international crises is that large amounts of data need to be collected and analyzed and the separating of intra-unit and inter-unit materials helps to keep the work to manageable proportions.

The systemic approach followed in the reporting of research in this chapter ignores the impact of public opinion, the effects of informal and non-governmental pressures, and the part played by the organizational, perceptual, motivational, and personality aspects of crisis behavior. No attention is given to the processes of making decisions within governments under crisis conditions. The focus is on the interflow of actions and responses of the crisis participants.

Findings will be presented to show how an international crisis can be identified and distinguished from at least some pseudo-crisis. Then the problem of accounting for changes in behavior which are thought to be important in the abatement phases of crises is considered from a systemic point of view.

THE BERLIN AND TAIWAN CONFLICT ARENAS

The research has been given specific direction through the study and comparison of two arenas of international conflict. One is the Berlin conflict. International crises are generally considered to have occurred in the long struggle to control Berlin and the accesses to the city. Data pertaining to the actions and responses of the contending parties were gathered for the period from January 1, 1948, through December 31, 1963. The other conflict arena that has been studied is that of the Taiwan Straits between 1950 and 1964. Reported interactions of the contending parties were gathered in the same general way as for the Berlin confrontations. Public sources (mainly contemporary news reports) were used in making these chronological collections of data. The selection of items was guided by the question: "Who did what to whom and when?" Both verbal actions and physical actions (deeds) were collected. During the sixteen years included in the analysis of the Berlin conflict 1,791 interaction items were identified; for the fifteen years of the Taiwan Straits conflict 2,625 items were recorded. The Berlin material was restricted somewhat by a selection of items related directly to access—that is, the events concerning movement and transport within, to, and from the occupied city. This limitation stemmed from the requirements of an earlier inquiry of subsystem phenomena for which the Berlin data were originally collected.

Far too much information was acquired to permit incorporating all of it into narrative accounts. The idea needs emphasis that the purpose of collecting the information was not to construct some historical descriptions of events but, rather, to allow the building of something resembling box scores of actions and responses. The research was attentive to the external behaviors of the conflict participants and has exploited quantitative information on the performance records of these participants in the two arenas of conflict.

The reasons for selecting these particular arenas for study and comparison become apparent when one considers a number of general similarities. The Berlin and Taiwan situations represent examples of the quasi-peace, quasi-war conditions described earlier as fairly typical of post–World War II international politics. At the time of this writing, the two conflicts have been chronic for a period approaching twenty years and remain "unresolved" to this day. In both there has existed the most common form of conflict in international politics: the struggle for territorial control. At Berlin the forces of the Soviet Union, East Germany, and East Berlin have contested persistently against the presence in Berlin of the American, French, British, West German, and West Berlin representatives and regimes. The latter have fought unrelentingly against the efforts to displace them. Similarly, in the Taiwan area the Nationalist and Communist Chinese governments have been engaged in a continuing struggle for possession of the coastal and main islands held by the Nationalists since the Chinese revolution of 1949. The United States efforts to uphold the claims of the Nationalist regime and the considerably less vigorous support of the Chinese mainland forces by the Soviet Union bridge, in a general way, the two conflict arenas. The involvement of great powers in the struggles is a significant common feature.

Very important from the standpoint of the research problem of identifying real crises has been the frequent fluctuations in the actions of the contesting parties in the two arenas. The underlying motivations of the contestants appear to have remained quite constant, at least in terms of the determination to displace and to resist displacement, but the campaigns to attain these goals have varied greatly across time periods. On five different occasions the confrontations have become active and intense to the extent that news commentators at the time characterized the situations as "crises."

In 1948 the Soviet occupation authorities in Berlin gave orders which resulted in the attempt to seal the city against access from the Western zones of Germany and beyond. The famous Soviet blockade and the countering Western airlift of supplies then followed. The blockade was lifted in 1949 by agreement between the Western and Soviet governments and the airlift was no longer needed.

Late in 1954 Communist China launched an effort to gain possession of a number of small islands along the China coast. In the "Tachens crisis" of 1955, the mainland regime succeeded partly in its objective although strenuous objections and resistance came from both the Nationalist Chinese and the United States.

Another attempt to possess the Nationalist terrain was made in 1958 when a large artillery barrage from the mainland was directed mostly at the Quemoy group of islands. This attack was so heavy and continuous that the Nationalist troops stationed on the big island of Quemoy were cut off from supplies and access from Taiwan. The Quemoy crisis was centered on this action and the efforts made to break through or halt the Communist Chinese attack. Minor diplomatic accommodations were made in a series of exchanges between Communist China and the United States; the Quemoy crisis declined before the end of 1958.

At about the time of the abatement of the Quemoy crisis the confrontation in the Berlin arena was intensified. In November 1958 the Soviet Union served notice on the Allied powers in Berlin that the occupation status of the city was to be ended and six months were allowed for Allied cooperation in concluding the occupation. Otherwise, the Soviet Union proposed to act unilaterally and to turn over its Berlin affairs to the East Germans. The press proclaimed this "Deadline crisis" the worst since 1948. Nevertheless, the deadline passed without serious consequences and perhaps face was saved sufficiently by the convening of a foreign ministers' conference in May 1959 to mark the decline and end of that particular episode.

In August 1961 the Berlin arena again became very active when the East began the construction of the wall, running for miles through the city and cutting the movement of Berliners between the East and West sectors. Many incidents occurred involving the occupation forces. On one day late in October 1961, Soviet and American military units were in a tense and extreme confrontation for several hours. Few observers failed to call the Berlin Wall affair a "crisis."

These five occasions, then, provide material for research.[1] The most recent pair of crises—Quemoy and the Berlin Wall—are of particular interest. Much experience in the thrust and parry of crisis interchange had accumulated before their occurrence and, presumably, these two crises illustrate the seasoned skills of the involved parties at crisis and conflict. If there are patterns of behavior that took shape earlier in these affairs, the two crises late in the series should reflect them. We should be able to demonstrate from the data whether or not some basic questions can be answered. Is it possible to identify crises by means other than the general feel of the situation or the judgments of contemporary observers and participants? Can the occurrence of a crisis be established by noting changes in the streams of action and response of the participants? In a chronic international conflict that is seldom far from a state of war, are there notable differences in behavior that mark a crisis?

THE QUANTITY AND VARIETY OF EVENTS

The most obvious way to approach these questions about observable changes in behavior is to look into the frequency of occurrence of the interactions within specified time periods. We can obtain results from the quantity of events data at once. The reader can identify "crisis years" in the two arenas by noting the main variations in Tables 1 and 2.

Even as rough a measure as the annual frequencies of occurrence of acts suggests that 1958 and 1961 stand apart in the Berlin arena. The same is true for 1955 and 1958 in the Taiwan arena. The single casualty of the annual frequency

1. Descriptive accounts and several analyses of the conflicts appear in the following: W. Phillips Davison, *The Berlin Blockade: A Study in Cold War Politics* (Princeton: Princeton University Press, 1958); Jean Edward Smith, *The Defense of Berlin* (Baltimore: Johns Hopkins Press, 1963); Tang Tsou, *The Embroilment over Quemoy: Mao, Chiang and Dulles* (Salt Lake City: Institute of International Studies, 1959); Tang Tsou, "Mao's Limited War in the Taiwan Strait," *Orbis*, 3 (Fall 1959), 332–350; Charles A. McClelland, "Decisional Opportunity and Political Controversy: The Quemoy Case," *Journal of Conflict Resolution*, 6 (September 1962), 201–213; and Charles A. McClelland, "Action Structures and Communication in Two International Crises: Quemoy and Berlin," *Background*, 7 (February 1964), 201–215.

TABLE 1. ANNUAL TOTALS OF ACTS COMMITTED IN THE BERLIN ARENA, 1948–1963

	1948	*1949*	*1950*	*1951*	*1952*	*1953*	*1954*	*1955*	*1956*	*1957*	*1958*	*1959*	*1960*	*1961*	*1962*	*1963*
East*	*210*	81	87	61	128	58	22	38	10	11	14	23	43	*149*	88	39
West†	*144*	44	57	39	69	36	16	27	7	7	7	22	33	*135*	63	23
Both	*354*	125	144	100	197	94	38	65	17	18	21	45	76	*284*	151	62

* "East" includes East Germany, East Berlin, and the Soviet Union.
† "West" includes West Germany, West Berlin, the United States, France, and Great Britain.

TABLE 2. ANNUAL TOTALS OF ACTS COMMITTED IN THE TAIWAN ARENA, 1950–1964

	1950	*1951*	*1952*	*1953*	*1954*	*1955*	*1956*	*1957*	*1958*	*1959*	*1960*	*1961*	*1962*	*1963*	*1964*
U.S.S.R. and Communist China	47	30	5	11	188	*297*	87	81	*399*	104	74	50	45	34	28
U.S. and Nationalist China	85	30	18	27	176	*291*	64	53	*298*	26	23	11	19	13	10
Both	132	60	23	38	364	*588*	151	134	*697*	130	97	61	64	47	38

indicator of crisis is the 1958–1959 Deadline crisis at Berlin. Clearly, the Soviet ultimatum did not have much effect on the access interactions. It did not trigger a crisis if a crisis is to be defined by a sudden increase in the frequency of interactions. On the other hand, the strength of the crisis years as measured by the volume of activity is shown by the fact that the two crisis years of 1948 and 1961 at Berlin took up 35.6 per cent of the total volume of the action in the period 1948–1963 while the two years of 1955 and 1958 constituted 51 per cent of the Taiwan total (1950 through 1964).

One possibility is that world news reporting becomes more attentive and, therefore, more voluminous during certain periods. The amount of news that sometimes is *not* reported is a very difficult problem to approach. In any case the simple volume indicator which increases appreciably in times ordinarily regarded as crisis periods is useful. It would be better if another indicator were used, particularly if it could show with more precision when international crises have started and how long they have lasted. In earlier research reports we have called the indicator capable of these accomplishments a *variety measure*.[2] The development of the variety measure depends on the categorization of the actions and responses by type for the conflict participants.

Obviously, there could be several different ways to group 4,416 reported events in the two conflict arenas. The method followed in the research was to develop a list of different *kinds* of actions and responses found in the data. Some acts are so definite and clear that classifying them under a heading presents no difficulties. For example, the delivery of a protest note by one government to another is a common occurrence and is readily typed as a PROTEST. On the other hand, a category such as REQUEST turns out to be a composite which puts together several specific subtypes of acts such as "ask for information," "ask for material help," "request action," "appeal to," and "seek policy support." The single word REQUEST does not truly describe all that is subsumed. At present the classification system consists of sixty specific types of acts committed by participants in international politics. Our current practice is to group these more generally under twenty-two not-entirely-descriptive labels as follows: YIELD, COMMENT, CONSULT, APPROVE, PROMISE, GRANT, REWARD, AGREE, PROPOSE, REJECT, ACCUSE, PROTEST, DENY, DEMAND, WARN, THREATEN, DEMONSTRATE, REDUCE RELATIONSHIP, EXPEL, SEIZE, and FORCE. The Berlin analysis was done in part with a shorter list of eighteen types of acts and with somewhat different labels. The Taiwan analysis employed a list of twelve types at one stage of the work but new research on the Taiwan data has used the current categorization. In addition, the standard time unit used in counting the number of acts was shortened from a year to a month for the development of the variety measure results. Later in the reporting, the time unit will be changed to a day when the details of crisis periods are examined.

Because the interaction data are organized chronologically, it is possible to count the frequencies of occurrences of acts, month by month, through the

2. Details on this measure are given in Wendell R. Garner, *Uncertainty and Structure as Psychological Concepts* (New York: Wiley, 1962). Applications using crisis data were reported in Charles A. McClelland et al., *The Communist Chinese Performance in Crisis and Non-Crisis: Quantitative Studies of the Taiwan Straits Confrontation, 1950–1964*, Report to Behavioral Sciences Group, Naval Ordnance Test Station, China Lake, Calif. Contract no. N60 530-11207 (1965); and Charles A. McClelland, "The Access to Berlin: The Quantity and Variety of Events, 1948–1963," in J. David Singer, ed., *Quantitative International Politics* (New York: The Free Press, 1967).

years 1948–1963 and 1950–1964 for the respective conflict arenas and for the respective behaviors of the participants. To simplify reporting, we have made the confrontations and crises two-sided affairs by counting the acts of all parties together on one side of the conflict and the acts of the other parties together on the other side of the conflict. Thus *East* and *West* are labels which reflect the combining although they may seem not entirely appropriate in the Taiwan case. To illustrate, in the Berlin arena in June 1962, *West* produced seven PROTESTS, two DEMANDS, two SEIZES, two REQUESTS, and a scattering of single acts in other categories for a total of seventeen. *East*, in the same arena and the same month, committed eight SEIZES, nine YIELDS, four DEMANDS, two ACCUSES, and a scattering of single acts in other categories for a total of twenty-nine. In order to remove the effect of variations in the volume of activity from time period to time period, we converted the frequency counts to percentages of the whole. Thus, in the illustration given above, *West*'s PROTESTS were 7/17 or 41.1 per cent of the whole, *East*'s DEMANDS were 4/29 or 13.8 per cent, and so on for the other categories. Thereafter, the percentages were transformed to corresponding logarithmic numbers to the base two.

There are two main reasons for converting the percentages to the corresponding logarithmic numbers. First, this operation permits a measurement to be achieved that allows comparisons on a common basis of changes in interactions in two or more international conflict arenas and at different time periods. Second, it has a normalization effect on the data so that small frequencies are somewhat enhanced and large frequencies are somewhat diminished. To illustrate the first advantage, let us consider a hypothetical case in which a party in a conflict could do only five different kinds of acts: *A*, *B*, *C*, *D*, and *E*. Let us say that this party committed fifty acts in a given time period. One possible distribution appears in Table 3. Although an observed instance with exactly equal

TABLE 3. EXAMPLE OF EQUAL DISTRIBUTION ACROSS THE CATEGORIES

	No. of Acts in Category	*Per cent*	Log_2
A	10	20	.464
B	10	20	.464
C	10	20	.464
D	10	20	.464
E	10	20	.464
Sum	50	100	2.320

distribution might be unusual, it could happen. Another distribution that one might observe appears in Table 4. Tables 3 and 4 show equal and unequal distributions of the same number of acts. The sums of the logarithmic numbers reflect the difference. The difference between the sum of the logarithmic numbers for any unequal distribution (as in Table 4) and a similar sum of the logarithmic numbers for an equal distribution (as in Table 3) provides the basis for the variety measure. We compare an observed sum such as that shown in Table 4 against the "standard" of Table 3 by taking the ratio: 1.652/2.320 or .712.

This ratio result (.712) is called "relative uncertainty" or *Hrel.* The uncertainty aspect is contained in the observation that in the equal probability instance, there is no way to judge if further occurrences would be more likely to fall in one category rather than another. In the distribution in Table 4, one can see that *A*, *D*, and *E* would be likely to receive more future occurrences than *B* and *C*. Hence it is said that "uncertainty is reduced" in this case. The smaller the *Hrel* figure, the "more certain" it is (i.e., the more the distribution departs from the equal condition). A common sense way to view a series of *Hrel* numbers is to think in terms of a "fanning out" toward equality of the distribution across the category system with the larger figures and a "channeling in" of the distribution toward relatively frequent occurrences in fewer categories with the smaller figures. As the ratio approaches 1.000, it suggests not only that almost everything that could happen has been occurring but also that the behaviors have shown increasing signs of disorderliness. The information measures do not tell us what

TABLE 4. EXAMPLE OF UNEQUAL DISTRIBUTION ACROSS THE CATEGORIES

	No. of Acts in Category	*Per cent*	Log_2
A	12	24	.494
B	5	10	.066
C	5	10	.066
D	13	26	.505
E	15	30	.521
Sum	50	100	1.652

the particular lack of ordering is, but they do give us a technical indication of a large amount of "variety" in the emissions. As the ratio decreases toward .000, the suggestion is that (1) there may be present a large amount of highly patterned and repetitive behavior and limited variety in the action, or (2) very little is occurring.

A long series of analyses has been carried out with the variety measure to establish how it functions on the data of the Berlin and Taiwan conflict arenas. The basic results are these:

1. With occasional exceptions, an *Hrel* of .700 or higher is associated with crisis months and only with crisis months. One or both parties will achieve this ratio or higher.

2. If we operationalize the beginning and duration of international crises with this *Hrel* criterion of .700 and higher, we are able to state when a particular crisis began and how long it lasted:

   a. The Berlin Blockade crisis began in April 1948 and lasted through August 1948.

   b. The Deadline crisis of 1958–1959 was not a crisis.

   c. The Berlin Wall crisis began in August 1961 and lasted through September 1961.

   d. Calculated with a twelve-type category system (the Berlin data were organized on an eighteen-type category system), the Tachens crisis of 1955 began in January and extended through March.

   e. The Quemoy crisis began in September 1958 and concluded by the end of October 1958.[3]

3. Slightly different results were obtained in the first study of the Taiwan arena by Warren Phillips and John Sullivan. They used the *Hrel* measure on a small collection of data to establish crisis dates. The results are found in John Sullivan, "Quemoy and Matsu: A Systematic Analysis," unpublished paper, 1964.

3. According to the calculations, only three months (April, May, and October 1948) in all the noncrisis time periods of the Berlin arena went over the .700 mark. Some questions may be raised about the months of April and May 1948 when the *Hrel* figures ranged between .738 and .784, yet the initial blockade announcement came late in June. Ordinarily, warning signs, if that is what they were in 1948, do not precede the dramatic onset of a crisis.

4. According to the calculations, only the month of June 1955 of all the noncrisis time periods of the Taiwan arena exceeded the .700 level while August 1958, the month of the beginning of the massive bombardment of Quemoy, did not reach the crisis level.

5. All noncrisis periods, except as just noted, have monthly *Hrel* figures below .700.

TURNING POINTS IN THE BERLIN WALL AND QUEMOY CRISES

The good success in identifying crises with the variety measure encouraged further inquiries directed toward still more precise findings. It will have been noted that the change from noncrisis periods to crisis periods has been a "fanning out" rather than a "channeling in" movement. Two questions arise from this interesting effect. First, one expects, on the basis of general knowledge about how conflicts take place, that the intense interchanges of a crisis should have a narrowing effect. There ought to be a shift toward a concentration of activity in a limited range during a crisis. The variety measure suggests the opposite conclusion. Interest is directed toward finding out what does, in fact, go on and in more detail. Are there any particular patterns or combinations of acts and responses peculiar to a crisis? The variety measure tells us about a shift of combination but not what that combination is. The second question reflects some dissatisfaction with the analyses of crises according to whole month periods. Can the beginning of a crisis be specified more closely? For example, can it be determined how long it takes in days for the beginning of a crisis to reach above the .700 level?

The second question is easy to investigate with a closer and more detailed application of the variety measure. The Berlin Wall and Quemoy crises were studied day by day to establish how fast they "ripened" into real crises, according to *Hrel* standards. Since, apparently, both began with dramatic initial events (building the wall, bombarding the island), the counting was begun with these occurrences. The numbers of acts were tallied according to category and the *Hrel* numbers were figured. This was done cumulatively. Results for the first day were computed, results for the first and second days were computed, results for the first, second, and third days were computed, and so on until the .700 level was passed. The acts of *East* and *West* were combined for this purpose so that the whole configuration might be revealed. Tables 5 and 6 show the results.

The difference in the beginnnings of the Berlin Wall and Quemoy crises is apparent in the tables. The Berlin Wall interactions achieved a crisis level almost at once whereas the Taiwan interactions very gradually spread across the categories and increased beyond the .700 level only after the thirteenth day. Here is the explanation of why August 1958 did not figure as a crisis month. The events of August were violent; other kinds of action occurred very infrequently with the result shown by the low *Hrel* numbers. The Quemoy encounter began, in fact,

TABLE 5. THE ONSET OF THE BERLIN WALL CRISIS ACCORDING TO CUMULATIVE *HREL*

	Day														
	*1**	*2*	*3*	*4*	*5*	*6*	*7*	*8*	*9*	*10*	*11*	*12*	*13*	*14*	*15*
No. of Acts Each Day	5	8	5	7	4	8	1	6	2	2	6	11	16	1	27
Cumulative No. of Acts	5	13	18	25	29	37	38	44	46	48	54	65	81	82	109
Cumulative *Hrel*	521	692	740	739	738	749	749	745	763	757	754	743	815	815	832

* Day 1 of the Berlin Wall crisis was August 13, 1961.

TABLE 6. THE ONSET OF THE QUEMOY CRISIS ACCORDING TO CUMULATIVE *HREL*

	Day														
	*1**	*2*	*3*	*4*	*5*	*6*	*7*	*8*	*9*	*10*	*11*	*12*	*13*	*14*	*15*
No. of Acts Each Day	9	11	9	10	8	11	5	4	3	8	5	6	9	9	8
Cumulative No. of Acts	9	20	29	39	47	58	63	67	70	78	83	89	98	107	115
Cumulative *Hrel*	543	431	399	450	468	518	568	596	608	609	622	640	665	701	710

* Day 1 of the Quemoy crisis was August 24, 1958.

with a "channeling in" movement giving way only slowly to the spreading effect which we believe may be a characteristic of international crisis.

There is an indication in Tables 5 and 6 that deserves some particular attention. The increases in the *Hrel*s on the thirteenth day in the Berlin case and on the fourteenth day in the Quemoy case are noteworthy. The variety measure was applied cumulatively for each of the succeeding fifteen days and by month (still cumulatively) to the end of the year in both cases. No comparable change of level appeared in these later time periods. The possibility is, therefore, that some change in the pattern of behavior of the contestants began to take place on the thirteenth and fourteenth days. One might expect, in fact, that the course of each crisis followed an "uptrend" for about two weeks and thereafter began a "downtrend." In other words, a turning point in each crisis may have appeared at about these times.

It would be worthwhile if one could determine by quantitative analysis whether or not turning points in crises can be located. In the two cases in hand, the shifts of the thirteenth and fourteenth days might be the beginnings of the decline of the crises. This observation leads us to speculate on the behavioral characteristics of an abatement phase in international crises. Further, we wonder if uptrends and downtrends in noncrisis periods in a given conflict arena are anything like uptrends (crisis mounting) and downtrends (crisis abating) in crisis episodes. Is there anything to be found in the data which would permit measurements of crisis abatement processes against the up-and-down fluctuations of noncrisis conflict?

PATTERNS OF CRISIS ABATEMENT

Pattern relationships in international politics are discussed sometimes as if they had been thoroughly investigated. How formidable the task is of actually carrying out intensive research on such relationships can be readily illustrated with the span of the subject matter of this chapter. We would have to consider 22 behavioral variables (or 60, if the subtypes are used) in various combinations, generated in two conflict arenas by nine main participants through four international crises and numerous subcrises across a span of time of about twenty years. This is enough complexity to challenge almost any amount of investigative enterprise and virtuosity. No doubt, a large number of relationships could be ferreted out of the data. The skeptic's question remains always to be faced in these matters: Is it worth all the effort and trouble to make such searches and to produce findings that, for the most part, can be regarded as only trivial?

Prevailing opinion seems to be that the important historical events of international relations follow each other in a unique succession with the result that productive comparisons across time are more in the nature of accidents than revelations of reality. The task of investigating regularities or recurrences such as turning points and changes in patterns of crisis behavior involves the possibility that one may be looking for something that is not there. In undertaking an inquiry of this sort, one needs to simplify things to avoid becoming overwhelmed with the work of analyzing quantities of complicated details and at the same time to direct research conservatively toward demanding tests which, if they produce poor results, will strongly suggest the wisdom of abandoning the project. In other words, a preliminary survey has much to recommend it. The following is a report on an effort of that type.

Simplification has been achieved and information has been combined in a way that should greatly reduce the likelihood of finding repetitive patterns. The actions and responses of all the conflict participants have been lumped together, although it is clear from the data already presented that the opposing sides did not behave similarly. The shifts of behavior of one side might either amplify or diminish the evidence of shifts of the other side. Whole year comparisons are going to be made against day-to-day data. It has been assumed, without any real knowledge of the matter, that the shifts from uptrend to downtrend behaviors in the Berlin Wall and Quemoy crises are located where the *Hrel* figures suggest they are. We shall want to test the assumption against the data, of course. Finally, the interaction data have been reorganized into a set of a very few simple and manageable categories. By drastically reducing our information, we have reordered all data within the framework of just five behavioral alternatives. These are:

1. *Conflict deeds* including the active physical events of violent force, seizure, expulsion, negative sanctions which intend to punish opponents and reduce relationships, and the shows of potential force as in demonstrations and mobilizations. Thus we have grouped together the data previously categorized under DEMONSTRATE, REDUCE RELATIONSHIP, EXPEL, SEIZE, and FORCE and we shall call this grouping CONFLICT for the present purpose.

2. *Verbal combat* which reflects the actions and responses of parties in conflict but are not active physical events. For present purposes, this grouping is called CONFRONTATION and it encompasses the interaction categories of REJECT, ACCUSE, PROTEST, DENY, DEMAND, WARN, and THREATEN.

3. *Probing, exploratory, and supportive acts* which move away from confrontation and violent conflict and contain the means for approaching settlement, abatement, accommodation, postponement, or conclusion of conflict. Here we call this grouping ATTEMPTS TO SETTLE; it contains the categories of APPROVE, CONSULT, PROMISE, REQUEST, and PROPOSE.

4. *Acts which mark outcomes*, however temporary and partial, of confrontation and conflict. This grouping is named SETTLEMENT and includes the items categorized previously under the headings of YIELD, GRANT, REWARD, and AGREE.

5. *Expressions which convey information and state positions and intentions* related to the conflict arena, but without the attributes of the other four groupings. Merely talking about the conditions in a conflict arena and stating one's place in the action may appear to be of little importance but such utterances often have an influencing purpose behind them and, perhaps, also serve the functions of release and orientation. The interaction category COMMENT is the sole member of this grouping.

A pattern of behavior is defined in this work as a particular combination of these five groupings, identified in frequencies and percentages. The overall patterns of the two conflict arenas are shown in Tables 7 and 8. The prevalence of force and violence is the notable feature in the conflict arenas. There are few other apparent consistencies within and across these tables. *East* and *West* do not behave very similarly and the two conflict arenas are obviously not identical in general configuration. If there are universal patterns of behavior in international conflict arenas, we shall need to study many more cases to establish what they are. Meanwhile, it is sufficient to search for signs of regularities within each conflict arena.

TABLE 7. WHOLE PATTERN OF THE BERLIN CONFLICT ARENA, 1948–1963*

	East		*West*		*Both*	
	No. of Acts	%	*No. of Acts*	%	*No. of Acts*	%
CONFLICT	482	45.4	191	26.2	673	37.6
CONFRONT	274	25.8	345	47.3	619	34.6
ATTEMPT SET.	35	3.3	57	7.8	92	5.1
SETTLEMENT	202	19.0	74	10.2	276	15.4
COMMENT	69	6.5	62	8.5	131	7.3

* Table includes both crisis and noncrisis interaction data for the 1948–1963 time period.

TABLE 8. WHOLE PATTERN OF THE TAIWAN CONFLICT ARENA, 1950–1964*

	East		*West*		*Both*	
	No. of Acts	%	*No. of Acts*	%	*No. of Acts*	%
CONFLICT	646	43.4	491	43.1	1137	43.3
CONFRONT	566	38.1	214	18.8	780	29.7
ATTEMPT SET.	190	12.8	189	16.6	379	14.4
SETTLEMENT	33	2.2	99	8.7	132	5.1
COMMENT	51	3.4	146	12.8	197	7.5

* Table includes both crisis and noncrisis interaction data for the 1950–1964 time period.

From a systemic standpoint, a reasonable definition of international crisis is that it is a particular kind of alteration of the pattern of the interflowing actions between conflict parties. The change takes place in a short time and is large enough to be recognized. Thus the uptrend stage of a crisis (if there is such) should establish a change from the noncrisis condition to the crisis condition and the downtrend should be another change of state in the interaction flow, perhaps different from both the uptrend and the noncrisis situations. A test of these possibilities can be made by comparing the crisis stages with the average noncrisis behavior pattern of the conflict arena. The noncrisis frequencies and averages appear in the first two columns of Tables 9 and 10. The values of crisis years have been removed and, in the Taiwan case, the data of 1954 have also been excluded because the increase in interactions in 1954 clearly led to the Tachens crisis of early 1955. How the hypothesized uptrend and downtrend phases in the Berlin Wall and Quemoy crises varied from the noncrisis averages of the respective conflict arenas is revealed by comparing the subsequent columns in Tables 9 and 10 with the first two columns.

The data in these tables confirm turning points in the crises previously located by the variety measure. The evidence is more convincing in the Taiwan-Quemoy comparisons than in the Berlin data. Yet both indicate substantial shifts in the distributions across the five behavioral categories. Conflict deeds increased slightly in the uptrend phase of the crises and decreased more strongly in the downtrend or abatement phase. Very interesting is the fact that in the downtrend phase the reported acts of force, show of force, and direct violence are fewer than the noncrisis average. Interactions that fall within the ATTEMPT TO

TABLE 9. CHANGES BETWEEN NONCRISIS, CRISIS UPSWING, AND CRISIS DOWNSWING FOR BERLIN ARENA

	No. of Acts in Noncrisis	*% of Acts in Noncrisis**	*% of Acts in Crisis Engagement†*	*% of Acts in Crisis Abatement‡*	*Difference between Noncrisis and Engagement*	*Difference between Noncrisis and Abatement*	*Difference between Engagement Downtrend and Abatemten Phases of Crisis*
CONFLICT	422	36.6	38.5	25.7	1.9	-10.9	12.8
CONFRONT	393	34.1	52.3	52.3	18.2	18.2	0.0
ATTEMPT SET.	60	5.2	0.0	4.6	-5.2	-0.6	-4.6
SETTLEMENT	206	17.9	7.7	9.2	-10.2	-8.7	-1.5
COMMENT	72	6.2	1.5	8.2	-4.7	2.0	-6.7

* Noncrisis percentages are based on the number of acts made by all parties during the years between 1948–1963 when data of crisis periods have been excluded.

† Crisis upswing percentages are based on the number of acts made by all parties during the first 12 days of the Berlin Wall crisis.

‡ Crisis downswing percentages are based on the number of acts made by all parties during the succeeding 25 days of the Berlin Wall crisis.

TABLE 10. CHANGES BETWEEN NONCRISIS, CRISIS UPSWING, AND CRISIS DOWNSWING FOR TAIWAN ARENA

	No. of Acts in Noncrisis	*% of Acts in Noncrisis**	*% of Acts in Crisis Engagement†*	*% of Acts in Crisis Abatement‡*	*Difference between Noncrisis and Engagement*	*Difference between Noncrisis and Abatement*	*Difference between Engagement Downtrend and Abatement Phases of Crisis*
CONFLICT	472	48.4	52.0	21.7	3.6	-26.7	30.3
CONFRONT	251	25.8	32.6	42.8	6.8	17.0	-10.2
ATTEMPT SET.	157	16.1	3.1	20.5	-13.0	4.4	-17.4
SETTLEMENT	34	3.5	2.1	7.8	-1.4	4.3	-5.7
COMMENT	60	6.2	10.2	7.2	4.0	1.0	3.0

* Noncrisis percentages are based on the number of acts made by all parties during the years between 1950–1964 when the data of crisis periods have been excluded.

† Crisis upswing percentages are based on the number of acts made by all parties during the first 13 days of the 1958 Quemoy crisis.

‡ Crisis downswing percentages are based on the number of acts made by all parties during the succeeding 15 days of the 1958 Quemoy crisis.

SETTLE and SETTLEMENT categories increased in the shift across the turning point from crisis uptrend to crisis downtrend. In both cases crisis abatement was accompanied by more than average amounts of harsh language directed at opponents, as is shown in the CONFRONTATION data. One is led to suspect that conflict parties in international crises are sometimes inclined to cover their retreats from violent deeds with a barrage of complaints, protests, accusations, denials, rejections, warnings, and threats. Overall, the usual pattern of behavior in noncrises is not like the pattern of behavior in crises, the crisis engagement patterns differ from the abatement patterns, and the patterns throughout in the two conflict arenas are unlike.

The last step in this preliminary survey of crisis turning points and patterns consisted of an exploration of particular noncrisis periods when marked fluctuations appeared to have occurred. These were used for matching against changes of pattern within the crises. We concentrated only on the examination of the abatement phases of the Berlin Wall and Quemoy crises and compared them with downtrend periods of noncrisis in the two conflict arenas.

A search was made through the quantity and variety data for noncrisis time to locate the years that were not preludes or aftermaths of crises and that had a shift from a high level of interaction to a lower level. One instance was found in the Taiwan arena data: the high activity level of 1950 was followed by a marked decrease in 1951. In the Berlin arena, the best instance was found in the high activity of 1952 followed by the low activity of 1953. These downturns of Taiwan (1951) and Berlin (1953) were the only clear choices that could be made from the yearly data. The suggestion of a downtrend in activity seems to imply relaxation of conflict. The analogy with the abatement phase of a crisis following a turning point is obvious. The differences in behavior patterns of 1950–1951 and 1952–1953 provide change indicators to be applied against the crisis downtrend evidence. The essential information is the up-down differences of noncrisis and crisis; Tables 11 and 12 organize these data conveniently for the two conflict arenas.

The data for the downtrend effects are simple enough in these tables to allow direct observation of certain tendencies. The abatement process in both noncrisis and crisis situations in the two conflict arenas contains some similarities. The reported instances of forceful and violent actions decreased and the reported

TABLE 11. UP-DOWN CHANGES IN BERLIN ARENA (1952–1953) AND THE WALL CRISIS

	1952 Uptrend %	*1953 Downtrend* %	*Difference*	*Wall Crisis Uptrend; 1st 12 Days* %	*Wall Crisis Downtrend; Next 25 Days* %	*Difference*
CONFLICT	30.3	29.0	−1.3	38.5	25.7	−12.8
CONFRONT	36.2	29.1	−7.1	52.3	52.3	0.0
ATTEMPT SET.	5.4	18.3	12.9	0.0	4.6	4.6
SETTLEMENT	21.1	15.0	−6.1	7.7	9.2	1.5
COMMENT	7.0	8.6	1.6	1.5	8.2	6.7

TABLE 12. UP-DOWN CHANGES IN TAIWAN ARENA (1950–1951) AND THE QUEMOY CRISIS

	1950 Uptrend %	*1951 Downtrend* %	*Difference*	*Quemoy Crisis Uptrend; 1st 13 Days* %	*Quemoy Crisis Downtrend; Next 15 Days* %	*Difference*
CONFLICT	55.3	43.3	-12.0	52.0	21.7	-30.3
CONFRONT	21.2	31.6	10.4	32.6	42.8	10.2
ATTEMPT SET.	6.8	15.0	8.2	3.1	20.5	17.4
SETTLEMENT	6.8	3.3	-3.5	2.1	7.8	5.7
COMMENT	9.8	6.7	-3.1	10.2	7.2	-3.0

instances of settlement efforts increased. There are also a few systematic contrasts. Noncrisis abatement shows a somewhat unexpected decline of acts in the SETTLEMENT category while crisis abatement exhibits a modest increase in this area, as one might expect on a common sense basis. The data indicate that tendencies in one conflict arena are different from those in another conflict arena. Thus abatement in the Taiwan arena included small declines in official explanations and policy comments but small increases in these behaviors in the Berlin arena. Increased verbal combat during the abatement phase appears to have been characteristic in the Taiwan arena but not as much so in the Berlin arena.

The difference figures for noncrisis abatement within each conflict arena show that the changes in pattern are much alike. Just how alike these changes are is not a critical consideration in a preliminary study such as this. Only in a more ambitious and complex analysis involving more cases and much more detailed data would it become important to adopt a specific method to establish the degree of pattern shift similarity. Nevertheless, the extent of downtrend pattern resemblance was calculated, using the simplified Taiwan and Berlin materials. The main purpose was to explore an approach to more complicated analyses which the preliminary survey now suggests should be undertaken.

MONITORING CRISIS CHANGES: A SIMPLE ILLUSTRATION USING GRAPH THEORY

The theory of directed graphs and adjacent matrices has not been used much in the study of international relations.[4] The application of even a few simple principles of graph theory appears to have much to offer to international relations analysis. If we faced the problem of tracing the downtrend change patterns in crisis and noncrisis using sixty behavioral variables on many cases, the graph and matrix procedures described below would be very helpful. With five variables and only two cases to handle, the graph and matrix procedure is less

4. See Frank Harary, "A Structural Analysis of the Situation in the Middle East in 1956," *Journal of Conflict Resolution*, 5 (June 1961), 167–178. For the theory see Frank Harary, Robert Z. Norman, and Dorwin Cartwright, *Structural Models: An Introduction to the Theory of Directed Graphs* (New York: Wiley, 1965).

impressive but it produces a calculation of how much alike are the noncrisis downtrend pattern and the crisis abatement pattern.

The differences in uptrend-downtrend change for the Berlin Wall crisis were ranked on the basis of "gained more than." As Table 11 shows, the COMMENT category "gained more" than any other. At the other end of the scale, the CONFLICT category "lost more" than any other. The other categories fall between these extremes. The rank ordering simply reflects the gain-loss status of each of the five categories in relationship; the Berlin Wall graph in Figure 1 pictorializes these relations. The connecting arrows are directed to show "gained more than" (or "lost less than"). The numbering in the circles identifies the category type. Thus the graph tells us that CONFRONTATION, ATTEMPT TO SETTLE, SETTLEMENT, and COMMENT gained more than CONFLICT, that SETTLEMENT gained more than CONFRONTATION and CONFLICT, and so on. The adjacency matrix labeled "A" in Figure 1 contains exactly the same information as the graph and may be read across the rows for the "gain" relations. The directed graph and its adjacent matrix "B" which show the noncrisis downtrend in the Berlin arena should be read and interpreted in the same way as the graph and matrix for the Berlin Wall crisis.

The third step in the analysis is to place one directed graph over the other to determine which relations changed and which remained the same. The union of A and B matrices is equivalent to the superimposition of one graph on the other (see part C of Figure 1). The lines on the combined graph that are in two directions record the shifts in relations between noncrisis and crisis. Six lines out of 20 (twenty relations are in the composite graph) represent the amount of divergence in pattern in the comparison of downtrends in the noncrisis and crisis situations. The difference is 30 per cent or the noncrisis and crisis patterns are alike to the extent of 70 per cent.

Under standard procedures of directed graph theory, one is permitted to group together "strong components" and "condense the digraph" in order to reveal fundamental structures. The two-way relations of CONFLICT and CONFRONTATION and of CONFLICT and SETTLEMENT in the combined graph of the Berlin Wall and Berlin arena changes are condensed properly to one "point." The two-way relation of ATTEMPT TO SETTLE and COMMENT constitutes another "strong component" and hence allows another condensation to one "point." The result is the condensed digraph (D) in Figure 1. Its interpretation is that the abating action in the Berlin conflict arena consisted of ATTEMPT TO SETTLE and COMMENT behaviors which overrode the CONFLICT, CONFRONTATION, and SETTLEMENT behaviors.

An analysis of the downtrend phenomena carried out with the Taiwan conflict arena data can be followed in the graphs and matrices of Figure 2. It is to be noted that the change pattern is different from that of Berlin. The Taiwan noncrisis change pattern (A of Figure 2) resembles the Quemoy crisis change pattern (B) even more closely than in the Berlin comparisons. Only two relations shifted (they are circled in matrix D) and only four lines of 20 are in two directions. This represents a 20 per cent divergence of noncrisis and crisis patterns. The basic abatement action structure at Taiwan (D) is also different from that at Berlin and it suggests that the main abatement movement in the arena was to override acts of force and violence by a pair combination of the other four types of behavior.

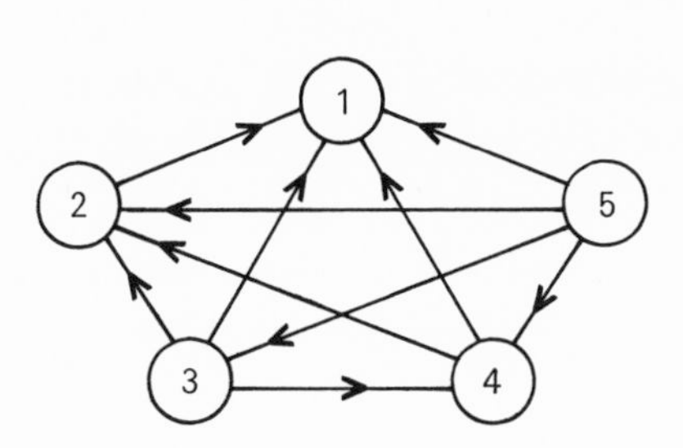

Categories	1	2	3	4	5
1	0	0	0	0	0
2	1	0	0	0	0
3	1	1	0	1	0
4	1	1	0	0	0
5	1	1	1	1	0

A. Relationships in Abatement Phase of Berlin Wall Crisis

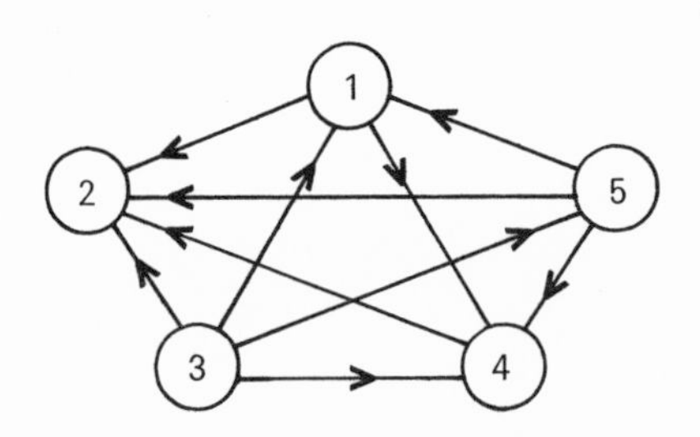

Categories	1	2	3	4	5
1	0	1	0	1	0
2	0	0	0	0	0
3	1	1	0	1	1
4	0	1	0	0	0
5	1	1	0	1	0

B. Relationships in Noncrisis Abatement Period of Berlin

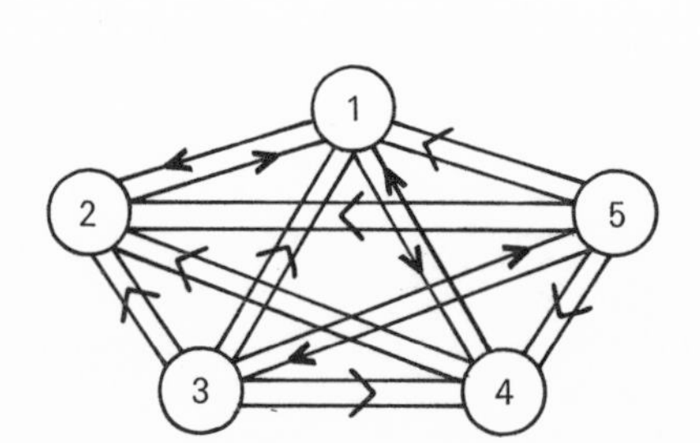

Categories	1	2	3	4	5
1	0	1	0	1	0
2	1	0	0	0	0
3	2	2	0	2	1
4	1	2	0	0	0
5	2	2	1	2	0

C. Comparison of Crisis and Noncrisis Action Categories in Berlin Arena

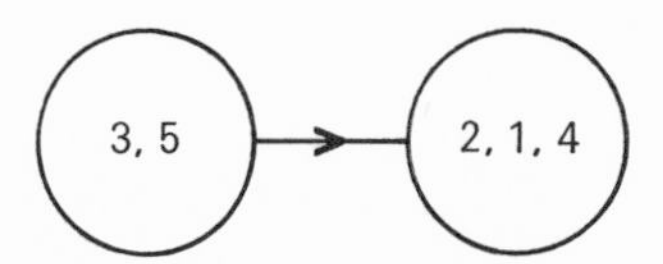

D. Basic Abatement Action Structure at Berlin

FIGURE 1. Directed graphs and matrices indicating patterns among five categories of action in crisis and noncrisis abatement periods for the Berlin arena. (*Note*: 1=Conflict; 2=Confrontation; 3=Attempt to settle; 4=Settlement; 5=Comment.)

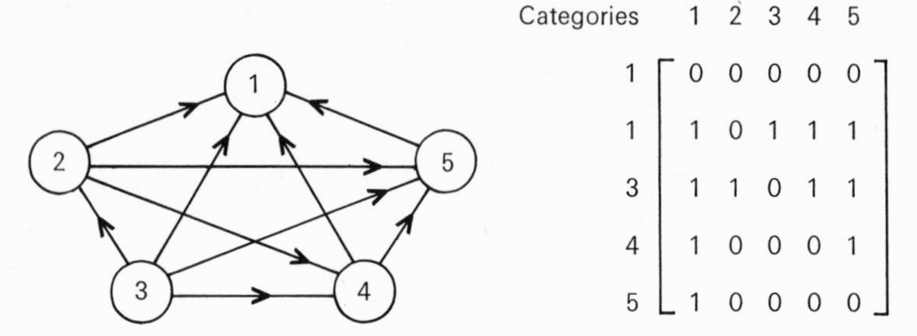

Categories	1	2	3	4	5
1	0	0	0	0	0
1	1	0	1	1	1
3	1	1	0	1	1
4	1	0	0	0	1
5	1	0	0	0	0

A. Relationships in Abatement Phase of Quemoy Crisis

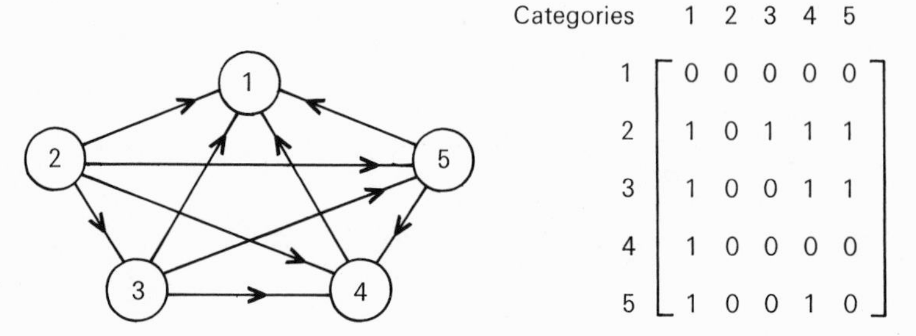

Categories	1	2	3	4	5
1	0	0	0	0	0
2	1	0	1	1	1
3	1	0	0	1	1
4	1	0	0	0	0
5	1	0	0	1	0

B. Relationships in Noncrisis Period of Taiwan Arena

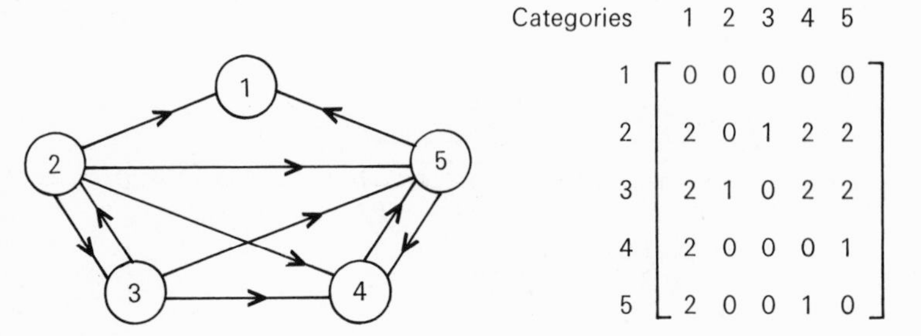

Categories	1	2	3	4	5
1	0	0	0	0	0
2	2	0	1	2	2
3	2	1	0	2	2
4	2	0	0	0	1
5	2	0	0	1	0

C. Comparison of Crisis and Noncrisis Action Categories in Taiwan Arena

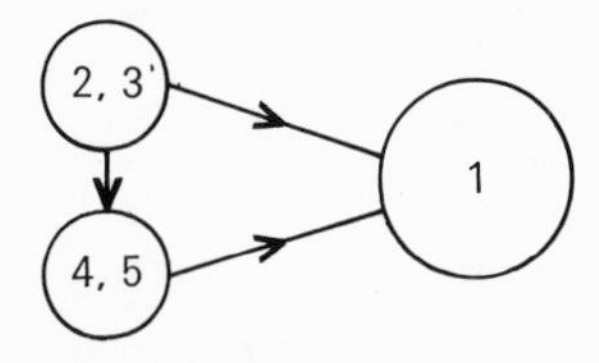

D. Basic Abatement Action Structure at Taiwan

FIGURE 2. Directed graphs and matrices indicating patterns among five categories of action in crisis and noncrisis abatement periods for the Taiwan arena. (*Note*: 1=Conflict; 2=Confrontation; 3=Attempt to settle; 4=Settlement; 5=Comment.)

THE DIRECTION OF FURTHER WORK

The findings from two case studies do not establish any reliable generalizations beyond the cases. No matter how intensive is the research, the investigation of one or two conflict arenas is insufficient. The outcomes of the preliminary survey of crisis turning points and pattern changes are, therefore, interesting, encouraging, and inconclusive. It is clear that further inquiries concerning the structures of action and the relations within international crises should now be turned to more cases. More crisis situations need to be analyzed to ascertain whether or not the patterning and recurring tendencies demonstrated for the Berlin Wall and Quemoy crises will hold widely. The liability of the moment is in the paucity of data organized for the type of analysis presented in this chapter. The facts are available but gathering and ordering them involve a substantial outlay of time and research resources. The difficulty will have to be overcome because, without a comparative study of many crises, almost all conclusions about their behavioral characteristics will remain merely tentative.

The next step in pattern analysis requires the removal of the simplifications in the preliminary survey. The demonstration that there are some fairly steady patterns in crisis behavior warrants the expense and trouble of more detailed research. It is possible that more sensitive or more decisive indicators of crisis patterns and crisis changes are to be found within that detail. The survey dealt with the whole configuration of crisis interaction. Obviously, the performance of each of the major conflict participants should be traced. Joint performance relationships should be delineated more precisely by some means.

A significant result of the studies reported here is the discovery of the potential importance of noncrisis data in forecasting some aspects of crisis behavior. One might expect some regularity and continuity in chronic conflict situations between countries but explicit demonstrations of such similarities have been lacking over time. The field of investigation will be much widened if lesser encounters and confrontations of international politics are included within the study of crises. The number of cases for investigation will be greatly increased and it is not beyond the realm of possibility that there will be success in establishing operational codes and behavioral tendencies of nations that take part in the perennial contests of international politics. Eventually, subcrisis analysis may contribute to the understanding of all the interpositional phenomena lying between peace and war.

part three

PERCEPTIONS OF CRISIS BY POLICY MAKERS

chapter six

EDITOR'S INTRODUCTION

The two chapters in this section deal with the perceptions that foreign policy makers have of crises and their attributes. In the present chapter their perceptions are obtained through interviews and questionnaires; in the following chapter the Zinneses and their collaborator use a content analysis of diplomatic communications authored by policy makers. The case studies by Paige and Holsti in the previous section gave some attention to policy makers' views of crises. In contrast with the next two chapters, however, neither author used an analytical framework that insured the exclusive use of perceptual material. Thus Paige included variables like the size and the nature of the group making the decision and Holsti referred to variables such as the volume of communications. The focus of the next two chapters allows their authors to address the broad question: How do policy makers—not observers—interpret the experiences referred to as crises?

Lentner's interview method of determining the perceptions of policy makers is obvious but, except for case studies, infrequently used in the systematic study of crises. He questioned individuals associated directly or indirectly with the Operations Center in the Department of State. Established early in the Kennedy Administration, the Operations Center has been judged by at least one former Assistant Secretary of State as a badly needed and valuable capability.

> *The Defense Department had its War Room, which served as a central nerve center, fully manned, and equipped with twenty-four-hour-a-day communications to United States military installations all over the world. Even the CIA had modern communications and coding equipment. But the State Department was hopelessly behind. Its cryptographic equipment was obsolescent, which slowed communications, and it had no central situation room at all. . . . Secretary Rusk directed that the Department should set up a room with communications tickers hooked to the military networks, scrambler phones, and so on, and man it with middle-grade foreign service officers who could at least make judgments about urgency in the middle of the night. . . . The improved communications and a place from which crises could be managed at night or on weekends were a great help.*[1]

In brief, the men in the Operations Center monitor events around the world, identify what appear as crisis-like situations, and then alert and support those who must handle the problems. These men would appear to be excellent respondents for a study designed to ascertain the kinds of situations that policy makers define as crises.

Two important questions arise in connection with such research. First, are policy makers tempted to define any situation as a crisis if it is politically advantageous to do so? If this question receives an affirmative answer, then little is gained by the systematic examination of the policy makers' perceptions of crisis. The only common property shared by an otherwise diverse set of

1. Roger Hilsman, *To Move a Nation* (Garden City, N.Y.: Doubleday, 1967), pp. 27–28. Reprinted by permission of the publisher.

events would be the opportunity they offered for political expediency if various domestic and foreign publics were convinced that the government faced a crisis. Waltz presents exactly this argument:

> *The American government since the war has been impressively ready to say that difficult situations abroad should be treated as though they were crises, which the United States should seek to meet or to mitigate. In no strict sense was it necessary to describe the plight of West European countries after the war as constituting a crisis for the United States. A similar statement can be made about the attack on South Korea, about Communist China's pressure upon the islands of the Formosa Strait, and about other cases.*[2]

Others, including the editor, believe that when policy makers perceive a situation to have certain immediate implications for their country, various processes and behaviors are then likely—not because the policy makers believe it is advantageous to act in that fashion, but because most men and organizations naturally react in that manner. As Hoffmann puts it:

> *There is an element of choice in the presentation of an issue as a crisis, and it is possible to argue either that certain issues ought not to have been presented as crises because no vital United States interest was involved (Lebanon, the Dominican Republic, or even Vietnam), or that others were presented as crises for tactical reasons only (the Truman Doctrine). However, an examination of the record shows that more often than not a crisis is to the policy-makers, not an event of debatable relevance to the U.S. interests which they* choose *to treat as an emergency, but an event believed, rightly or wrongly, to be of indisputable importance, creating a* compelling necessity *for action.*[3] [emphasis in original]

The second question concerns the particular foreign policy officials that Lentner interviewed. We know the contraction of authority that normally occurs in a crisis confines the decision-making group to a small number of individuals usually holding the highest level positions in the government. Clearly, the middle-level officers associated with the Operations Center are not such a group. Of what value, therefore, are their perceptions of international crises? Lentner addresses this question in his chapter, but several additional points seem appropriate. Even in noncrisis situations the individuals in one or another of the foreign policy bureaucracies often resist the designation of themselves as "policy" or "decision" makers. They argue that policies and decisions are made by the "principals" (i.e., assistant secretaries or above) and that as subordinates they undertake the sizable twin tasks of gathering the information necessary for higher-level decisions and executing policy decisions once they have been reached by their superiors. Such a self-view on the part of lower- and middle-level officials may reflect modesty or a desire to duck responsibility, but it does not square with considerable evidence.[4] The information that gets relayed, the

2. Kenneth N. Waltz, *Foreign Policy and Democratic Politics* (Boston: Little, Brown, 1967), p. 108.

3. Stanley Hoffmann, *Gulliver's Troubles* (New York: McGraw-Hill, 1968), p. 295.

4. For example, see Richard Neustadt, *Presidential Power* (New York: Wiley, 1960); and Dean G. Pruitt, *Problem Solving in the Department of State*, no. 2 (1964–

options that are argued with special vigor by the country director, or the instructions that are complied with in the most minimal way—all these and other techniques give the lower-level officers considerable ability to shape policy.

To a degree the same is true in crisis. If the decision-making group in a crisis considers a contingency plan prepared previously by middle-level officers, then the latter will have made a vital input. If in a crisis a Navy captain is ordered to intercept the vessel of an opposing country without sinking it, how he carries out that instruction can spell the difference between success and disaster.

With respect to the Operations Center, the men associated with that facility can be expected to have an even more certain effect on crisis decision making. Technically, it may be correct to say that "it is not its [the Operations Center's] task to make decisions, but to make available to the decision-makers all information available, maps, data and communications."[5] In performing that information role, however, the officers subtly but surely affect the outcome. Furthermore, because it is the watch officers in the Operations Center who decide which situations warrant the immediate attention of higher officials, the correspondence must be good between their perceptions of crises and those of the senior officials in the Department of State. If a watch officer too frequently wakes his superiors in the middle of the night for situations they do not regard as emergencies, that watch officer may soon find himself at another post—far from Washington.

Howard H. Lentner is the Chairman of the Department of Political Science at McMaster University in Ontario, Canada. In addition to the research reported in this chapter, Lentner's contributions to the study of crisis include an article on the seizure of the *Pueblo*.[6]

1965), Monograph Series in World Affairs, The Social Science Foundation and the Department of International Relations, University of Denver, Denver, Colo. In a book he is writing, Morton Halperin makes this point with considerable force.

5. Lloyd Armour, " 'Flap House' Stays Busy as War Tensions Mount," Nashville *Tennessean*, June 4, 1967, p. 1-B.

6. Howard H. Lentner, "The *Pueblo* Affair: Anatomy of a Crisis," *Military Review*, 49 (July 1969), 55–66.

chapter six

THE CONCEPT OF CRISIS AS VIEWED BY THE UNITED STATES DEPARTMENT OF STATE*

Howard H. Lentner

This study is an attempt to elucidate the concept of crisis by investigating the Department of State's machinery for crisis management. The aim is to contribute to the search for an analytically precise and theoretically useful definition of crisis in the study of international politics and foreign policy.

Two analyses are undertaken. The first attempts to discover the manner in which crisis is defined by some of those in the Department of State who deal with crises. The second is an inquiry into the reactions of these officers to several propositions concerning crisis.

Apart from the principal officers of government who make important decisions but to whom it is difficult to gain access, the personnel most closely associated with crisis management are those who serve in the Operations Center and on task forces for particular crises. The officers who work in the Operations Center have a unique vantage point from which to view crises. As a collectivity, they observe all crises and perform certain staff functions in identifying and responding to crises. Foreign Service Officers who have served on task forces for crisis management have the advantage of having worked on at least one crisis and can thus draw on their experience in describing both what occurs and their own perceptions of the differences between crisis and routine.

DESCRIPTION OF THE OPERATIONS CENTER

The Operations Center was established as part of Secretary of State Rusk's office following the Bay of Pigs incident. Headed by Theodore Achilles, who was assisted by Steven Smith, a White House appointee, it was initially staffed at the FSO-1 and FSO-2 level.[1] In its early days the Operations Center was manned eight to nine hours per day by fifteen people, including "permanent high level representatives of the Department of Defense, the Central Intelligence Agency, and the United States Information Agency."[2]

* The author gratefully acknowledges a grant from the Graduate Council of Western Reserve University which made this study possible. Without the participation of the Foreign Service Officers who gave of their time and thought, no study could have been done. The author wishes to express his appreciation to these participants. He would like to acknowledge the late Douglas W. Coster for his assistance in arranging for the study and carrying it out. The author expresses his gratitude to Professor Alan Arian for his assistance in developing the interview schedule and to Professor Douglas P. Bwy for his help on the technical aspects of the statistical analysis.

1. That is, they were at a relatively high level. FSO-1 is approximately equivalent to GS-14 in the Civil Service, and FSO-2 is equivalent to GS-13.

2. *Department of State News Letter*, no. 2 (June 1961), p. 4.

As originally conceived, the Operations Center was to serve the Secretary in the functions of "setting in motion and supporting major interdepartmental task forces . . ., conducting informal interdepartmental reviews of emerging foreign policy problems, and . . . following up government-wide action in the field of foreign affairs."[3] In addition, the Center acted as "an instrument for keeping special watch on an emerging or potential crisis, when so assigned by the Secretary."[4] A task force, called into existence by the Secretary and headed by the Assistant Secretary of a geographical bureau, acted as an information-and-analysis-processing unit for helping the Secretary "manage crisis." In addition, an officer (usually FSO-3) was maintained on duty twenty-four hours per day.

In January 1962, after the retirement of Achilles and the resignation of Smith, the Operations Center was reorganized. A staff consisting of a Senior Watch Officer, an Associate Watch Officer, and an Editor maintained a twenty-four-hour-per-day watch. The Operations Center was given an alerting function which had previously been performed by the Communications Center. Twice-daily summaries, which had previously been prepared in the Secretariat, were written by the Editor under the supervision of the Senior Watch Officer (SWO).

In the Cuban missile crisis, principal officers of the Department focused their attention on the Operations Center, and five watch officers were detailed to the Defense Department's Joint War Room (now called the National Military Command Center). Since that time the principal officers of the Department of State have used the Operations Center more than before. The Operations Center was transferred from the Secretary's office to the Executive Secretariat, the Director serving as a deputy to the Executive Secretary. In 1963 interagency agreements provided for exchanges of personnel on a permanent basis between State and Defense.

Additional manpower, equipment, and responsibilities have been added. The Operations Center "is clearly identified with the central staff function of managing the information flow to the Department's top policymakers."[5] The Operations Center handles "more urgent categories of information"[6] by monitoring wire service tickers, urgent categories of telegrams, and telephones. It alerts both high-level officers and the substantive bureaus to information requiring "quick action."[7] Watch officers must be prepared to brief principals on events affecting major American foreign policy interests. Liaison is maintained with other watch centers throughout the national security agencies in Washington. When a crisis develops, the Operations Center provides both physical facilities and technical assistance to task forces which gather there to manage crises. Thus an office and a bureaucratic technology has developed to facilitate the handling of foreign policy crises and trouble spots by the Department of State.

The Operations Center, although performing several functions, is, above all, a nodal point in the communications network at the service of top-level foreign affairs decision makers. It receives, processes, and distributes high-speed and high-precedence communications. In addition to telephone messages and

3. *Ibid.* 4. *Ibid.*

5. William B. Connett, "Operations Center—Locus of 'Crisis Management,'" *Department of State News Letter*, no. 40 (August 1964), p. 16.

6. *Ibid.*

7. *Watch Manual.* The *Watch Manual* is an internal document prepared by senior officers in the Operations Center as a reference for watch officers. Citations from the *Watch Manual* are from unclassified sections to which the author had access.

wire service tickers which are monitored by watch officers, approximately one hundred and seventy-five advance copies of telegrams come to the Operations Center each day. The originators of these cables tag them with precedence indicators. One of the tasks of the watch officer is to judge whether, in the context of his knowledge, messages should be distributed immediately or whether to wait for further information before distributing messages to the intended recipient.

Certain communications traffic is watched for because of the interest of principal officers of the Department in the subject matter. This traffic may be called to the attention of a particular principal officer, if he wishes, or it may be used by the watch officers as a means of keeping informed for purposes of briefing the principal officer interested. Such interest on the part of a principal officer does not necessarily focus on "crises."

Should the information coming into the Operations Center require "quick reaction"[8] procedures, watch officers must notify appropriate personnel immediately, usually at the Assistant Secretary level. Further notification is given when warranted, and is demanded for "major crisis alerting."[9]

Should an Assistant Secretary make a determination, after consultation with the Senior Watch Officer on duty, that the situation requires abnormal procedures, he may call a task force or working group into being. (A task force is inter-departmental; a working group is composed of State Department personnel only.) The task force is located physically in the Operations Center. During the day the task force is an inter-departmental committee engaged in dealing with a single situation. At least one task force representative remains on duty overnight to follow the development of the crisis. During a crisis relevant cable traffic into the Operations Center increases substantially, and total cable traffic can be more than four times its normal flow.

In a crisis situation watch officers must read the increasing cable traffic, notify various officials and other "command and control" posts, assist in the setting up of a task force, brief senior officers, and keep abreast of other events besides those in the crisis situation. As the task force takes over the crisis, the Operations Center staff returns to its normal functions, although with heavier message traffic. During the period between the initial vast increases in cable traffic and the assemblage of a task force, the normal complement of Operations Center personnel may be strengthened by bringing in additional help. After the task force is established, the watch officers cooperate with it in routine ways—exchange of information and so forth.

Because the Operations Center plays an important role in the process of crisis management in the State Department, it was thought that the views of crisis held by those who have worked in or with the Operations Center would be helpful in arriving at a conception of crisis.

8. This is a term used in a memorandum dated October 1, 1964, in the *Watch Manual.* This memorandum describes incidents requiring quick reaction procedures as follows: "They are or might become of substantial importance to the national security; . . . they are fast-moving enough to demand rapid operational responses; [and] . . . they are likely to require inter-agency coordination and liaison."

9. Para. 141.1 of *Watch Manual.*

METHODS OF INVESTIGATION AND ANALYSIS

The views reported here are based on forty-two interviews held in Washington in June and August 1966 with Foreign Service Officers, thirty of whom were serving or had served as watch officers in the Operations Center. The other twelve interviewees ranged from desk officers to Deputy Assistant Secretaries, all of whom had served on a task force in the Operations Center or were in some other way familiar with its work. In addition, the views are based on responses to a questionnaire about crisis. One hundred two written forms each containing fifty statements concerning crisis were distributed to the persons interviewed and others with similar experience; seventy-nine of these individuals responded. See the Appendix for a description of the participants in this study.

On the one hand, the interview questions were open-ended, and the responses varied considerably but with repeated references to a few points. The questionnaire, on the other hand, contained statements followed by four choices ("always," "often," "sometimes," "never") and respondents were asked to indicate the degree to which each statement applied to crisis. Some divergence of views occurs in the responses to the two methods of data collection.

The questionnaire items included many propositions culled from the literature on crisis in foreign affairs and foreign policy decision making. Although the responses of Foreign Service Officers cannot be considered a complete test of these hypotheses, the views of people who deal with foreign affairs crises might lead to a reexamination of some propositions. The interview and questionnaire data also permit scholars and public officials to compare their perceptions of crisis.

Interpretations of these data, however, must be made with caution because this study suffers from certain substantive and methodological disabilities. The author had no access to classified information. The study, therefore, is of process divorced from substance. Although the study seems worthwhile in spite of this deficiency and incompleteness, it must be recognized that it is inadequate as a complete treatment of its subject matter. When the documents become open to scholars, a partial test of the observations in this study may be made. Even that, however, will be incomplete, for many of the written materials will not be kept, the personality and group dynamic factors will not have been recorded, and the verbal behavior of participants will not be available.

The study also suffers from certain other deficiencies. First, the most important views of crisis are those held by principal officers in government. These men were not interviewed. One does not know if their views are reflected by their subordinates. Because all the material is aggregated to create a composite view of the Foreign Service Officers interviewed and questioned, one might infer that the responses presented below approximate the views of the principals. Second, in interviewing, one does not know why particular responses are given. The interviewee may conceptualize inadequately, or he may simply have a negative reaction to the interviewer. In this study the interviewer attempted to get respondents to deal in concepts (including the concept of crisis) that a few of them were reluctant to use. In spite of efforts by the interviewer to allow reluctant interviewees to employ their own concepts or even to refuse to deal conceptually with the subject matter, he does not know precisely how the interview situation affected the responses.

The written forms contained some ambiguous statements and forced answers into a restricted number of choices. These are both deficiencies of this particular technique.

Another difficulty is that views of crisis may change over time and by situation. Account of this problem is taken by contacting personnel who had served in different periods, but one cannot be certain that it is dealt with adequately. For the most part, the study focuses on the Operations Center as it existed in the summer of 1966 and at relevant periods in the memories of those who served there.

The responses in this study offer some difficulties in reporting and interpretation not only because of the methodological problems cited above but also because there was no uniform agreement on what constitutes crisis. This is a two-fold problem. First, there were some differing frames of reference among respondents. Second, any single respondent may have employed multiple frames of reference in replying to different interview or questionnaire items. Where possible, the consequences of different frames of reference are cited in the report of findings below. To check the impact of shifting frames of reference in answer to different questions, items which were equivalent or opposites were compared. No significant inconsistencies were found.

VIEWS OF CRISIS HELD BY STATE DEPARTMENT OFFICERS[10]

This section utilizes the first type of analysis mentioned in the introduction to this chapter: an examination of the way in which crisis is defined by some of those who have dealt with crises. Initially, information from all the officers will be aggregated to form a composite view of the characteristics most often associated with crisis. An illustration later in the section will show a possible difference in some officers' interpretation of crisis.

Threat to goals. The most frequent response to every question asking for a definition of crisis and for the characteristics of crisis was a reference to the possible or actual involvement of American national interests. Various references to U.S. interests were made, including national security, danger to American citizens, general diplomatic relations with another country, and so forth. A related questionnaire item also dealt with threat to United States policy. The exact format of the statement and responses appears in section (a) of Table 1. The results reveal that slightly over half the officers either always or often associated a crisis with a threat to American goals.

Threat to the decision-making unit is one characteristic of crisis accepted by some analysts attempting to define the concept precisely. "In international relations, one typically thinks of threats as involving potentially severe damage to the goals or objectives of the decision makers of a nation-state."[11] Without a specification of goals, one can presume that these authors either hold an unspecified but restricted view of the goals they have in mind or that they accept all

10. This section is based both on the views given in response to the interview questions and, when related to these responses, the replies to questionnaire items.

11. James A. Robinson, Charles F. Hermann, and Margaret G. Hermann, "Search Under Crisis in Political Gaming and Simulation," in Dean G. Pruitt and Richard C. Snyder, eds., *Theory and Research on the Causes of War* (Englewood Cliffs, N.J.: Prentice-Hall, 1969), pp. 80–94. See also the chapter on simulation by Hermann in this volume.

goals (e.g., personal, organizational, national) which can reasonably be imputed to decision makers. As defined, this property of crisis is highly ambiguous, but it does accord with the views of the Foreign Service Officers interviewed and over half of those who completed the questionnaire.

The present study noted that policy makers were attentive to a considerable array of goals. In addition to foreign policy goals—in the sense of American external relations with specific areas—decision makers in the Department of State pursue such goals as maintaining good relations with Congress, obtaining

TABLE 1. FREQUENCY OF THREATS TO NATIONAL, ORGANIZATIONAL, AND PERSONAL GOALS IN CRISIS

	*No Response**	*Always*	*Often*	*Sometimes*	*Never*
(a) A crisis threatens the goals and objectives of American foreign policy	0	12 (15.2%)	32 (40.5%)	35 (44.3%)	0
(b) A crisis threatens the goals and objectives of the Department of State	1	9 (11.5%)	27 (34.6%)	41 (52.6%)	1 (1.3%)
(c) A crisis threatens your goals and objectives	0	9 (11.4%)	31 (39.2%)	37 (46.8%)	2 (2.5%)

* Excluded in calculating percentages.

the support of the public, and providing effective service to the White House. Interviewees noted that a crisis can occur with respect to any of these goals. For example, merely by taking an active interest in an issue, Congressmen, the press, or the White House can create a crisis for the State Department in the sense that they may produce the organizational and psychological responses associated with crises in the realm of international politics.

In an attempt to differentiate departmental and personal goals from those of the United States, two additional questionnaire items referred to these subnational objectives. As the comparison of items (b) and (c) with item (a) in Table 1 reveals, the frequency with which crises are associated with personal or departmental goals is only slightly less than the frequency with which national goals are involved. These findings, plus remarks made in the interviews, indicate that the respondents did not make distinctions between the involvement of personal, organizational, and national threat in times of crisis.

According to these data, the behavior within the decision-making unit associated with crisis may occur when any of various kinds of goals is threatened. If crisis is defined exclusively with reference to matters of state in international politics, the definition will have to specify which goals are relevant to foreign affairs. In short, "threat [which is] presented to the decision-making unit"[12] is not sufficiently precise for an exploration of international crisis behavior.

12. *Ibid.*

Instability and violence. Apart from the involvement of American interests, the characteristic of crisis most often mentioned during the interviews was some aspect of political instability or violence. The general impression given by respondents was that such factors as coups d'état, street rioting, and so forth are indices of possible crisis. A coup d'état, for example, draws the immediate attention of the Department of State until the composition and policies of the new government are known. The respondents implied that a crisis ensues if problems involving U.S. interests are generated by the change of government.

Questionnaire items dealing with instability and military action provided a means of exploring further the observations made in the interviews. One item asserted, "A crisis may involve United States relations with an unstable area of the world." In contrast, a second statement associated crises with stable areas. The results in section (a) and (b) of Table 2 confirm the pattern established in

TABLE 2. FREQUENCY OF INVOLVEMENT OF UNSTABLE AREAS AND MILITARY ACTION IN CRISES

	*No Response**	*Always*	*Often*	*Sometimes*	*Never*
(a) A crisis may involve U.S. relations with an unstable area of the world	0	1 (1.3%)	55 (69.6%)	23 (29.1%)	0
(b) A crisis may involve U.S. relations with a stable area of the world	0	0	7 (8.9%)	72 (91.1%)	0
(c) A crisis involves the threat of military action	0	0	17 (21.5%)	62 (78.5%)	0
(d) A crisis involves military action	0	0	13 (16.5%)	66 (83.5%)	0
(e) A crisis involves the possibility of war	2	0	12 (15.6%)	65 (84.4%)	0
(f) A crisis involves the possibility of nuclear war	1	0	3 (3.8%)	75 (96.2%)	0

* Excluded in calculating percentages.

the interviews. Crises were viewed by fifty-six officers as always or often involving unstable areas, whereas only seven officers made comparable replies about stable areas.

The questionnaire did not include any items which might have given collaborative evidence on the presence of political instability and violence. Included in the questionnaire, however, were several items which related crises to (1) the threat of military action, (2) the actual occurrence of military action,

(3) the possibility of war, and (4) the possibility of nuclear war. To these four items no respondent used either extreme category (that is, "always" or "never"). As shown in sections (c) through (f) of Table 2, a majority of officers selected the sometimes classification for each of these statements with the percentage in that category varying from 78.5 for the threat of military action to 96.2 for the possibility of nuclear war. Given the responses to the questionnaire items, the officers appear to consider neither military action nor its threat as necessary qualities of crisis. Instability was more often viewed as a concomitant of crisis than military action.

Uncertainty. Although only three interviewees volunteered a statement that uncertainty was a characteristic of crisis, many more respondents indicated that an element of uncertainty existed in establishing whether a situation would develop into a crisis. This interpretation is reinforced by the replies to two other questions asked during the interviews. In response to the question, "Are there different kinds of crises?" sixteen of the thirty (53.3%) Operations Center respondents mentioned some variation of a cyclical process in crisis. That is, they hold that a crisis proceeds through an initiation stage to increasing tension to a peak and, finally, a resolution. Many also mentioned that in numerous cases a crisis never reaches the peak of the cycle, for the indicators do not prove to presage a "real" crisis. It appears that an element of uncertainty pervades this stage. When events occur, it is uncertain whether they are accurate forewarnings of further events. Until the uncertainty is resolved, one does not know whether a crisis is occurring.

The other data which appear to verify uncertainty as associated with crisis are those given in reply to the questionnaire item found in section (a) of Table 3. Combining the "often" and "always" categories, one finds that 86 per cent of the State Department officials found uncertainty to be an element usually present in crises.

TABLE 3. FREQUENCY OF TYPES OF UNCERTAINTY IN CRISES

	Always	*Often*	*Sometimes*	*Never*
(a) A crisis produces uncertainties in assessing a situation	22 (27.8%)	46 (58.2%)	10 (12.7%)	1 (1.3%)
(b) A crisis produces uncertainties in formulating alternatives for dealing with a situation	12 (15.2%)	39 (49.4%)	28 (35.4%)	0
(c) A crisis reduces control over events and their effects	12 (15.2%)	43 (54.4%)	24 (30.4%)	0

Two related questionnaire statements deal with uncertainty in establishing alternatives and in the ability to maintain control over events.[13] The results are

13. These two questionnaire items together with the one in section (a) of Table 3 were drawn from the list of crisis traits described by Anthony J. Wiener and Herman Kahn, *Crisis and Arms Control* (Harmon-on-Hudson, N.Y.: Hudson Institute, 1962).

reported in sections (b) and (c) of Table 3. These findings suggest that uncertainty is present not only in the identification of crises but also in the response to them.

Short response time. An additional characteristic of crisis situations mentioned frequently by the interviewees was the factor of immediacy or short response time. Roughly half of the respondents in both categories—Operations Center personnel and others—observed that a crisis requires immediate attention and/or decision. This observation confirms various academic analyses of crisis.[14] Moreover, responses to two similar questionnaire items, presented in Table 4,

TABLE 4. FREQUENCY OF INCREASED TIME PRESSURE AND REDUCED DECISION TIME IN CRISES

	Always	*Often*	*Sometimes*	*Never*
(a) A crisis increases time pressures for those involved	53 (67.1%)	23 (29.1%)	3 (3.8%)	0
(b) A crisis lessens the decision time available for response	32 (40.5%)	41 (51.9%)	6 (7.6%)	0

lend further emphasis to this view. The divergence of replies to these two items (between "always" and "often") might represent a distinction between "time pressures" as a psychological phenomenon of decision makers, on the one hand, and the external time dimension established by the pace of events, on the other. This interpretation is in conformity with the observations of several respondents.[15]

Change from routine. Another factor which was frequently mentioned in the interviews was that a change in routine occurred in a crisis. Even more impressive in this regard was the virtually unanimous response by the watch officers to the question, "How does one know when a crisis is over?" That response was, "a return to routine." Without specification of precise divergences from routine in a crisis, the response can tell us only that the Operations Center watch officers clearly and almost unanimously regard crisis as embodying unusual organizational behavior. It does suggest that, in spite of denials of the utility of the concept of crisis, they do recognize that things go differently on occasion. One may draw the conclusion that there are periods when departure from routine is sufficiently great to be apparent to all participants. This does not

14. For example, Robinson, Hermann, and Hermann, "Search Under Crisis." The specific phrasing for item (a) in Table 4 was drawn from Wiener and Kahn, *Crisis and Arms Control.* Item (b) in that table represents a statement appearing in James A. Robinson, "The Concept of Crisis in Decision-Making," in *Series Studies in Social and Economic Studies*, no. 11 (Washington, D.C.: National Institute of Social Behavioral Science, 1962).

15. For example, several interviewees mentioned that there is a tendency for task forces to remain in existence after the actual external events creating time restrictions have dissolved. Others noted that there are varied psychological responses among decision makers, some having "lower panic points" or being more "flappable" than others.

close the question of whether every departure from routine should be called a crisis.[16]

Creating crises. The only other interview question on which there was a large measure of agreement was, "Does an action by the United States ever result in a crisis for the United States?" Although the responses to this question were interesting because some respondents were made uncomfortable by it, no one answered no, only one refused to answer, and thirty-five of the forty-two either answered or implied yes. The thirty-five varied in their interpretations of whether such actions were deliberate or unintentional, recognized or unrecognized. A few interviewees answered neither yes nor no but instead cited examples which, they allowed, the interviewer might interpret in his own way. Even though many officers acknowledged that crises were occasionally self-created, this quality was clearly not viewed as a necessary characteristic of all crises.

The impression formed from the interviews is supported in the questionnaire responses. That instrument contained four statements about the origin of crises including whether such a situation might be initiated by a foreign government, a foreign nongovernmental group, the United States government, or an American nongovernmental group. As shown in Table 5, most officers considered

TABLE 5. FREQUENCY WITH WHICH CRISES ARE INITIATED BY VARIOUS SOURCES

	*No Response**	*Always*	*Often*	*Sometimes*	*Never*
(a) A crisis may be initiated by a foreign government	1	0	49 (62.8%)	29 (37.2%)	0
(b) A crisis may be initiated by a foreign non-governmental group	2	0	18 (23.4%)	59 (76.6%)	0
(c) A crisis may be originated by the United States government	2	0	2 (2.6%)	71 (92.2%)	4 (5.2%)
(d) A crisis may be originated by an American non-governmental group	3	0	1 (1.3%)	67 (88.2%)	8 (10.5%)

* Excluded in calculating percentages.

16. If psychological and organizational behavior induced in a foreign policy crisis can be determined to be the equivalent of behavior induced in other ways, research on crisis behavior can be conducted not only by foreign policy simulations, but also by creating the kind of situation which results in "crisis behavior." For example, small group experiments in the laboratory or the study of crisis behavior in business might yield findings useful for the understanding of foreign policy crises.

each of these sources as a possible source of crisis but none was recognized as always responsible for its occurrence. Only four of the seventy-seven officers replying to the item thought that their own government never originated a crisis. Foreign governments and foreign nongovernmental groups were more frequently recognized as originators. Besides indicating that officers find self-induced crises possible though infrequent, the questionnaire results also suggest that these officers do not exclusively associate crisis with any particular source.

Duration of a crisis. When asked about the duration of crises ("How long do crises last?"), the respondents gave widely varied answers. By collapsing the replies, one can say that the officers interviewed consider crises relatively short-term occasions, lasting from twenty-four hours or less to one month. Of the thirty-six classifiable replies,[17] all minimum times fell into the categories above. The maximum times and the number of responses were as follows: twenty-four hours or less (3 replies); two to five days (5); one week to a month (14); more than a month to four months (4); one year or longer (10).

Unexpectedness. In academic studies of crisis,[18] the element of unexpectedness or lack of anticipation is frequently included in the definition. In the questionnaire portion of this study, six statements were introduced concerning this attribute. These items, together with the replies of the State Department respondents, appear as sections (a) through (f) in Table 6. The results suggest that these officers did not consider unexpectedness a necessary attribute of crisis. About half of them seemed to feel that crises are often unanticipated (section [a]), whereas about the same proportion considered such situations to contain clear warning signs (section [c]).

In addition to noting that these data tend to cast doubt on the proposition that unexpectedness is a necessary element of crisis, one may make certain other observations about them. The data suggest that the Foreign Service Officers feel that "warning signs" are more often seen than missed (Table 6, sections [c] and [d]). The officers also seem to evidence some respect for intelligence estimates (section [e]). It is more difficult to interpret the heavily weighted "often" and "always" replies to the question on surprise which seem to contradict the other answers in this series (section [f]). Without further information, one might suggest that the concept of unexpectedness is particularly ambiguous, relative, and imprecise. Alternatively, it is possible that a crisis in general may be anticipated, but that its particular form and dynamics will contain an element of surprise.

The relationship between unexpectedness and planning merits a brief digression. Writers such as Ausland and Richardson[19] have been concerned about the lack of contingency planning for crises. Because the officers responding to the questionnaire failed to identify crisis with a lack of anticipation, it might be assumed that they feel that contingency plans are more frequently created and

17. Three respondents refused to answer the question, and three gave replies that could not be put into a time frame of reference.

18. For example, see Alastair Buchan, *Crisis Management* (Boulogne-sur-Seine, France: Atlantic Institute, 1966); and Charles F. Hermann, *Crises in Foreign Policy* (Indianapolis: Bobbs-Merrill, 1969).

19. See John C. Ausland and Colonel Hugh F. Richardson, "Crisis Management: Berlin, Cyprus, Laos," *Foreign Affairs*, 44 (January 1966), 291–303.

TABLE 6. FREQUENCY WITH WHICH CRISES ARE UNEXPECTED

	Always	*Often*	*Sometimes*	*Never*
(a) A crisis may be unanticipated	0	39 (49.4%)	39 (49.4%)	1 (1.3%)
(b) A crisis may be anticipated	0	29 (36.7%)	49 (62.0%)	1 (1.3%)
(c) A crisis involves warning signs	4 (5.1%)	43 (54.4%)	32 (40.5%)	0
(d) A crisis involves warning signs which can be seen in retrospect to have been involved but which are not perceived in time for action to deal with the crisis	1 (1.3%)	15 (18.9%)	62 (78.5%)	1 (1.3%)
(e) A crisis represents a deviation from intelligence estimates	1 (1.3%)	22 (27.8%)	56 (70.9%)	0
(f) A crisis involves an element of surprise	11 (13.9%)	52 (65.8%)	16 (20.3%)	0
(g) A crisis leads to putting contingency plans into effect	2 (2.5%)	17 (21.5%)	58 (73.5%)	2 (2.5%)

applied in crises than some observers have implied. As evident from section (g) of Table 6 that is not the case. Sixty of the seventy-nine responding officers said "never" or "sometimes" when asked to rate the applicability of the statement, "A crisis leads to putting contingency plans into effect." Considering that 37 per cent of the respondents held that crises were often anticipated while only 24 per cent found contingency plans frequently employed, a number of officers would probably agree that the period of expectancy prior to a crisis is not being used to the best advantage in developing contingency plans. The analysts who urge greater use of planning for crises are addressing themselves to a problem recognizable to those men who regularly experience such situations.

Crisis as a turning point. Another common definition of crisis is that it is a turning point.[20] Five statements in the questionnaire attempted to represent the concept of turning point as it has been described in other studies. Three of the statements in Table 7 are drawn from Wiener and Kahn (items [a], [c], and [d]), and one from Robinson (b).[21] A fifth item (e) designed by the author has some implications for the turning point formulation. Again, the results are negative in terms of the number of officers who always associated crises with turning points, but some contradiction appears between responses to the items.

20. See, for example, Robert C. North, Ole R. Holsti, M. George Zaninovich, and Dina A. Zinnes, *Content Analysis* (Evanston, Ill.: Northwestern University Press, 1963), pp. 4–5.

21. Wiener and Kahn, *Crisis and Arms Control*; Robinson, "Concept of Crisis."

TABLE 7. FREQUENCY WITH WHICH CRISES APPEAR AS TURNING POINTS

	*No Response**	*Always*	*Often*	*Sometimes*	*Never*
(a) A crisis is a turning point in an unfolding sequence of events	1	11 (14.1%)	35 (44.8%)	31 (39.7%)	1 (1.4%)
(b) A crisis is a turning point that distinguishes the outcome of an event	2	3 (3.9%)	21 (27.3%)	51 (66.2%)	2 (2.6%)
(c) A crisis consists of a convergence of events that results in a new set of circumstances	0	10 (12.7%)	39 (49.4%)	30 (37.8%)	0
(d) A crisis is followed by an important outcome whose consequences shape the future of the United States	0	0	12 (15.2%)	67 (84.4%)	0
(e) A crisis fits into a pattern of events involving American foreign policy	0	9 (11.4%)	21 (26.6%)	47 (59.5%)	2 (2.5%)

* Excluded in calculating percentages.

On the face of it, one might interpret these data first by comparing items (a) and (b). Collapsing categories for simplicity of argument, one finds that 58.9 per cent of the respondents regard crisis usually as a turning point, but 68.8 per cent think it seldom determines the outcome of an event. Comparing item (d) with items (a) and (b), one sees that most respondents (84.4%) think that a crisis does not often shape the future of the United States. Looking at item (e), one can see that somewhat more respondents (62%) think that a crisis seldom fits a pattern of events than think that it usually does (38%). One might then infer the opposite: that 62 per cent of the respondents think a crisis usually disrupts (i.e., represents a sharp break from) a pattern.

The comparability of these five items, however, is limited. To check consistency of responses, statement (a) was compared with the approximately similar statement, (c). Inspection of the figures in Table 7 shows a reasonable fit between responses on these items. However, in examining the actual responses, it was found that eleven respondents answered one of the statements "always" but the other statement differently. A thorough search for explanation was not made, but it was found that a large proportion of those replying "always" to item (c) but another response to item (a) were officers with a generally economic rather than political background.

Summary. Now one can draw a summary of the composite views of the State Department officers on the definition of crisis, even though it is a definition containing qualifications. According to the interview and questionnaire data from all respondents, a crisis is a situation that (1) does or may involve United States national interests, (2) often occurs in unstable areas of the world, (3) often includes an element of violence or political instability, (4) is of relatively short duration, (5) allows only a short response time, (6) includes an element of uncertainty, and (7) may be initiated from various sources. The interviews alone indicate a change in routine in a crisis, and the questionnaire responses point to an element of surprise in such situations.

Two conceptualizations of crisis. The summary definition of crisis presented above is based on the composite view of that concept formed by examining the replies of all the State Department officers who participated in the study. Not all officers can be expected to conceive of a crisis in exactly the same way. Some slight variations in conceptualizing crisis may make very little difference in the manner in which the term is used. However, individuals who maintain that crisis must always contain some critical element may have a conceptualization of the phenomenon of crisis that is quite distinctive from that of other officers.

One initial effort to explore the possibility of major differences in the officers' definition of crisis was based on the statement: "A crisis is acute rather than chronic."[22] The distribution of replies to that statement appears in Table 8.

TABLE 8. FREQUENCY WITH WHICH CRISES ARE ACUTE RATHER THAN CHRONIC

	Always	*Often*	*Sometimes*	*Never*
Crisis is acute rather than chronic	22 (27.9%)	37 (46.8%)	20 (25.3%)	0

Two hypothetical groups of officers were created from their responses to this item. Those who conceived of crises as "always" (that is, necessarily) acute were separated from those who viewed crises as only occasionally acute (that is, responded "often" or "sometimes"). All replies to other questionnaire items were then examined for each of the two groups. The responses of the two groups varied substantially on at least six other statements characterizing crisis.[23]

This limited number of items makes clear a distinction between those who think of crises as acute rather than chronic and those who do not think so. Those who do not think crisis is always acute are highly likely to think that uncertainty is not always an element in crisis whereas those who think that crisis is always

22. This item is based on the observations of Kent Miller and Ira Iscoe, "The Concept of Crisis: Current Status and Mental Health Implications," *Human Organization*, 22 (Fall 1963), 195–201.

23. The acute-chronic reponses were cross-classified with forty other statements. Table 9 is composed of the six statements in which ten or more respondents replied always to both the chronic-acute statement and the other item with which it was cross-classified.

acute are evenly divided on the question of whether uncertainty is always an element. Those who think that crisis is always acute also tend to think that crisis always precipitates higher level concern and tend to think that crisis always precipitates higher level decision making. Those who do not think that crisis must always be acute are less likely to associate such situations with higher level concern and higher level decision making.

Those who think that crisis is always acute are highly likely to think that crisis lessens decision time available for response as contrasted with those who think that crisis is not always acute: they tend to think that crisis does not always

TABLE 9. EFFECT OF THE ACUTE-CHRONIC DISTINCTION ON THE REPLIES TO SIX ITEMS

A crisis produces:		*Crisis is acute rather than chronic:* Always	*Often/Sometimes*
(a) Uncertainties in situation	Always	10	11
	Often/ Sometimes	11	45
			$X^2 = 11.49^{**}$
(b) Higher level concern	Always	18	35
	Often/ Sometimes	4	21
			$X^2 = 6.22^{*}$
(c) Higher level decision	Always	15	24
	Often/ Sometimes	7	31
			$X^2 = 4.27^{*}$
(d) Lessened decision time	Always	15	16
	Often/ Sometimes	7	40
			$X^2 = 7.81^{**}$
(e) Increased time pressures	Always	17	35
	Often/ Sometimes	5	21
			$X^2 = 5.88^{*}$
(f) Heightened tensions	Always	11	13
	Often/ Sometimes	11	42
			$X^2 = 9.00^{**}$

$^{*}p < .05$
$^{**}p < .01$

lessen decision time. Those who think crisis is always acute are more likely than those who do not to think that time pressures for those involved are always increased. Finally, those who do not think that crisis is always acute are strongly inclined to think that crisis does not raise tensions whereas those who think that crisis is always acute are evenly divided on the question of raising tensions.

As shown in Table 9, the difference between the acute-nonacute groups was statistically significant with each of the six variables. These data suggest that the State Department officers did not fully agree on their conceptualization of crisis and that their replies to at least six questions varied substantially depending on whether or not they viewed crises as necessarily acute. Other key properties may exist that can be used to distinguish between alternate views of crisis. The acute-chronic division serves only as an illustration to caution the reader against concluding that the composite definition presented earlier represents a consensus among the members of the Department of State on the nature of crisis.

RESPONSES OF STATE DEPARTMENT OFFICERS TO PROPOSITIONS ABOUT CRISES

In addition to exploring the definition of crisis used by State Department officials, this study sought to obtain their reactions to a number of propositions about crisis which have been advanced by various observers of international affairs. The questionnaire presented the hypotheses culled from the literature as descriptive statements about crises. As with the items dealing with definition, the respondents indicated how frequently the statement applied to crises they experienced.

Information in crises. One recurrent variable in crisis research has been the availability of information for decisions. Information has been described as

TABLE 10. FREQUENCY WITH WHICH CRISES ALTER INFORMATION PROCESSES

	*No Response**	*Always*	*Often*	*Sometimes*	*Never*
(a) A crisis is a situation in which information available to participants is adequate	2	0	8 (10.4%)	55 (71.4%)	14 (18.2%)
(b) A crisis is a circumstance in which information available to participants is inadequate	0	9 (11.4%)	25 (31.6%)	44 (55.7%)	1 (1.3%)
(c) A crisis is a circumstance in which information available to participants is overwhelming	1	0	6 (7.7%)	44 (56.4%)	28 (35.9%)
(d) In a crisis, it is clear who needs to receive information about it	0	16 (20.3%)	48 (60.8%)	15 (18.9%)	0

* Excluded in calculating percentages.

narrowing to a single channel in crisis.[24] Others have noted that information increases and may even reach overload proportions.[25] The State Department officers were asked about the adequacy of information, the possibility of being overwhelmed by the flow of communications, and the clarity of communication channels (who needs information). The specific items and the replies appear in Table 10.

In comparison to the remainder of the questionnaire, the most striking feature of these responses is the large number of "never" replies to the statements about the adequacy and overwhelmingness of information in a crisis (items [a] and [d] in Table 10). The alternative adequate-inadequate formulations were included merely to check consistency.[26] The majority of respondents did think that it is usually clear who needs information in a crisis (81.1%), but it is also interesting to observe that nearly one out of five (18.9%) thought that this was only sometimes true. It would appear that information is seldom perceived as inadequate (89.6%) in a crisis, and that is not surprising. What is surprising, however, is that the respondents think that information is seldom (92.3%) overwhelming.

Some authors hold not only that minimal information forms the basis for decision making in a crisis but also that alternatives for action are reduced.[27] One statement on the questionnaire of the present study dealt with this consideration; it appears in Table 11. In addition to the findings presented in Table 11, it should be noted that one respondent volunteered that crises, on occasion, open up alternatives that were not present before the crises. These responses offer some evidence contradictory to the proposition that crises lead to a reduction of alternatives for action.

TABLE 11. FREQUENCY OF REDUCED ALTERNATIVES IN CRISES

	Always	*Often*	*Sometimes*	*Never*
A crisis reduces the alternatives for action by decision makers	3 (3.8%)	27 (34.2%)	47 (59.5%)	2 (2.5%)

Psychological stress, anxiety, and tension. Some analysts of foreign policy crises have borrowed hypotheses from the psychological literature on

24. Richard C. Snyder and Glenn D. Paige, "The United States Decision to Resist Aggression in Korea," *Administrative Science Quarterly*, 3 (December 1958), 342–378. Statement (b) in Table 10, which is consistent with this proposition, is drawn from Wiener and Kahn, *Crisis and Arms Control.*

25. See the chapters by Holsti and Charles F. Hermann in this volume.

26. To check consistency, the questionnaires of those persons answering "always" or "never" to both questions were examined. There were a total of 24 such responses (fourteen "never" replies to item [a] in Table 10, nine "always" responses to item [b], and one "never" reply to item [b]). The examination showed that eight persons responded "always" or "never" to one of the questions and "often" or "sometimes" to the other. The categories were apparently not considered mutually exclusive by some respondents.

27. Robinson, Hermann, and Hermann in "Search Under Crisis" state the following hypothesis which is supported by one of their studies but not the other: "In crisis as compared with noncrisis, fewer alternatives will be identified by the national decision makers" (p. 88). See, however, the chapter by McClelland in this volume.

stress.[28] Two of these concerning stress, anxiety, and tension were included in this study's questionnaire. The results in Table 12 tend to confirm the propositions, particularly when the "always" and "often" categories are combined and compared with the "sometimes" and "never" responses.

TABLE 12. FREQUENCY OF PSYCHOLOGICAL STRESS, ANXIETY, AND TENSION IN CRISES

	*No Response**	*Always*	*Often*	*Sometimes*	*Never*
(a) A crisis heightens urgency which produces stress and anxiety among those alerted	1	30 (38.4%)	36 (46.2%)	12 (15.4%)	0
(b) A crisis raises tension among the participants handling it	0	24 (30.4%)	35 (44.3%)	19 (24.0%)	1 (1.3%)

* Excluded in calculating percentages.

Yet one is faced with the difficulty of interpreting the significance of these variables. Does personal stress and anxiety serve the function of producing clearer thought and enhanced proclivity to decisiveness or does it produce irrational behavior and a tendency to withdraw from making decisions? Does interpersonal tension sharpen thinking about alternatives and lead to a situation wherein participants are led to lay bare their arguments for rational and detailed examination or does it lead to animosities and a reduction of group thinking to group hysteria?

It is generally assumed that within limits the biological mechanisms for producing "stress" are functional for the human organism. They induce a sharper perception and keenness of mind and senses. In the realm of cerebral activity affecting foreign policy, however, the evidence is lacking for either confirming or disconfirming this interpretation. The same may be said regarding interpersonal tension. One can remark that public reports of some crises handled by the United States government tend to indicate that the stresses and tensions are functional.[29]

These questions might be approached by interviewing participants in the

28. For example, see Wiener and Kahn, *Crisis and Arms Control.* Phrases drawn from their study provided the basis for the two statements reported here.

29. Compare the Cuban crises of 1961 and 1962, for example. In handling the Bay of Pigs invasion, there seemed little stress and tension. Confidence and agreement prevailed. Only Senator Fulbright openly disagreed with the consensus. In the missile crisis of 1962, on the other hand, we are told that there was a large measure of disagreement and tension among the decision makers, and we may safely infer personal stresses and anxieties. The first crisis was a rare case of virtually total failure; the second had a more nearly successful outcome. For a full account of these crises see Arthur M. Schlesinger, Jr., *A Thousand Days* (Boston: Houghton Mifflin, 1965), Chaps. 10 and 30.

crisis management undertaking or by observing them in a crisis situation if that could be arranged. Simulation might also be used in such an inquiry.

Organizational level. One frequently advanced proposition is that crises lead to centralization—that is, in crises the officers at higher levels in the department become involved in the problem.[30] The first of two relevant statements contained in the questionnaire asserts that in a crisis the officers "concerned" about the problem are likely to be at high levels of the organization. The second statement goes further by maintaining that higher level officers would not only be attentive to a crisis but would also enter directly into the decision making. Compared to the replies given other items in the questionnaire, the responses summarized in Table 13 contain an extremely large number of entries in the

TABLE 13. FREQUENCY OF INVOLVEMENT OF HIGH-LEVEL OFFICERS IN CRISES

	*No Response**	*Always*	*Often*	*Sometimes*	*Never*
(a) A crisis precipitates concern at a higher level than normal	0	54 (68.4%)	22 (27.8%)	3 (3.8%)	0
(b) A crisis precipitates decision making at a higher level than normal	1	40 (51.3%)	37 (47.4%)	1 (1.3%)	0

* Excluded in calculating percentages.

"always" category. The data in the table clearly support the proposition. Further evidence emerged during the interviews in which several respondents indicated that they tended to take their cues as to what situations were crises from the interests of their superiors. In considering these findings, however, one observation should be noted. If all crises are important problems, but not all important problems are crises, then the increased involvement of high-level officers may be a function of the larger class of phenomena rather than crisis. A decision to dispatch troops, for example, is made by the President, regardless of whether a crisis exists as defined by all other characteristics. Briefly, high-level concern and/or decision making may occur because of the importance of the decision, and thus crisis may not be the actual independent variable.

Parties to crises. A final series of statements in the questionnaire was designed to explore propositions about the parties most often involved in crises. Some views of the officers on this subject have been presented earlier in the chapter. For example, Table 2 and the accompanying discussion revealed the tendency of the State Department officers to consider crises more likely in

30. This proposition appears in the summary of social science findings prepared by Bernard Berelson and George A. Steiner, *Human Behavior* (New York: Harcourt, Brace, & World, 1964). See also Wiener and Kahn, *Crisis and Arms Control*; and Buchan, "Crisis Management," pp. 40–41.

unstable areas of the world. Moreover, they tended to see foreign governments as the most frequent initiators of crisis. An additional proposition about the conditions under which parties engage in crisis emerges from the question: "Are the events that trigger a confrontation between two or more parties more likely to occur on land or at sea?" According to most officers, crises are more frequently land encounters than naval ones. (See sections [a] and [b] of Table 14.) One suspects that a sample of high-level Navy policy makers—whose preoccupation is with the sea—might have altered this evaluation. Perhaps even foreign affairs personnel would have responded differently at a time when they

TABLE 14. FREQUENCY OF INVOLVEMENT OF VARIOUS PARTIES IN CRISES

	*No Response**	*Always*	*Often*	*Sometimes*	*Never*
(a) A crisis may involve an incident or event on land	0	1 (1.3%)	45 (57.0%)	33 (41.8%)	0
(b) A crisis may involve an incident or event at sea	0	1 (1.3%)	1 (1.3%)	77 (97.5%)	0
(c) A crisis may involve an adversary country	0	0	31 (39.2%)	48 (60.8%)	0
(d) A crisis may involve an allied country	1	0	20 (25.6%)	58 (74.4%)	0
(e) A crisis may involve a neutral country	0	0	19 (24.0%)	59 (74.7%)	1 (1.3%)
(f) A crisis may involve U.S. relations with a Communist country	0	1 (1.3%)	30 (37.9%)	48 (60.8%)	0
(g) A crisis may involve U.S. relations with a non-Communist country	0	1 (1.3%)	39 (49.4%)	39 (49.4%)	0
(h) A crisis for the United States may not be a crisis for another country	2	2 (2.6%)	40 (51.9%)	31 (40.3%)	4 (5.2%)

* Excluded in calculating percentages.

perceived either an increased threat to the position of the United States Navy and the American merchant marine or a greater association between various national interests and naval mobility.

The categories of adversary, ally, and neutral were used as a means of identifying the other parties to crises involving the United States. The questionnaire statements and the responses to these items appear in sections (c), (d), and (e) of Table 14. The replies indicate that crises tend to involve an adversary country somewhat more often than either an ally or neutral country. However, the difference between the three types of parties is not large. Particularly interesting is the virtual absence of a difference between the frequency of crises with allies and with neutrals.

Inasmuch as most American Foreign Service Officers could be expected to associate Communist states with adversary nations, statements on the relative frequency of crises with Communist and non-Communist countries provided a check on the consistency of responses to the questionnaire. Sections (f) and (g) of Table 14 present these findings. The responses to the statements on crises with adversary countries and with Communist countries are practically identical.

The questionnaire contained an item to determine whether symmetry occurred in a crisis—that is, whether an incident that appeared as a crisis to one party (the United States) would seem to be a crisis to other parties. The statement was: "A crisis for the United States may not be a crisis for another country." As indicated in section (h) of Table 14, slightly over half the respondents agreed that this condition occurred "always" or "often." If one thinks of crises as international events, these responses suggest a lack of symmetry in approaching the same set of events. The United States Government may see things as crises when other governments do not. If this is so, it may mean that the United States may respond uniquely to events. It may mean that the United States, organized to manage and monitor crises, has created a view of the world that is not shared by others.

SUMMARY AND CONCLUSIONS

This study presents data collected through interviews and questionnaires in which the respondents were Foreign Service Officers familiar with the Department of State's crisis management functions. Their responses have been used (1) to ascertain the meaning they attribute to the concept of crisis, and (2) to obtain their reactions to propositions about the effect of crisis.

The composite view derived from the interview and questionnaire data associated crisis with the potential or actual involvement of United States national interests, with violence and political instability in unstable areas of the world, with short response time and short duration, and with an element of uncertainty. The conception that crisis may be initiated from a variety of sources was also established in the composite view presented previously. Moreover, disruption of routine and surprise were to some degree associated with crisis. As suggested by the decompositon of the replies along the acute-chronic dimension, the officers did not share a uniform view of crisis. Given the difference among the governmental officials themselves it is not surprising that their composite view of crisis does not parallel any of the recent scholarly efforts to assign a more precise meaning to the term.

Even if a precise conception of crisis is formulated, it will not become an *analytically* useful one until it is related to a more general theory of international politics and foreign policy. Moreover, such a definition obviously will not have *applied* utility until policy makers can use the concept in a comparable manner to designate some meaningful set of situations.

In summarizing the hypotheses, it must be remembered that not only the concept of crisis but also the other variables in the propositions were subject to the individual interpretations of the respondents. With this caveat, the State Department officers appeared to support the following propositions:

1. It is usually clear who needs information in a crisis.
2. Crises raise tensions among the policy makers involved and heighten the stress and anxiety they experience.
3. Crises involve high-level officers.
4. Crises occur more frequently over incidents on land than over those at sea.
5. Crises somewhat more frequently involve adversaries than allies or neutral nations.

The responses of the officers reveal no clear-cut positions on the adequacy of information, the relative frequency of allies as compared to neutrals as parties to crisis, and the number of alternatives examined in a crisis. They did reject the proposition that the amount of information generated during a crisis overwhelms the participants. The significance of all these data lies less in their confirmation or rejection of some relationships assumed to exist in reality—although their implications for the plausibility of some hypotheses must not be ignored—than in their indication of what officers at the operating level in the Department of State perceive to be true. The perceptions of policy makers will be one important factor which determines their behavior in crises.

APPENDIX

INTERVIEW AND QUESTIONNAIRE SAMPLES

Characteristics of Operations Center Personnel Interviewed

Total Number = 30

Rank

FSO-2 = 1; FSO-3 = 9; FSO-4 = 6; FSO-5 = 1; FSO-6 = 10; FSO-7 = 2; GS-11 = 1

Area Assignment

Operations Center = 10; National Military Command Center (NMCC) = 5; Executive Secretariat = 2; International Organization Affairs = 2; African Affairs = 2; Asian Affairs = 1; Other State Department = 7; Other Government Agency = 1

Highest Position in Operations Center

Deputy Director = 2; Senior Projects Officer = 4; Senior Watch Officer = 6; Senior Watch Officer—NMCC = 5; Associate Watch Officer/Editor = 12; Other = 1

Length of Time in Operations Center or NMCC

Less than six months = 3; Six months to one year = 16; One year to 18 months = 5; 18 months to two years = 3; More than two years = 3

Latest Year Served in Operations Center/NMCC

1966 = 21; 1965 = 7; 1964 = 1; 1963 = 0; 1962 = 1

Characteristics of Other Personnel Interviewed

Total Number = 12

Position

Deputy Assistant Secretary = 2; Officer in Charge (of Office of Regional Affairs) = 1; Deputy Director (of Office of Regional Affairs) = 2; Assistant Director (of Office of Regional Affairs) = 2; Desk Officer (for country affairs) = 3; Staff Assistant (to Undersecretary of State) = 1; Staff Aide (to Deputy Assistant Secretary) = 1

Area

African Affairs = 2; European Affairs = 1; Inter-American Affairs = 2; Secretariat = 1; South Asian Affairs = 2; Southeast Asian Affairs = 4

Crisis Involved in

Cyprus = 1; Dominican Republic = 2; India–China = 1*; India–Pakistan = 2*; Indonesia = 2; Vietnam = 2; West African Coups = 1; Several unspecified = 2

* One person interviewed was involved in both.

Characteristics of Questionnaire Respondents

Total Number = 79

Assignment

Operations Center = 13; National Military Command Center = 5; Other State Department in Washington = 32; Embassy or Consulate = 20; Other Government = 3; Training = 2; Not in government = 2; Information not available = 2

Area Assignment

African Affairs = 7; Asian Affairs = 9; European Affairs = 11; Inter-American Affairs = 3; International Organization Affairs = 4; Middle East Affairs = 2; Operations Center/NMCC = 18; Other State Department = 16; Information Not Available = 4; Not Applicable = 5

Latest Year Served in Operations Center/NMCC

1966 = 26; 1965 = 19; 1964 = 12; 1963 = 5; 1962 = 3; 1961 = 2; Not applicable = 12

Length of Time Served in Operations Center/NMCC

Less than six months = 11; Six months to one year = 34; One year to 18 months = 12; 18 months to two years = 6; More than two years = 4; Not applicable = 12

chapter seven

EDITOR'S INTRODUCTION

The acquisition of perceptual data through interviews and questionnaires—as Lentner did in the preceding chapter—requires the full cooperation of the relevant policy makers. For many international crises subsequent access to those who participated is simply impossible. Even the researcher who obtains interviews faces the problem of determining whether the policy makers' current recollections correspond to their perceptions at the time of the crisis. The authors of the present chapter illustrate the use of content analysis as an alternative technique for establishing the perceptions of policy makers at the time they are confronting the crisis. Although the Zinneses and McClure apply research techniques that differ from those of Lentner, the authors of both chapters seek to examine the policy makers' interpretation of crisis. The grouping of the two chapters into this section rests upon the assumption that the reconstruction of crises from the perspective of the actors rather than that of the observers can have important implications for the confirmation of hypotheses.

This chapter offers linkages to other research in the volume as well. Both Dina Zinnes and Holsti (Chapter 4) worked with the Conflict and Integration Project directed by Robert North at Stanford University and used that project's rich data base on the 1914 crisis in their analyses. Although they approach the crisis that precipitated the outbreak of World War I in quite distinctive ways, they both possess an expert's knowledge of the diplomatic communication exchanged during the summer of 1914. Similar to McClelland in Chapter 5, the authors of this chapter study the interactions that transpire in a crisis. Both analyses treat the reaction of one country or alliance as a function, in part, of the actions of the other parties in the crisis. The present researchers, however, insist that the actions of others be examined after they have filtered through the perceptual mechanisms of the policy makers whose responses are to be predicted. This chapter also shares with both McClelland and Snyder (Chapter 10) an emphasis on the behavior taken in a crisis. The centrality of hostility in the Zinnes–Zinnes–McClure research parallels McClelland's use of conflict in the sense that both variables represent part of the broader effort to understand the conditions under which crises lead to war.

Although they share concerns with many other contributors, Dina and Joseph Zinnes and Robert McClure provide an extremely original and significant approach in their research on crisis. More than any others in this collection, these authors present a defined and limited model tested with the crisis data. Their model has applicability for noncrisis periods as well as crises—an observation that reveals something about their definition of crisis. Some authors view crises as triggering behaviors that are different and perhaps nonrational when compared to those in noncrises (e.g., see Milburn in Chapter 11). In that interpretation, misperception and distortion are frequently used to explain crisis behavior. In contrast to such a view, the model in this chapter indicates that crisis behavior differs from noncrisis behavior not in kind, but in amount or intensity. In a crisis policy makers process and react to the hostility directed at their country as they would in a noncrisis, but their response reflects the increased amount of perceived hostility they have received in the present and in the immediate past.

The authors' model of hostility is based on Markov chains, a method that requires a brief introduction. The Russian mathematician A. A. Markov introduced the Markov chain concept in 1907. It consists of a chance process having the special quality that one can predict the future state of a system from knowledge of its present state and its immediate past state equally as well as one could with knowledge of the entire past history of the system. No natural systems appear to exactly satisfy the Markov chain condition, but some approximate it to such an extent that the model becomes quite useful. To date, Markov models have been applied to such diverse areas as industrial inspection, sickness and accident statistics, and social mobility. In general, Markov models prove fruitful for describing systems that change state from trial to trial in response to reinforcement in a learning process. In this chapter the consecutive days of the 1914 crisis become the trials and the reinforcement appears as the presence or absence of hostility perceived on a given day and on the immediately preceding day. The authors hypothesize that a crisis so described approximates a first-order Markov chain and check their hypothesis with the 1914 data.

Patrick Billingsley offers the following formal definition of the Markov model:

> *Imagine a system (family, society, person, organism) that passes with each unit of time (minute, hour, generation) from one to another of the s states* $E_1, E_2, \ldots E_s. \ldots$
>
> *Assume that a chance process governs the evolution of the system; the chance process is the collection of probability laws describing the way in which the system changes with time. The system is that which undergoes change; a particular analysis may involve many systems of the same kind (many families, or many societies, etc.), all obeying the same process or set of probability laws. Since the system passes through various states in sequence, time moves in jumps, rather than continuously; hence the integers* 1, 2, 3, ... *provide a natural time index. Denote by* $P(E_k | E_i, E_j)$ *the conditional probability that at time* $n+2$ *the system is in state* E_k*, given that at times* n *and* $n+1$ *it was in states* E_i *and* E_j *in that order; and similarly for longer or shorter conditioning sequences of states. We make the usual assumption that the conditional probabilities just defined do not depend on* n *(that is, the conditional probabilities do not change as time passes). The process is a Markov chain if* $P(E_k | E_i, E_j) = P(E_k | E_j)$, $P(E_1 | E_i, E_j, E_k) = P(E_1 | E_k)$, $P(E_m | E_i, E_j, E_k, E_1) = P(E_m | E_1)$, *etc.*[1]

The reader not previously acquainted with this kind of analysis should be cautioned against certain premature judgments. After the authors define key terms, they use symbols to represent the longer verbal descriptions, thus avoiding the tedium of repeating the formal definition phrase over and over again. This procedure should in no way be associated with the kind of sophistry that Kaplan rightly chastises.[2] For carefully defined terms the symbols combine precision with brevity. Another misinterpretation that might result from a casual first reading is that the explored relationships represent common sense. (One can

1. Patrick Billingsley, "Markov Chains," in David L. Sills, ed., *International Encyclopedia of the Social Sciences*, 9 (New York: The Macmillan Company and The Free Press, 1968), 582. Reprinted by permission of publisher.

2. See the discussion on "Overemphasis on Symbols" by Abraham Kaplan, *The Conduct of Inquiry* (San Francisco: Chandler, 1964), pp. 277–278.

almost hear the wit suggesting that the findings are: "As someone gets madder at you, you get madder at them.") Two observations should make evident the foolishness of such comments. First, as is rather more often the case than we would like, the data do not support the common sense assertion. Second, and more important, the larger issue at stake in this chapter is an initial fitting of crisis to a Markov model—a model whose implications for predicting crisis behavior are far from commonplace.

Dina A. Zinnes is an Associate Professor of Political Science at Indiana University whose continuing research on hostility, using data from crisis situations, has been reported in several publications.[3] Associate Professor Joseph L. Zinnes, a mathematical psychologist at Indiana University, collaborated with his wife on some of their recent research with Markov chains.[4] The third author, Robert D. McClure, was a graduate student at Indiana University at the time of this research and is now an Assistant Professor of Political Science at Syracuse University.

3. These writings include Dina A. Zinnes, Robert C. North, and Howard E. Koch, Jr., "Capability, Threat, and the Outbreak of War," in James N. Rosenau, ed., *International Politics and Foreign Policy* (New York: The Free Press, 1961), pp. 469–482; Dina A. Zinnes, "A Comparison of Hostile Behavior of Decision-Makers in Simulate and Historical Data," *World Politics,* 18 (April 1966), 474–502; and Dina A. Zinnes, "The Expression and Perception of Hostility in Prewar Crisis: 1914," in J. David Singer, ed., *Quantitative International Politics* (New York: The Free Press, 1968), pp. 85–119.

4. Other publications of Joseph L. Zinnes include Patrick Suppes and Joseph L. Zinnes, "Basic Measurement Theory," in Robert R. Bush and Eugene H. Galanter, eds., *Handbook in Mathematical Psychology*, 1 (New York: Wiley, 1963), 1–76; Joseph L. Zinnes and R. Kurtz, "Matching, Discrimination, and Payoff," *Journal of Mathematical Psychology*, 5 (1968), 392–421; and Joseph L. Zinnes, "Scaling," in Paul H. Mussen and Mark R. Rosenzweig, eds., *Annual Review of Psychology*, 20 (Palo Alto: Annual Reviews, 1969), 447–478.

chapter seven

HOSTILITY IN DIPLOMATIC COMMUNICATION: A STUDY OF THE 1914 CRISIS*

Dina A. Zinnes, Joseph L. Zinnes, and
Robert D. McClure

INTRODUCTION

Recent studies on crisis decision making imply, either explicitly or implicitly, that in a crisis decision makers become "irrational," "panicky," or even "paranoid." For example, one study of the six-week crisis prior to the outbreak of World War I concluded: "If the decisional process were rational it would have followed . . . that the pattern of perceptions prior to involvement in armed conflict would have been characterized by almost arithmetic appraisals of capability. As the results of the analysis tend to demonstrate, however, perceptions of hostility far exceeded perceptions of capability, suggesting that rational considerations may exert limited influence on the decision to wage war."[1] In a subsequent study on the same data, Holsti and North[2] construct an "index of injury" which reflects the extent to which decision makers perceive themselves as the objects of another state's hostility. The authors then suggested that this "might also be used as an 'index of paranoia.' "[3] These two studies seem to imply that decision makers are manufacturing perceptions in the absence of stimuli from other states; that the decision makers are in effect reacting out of proportion to actual environmental stimuli.

Several conclusions from the above two studies are based on graphs that show the frequency and intensity of perceptions and expressions of hostility increasing as the crisis progresses. While this is an interesting first-stage analysis, it can obscure the interaction process. By looking at only total perceptions and expressions of hostility, the link between a given perception and a prior incoming message may be missed. For example, it is possible that when a critical event occurs—such as the assassination of the Archduke on June 28, 1914—it is

* This research has been supported, in part, by Grant GS 663 from the National Science Foundation. Some of the work also was carried out while the first author was in residence at the Center for International Studies, Princeton University, and the second author was at the Educational Testing Service, Princeton, N.J. We wish to thank Richard Liniger, Elaine Marikakas, and Jonathan Wilkenfeld for their extensive help with the computational aspects of the chapter. We also wish to thank Henry Alker and the editor for their careful and critical review of the manuscript.

1. Dina A. Zinnes, Robert C. North, and Howard E. Koch, Jr., "Capability, Threat, and the Outbreak of War," in James N. Rosenau, ed., *International Politics and Foreign Policy* (New York: The Free Press, 1961), p. 476.

2. Ole R. Holsti and Robert C. North, "The History of Human Conflict," in Elton B. McNeil, ed., *The Nature of Human Conflict* (Englewood Cliffs, N.J.: Prentice-Hall, 1965), pp. 155–171.

3. *Ibid.*, p. 163.

interpreted by Austro–Hungarian policy makers as a hostile act against them perpetrated by Serbian policy makers. Austro–Hungarian leaders then reciprocate with a hostile message. This begins a cycle of hostile messages as the two sets of decision makers reply to each other with hostile communications. The frequency and intensity of hostile perceptions and expressions increases, yet there is nothing necessarily paranoid about these responses. In fact, it could be said that the decision maker's behavior resembles typical learning behavior if he modifies his perception and expressions of hostility to match the messages he receives.

The present study will examine the relationship between incoming and outgoing messages during the 1914 crisis. The model, described in greater detail below, postulates (1) that changes in the intensity level of perceptions of hostility (P) depend on the immediately preceding perception and on the most recently received messages (R), and (2) that the expression of hostility (E) depends on the immediately preceding expression of hostility and on the current perception of hostility. In short, it is assumed that decision makers are not behaving in a "paranoid" fashion during a crisis. In crises, as well as in "noncrises," decision makers react to incoming stimuli. The difference between the crisis and "noncrisis" situation lies in the amount and intensity of hostile messages exchanged, *not* in distorted (paranoid) reactions to incoming messages.

The following sections contain further details of the basic model, the type of data used, some of the basic problems encountered in applying a probabilistic model to historical materials, and some preliminary results. It should be emphasized that the findings reported here reflect only very general and very preliminary tests of the model.

THE GENERAL MODEL

Our general model can be divided into two stages or submodels. The first stage is referred to as the reception-perception submodel (*RP*) and the second as the perception-expression (*PE*) submodel.

Reception-perception stage. It is assumed in this first stage that a decision maker's perception on a given day is a consequence of two factors, the hostile messages that he receives that day and his previous perception. Although the first factor, the hostile messages received, was treated previously,[4] the second factor, the prior perceptions, was not. It appears intuitively reasonable, however, to assume that an incoming message is read within the context of a previous perception. If the decision maker perceives another state as extremely hostile and then receives a very mild message, he is likely to alter his perception, but he is not likely to do so drastically. The first stage of the model, then, can be represented as follows:

$$P_n, R_{n+1} \rightarrow P_{n+1},$$

where P_n represents the decision maker's previous perception, R_{n+1} indicates the hostile messages the decision maker receives on the $(n+1)$st day and P_{n+1}

4. Dina A. Zinnes, "A Comparison of Hostile Behavior of Decision Makers in Simulate and Historical Data," *World Politics*, 18 (April 1966), 474–502; and Dina A. Zinnes, "The Expression and Perception of Hostility in Pre-War Crisis: 1914," in J. David Singer, ed., *Quantitative International Politics* (New York: The Free Press, 1968), pp. 85–122.

represents the decision maker's perception, presumably revised on the basis of P_n and R_{n+1}.

Perception-expression stage. The second stage of the model postulates that a decision maker's expression of hostility on a given day is a consequence of both his perception on that day *and* his previous expression of hostility. Again, this second factor seems intuitively plausible: a decision maker generally does not drastically change his expressions from day to day, even given sudden shifts in his perception of the situation. Stage two of the model can be represented by

$$E_n, P_{n+1} \rightarrow E_{n+1},$$

where E_n represents the decision maker's hostile expressions on day n, P_{n+1} indicates his perceptions of hostility on the following $(n+1)$st day, and E_{n+1} represents his subsequent expression.

Testing the two stages of the model. The analyses to be reported here involve testing two implications inherent in both stages of the general model. First, stage one of the model implies that for incoming messages containing a given amount of hostility, the decision maker's subsequent perception is only a function of his previous perception. And, similarly, stage two of the model implies that whenever the decision maker perceives hostility at a given level, his subsequent expression is solely a function of his prior expression. More specifically, the two stages of the model imply, respectively, that when R_{n+1} is held constant, P_n is a first-order Markov chain, and when P_{n+1} is held constant, E_n is a first-order Markov chain. That is, when R_{n+1} is fixed, it is assumed that the probability of P_{n+1} depends on P_n and only on P_n, and when P_{n+1} is fixed, the probability of E_{n+1} depends on E_n and only on E_n.

The second implication of the model to be tested concerns the effects of R and P on the two stages of the model. Specifically, it is assumed that the P transition probabilities depend on R. This means that the probability of changing from one level of P to another level depends in part on the message received. Analogously, it is assumed that the E transition probabilities depend on P. These two types of analyses will be made more explicit in the results section.

DESCRIPTION OF THE DATA

Data used in this study have been described at length elsewhere.[5] The discussion here is, therefore, limited to a brief summary of the sources and collection techniques used. These data were collected from the collated volumes of documents relevant to the pre–World War I crisis. These documents are the international communications, or messages, exchanged between the key decision makers of Germany, Austria–Hungary, France, England, Russia, and Serbia from the assassination of the Archduke on June 28, 1914, to the general outbreak of war about August 4, 1914.

Data were collected from these documents by a special form of thematic content analysis. Using a list of *tip-off* words—that is, synonyms for the variable being coded—the coders were instructed to count those tip-off words which

5. Dina A. Zinnes, "Expression and Perception of Hostility."

appeared in the "appropriate" context. The appropriateness of the context was determined by the extent to which the tip-off word was in fact being used in the sense in which it had been listed as a synonym for the variable. Extensive training sessions helped the coders identify these "appropriate" contexts. Before the actual coding began the coders passed tests to demonstrate their ability to correctly code the documents, and a reliability check was made between the various coders. (Using a modified, conservative reliability formula the reliability was .67.)

A number of variables were measured using these content analytic techniques. The variable of interest to us, and the one which showed the greatest degree of coding reliability, was the hostility variable. Figure 1 gives examples

CODING SHEET

1. Number of Hostility Themes 4
2. Recipient of Document Austria-Hungary (Francis Joseph)
   Interlocutor ____
3. Author of Document Germany (Wilhelm II) Person Quoted ____
4. Source Kautsky #503 31 July 1914
5. "Perceiver:" Author X Recipient ____ Persons Quoted ____
   Interlocutor ____ Other ____
6. "Perceived:" Author X Recipient ____ Persons Quoted ____
   Interlocutor ____ Other ____
7. Target of Perception H1—General; H2—Russia; H3—France; H4—France
8. Text of Document:
   "The introductory mobilization of my entire army and the navy which I have ordered today will be followed shortly by the actual mobilization. I am planning on the second of August as the first day of mobilization and I am prepared in fulfillment of the obligations of my alliance, to start war at once against Russia and France. It is of utmost importance in this grave struggle that Austria oppose her principal forces to Russia and not splinter her strength by a simultaneous offensive against Serbia. This is of all the more importance as a great part of my army will be employed against France. Serbia plays in this gigantic fight which we are entering shoulder to shoulder a very ordinate role, which requires of us only the defensive measures absolutely necessary."
9. Capsule statement(s):
   H1. "The introductory mobilization of my entire army and the navy which I have ordered today will be followed shortly by the ACTUAL MOBILIZATION."
   H2. "I (Wilhelm II) am prepared . . . TO START WAR at once against . . . Russia . . ."
   H3 "I (Wilhelm II) am prepared . . . TO START WAR at once against . . . France . . ."
   H4. ". . . a great part of my army will be EMPLOYED AGAINST FRANCE . . ."

FIGURE 1. Example of relevant parts of the coding sheets used to classify the hostility themes. Line 1 indicates the number of hostility themes in the text being coded. Lines 2–4 identify the document and source. Line 5 indicates the person having the perception and line 6 the party who is being perceived. The capsule statements at the bottom of the coding sheet designate the specific statement upon which each classification is based.

of hostility themes as abstracted from the documents and as coded on the original coding sheets. Using the material on these code sheets, it is possible to put all hostility statements into the following general format:

w writes: x says that y is hostile to z: and sends this message to v, where
w = author of document,
x = perceiver,
y = perceived,
z = target,
v = recipient (see Figure 1).

On the basis of the above "general hostility" statement, the three main variables can be defined:

1. A PERCEPTION of hostility (P') is said to occur whenever the perceiver and target are equal—that is, when w writes, "x says that y is hostile to x," and sends this to v.

2. An EXPRESSION of hostility (E') is said to occur whenever the perceiver and perceived are equal—that is, when w writes, "x says that x is hostile to z," and sends this to v.

3. And a RECEPTION (R') is an expression of hostility received by the target of the statement—that is, when w writes, "x says that x is hostile to z," and sends this to z.

Primes on P, E, and R are used to distinguish between these initial definitions and a set of parallel definitions (to be given later) that were used for most of the analyses. Using these definitions, the number of PERCEPTIONS, EXPRESSIONS, or RECEPTIONS can be counted for any particular country.

Vast differences in the content of hostility statements indicated the need for a scaling technique which would assign weights on the basis of the intensity of the statement. Random samples, consisting of about twelve statements from the data, were rank-ordered from pair comparison judgments. From several such rank-ordered sets of hostility statements, the following twelve-point abstract scale was derived.

1. Shirking obligations.
2. Preventing press from misleading public opinion; denying; putting an end to.
3. Using events against opponent; refusal; making others responsible; misrepresentation; spreading false news.
4. Cool relationship; undermining credit of opponent, undermining opponent's position in world.
5. Tolerating agitation against others; weakening opponent directly; warning opponent; possibility of intervention; will not tolerate.
6. Reproaching; agitating against opponent; anti-x feeling; difficulties.
7. Conspiracy; committing crimes against opponent or so implicated; provoking; inciting others against enemy.
8. Making demands; diplomatic ruptures; démarche; danger; conflict; taking steps.
9. Getting maximum; intimidating; humiliating; ultimatums; menace.
10. Mobilization; troop concentrations; troop movements.
11. Declaration of war; attacks; bombing.
12. Destruction; annihilation; disposal.[6]

6. For a specific discussion of this scaling procedure, see Dina A. Zinnes, "Expression and Perception of Hostility," pp. 96–99. A more general examination of such

All 2,000 statements were compared with this scale and assigned an intensity value.

PROCEDURE

Two problems were encountered in applying these models to the 1914 data: (1) a large number of zero entries for perceptions, receptions, and expressions—there were many days during the crisis when the decision makers did not perceive, receive, or express hostility; and (2) the absence of dates and times when messages were in fact received; frequently, only the date the message was sent is known. These two problems required that several assumptions be made concerning the data.

Solution to the zero perception and expression days. The first solution involved a redefinition of the international system. Data for the individual countries were aggregated according to historical alliances that existed prior to World War I. Following historical analysis, it was assumed that Germany and Austria–Hungary belonged to the Dual Alliance (D) and that the remaining four countries—England, France, Russia, and Serbia—formed a loose but cooperative unit, referred to here as the Serbia–Entente Alliance (S). By so combining these data for all countries in each bloc, it was assumed that an alliance operated as a single unit. This assumption is analogous to our original assumption that the various decision makers in a foreign office worked as a single unit. Thus, for example, an expression of hostility by either Germany or Austria–Hungary directed toward any member of the Serbia–Entente Alliance was considered an expression of hostility by the Dual Alliance directed toward the Serbia–Entente Alliance.

This set of pooled data produced the following revised definitions of the main three variables:

1. A PERCEPTION (P) is a hostility statement in which the perceiver and target belong to one alliance but the perceived belongs to the other alliance.
2. An EXPRESSION (E) is a hostility statement in which perceiver and perceived belong to one alliance and the target belongs to the other alliance.
3. And a RECEPTION (R) is an expression of hostility by one alliance received by the target alliance.

It should be emphasized that when primes are absent on P, E, and R, these variables are based on the revised alliance definitions. With the exception of the descriptive statistics, all analyses reported in this chapter are based on alliances.

Solution to the lack of arrival dates. The second problem concerns the absence of official reception dates and times. The documents indicate only when the message was sent. A systematic review of the documents shows that most of the communications were telegrams and therefore, were frequently received the same day of dispatch. But this information does not entirely solve the problem because of the diplomatic communication structure. A message from

---

scaling appears in Dina A. Zinnes, " 'Pair Comparison' Scaling in International Relations," in Robert C. North, Ole R. Holsti, M. George Zaninovich, and Dina A. Zinnes, *Content Analysis* (Evanston, Ill.: Northwestern University Press, 1963), pp. 78–89.

the decision makers of state X to their counterparts in Y usually travels by way of X's ambassador stationed in Y. Thus, even if it is assumed that the ambassador receives his instructions on the day they are sent, there are no clues as to when the ambassador communicates the information to the decision makers of the country to which he is accredited. It seemed advisable, then, to introduce three different time-lag assumptions.

Lag = 0. Messages are communicated to the decision makers of the host country the *same day* they are sent.
Lag = 1. Messages are communicated to the decision makers of the host country *one day after* they are sent.
Lag = 2. Messages are communicated to the decision makers of the host country *two days after* they are sent.

Because the different time-lag assumptions directly affect only the reception messages, they play a direct role in the first stage of the model (*RP*) but not in the second, *PE*, stage.

IMPORTANT CHARACTERISTICS OF THE DATA

Tables 1 and 2 summarize some of the general features and limitations of the data that form the basis of our analyses. Unlike the tables that follow, these tables do not involve tests of any specific hypotheses.

Table 1 gives the number of various types of hostility themes for each of the six countries before the revised alliance definitions were introduced. The decision makers in these six countries are the authors of the documents that were content analyzed. The category "Other Countries" is included in this table to show the number of messages sent out of the system, that is, messages that were not sent to one of the six countries. As indicated in Table 1, no message in these data originated from countries other than the six indicated. The category "Other Themes" in Table 1 refers to hostile themes that are neither E' nor P' themes. These messages are of the form "x says that y is hostile to z," where x, y, and z are different countries.

The bottom entry in the last two columns of Table 1 shows that the entire set of data consists of 2,315 hostile themes (and, equivalently, 2,315 punch cards). What Table 1 mainly demonstrates, therefore, is how these 2,315 themes distribute themselves over various classifications and subclassifications. It should be emphasized that although most of our efforts have been directed at maximizing the number of these themes that are directly involved in the analyses that follow, this effort is limited by the 2,315 themes available.

The significant aspect of Table 1 is that nearly one half of the 2,315 themes (1,059) are neither E' nor P' themes as these variables were originally defined. Thus the use of these initial definitions would mean that one half of the data would be ignored. By redefining the variables in terms of alliances, an additional 36 percent of the data is used. This will be shown in Table 2. The effect of redefining the variables was to reclassify some of the "Other Themes" as expression or perception themes; for example, after the revision a theme is classified as an expression if the perceiver and perceived belong to the same alliance, rather than requiring them to be the same country.

The daily perception and expression intensities are summarized in Table 2. This table shows the effect of the use of a two-alliance system on the amount

TABLE 1. NUMBER OF HOSTILITY THEMES AUTHORED AND RECEIVED OVER ALL DAYS OF THE CRISIS

	Expressions		*Perceptions*		*Other Themes*[d]		*Total*	
Countries	*Authored*[b]	*Received*[c]	*Authored*[b]	*Received*[c]	*Authored*	*Received*	*Authored*	*Received*
Great Britain	22	53	13	129	302	146	337	328
France	84	40	131	97	550	136	765	273
Russia	24	34	13	76	57	140	94	250
Serbia	31	6	69	17	8	36	108	59
Austria	142	50	540	66	57	139	739	255
Germany	59	78	128	156	85	191	272	425
Other Countries[a] (52 countries)	—	101	—	353	—	271	—	725
Total	362	362	894	894	1,059	1,059	2,315	2,315

NOTE: These entries are not based on alliances.

[a] These are themes sent by one of the six countries to another country not in our "system." No themes authored by these other nations are included in the present analysis.

[b] The author of these expressions and perceptions is not necessarily the perceiver.

[c] The target of these hostility themes is not necessarily the recipient.

[d] These are hostility themes which were neither expressions nor perceptions.

TABLE 2. SUM OF THE DAILY INTENSITIES OF PERCEPTIONS AND EXPRESSIONS BY ALLIANCE

	Days[a]																			
	1	*2*	*3*	*4*	*5*	*6*	*7*	*8*	*9*	*10*	*11*	*12*	*13*	*14*	*15*	*16*	*17*	*18*	*19*	*Frequency*
	20	*21*	*22*	*23*	*24*	*25*	*26*	*27*	*28*	*29*	*30*	*31*	*32*	*33*	*34*	*35*	*36*	*37*	*38*	*Totals*[b]
Serbia-Entente Alliance																				
Perceptions	0	0	7	62	0	0	0	0	6	6	14	7	0	0	0	0	0	0	0	
	0	0	75	28	8	60	0	240	342	533	619	181	1,060	412	594	820	1,008	460	129	748
Expressions	0	0	0	2	0	0	0	0	0	0	14	0	0	0	0	0	0	0	0	
	0	5	55	7	0	7	0	339	160	210	193	83	264	416	533	251	56	622	145	398
Receptions	0	0	0	0	12	0	0	0	0	0	0	0	0	6	0	0	0	0	0	
	0	0	0	42	0	0	0	24	67	102	54	63	40	61	35	82	48	44	0	83
Dual Alliance																				
Perceptions	0	0	0	0	136	0	0	37	0	31	75	0	0	0	0	0	38	0	7	
	0	0	0	515	22	156	551	458	557	374	35	112	313	139	463	44	404	428	43	708
Expressions	0	0	0	0	20	0	0	43	0	15	19	0	0	24	25	0	34	0	0	
	0	0	0	95	23	8	34	48	103	224	110	94	181	123	297	114	167	65	11	235
Receptions	0	0	0	0	0	0	0	0	0	0	0	0	0	0	0	0	0	0	0	
	0	0	22	0	0	0	0	42	40	60	79	31	79	145	126	45	0	60	41	101

NOTE: All entries are tallied by perceiver who is not necessarily the author. Intensity refers to the weighting on a twelve-point scale of each statement according to the degree of hostility it contains.

[a] First line of each variable refers to days 1–19, second line to days 20–38.

[b] Frequency totals are the number of Perceptions, Expressions, and Receptions based on the alliance. Total number of P and E=2,089.

of data available for analysis. As indicated above, the Serbia–Entente Alliance in this table refers to Great Britain, France, Russia, and Serbia, while the Dual Alliance refers to Austria–Hungary and Germany. The intensity values of the daily P and E themes given for each alliance in this table are based on summing corresponding intensities for all countries in each alliance. This pooling of the P and E intensities for the countries of each alliance gives a general picture of how the intensities change from day to day for each alliance. However, it must be pointed out that the actual analyses that follow were not based on *this* pooled data. We did *not* sum all P (or E) themes for the members of an alliance on each day, thereby obtaining a total of only 38 observations (days) for each alliance. Rather, in the analyses that follow, each country was treated separately *using the revised alliance definitions* to provide $4 \times 38 = 152$ observation (days) for the Serbia–Entente Alliance and $2 \times 38 = 76$ observations for the Dual Alliance.

Table 2 demonstrates several important characteristics (and limitations) of the data. First, a comparison of Table 2 with Table 1 shows the increase in data obtained by the use of the alliance definition. The E intensities indicated in Table 2 are based on a total of 633 E themes while the P intensities are based on 1,456 P themes. The total number of E and P themes involved in the revised definition of these terms is, therefore, equal to 2,089. This means that out of the 2,315 available themes, the analyses based on the alliance concept ignore only 226 themes or, equivalently, use over 90 per cent of the available themes. Comparing these numbers with those given in Table 1, the effect of the revised definitions of E and P themes is to increase the number of themes utilized from 1,256 to 2,089, or from 54 per cent to 90 per cent of the available themes.

The other two features of the data evident from Table 2 are (1) the very small number of themes present during the first 19 days and (2) a general tendency for all intensity measures to increase during the last 19 days.

RESULTS

As noted earlier, the present paper reports the results of only one preliminary set of analyses. These analyses are based on treating the three variables R, P, and E as dichotomous variables. For a given alliance we let $R_n = 0$ indicate that no message containing any degree of hostility was received on day n by that alliance. For a given alliance, $R_n = k$ indicates that some message was received on day n containing some degree of hostility. The two values of the variables P and E are similarly defined. Thus the RP and PE submodels being tested here are in terms of two types of messages: those having some degree of hostility and those having none.

Reception–perception (RP) stage. Table 3 gives the transition probabilities for the RP submodel or stage for both the Dual and Serbia–Entente Alliances. The entries in each matrix are proportions and the values in each row add to 1.00. The matrices are arranged in rows corresponding to the three lag conditions defined previously, and in columns on the basis of the value of the incoming messages ($R = 0$ or k). For example, the matrix in the top left-hand corner gives the transition probabilities under the lag $= 2$ condition when no message was received by any member of the Serbia–Entente Alliance ($R = 0$). Similarly, the second matrix in the first row gives the transition probabilities for the lag $= 2$ condition when the Serbia–Entente Alliance received some messages ($R = k$).

TABLE 3. TRANSITION MATRICES FOR THE *RP* MODEL

			Serbia-Entente				*Dual*			
			Perception on Following Day (P_{n+1})				*Perception on Following Day* (P_{n+1})			
			No Messages Received		*Some Messages Received*		*No Messages Received*		*Some Messages Received*	
			k	0	k	0	k	0	k	0
Lag = 2	Perception on given day (P_n)	k	0.48	0.52	0.87	0.13	0.40	0.60	0.87	0.13
		0	0.15	0.85	0.67	0.33	0.28	0.72	0.20	0.80
			$N=119$		$N=29$		$N=54$		$N=20$	
Lag = 1	Perception on given day (P_n)	k	0.38	0.62	0.92	0.08	0.38	0.63	0.93	0.07
		0	0.17	0.83	0.33	0.67	0.25	0.75	0.38	0.63
			$N=117$		$N=31$		$N=52$		$N=22$	
Lag = 0	Perception on given day (P_n)	k	0.46	0.54	0.95	0.05	0.33	0.67	0.93	0.07
		0	0.13	0.87	0.55	0.45	0.31	0.69	0.11	0.89
			$N=117$		$N=31$		$N=50$		$N=24$	

NOTE: In each matrix, k = some hostility and 0 = no hostility. N is the number of nations times the number of days for which data were available under the conditions specified for a particular matrix.

The entries in each of the matrices for the Serbia–Entente Alliance shown in Table 3 indicate the proportion of times members of this alliance made a transition from one level of hostility to another on the following day. Here there are only *two* levels of hostility: no hostility and some hostility. For example, the first matrix in the top row of Table 3 (lag -2, $R=0$) indicates that when the Serbia–Entente Alliance perceived some degree of hostility on a given day ($P_n=k$ for a member of that alliance), 48 per cent of the time it continued to perceive some hostility ($P_{n+1}=k$) on the following, $(n+1)$st, day. Similarly, when $P_n=0$, 85 per cent of the time $P_{n+1}=0$. The transition probabilities are computed by determining the proportion of times a perception at level i ($i=0$ or k) on day n is followed by a perception at level j ($j=0$ or k) on the following, $(n+1)$st day. Thus, as described above, in the first matrix of Table 3, 48 per cent of the time $P_n=k$ is followed by $P_{n+1}=k$.

Table 3 again demonstrates the problem described earlier concerning the number of days of zero R and P. The greatest number of cases occurs in the $R=0$ matrix, and in this matrix the greatest number of cases is in the $P_n=0$ row. The larger number of total cases for the Serbia–Entente Alliance is due to the fact that this alliance contains four nations, while the Dual Alliance contains only two.

Order properties of the RP submodel. A test of the first implication of the model involves determining whether the P on one day influences the P on the next day. If the level of incoming hostility (R) is fixed, do decision makers perceive hostility on day $(n+1)$ as a function of their perception of hostility on day n? Answering this question is equivalent to determining whether the proportions in the rows of a given matrix differ from each other significantly. Thus we wish to reject the null hypothesis that the rows come from the *same* binomial distribution (i.e., there is no difference between the rows). In the terminology of Markov chains, this null hypothesis is equivalent to asserting that the Markov chain represented by the given transition matrix is a zero-order, rather than a first-order, chain.

The results of the test of this implication of the model can be found in Table 4. The last three columns of the table give the total results when the $R=0$ and $R=k$ matrices are analyzed together. The chi-square values reported here are based on the summation of the chi squares for the two individual matrices. The larger the chi square for a fixed degree of freedom, the less likely it is that the null hypothesis is true. It should be pointed out that these chi squares are not entirely accurate due to the small sample sizes in each of the two matrices. For this reason the individual matrices reported in the first six columns of Table 4 were analyzed using exact tests; the exact probability level (p) given in this table was determined from a two-tailed hypergeometric distribution. The smaller the p value, the less likely it is that the null hypothesis is true though, following the accepted standards for rejecting the null hypothesis, one would hope for a p value less than .05. While it is possible to compute an exact p over two or more matrices, such calculations are extremely tedious and time consuming, even on a high-speed digital computer. Thus we have reported only chi squares for the total case.

Table 4 shows that the total chi squares (last three columns) are significant at the $p=.05$ level for both alliances and all lags. On the basis of the total chi squares, then, it is possible to reject the hypothesis that the perceptual

TABLE 4. EXACT AND CHI-SQUARE TESTS OF THE ORDER PROPERTIES OF THE *RP* TRANSITION MATRICES

		$R=0$			$R=k$			*Total*		
		p	df	N	p	df	N	X^2	df	N
Lag = 2	Serbia-Entente	.001	1	119	.269	1	29	13.729*	2	148
	Dual	.535	1	54	.013	1	20	8.635*	2	74
Lag = 1	Serbia-Entente	.040	1	117	.006	1	31	15.522*	2	148
	Dual	.527	1	52	.011	1	22	8.709*	2	74
Lag = 0	Serbia-Entente	.001	1	117	.013	1	31	20.920*	2	148
	Dual	1.000	1	50	.000	1	24	16.243*	2	74

* $p \leq .05$.

process is a zero order Markov chain. Alternatively, P on day n evidently affects P on day $(n+1)$. An alliance's perception of hostility on day $(n+1)$ is determined, in part, by whether or not it perceived hostility on the previous, nth, day.

Table 4 also indicates a slight difference between the three lag assumptions. For the no-lag condition (lag $=0$), the chi squares for both Serbia-Entente and Dual Alliances are larger than those obtained under the other two conditions. However, since all the chi-square values are significant, this difference between lags is not striking.

The results for the individual matrices, unfortunately, do not present the same consistent results found for the total case. When $R=0$ none of the Dual Alliance results are significant, and when $R=k$ the Serbia-Entente Alliance does not produce significant results for lag $=2$. Apparently, in the case of the Dual Alliance, P_n affects P_{n+1} only when messages are received; when no messages are received by either Germany or Austria, their perceptions on day $(n+1)$ are independent of perceptions on the previous day. In contrast, with the exception of the two-day lag condition (lag $=2$), the individual matrices for the Serbia-Entente Alliance are consistent with the total chi-square results; a previous perception has an effect on a subsequent perception for the members of the Serbia-Entente Alliance.

While we have reported simply the existence of statistically significant differences between the rows of the matrices shown in Table 3, an inspection of those matrices shows that the differences are in the direction that might be anticipated in a typical learning situation. To demonstrate this let $p(P_{ij}|R_k)$ indicate the probability of a transition from a perception at level i on day n to a perception at level j on day $(n+1)$ when messages at level k are received. Thus $p(P_{oo}|R_o)$ indicates the probability of a transition from $P_n=0$ to $P_{n+1}=0$ when no messages containing hostility are received. Then, in terms of this notation, the above order analyses have shown that

$$p(P_{oo}|R_o) \neq p(P_{ko}|R_o)$$

and that

$$p(P_{kk}|R_k) \neq p(P_{ok}|R_k).$$

While all four transitions in these inequalities represent correct responses, since the perception on day $(n+1)$ reflects appropriately the message received just prior to it, it is reasonable to expect in each case that the terms on the left-hand side of these inequalities will be larger than the terms on the right. The left-hand term in each inequality refers to the probability of "correctly" maintaining the prior perception, while the right-hand term refers to the probability of "correctly" changing perceptions. Ordinarily, the probability of repeating a "reinforced" response in learning situations is greater than the probability of changing responses following a nonreinforced response.

For all lags and both alliances we find that the predicted inequalities are verified. This can be seen in Table 5. The asterisks in this table show which pairs of probabilities are significantly different.

One other interesting comparison can be made using the data in Table 3. Pursuing the argument that decision makers do not manufacture hostile perceptions in the absence of hostile stimuli, and do not ignore hostile comments in messages received, the following predictions can be made:

$$p(P_{oo}|R_o) > p(P_{ok}|R_o) \quad (1)$$

$$p(P_{kk}|R_k) > p(P_{ko}|R_k) \quad (2)$$

$$p(P_{ko}|R_o) > p(P_{kk}|R_o) \quad (3)$$

$$p(P_{ok}|R_k) > p(P_{oo}|R_k). \quad (4)$$

Inequality (1) above indicates that in the absence of hostile messages and when there is no prior perception of hostility, decision makers should continue to perceive no hostility. Inequality (2) indicates that decision makers should continue to perceive hostility when it exists. Inequality (3) indicates that decision

TABLE 5. A COMPARISON OF INEQUALITIES BETWEEN TRANSITIONAL PROBABILITIES BASED ON THE ORDER PROPERTIES FOR THE *RP* MODEL

	$p(P_{oo}|R_o)$	$>p(P_{ko}|R_o)$	$p(P_{kk}|R_k)$	$>p(P_{ok}|R_k)$
Serbia-Entente				
lag = 2	.85	.52**	.87	.67
lag = 1	.83	.62**	.92	.33**
lag = 0	.87	.54**	.95	.55*
Dual				
lag = 2	.72	.60	.87	.20*
lag = 1	.75	.63	.93	.38*
lag = 0	.69	.67	.93	.11**

* $p \leq .05$.
** $p \leq .01$.
NOTE: The first inequality statement in the table heading is confirmed when a transitional probability in the first column exceeds the corresponding value in the second column. Similarly, the second inequality statement is confirmed when probabilities in the third column exceed those in the fourth. The relative magnitude of all such adjacent terms are in the predicted direction. Asterisks indicate those differences between compared probabilities that are statistically significant. Exact p values are given in Table 4.

makers should modify their prior perceptions of hostility when no hostility is received. And inequality (4) indicates that decision makers should perceive hostility when it exists. Each of these comparisons implies that a "correct" or "appropriate" response, in the sense of matching the level of hostility in the incoming message, should be more probable than an "incorrect" or "inappropriate" one. Table 6 gives the results of the comparison. All inequalities but the last support these predictions. For the last inequality only two of the six pairs of probabilities are in the predicted direction.

Thus in most instances it appears to be the case that not only does the perception of hostility on one day have an effect on the perception of hostility on the following day, but also that decision makers respond appropriately to incoming stimuli. They do not perceive hostility in the absence of hostile messages, and they do perceive hostility when hostile messages are received. The one exception to these latter findings appears to occur in the Dual Alliance. However, it should be pointed out that even for the Dual Alliance the misperception

TABLE 6. A COMPARISON OF CORRECT AND INCORRECT TRANSITIONAL PROBABILITIES FOR THE *RP* MODEL

	$p(P_{oo}\|R_o) > p(P_{ok}\|R_o)$		$p(P_{kk}\|R_k) > p(P_{ko}\|R_k)$		$p(P_{ko}\|R_o) > p(P_{kk}\|R_o)$		$p(P_{ok}\|R_k) > p(P_{oo}\|R_k)$	
Serbia-Entente								
lag = 2	.85	.15	.87	.13	.52	.48	.67	.33
lag = 1	.83	.17	.92	.08	.62	.38	.33[a]	.67[a]
lag = 0	.87	.13	.95	.05	.54	.46	.55	.45
Dual								
lag = 2	.72	.28	.87	.13	.60	.40	.20[a]	.80[a]
lag = 1	.75	.25	.93	.07	.63	.38	.38[a]	.63[a]
lag = 0	.69	.31	.93	.07	.67	.33	.11[a]	.89[a]

[a] Indicates terms whose relative magnitudes are *not* in the predicted direction.

is *not* in the direction that would be predicted from the hypothesis that decision makers manufacture perceptions in the absence of, or out of proportion to, incoming stimuli. For this alliance the probability is greater than .5 that, *having received a hostile message* and having no prior perception of hostility, the decision makers of Austria and Germany will continue *not to perceive any hostility*. Considering the fact that Austria was one of the main protagonists of the crisis and, therefore, one would assume, the most likely to misperceive and perhaps be paranoid, it is interesting to find that the misperception is not in the paranoid direction (seeing enemies where none exist), but rather in the "day-dreamer's" direction of not seeing danger when it really exists. This would seem to indicate that the exclamation uttered by the German Kaiser and frequently quoted to demonstrate the paranoid perceptions of decision makers in crises is not typical of the behavior of most decision makers, even in the 1914 crisis.[7]

Equality properties of the RP submodel. That decision makers respond in relationship to incoming messages is further substantiated by the test of the second implication of the *RP* submodel. This second analysis considers whether incoming messages have an effect on the *P* transition probabilities. In terms of Markov chain terminology, we are interested in testing whether the two transition matrices corresponding to $R=0$ and $R=k$ represent the same Markov chain. This is equivalent to asking whether corresponding rows in the two matrices are samples from the same binomial distribution. For convenience, we refer to this test as a test of the equality properties of the *RP* model.

The appropriate statistical test is carried out by regrouping the matrices of Table 3. One matrix is obtained by bringing together the first rows, the $P=k$ rows, of the two matrices for each alliance (and each time lag) in Table 3. This new 2×2 matrix can then be referred to as the $P=k$ matrix. Similarly, the $P=0$ matrix refers to a 2×2 matrix consisting of the $P=0$ rows of the two matrices in Table 3 for a given alliance and lag. The same chi-square and two-tailed hypergeometric tests described earlier can now be performed on these new matrices. Once again, we wish to reject the null hypothesis that rows of these new matrices are the same, and the larger the chi square for a fixed degree of freedom, or the smaller the exact p, the less likely it is that the null hypothesis is true.

The results of this analysis are reported in Table 7. We find that the total

7. For example, the Kaiser is paraphrased as having said:

The whole world, of a sudden, was to be plunged "into the most frightful war"—aimed at Germany's destruction. The case was clear: England, and France "after laying the foundation of the *casus foederis* through Austria," had agreed among themselves to wage a "war of extermination" against Germany. Thus by sheer unprincipled craft, Germany had been "brought into a situation" that offered England the desired pretext for "annihilating" Germany—"the net has been suddenly thrown over our head," the Kaiser asserted, ". . . . *and England sneeringly reaps the brilliant success of her persistently prosecuted purely anti German world policy, against which we have proved ourselves helpless, while she twists the noose of our political and economic destruction out of our fidelity to Austria, as we squirm isolated in the net.*"

Dina A. Zinnes, Robert C. North, and Howard E. Koch, Jr., "Capability, Threat, and the Outbreak of War," p. 476.

TABLE 7. EXACT AND CHI-SQUARE TESTS OF THE EQUALITY PROPERTIES OF THE *RP* TRANSITION MATRICES

		$P=0$			$P=k$			Total		
		p	df	N	p	df	N	X^2	df	N
Lag = 2	Serbia-Entente	.009	1	102	.006	1	46	18.554*	2	148
	Dual	1.000	1	44	.021	1	30	7.184*	2	74
Lag = 1	Serbia-Entente	.288	1	102	.000	1	46	16.170*	2	148
	Dual	.663	1	44	.003	1	30	10.369*	2	74
Lag = 0	Serbia-Entente	.004	1	102	.001	1	46	23.824*	2	148
	Dual	.406	1	44	.001	1	30	13.117*	2	74

* $p \leq .05$.

chi squares for all lags and both alliances are all significant though, once again, in terms of the magnitude of the chi-square values, the zero lag (lag $=0$) condition appears to be the better for both alliances. Thus, in terms of the total results, we can conclude that R does affect the P transition probabilities. As we have seen thus far, perceptions of hostility are made in the context of the receipt of hostile messages.

Again, however, as we indicated in the first analysis, the results for the individual matrices do not present the same consistent picture. While, as found before, nearly all individual results for the Serbia-Entente Alliance are consistent with the total chi-square values (there is just one exception, lag $=1$, $P=0$), none of the results for the $P=0$ condition for the Dual Alliance are significant. Thus for Austria and Germany, in the absence of a previous perception of hostility, the receipt of hostile messages has little effect on a subsequent perception.

It is also the case that all the statistically significant inequalities are in the predicted direction. The relevant inequalities for these equality analyses are

$$p(P_{kk}|R_k) > p(P_{kk}|R_o) \tag{5}$$

$$p(P_{oo}|R_o) > p(P_{oo}|R_k) \tag{6}$$

In both cases the left-hand terms should be larger than the right-hand terms if the perception of hostility is to accurately reflect the level of hostility in the incoming message. For convenience, the corresponding numerical values are grouped together in Table 8. It may be seen from this table that for the Serbia-Entente Alliance these inequalities are supported in each instance (even for the one case in which the results were not statistically significant), but for the Dual Alliance only one of these inequalities, (5), is supported for all lags. However,

TABLE 8. A COMPARISON OF INEQUALITIES BETWEEN TRANSITIONAL PROBABILITIES BASED ON THE EQUALITY PROPERTIES FOR THE *RP* MODEL

	$p(P_{kk}\|R_k) >$	$p(P_{kk}\|R_o)$	$p(P_{oo}\|R_o) >$	$p(P_{oo}\|R_k)$
Serbia-Entente				
lag $=2$	.87	.48**	.85	.33**
lag $=1$	.92	.38**	.83	.67
lag $=0$	.95	.46**	.87	.45**
Dual				
lag $=2$	.87	.40*	.72[a]	.80[a]
lag $=1$	.93	.38**	.75	.63
lag $=0$	.93	.33**	.69[a]	.89[a]

* $p \leq .05$.
** $p \leq .01$.

NOTE: The first inequality statement in the table heading is confirmed when a transitional probability in the first column exceeds the corresponding value in the second column. Similarly, the second inequality statement is confirmed when probabilities in the third column exceed those in the fourth. Asterisks indicate those differences between comparable probabilities that are statistically significant. Exact p values are given in Table 7.

[a] Indicates terms whose relative magnitudes are not in the predicted direction.

as indicated by the results of the equality analyses, the probabilities in (6) for the Dual Alliance are not significantly different for any lag. So it seems correct to say that for the Dual Alliance the $P=0$ state is not sensitive to the incoming message, rather than to say that for this state the effect of the incoming message is the opposite from what would be expected.

Perception-expression submodel. Having considered the effects of the receipt of hostile messages and previous perceptions of hostility on the subsequent perception of hostility, we turn now to the question of whether perceptions influence the expression of hostility. On the basis of the argument presented here, we would assume that when $P_n=0$ there should be less tendency to express hostility than when $P_n=k$. The analyses for the second stage of the model will answer this question as well as examine the compounding effect of a previous expression of hostility on a subsequent one.

The transition probabilities for the *PE* submodel are given in Table 9 for both the Serbia-Entente and the Dual Alliances. As explained above, because the lags pertain only to the arrival time of receptions (*R*) they are not explicitly involved in the *PE* model. Except for the absence of time lags, the matrices in Table 9 are completely analogous to those found in Table 3.

TABLE 9. TRANSITION MATRICES FOR THE *PE* MODEL

Serbia-Entente

		Expression on Following Day (E_{n+1})			
		No Perception		Some Perception	
		k	0	k	0
Expression on given day (E_n)	k	0.13	0.88	0.71	0.29
	0	0.04	0.96	0.67	0.33
		$N=99$		$N=49$	

Dual

		Expression on Following Day (E_{n+1})			
		No Perception		Some Perception	
		k	0	k	0
Expression on given day (E_n)	k	0.18	0.82	1.00	0.00
	0	0.03	0.97	0.75	0.25
		$N=43$		$N=31$	

NOTE: In each matrix, k = some hostility and 0 = no hostility. N is the number of nations times the number of days for which data were available under the conditions specified for a particular matrix.

Order properties of the PE model. This first test involves a consideration of the effect that E_n has on E_{n+1}, when P_{n+1} is held constant. When the perception of hostility is held constant, do decision makers express hostility on one day as a function of the hostility they expressed on the previous day?

Using the same chi-square and two-tailed hypergeometric tests described earlier, the results of this first analysis are reported in the top half of Table 10. We find that only for the Dual Alliance is the total chi square significant and,

TABLE 10. EXACT AND CHI-SQUARE TESTS OF THE ORDER AND EQUALITY PROPERTIES OF THE *PE* TRANSITION MATRICES

	Order Properties								
	$P=0$			$P=k$			*Total*		
	p	*df*	*N*	*p*	*df*	*N*	X^2	*df*	*N*
Serbia-Entente	.350	1	99	.782	1	49	1.135	2	148
Dual	.156	1	43	.049	1	31	8.118*	2	74
	Equality Properties								
	$E=0$			$E=k$			*Total*		
Serbia-Entente	.000	1	112	.005	1	36	57.941*	2	148
Dual	.000	1	44	.000	1	30	47.880*	2	74

* $p \leq .05$.

in fact, that this result seems to be based principally on the data for the $P=k$ condition. Thus, in this alliance, E_n affects E_{n+1} only when $P_{n+1}=k$, that is, when no hostility is perceived, expressions of hostility are independent of previous expressions. For the Serbia-Entente Alliance, when the perception of hostility is held constant, the existence of a previous expression seems to have no effect on whether or not the members of the Serbia-Entente Alliance express hostility on the following day.

Although the tests of the order properties of the *PE* model do not produce consistently significant results, it is noteworthy that all the inequalities are in the predicted direction. The predictions are that

$$p(E_{oo}|P_o)>p(E_{ko}|P_o) \tag{7}$$

and

$$p(E_{kk}|P_k)>p(E_{ok}|P_k). \tag{8}$$

The matrices in Table 9 support these predictions. For convenience, the relevant terms are grouped together in the top of Table 11, under "Order Properties."

Although the above findings seem to suggest that an earlier expression of hostility is not a highly relevant variable for understanding expressions of hostility, this does not imply that P_{n+1} does not affect E_{n+1}. In fact, an inspection of the transition matrices of Table 9 shows that such a relationship does exist. The predictions made for the *RP* model are directly analogous here: "correct" responses in the sense defined previously should be more probable than "incorrect" ones, specifically:

$$p(E_{oo}|P_o)>p(E_{ok}|P_o) \tag{9}$$

$$p(E_{kk}|P_k)>p(E_{ko}|P_k) \tag{10}$$

$$p(E_{ko}|P_o) > p(E_{kk}|P_o) \quad (11)$$

$$p(E_{ok}|P_k) > p(E_{oo}|P_k). \quad (12)$$

Table 12 shows that these inequalities are supported by the data in every instance.

Thus expressions of hostility appear to be based principally (on the basis of the first analysis) on the perception of hostility. This finding is further substantiated by the results obtained for the second set of analyses performed on the *PE* model.

TABLE 11. A COMPARISON OF INEQUALITIES BASED ON THE ORDER AND EQUALITY PROPERTIES OF THE *PE* MODEL

	Order Properties			
	$p(E_{oo}|P_o)$ >	$p(E_{ko}|P_o)$	$p(E_{kk}|P_k)$ >	$p(E_{ok}|P_k)$
Serbia-Entente	.96	.88	.71	.67
Dual	.97	.82	1.00	.75*
	Equality Properties			
	$p(E_{kk}|P_k)$ >	$p(E_{kk}|P_o)$	$p(E_{oo}|P_o)$ >	$p(E_{oo}|P_k)$
Serbia-Entente	.71	.13**	.96	.33**
Dual	1.00	.18**	.97	.25**

* $p \leq .05$.
** $p \leq .01$.
NOTE: Values of *p* are for the differences between adjacent pairs of terms. Exact *p* values are given in Table 10. The relative magnitude of all adjacent pairs of terms are in the predicted direction.

Equality properties of the PE model. This analysis is directly comparable to the second analysis performed on the *RP* model and involves the rewriting of the transition matrices found in Table 9 to hold *E* constant. The same chi-square and exact *p* tests are used. The results in the lower half of Table 10 support the argument just outlined. The total chi squares in the lower half of Table 10 are highly significant for both alliances; and this is further substantiated by the exact *p*'s given for the individual matrices. It may also be seen from the lower part of Table 11 that in every instance all inequalities are in the predicted direction. These results seem to indicate that *P* clearly has an effect on the *E* transition matrices: when there is no perception of hostility there is no expression of hostility, but when hostility is perceived it is replied to with hostility.

CONCLUSION

The argument we have attempted to present here is that decision makers do not perceive or behave differently in a crisis. In a crisis, as in a noncrisis, they react in proportion to incoming stimuli. They do not perceive hostility when none exists, and they express hostility directly in terms of their perception of hostility. On the basis of the 1914 evidence, it does not appear that decision makers become paranoid under the pressures of the situation.

TABLE 12. A COMPARISON OF CORRECT AND INCORRECT TRANSITIONS FOR THE *PE* MODEL

	$p(E_{oo}\|P_o) >$	$p(E_{ko}\|P_o)$	$p(E_{kk}\|P_k) >$	$p(E_{ko}\|P_k)$	$p(E_{ko}\|P_o) >$	$p(E_{kk}\|P_o)$	$p(E_{ok}\|P_k) >$	$p(E_{oo}\|P_k)$
Serbia-Entente	.96	.04	.71	.29	.88	.13	.67	.33
Dual	.97	.03	1.00	.00	.82	.18	.75	.25

NOTE: The relevant magnitudes of all adjacent pairs of terms are in the predicted direction.

However, while we wish to maintain that a distortion does *not* exist in the perception and expression of hostility during a crisis, we wish to make it plain that we have not demonstrated that decision makers are necessarily "rational" in times of crises. Rationality seems to imply the matching of alternative courses of action and their probable outcomes with ultimate goals. This study cannot answer the question of whether optimal strategies are chosen to achieve stated goals. It can only contend that distortion or misperception of incoming messages is not a part of this process.

One of the limitations of this type of study should be pointed out. We have been speaking somewhat loosely as though the statistically significant results reported here establish a causal relationship between two or more variables. For example, we have suggested that the close relationship between a perception and expression of hostility suggests that perception is, at least in part, a cause of the expression of hostility. Such an interpretation is generally reasonable when the independent variables have been carefully manipulated by an experimenter in a laboratory setting. The difficulty with historical data, however, is that the variables cannot be explicitly manipulated and, consequently, an observed correlation between two variables can all too easily be attributed to a third unknown variable. The simultaneous increase in both the perceptions and expressions of hostility, for example, could be due to a third factor.

The problem here is analogous to the cigarette and cancer issue. Without random and *a priori* assignments of subjects to a smoking and nonsmoking group, it is all too easy to argue that the observed correlations between cigarette smoking and cancer are due to a third factor, such as heredity or nervous tension. Generally, the only way to eliminate the possibility of such alternative interpretations is by obtaining a large amount of indirect evidence, all of which supports the thesis that one variable is indeed a cause of the other. In the context of the present historical data, this means showing that the results obtained here apply to other historical periods and that these results are also consistent with other known aspects of this historical period. Establishing this indirect kind of evidence is a long-term undertaking. This paper can be only one step in that direction.

One obvious extension of these analyses would involve a consideration of different levels of hostility for each of the three variables, R, P, and E. Are comparable results obtained when the variables assume more than just two values? Beyond this, following the argument described in the inspection of the matrices, we would like to propose and test the specific process taking place. What transition probability would one predict between $P_n = 0$ and $P_{n+1} = k$ when a hostile message is received ($R = k$)? These two general questions form the bases of our present research.

part four

GAMES AND SIMULATIONS OF CRISIS

chapter eight

EDITOR'S INTRODUCTION

Until this chapter the attempts to understand crisis behavior have been based exclusively on the reconstruction of actual international crises. The previous authors have indicated the inherent difficulties in such efforts: (1) Official documents often remain unavailable for years after the event. (2) Participants, when interviewed after the event, suffer from faulty memories or were not in a position to observe important aspects of the situation. (3) Memoirs are frequently written more to justify the author's activities than to clarify the crisis. (4) Journalists and scholars alike have scant opportunities for direct observation of policy makers during a crisis. One controversial adjunct to the direct investigation of actual crises is the use of political gaming and simulation. The research in this chapter introduces the use of gaming for the study of crisis. The chapter also makes a number of important linkages between different aspects of crisis research.

With respect to simulation, Schwartz's research provides a useful bridge between studies of actual international crises and those created in a laboratory setting. The author analyzes data from two of his related studies—one study uses experts to judge features of eight historical crises and the other simulates certain properties of the same eight crises. Not only are findings between these two projects examined, but they are compared with a prior study of the 1914 crisis and another that used simulation data.

There is a tendency among social scientists to heap professional rewards upon those who, after dismissing all previous research in an area of inquiry, chart a new and independent course. Thus we often find ourselves with basic hypotheses or fragments of a theory that have never been replicated. In this chapter Schwartz may signal that, at least with respect to the study of crisis, we are overcoming that unhealthy habit. The author builds on the previous work of Dina A. Zinnes by verifying and elaborating her hypotheses on the perception and expression of hostility in crisis. (These hypotheses were forerunners of the research that she and her colleagues describe in the preceding chapter.) By his use of operational definitions and research methods different from those that Zinnes had employed to test the same hypotheses, Schwartz has made possible the multi-trait, multi-method validity test of research findings first advocated by Campbell and Fiske.[1]

Other linkages in this chapter should be noted. Although concerned with perceptions and similar problems associated with decision making, Schwartz maintains an interest in interaction effects between parties to a crisis which leads him to introduce variables relevant to a systemic perspective. For example, his extension of the Zinnes work is concerned with the problem of alliance cohesion and escalation processes. The interaction emphasis is also reflected in his definition of an international crisis, which he views as a critical point in the conflict between two or more nations. Such a definition can be contrasted with that advanced by other contributors who define crisis in terms of the perceptions of one set of decision makers. (See, for example, Chapter 9.) Schwartz, however,

1. Donald T. Campbell and D. W. Fiske, "Convergent and Discriminant Validation by the Multi-trait–Multi-method Matrix," *Psychological Bulletin*, 56 (1959), 81–105.

does not exclude analysis based on the decision makers' perceptions of crisis. In a section of his chapter somewhat similar to Lentner's interviews in the Department of State (Chapter 6), Schwartz asked his simulation participants when they thought they were in a crisis. He then determined what other features were correlated with self-defined crises. One hopes for future research in which the same potential correlates of perceived crisis are studied with both actual policy makers and participants in simulations. The present chapter establishes a reference point for such work by introducing a multi-method research strategy for moving between historical and simulated crises.

David C. Schwartz is an Associate Professor of Political Science at Livingston College and a member of the Graduate Faculty of Rutgers University. He has published two articles that are quite relevant to the research reported here—one concerns political gaming techniques and the other deals specifically with crises.[2] He is currently preparing a volume on alliance behavior that draws on some of the research presented in this chapter.

2. David C. Schwartz. "Problems in Political Gaming," *Orbis*, 9 (Fall 1965) 677–693; and David C. Schwartz, "Decision Theories and Crisis Behavior," *Orbis*, 11 (Summer 1967), 459–490.

chapter eight

DECISION MAKING IN HISTORICAL AND SIMULATED CRISES*

David C. Schwartz

INTRODUCTION

It is an axiom of scientific inquiry that the accepted validity of a proposition varies directly with the frequency of its confirmation and also with the range of contexts and the number of observation techniques in which it is confirmed. As the study of international politics has moved, however fitfully, toward acceptance of scientific standards, the desirability of research replication and of linked, multi-method research (that is, applying different techniques to investigating the same hypotheses) has become increasingly accepted. The present chapter is an attempt to contribute to this research practice by comparing the author's findings on the causes, characteristics, and consequences of international crises with the findings from studies at Stanford, Northwestern, and elsewhere.

Substantive propositions of considerable theoretical importance have emerged from recent research on both historical and simulated crises. By investigating these propositions in different real and experimental contexts, we not only attempt to test the power of these formulations but also try to make further comparisons between the decision making of real world leaders and student surrogates. In this manner, it may be possible to increase our confidence in both the validity of our developing theories and the power of our emerging methodologies.

RESEARCH PROBLEM

Whether explicitly called "decision-making research" or not, most contemporary studies of international crises seek to take at least some account of the perceptions, attitudes, and other psychological attributes of the human actors involved.[1] Indeed, students of crisis have increasingly sought the explanation of crisis behavior in regular patterns of psychological conditions and processes. Accordingly,

* The research on which this paper is based was conducted at the Foreign Policy Research Institute of the University of Pennsylvania with the support of the USACDA (ACDA ST-64) and the USAF (AF 496 382 349). I wish to acknowledge the encouragement of Professors William R. Kinter, Roger L. Sisson (University of Pennsylvania), and Harold Guetzkow (Simulated International Processes Project, Northwestern University) and the assistance of Mr. Daniel L. Dolan. I am also grateful to Drs. Richard A. Brody and Dina Zinnes for permission to use their data. My gratitude is also extended to Professor Charles F. Hermann (Ohio State University) for his most useful critique of an earlier version of this paper.

1. For the theoretical bases on which much of this proceeds, see Richard C. Snyder, H. W. Bruck, and Burton Sapin, *Foreign Policy Decision Making* (New York: The Free Press, 1962).

there has been a recent burgeoning of professional literature on international decision making.[2]

But if few scholars now seem disposed to dispute the relevance of psychological factors, it may be well to ask ourselves what, specifically, we know both about the relationships among these admittedly pertinent factors and between them and the behavior they are supposed to predict. Is there a recurrent "crisis decisional mind-set" or "psychological decisional system" which is regularly associated with the recognition of a conflict as a crisis? How does variation in the magnitude of one perceptual factor affect others in the set; that is, how functionally integrated is the psychological decisional system? What crisis behaviors are associated with alternative states of that system?

To these questions we seem to have the beginnings of what may eventually become adequate answers. We have at least some consensus on the topics worthy of concern—that is, a set of commonly recognized problems. Although emphasis differs from scholar to scholar, central to many studies of crisis are such variables as the impact of alliances, the perceived threat and hostility from potential enemies, and the communication patterns and behaviors of leaders in crises. It is on these topics that we now have some comparative results—that is, some relationships which have been investigated by different researchers working in different contexts and using different methods. We now consider some hypotheses investigated in this manner.

Hypotheses. One of the most clearly focused efforts at comparative investigation of basic decision factors in crises is the article by Dina A. Zinnes.[3] This study links some of the crisis-relevant results of simulation research at Northwestern University[4] with the historical, content-analytic research on the 1914 crisis conducted at Stanford University and elsewhere. While "the choice of hypotheses was dictated by the availability of comparable data in both studies,"[5] we are fortunate in that the variables utilized and the propositions profferred are familiar, fundamental ones.

The hypotheses stated in Zinnes' work postulated relationships among the following four variables:

1. *A perception of threat*: state x's perception that y threatens x, denoted by xTy.
2. *A perception of unfriendliness*: state x's perception that y is hostile to x, denoted by xUy.
3. *An expression of hostility* by state x to state y, denoted by xEy.

2. The growing literature and the need for integration can be seen in a publication by Richard C. Snyder and James A. Robinson, *National and International Decision-Making* (New York: Institute for International Order, n.d.). This study lists twenty-one other bibliographies on related topics and some eight hundred books and articles on decision making.

3. Dina A. Zinnes, "A Comparison of Hostile Behavior of Decision-Makers in Simulate and Historical Data," *World Politics*, 18 (April 1966), 474–502.

4. See, specifically, Richard A. Brody, "Some Systemic Effects of the Spread of Nuclear Weapons Technology," *Journal of Conflict Resolution*, 7 (December 1963), 663–753; Michael J. Driver, *Conceptual Structure and Group Processes in an Inter-Nation Simulation*, Research Bulletin RB-62-15, Educational Testing Service and Princeton University, Princeton, N.J., 1962.

5. Dina A. Zinnes, "Comparison of Hostile Behavior," p. 477.

4. *The frequency of interaction* between two states as measured by the number of messages sent by x to y, denoted by xIy.[6]

The following thirteen hypotheses explore the effects of alliance systems or blocs on perceptions; the relationship between perception, on the one hand, and expression of hostility and amount of interaction on the other; and, in turn, the consequences of expressions of hostility on subsequent perceptions, expressions, and interactions.

Hypothesis 1. Nations outside the bloc will be seen as more threatening (xTy) than nations within the bloc.

Hypothesis 2. Nations outside the bloc will be seen as more unfriendly (xUy) than nations within the bloc.

Hypothesis 3. There will be more hostility transmitted (xEy) between blocs than within blocs.

Hypothesis 4. There is a positive relationship between perceptions of threat (xTy) and perceptions of unfriendliness (xUy).

Hypothesis 5. There is a positive relationship between x's expression of hostility to y (xEy) and y's perception of threat (yTx).

Hypothesis 6. There is a positive relationship between x's expression of hostility to y (xEy) and y's perception of unfriendliness (yUx).

Hypothesis 7. There is a positive relationship between the perception of threat (xTy) and the expression of hostility (xEy).

Hypothesis 8. There is a positive relationship between the perception of unfriendliness (xUy) and the expression of hostility (xEy).

Hypothesis 9. There is a positive relationship between x's expression of hostility to y (xEy) and y's expression of hostility back to x (yEx).

Hypothesis 10. Frequency of interaction (xIy) within the bloc will be greater than frequency of interaction between blocs.

Hypothesis 11. There is a negative relationship between the perception of threat (xTy) and the frequency of interaction (xIy), that is, the greater the perceived threat the less the interaction.

Hypothesis 12. There is a negative relationship between the perception of unfriendliness (xUy) and the frequency of interaction (xIy).

Hypothesis 13. There is a negative relationship between x's hostility to y (xEy) and y's frequency of interaction with x (yIx).[7]

It will be noted that a good bit of the entire decision dynamic is at least touched upon in these formulations. The relationship between reality and perception (Hypotheses 5 and 6), as potentially modified by perception bias (Hypotheses 1 and 2), results in a related set of perceptions (Hypothesis 4) that yield hostile and/or communicative behavior (Hypotheses 7, 8, 11, 12, and 13). Accordingly, these propositions may constitute a useful baseline for movement toward a more integrated theory of crisis decision making.

That theoretical development, however, requires knowledge beyond the substantiation of the Zinnes hypotheses. What is the relationship between alliance conditions and perceptions of potential enemies? Does alliance cohesion affect a leader's perception of threat and hostility from outside the bloc? In turn, what effect has such perceived threat upon the state of alliance systems? Similarly, what is the relationship between expressed hostility (e.g., escalation)

6. *Ibid.*, p. 476.

7. *Ibid.*, p. 476ff.

and other communicated acts in crises? How do behavior preferences mediate between perception and behavior.

As with any successful piece of research, additional work is encouraged both by what has been accomplished and by what has been left undone. We shall see below that other vital questions flow from the results and interpretation of Zinnes' work. As indicated, we have retested the fundamental propositions and used them in building a somewhat more complete theory of crisis behavior.

The organization of this chapter is as follows. First, the research designs the author used to test the Zinnes hypotheses are presented. Then, the designs and findings from the author's studies are compared with those of Zinnes and of Brody. Third, some new findings which may account for similarities and differences among the studies are set forth. Finally, an effort is made at a preliminary synthesis and interpretation of the studies.

TWO RESEARCH DESIGNS: HISTORICAL CASES AND SIMULATION

Variables in case studies. In the first of the two research projects, we were primarily interested in the influence of strategic factors such as weapons systems and force structures on crisis decision making. Therefore, perceptions of strategic factors served as the independent variables. Other decision-relevant perceptions, like threat and hostility, constituted intervening variables which were expected to link strategic perceptions to crisis behavior—the dependent variable. In addition, some variables descriptive of crisis contexts were included in order to identify and consider various relationships between situational-systemic variables and decision-perceptual factors. The relationships between all these variables were observed in a commonly conceptualized set of historical cases—that is, cases to which were applied a common operational definition of crisis and a comparable set of time periods. The overall research project, described elsewhere,[8] is not relevant to the immediate concerns of this chapter. What is relevant, however, is the inclusion of five variables in the study that can be used to investigate the Zinnes hypotheses. These variables were as follows:

1. *Perceived threat*. This variable concerns the degree of anticipated harm to the nation observed in both the semantics of crisis communication (such as "serious," "grave," "awesome," "calamitous") and in the character of situational fears (such as loss of prestige, loss of strategic bases, loss of bloc partners, attack on nation). It should be evident that this variable is similar to Zinnes' "perception of threat."

2. *Perceived opposing hostility*. This variable, intended to correspond to Zinnes' "perception of unfriendliness," represents the degree to which salient others are seen as intending harm to the nation as observed in strategic and tactical operations and diplomatic actions. The factors utilized in assessing perceived hostility included the perception of others' intentions, negotiability, and reasonableness.

3. *Use of strategic forces*. This variable includes the level of alert, deployment, and/or dispersal of long-range bombers and missiles, including sea-based missiles and such support capabilities as refueling tankers and systems for

8. David C. Schwartz, "Decision Theories and Crisis Behavior," *Orbis*, 11 (Summer 1967), 459–490.

command and control of these weapons systems. This variable and the one below correspond to the Zinnes variable, "expression of hostility."

4. *Use of tactical forces*. This variable consists of the level of alert, deployment, maneuver, and firepower expended by general purpose (that is, non-strategic) forces.

5. *Receptivity to communications*. This variable comprises the degree to which top-level decision makers initiate, maintain, and attend to information-seeking behavior such as the dispatch of envoys and observers, the receival of foreign diplomats, requests for clarification of positions, and the use of special communications media and processes. Receptivity to communications will be compared to the Zinnes variable described as "frequency of interaction."

Selecting the historical crises. For this exploratory study, we defined crisis as a hostile confrontation of two or more nations arising from conflicting policies toward a geographic or problem area which, by virtue of the use or suggested use of force, engenders a substantial increase in and high level of tension.

In addition, two classifications of these crises have seemed most useful: (1) the level of crisis as defined by the quality or quantity of committed capability (military and political); and (2) the directness of crisis confrontation as, for example, a clash between the United States and the Soviet Union, rather than between allies or "proxies." In order to facilitate a more detailed evaluation of strategically relevant influence, crisis *periods* were divided into three phases: initiation of crisis, peak of crisis, and resolution of crisis.

We selected eight major crises of the nuclear age as examples of crisis decision making. Our interest in the contemporary international setting suggested that we include only post-1950 crises. Beyond this, a sensitivity to the potential importance of regional differences argued for including cases representing considerable geographic diversity. Accordingly, we selected the following crises for investigation: Korea (1950), Suez (1956), Lebanon (1958), Quemoy (1958), Berlin (1961), Cuban missile crisis (1962), Tonkin Gulf (1964), Cyprus (1964).

To divide the crisis into separable periods for analysis, an extensive annotated chronology of events for each crisis was developed from the *New York Times*, *Foreign Broadcast Information Service*, *Deadline Data*, public documents and research memoranda, as well as the professional literature on these crises. From these chronologies we established: (1) the initiation phase of each crisis—that is, the time period in which initial deviation from pre-existing arrangements, tension levels, and so on, occurred; (2) the peak period, that is, that period wherein the major strategic, tactical, diplomatic, and economic operations were carried out and wherein, apparently, basic decisions were taken; and (3) the resolution-of-crisis stage, wherein relatively persistent arrangements, tension levels, and so on were established. Table 1 summarizes the crises and the observation points in the crises with which we worked.

Estimating variables in cases. The first step in the measurement procedures was to score the magnitude of each variable as perceived by Soviet and American leaders during the initiation, peak, and resolution of the selected crises. Each variable was operationalized using a "guideline index," with explicit coding rules but with some limited discretion left to the coder on weighting procedures.

This procedure was employed because our coders included high-level military and diplomatic personnel whose personal knowledge of American—and, in one case, Soviet—perceptions in crises seemed as important as absolutely identical weighting procedures. The indicators were researched in the same open sources as were the chronologies. The author developed the guideline indexes in conjunction with the professional staff of the Foreign Policy Research Institute. In obtaining a score for each variable in each crisis period, two to six coders reviewed the published material. Acceptable levels of intercoder agreement were consistently achieved.

In the second step, the researchers observed and recorded the direction of changes in perceptions between the initiation and peak of crises and between peaks and resolutions. A third step involved a determination of the relationships

TABLE 1. THE SAMPLE OF CRISES STUDIED BY HISTORICAL-ANALYTIC METHODS

Crisis	*Year*	*Initiation*	*Peak*	*Resolution*
Korea	1950	June 24–25	June 26–29	June 30–July 1
Suez	1956	Oct. 29–Nov. 3	Nov. 4–6	Nov. 7
Lebanon	1958	July 14–15	July 16–19	July 20–Aug. 3
Quemoy	1958	Aug. 29–31	Sept. 1–7	Sept. 8–Oct. 15
Berlin	1961	Feb.–June	July–Sept.	Oct.–Dec.
Cuba	1962	Oct. 22–24	Oct. 25–27	Oct. 28
Tonkin	1964	Aug. 2–3	Aug. 4	Aug. 5
Cyprus	1964	Aug. 8–9	Aug. 10–11	Aug. 12–15

between intensity levels and directional changes in any given time period for every pair of variables. Fourth, the researchers computed the frequency of association, that is, the number of crises or crisis time periods in which the hypothesized relationship held.

Design of the simulation. In order to generate a body of data sufficient to support statistically meaningful interferences, to increase observational control (i.e., to manipulate the model and the setting of crisis decision making), and to overcome difficult problems of access to real crisis decision makers, it was decided to conduct a large-scale simulation study. The simulations were to be sufficiently similar to the historical research to provide comparable data, of course, but there were also some differences (principally some additions and refinements). In brief, we utilized the same variables in the second study as in the first, but added some new factors in order to examine the bases of alliance cohesion and its consequences for crisis behavior.

The international setting for the simulation paralleled that for the case studies—that is, we attempted to represent the essential structures, processes, and constraints of the post-1950 international system. Our board of consultants found substantial "face validity" in the simulation's representation of selected features of the international system. Five of the eight crises which had been used as historical case studies were selected for the simulation: Korea, Suez, Berlin, Cuba, and Tonkin Gulf. These situations were presented to the subjects as disguised historical scenarios in seriatim fashion. Each scenario represented the crisis situation at the initiation of the crisis and the subjects played through the peak period.

The basic experimental form used in this project was a multiple-team, multiple-move period, manual gaming exercise with one individual or a small group of players representing the decision structure of abstract nation-states. Pregame indoctrination programs and background papers provided instruction for the roles. Move periods were discontinuous. Game time generally telescoped real time but was established with reference to processes dependent upon certain real-time relationships (for example, saliency and memory-forgetting).

Students at the University of Pennsylvania served as subjects. The selection of participants was based, wherever possible, on a "political knowledge—political awareness" filter. Subjects received $1.75 per hour for their participation.

Measurement techniques used in the simulation included: (1) questionnaires administered before, during, and after the game; (2) analysis (including content analysis) of formal moves, of required strategy papers, and of briefings to the investigators by game participants; (3) rapporteurs and interpersonal analysis of decision making and group interaction (as recorded on tape); (4) administration of standardized personality schedules and other psychological instruments.

We ran 45 experiments, a total of 225 gross "moves," observed 411 subjects and—except for escalation data—made 2,393 observations for each item on both our premove and postmove questionnaires. The escalation material was developed from a content analysis of behavioral (not questionnaire) responses. Intercoder reliability for the escalation measure was approximately .90 (determined by double-coding every tenth message).

Three variations. We employed three basic experimental variations which involved changes in the number of players per side, the number of moves, and the type of communications. In each type of experiment, subjects were: (1) informed as to experimental purposes and procedures; (2) taught an experimental role and experimental history and culture; (3) tested as to learning; (4) presented with a series of world and alliance problems (by scenario, one world and one alliance problem per move); (5) subjected to a premove questionnaire; (6) asked to react behaviorally (to "make moves," and send messages, commit resources, etc.) to the problems; (7) subjected to a postmove questionnaire to ascertain what changes their action caused, even in the absence of information on success; (8) requested intermittently to make budget allocations; (9) subjected to a postgame instrument; (10) debriefed.

In the first series of games there were six moves, six individual players per game, and all communications (one round of messages) were handled by a control team which made all responses for the purpose of experimental manipulation. Thirty such experiments were conducted.

We used a flexible preprogrammed set of experimenter responses to subject moves in order to control restimulation in directions and degrees which comported with the actual historical events. If, for a given real-world alliance, the historical pattern of national satisfactions (S) and dissatisfactions (D) over the outcomes of our modeled crises were, say, S–D–S–D–D, then the simulation subject received from control written outcomes to his moves which replicated this pattern—irrespective of the content of his moves. These preprogrammed manipulations were pretested for clarity and experimental effect. In the second series of games individual decision makers played through three of the standardized moves with three rounds of free communications. Also, there was a third series, consisting of five games, which had teams of three players per side play through three moves.

Validating the simulation. We utilized a "mixed strategy" of simulation validation. Initially, to ascertain the structural constraints of international alliances and their effects on national decision makers, scholars expert in the organization and history of NATO, SEATO, and OAS constructed a set of requirements for our experiments and background papers, then checked these and the operation of the games to insure that their specifications were being met. This is a form of both input validation and operational validation.

To be certain that our experimental manipulation of satisfaction patterns modeled the real world, "cohesional histories" of the three alliances were written. The conflict patterns introduced and the experimental manipulation were selected to match these histories. This is an example of input validation. The outcomes of the games were checked by the expert scholars for "cultural consonance." This is a new form of output validation in which events generated in games are checked not only against history (an event output validation) but for "fit" with the behavior-repertoire of the alliance or regional culture.

A BRIEF COMPARISON OF THE BRODY, ZINNES, AND SCHWARTZ DESIGNS

As noted previously, Zinnes' comparative essay is based upon simulation data generated by Brody and Driver utilizing the now widely known Inter-Nation Simulation and upon her own content analysis of communications between the six major states which participated in the six-week European crisis preceding the outbreak of World War I. The research designs of both these studies have been described in detail elsewhere.[9] Accordingly, the very brief descriptions of those projects in this section are intended merely to permit specification of the similarities and differences between those two studies and the research just described.

The comparability of the four studies depends upon two related matters. First, the similarity—if not isomorphism—of the measures of basic variables; and, second, the similarity in the conceptual meanings and the referents of the concepts. The former is the easier matter to determine; the latter raises certain fundamental questions about cross-project comparisons.

Perception of threat (*xTy*) was measured by Brody in a system-exogenous fashion. Simulation participants were asked to rate on a nine-point scale the likelihood of each of the other six nations becoming involved in a war with their nation. Zinnes, noting that Brody's measure concerns the intensity of a perception about future events, scanned the memos, messages, and so on of her 1914 decision makers for "perceptions of hostility statements made in the future tense."[10] As with most of these variables, our historical studies resemble Zinnes' procedures; our simulation measures are similar to Brody's. Threat, in the case studies, was assessed by aggregating decision-maker statements *both* as to the intensity and emotionality of each relevant phrase and as to the gravity of the

9. In addition to the previously cited references to Zinnes, Brody, and Driver, see the chapter by Zinnes in this volume for a somewhat related analysis.

10. Dina A. Zinnes, "Comparison of Hostile Behavior," p. 482ff. For a description of the scale see Brody, "Some Systemic Effects," item 2, p. 749.

envisaged future situation. For example, general war was rated as more threatening than limited war. In the simulation we inquired directly as to threat perceived by the subjects which emanated from "this world problem" as well as from other future-oriented situational fears. Thus our measure is less oriented to a specific situation. The original four-point, forced-choice scale, which offered no neutral point, was treated dichotomously in this analysis.

Perception of unfriendliness (*xUy*) was ranked on a nine-point scale in Brody's work where it was designated as "the friendliness to your nation of the other six nations."[11] Zinnes interpreted this as an intensity measure of past and present hostility statements and scanned her materials accordingly. Our simulation questionnaires asked participants to rate their perceived hostility emanating from the abstract surrogates of the Soviet Union and Communist China on an eight-point scale. For the analysis in this chapter, the scale was collapsed to a dichotomy between high and low perceived hostility.

Expression of hostility (*xEy*) was measured by Brody from a content analysis of messages in his simulation. Zinnes sought the intensity levels of all expressions of hostility in her 1914 data. Both of these are derived from system-endogenous sources. So, too, are those in the author's studies. In the historical case studies the intensity of expressed hostility was measured in terms of strategic and tactical forces and declaratory policy regarding those forces. In the simulation study we rated the intensity of all moves that expressed increases in hostility. Unlike those in the Brody and Zinnes studies, these measures are based more on action data than on message content, a fact which may raise questions regarding comparability but which also makes the findings relevant to the relationship of verbal to nonverbal crisis behavior.

Similarly, the author's studies used a somewhat different measure of communications between nations in crisis. Whereas both Brody and Zinnes counted the number of messages exchanged, this procedure did not seem feasible for the real crises of the nuclear era. Accordingly, in both the historical cases and their simulates, we concentrated on the desire for, receptivity to, and satisfaction with, crisis communications. These variables may be regarded as the behavioral tendencies or preferences of decision makers in crises and hence may help to explain some findings of Brody and Zinnes.

If the similarities (and recognized differences) between the procedures of the four studies suggest that we may cautiously compare at least some of their results as independent-but-linked tests of the same hypotheses, there are some additional problems of comparability which are not immediately procedural. I refer to the comparability of the settings of research and, more basically, to the conceptual meanings and referents of the variables.

Clearly, the international system under investigation was very different in the four studies. The alliances of 1914 contrast sharply with the more institutionalized, semipermanent blocs of the 1950–1964 period. In the former, lasting loyalties contravene the rules of the international system, whereas in the latter they constitute part of the norms of international life. Brody's abstract simulated alliances, too, are different in size, structure, character, and constraints from the real-modeled alliance structures we examined. The resources, power factors, decision structures, and obviously the personnel of nations in crisis are very different.

11. Brody, "Some Systemic Effects," item 1, p. 749.

But these differences offer a potential strength of this kind of comparison. One can intuitively assert, of course, that the world of 1914 is no more. One can counter-hypothesize that human nature is at best considerably similar across such short time spans as fifty years. Such intuitions and speculations may be the beginning of inquiry; they must not be its resting place. Through the reasonably systematic comparison of these researches, we may hope to determine how our era and Brody's simulated "multinuclear future" are similar to the recent past. We seek to know not whether, but in what ways, humans in crisis react similarly across history.

We take a similar position on the conceptual differences between these studies. Is "threat" the same thing in the Europe of 1914 as in Havana, Washington, Moscow, or Hanoi today? The answer may be found, in part, by determining whether in studies of more recent crises threat produces the same effects as those found in the 1914 case. In sum, these studies seem similar enough to be comparable, but different enough to be interesting.

RESULTS

The results from the four studies on the thirteen hypotheses advanced by Zinnes are treated first in numerical order. Then, with the addition of new data from the author's studies, the findings are used to consider a possible theory of crisis decision making. Before proceeding with the results, a brief description should be given of the nature of the data reported from the author's two studies.

The variable magnitudes identified in our historical case studies are shown in Tables 2 and 3. The vertical space of each cell is to be construed as a ten-point scale; the three bars in each cell represent the assessed variable magnitude at the initiation, peak, and resolution of a crisis, respectively. A variety of simple statistical tests, including the Fisher exact probabilities test and the chi square, were performed on these data but—owing to the extremely small sample size—the results seem better presented discursively from simple inspection and interpretation of the data. The generalizations regarding crisis behavior drawn from this material are advanced within the limitations of the approximate character and restricted scope of the data.

The data generated in our simulation study were analyzed initially by simple cross-tabulations. These results will be presented discursively. Unless otherwise noted, all relationships reported were statistically significant using chi-square tests ($p \leq .01$).

Comparison of results. The first three of Zinnes' hypotheses postulate that perceptions of threat, unfriendliness, and expressions of hostility will be greater between two nations belonging to different alliances than between two nations within the same bloc. These assertions may seem intuitively obvious today, but the findings prove of somewhat greater consequence for the 1914 case by suggesting some limits on the "game of musical alliances" which sometimes seemed to characterize the pre–World War I international system. Moreover, from these generally confirmed formulations, we might inquire how great the ratio of ingroup to outgroup hostility must be in order to maintain the alliance—that is, what is the "switching matrix" of alliance maintenance? No data collected on the historical case studies applied to these three initial hypotheses, nor did the author's simulation data permit an evaluation of the third. However, each of

TABLE 2. ASSESSMENTS OF AMERICAN PERCEPTIONS IN EIGHT CASE STUDIES OF CRISIS

Variables	*Korea*	*Suez*	*Lebanon*	*Quemoy*	*Berlin*	*Cuba*	*Tonkin*	*Cyprus*
Use of strategic forces								
Use of tactical forces								
Level of threat								
Level of opposing hostility								
Receptivity to communication								
	I P R	*I P R*	*I P R*	*I P R*	*I P R*	*I P R*	*I P R*	*I P R*

NOTE: *I* = Initiation period of crisis.
P = Peak period of crisis.
R = Resolution period of crisis.

TABLE 3. ASSESSMENTS OF SOVIET PERCEPTIONS IN EIGHT CASE STUDIES OF CRISIS

Variables	*Korea*	*Suez*	*Lebanon*	*Quemoy*	*Berlin*	*Cuba*	*Tonkin*	*Cyprus*
Use of strategic forces								
Use of tactical forces								
Level of threat								
Level of opposing hostility								
Receptivity to communication								
	I P R	*I P R*	*I P R*	*I P R*	*I P R*	*I P R*	*I P R*	*I P R*

NOTE: *I* = Initiation period of crisis.
P = Peak period of crisis.
R = Resolution period of crisis.

these alliance-relevant propositions was supported in the studies that allowed their investigation. Table 4 summarizes the results of the four-study comparisons for the initial three hypotheses as well as for the others advanced by Zinnes.

Hypothesis 4 suggests a positive correlation between the decision makers' perception of threat to their nation from another state and their perception that the other state is unfriendly. All four studies furnished data on this fundamental hypothesis, and in each study the hypothesis was confirmed. As shown in Table 4, data from the historical crises may be used both to convey an overall pattern and to indicate the separate perceptions of Soviet and American policy makers in different periods or phases of the crisis. With respect to Hypothesis 4, the shift in perceptions from one period in a crisis to another supports the proposition from both the American and Soviet viewpoints.

Hypotheses 5 through 9 deal with relationships involving the expression of hostility by policy makers in one state toward those in another. Regarding these hypotheses, both the strategic and tactical force variables are used to indicate the amount of expressed hostility in the historical cases. The fifth hypothesis contends that x's expressed hostility to y is positively related to y's perception of x as threatening. Except for the author's simulation, which provided no data on the hypothesis, the studies confirm the relationship.

A positive relationship is asserted in Hypothesis 6 between x's expressed hostility to y and y's perception that x is unfriendly. Again, no data gathered in the author's simulation apply to this hypothesis. The other three studies, however, confirm the relationship. This confirmation includes both the tactical and strategic measures of hostile expression in the historical cases.

Both the Brody and the author's simulations as well as the Zinnes study of the crisis prior to World War I confirm Hypothesis 7. That hypothesis indicates a positive relationship between x's perceived threat and x's expression of hostility. However, the two measures of hostile expression in the historical case studies yield conflicting results. For neither country is the strategic force expression of hostility associated with perceived threat, but the latter variable does seem to be related to the use of tactical forces by the United States.

Hypothesis 8 postulates that x's perceived unfriendliness toward y relates positively to x's expressed hostility toward y. The 1914 crisis research and both simulation studies support the hypothesis as do the estimates of American perceptions and behavior in the eight case studies. The hypothesis is disconfirmed with respect to the Soviet Union—suggesting, perhaps, that international power ratios constrain the ordinary relationship between these decision and behavior processes.

Hypothesis 9 asserts a reciprocal relationship between expressions of hostility. This important proposition pertains to the utility of escalation as a crisis response. If every expressed hostility produced counter-hostility, escalation would be a self-defeating strategy. This hypothesis—untestable with the author's simulation data—is supported by the Brody and Zinnes data but must be rejected in the author's analysis of eight crises during the Cold War. The differences among the international systems as presented in 1914, in the bipolarity of the Cold War, and in the Brody simulation provide potential explanations for the pattern of these findings.

The final set of hypotheses (10–13) relate to the interplay of perceptions and communications. Here Brody and Zinnes dealt with the volume of communications as an indicator of interaction. The author's studies concerned the

TABLE 4. A SUMMARY OF RESULTS FROM THE FOUR STUDIES

Hypothesis No.	*Brody Simulation*	*Zinnes 1914 Case*	*Schwartz Simulation*	*Schwartz Historical Cases*	*Proportion of Confirming Observations in Historical Crises**
1	Confirmed	Confirmed	Confirmed	Not directly testable	–
2	Confirmed	Confirmed	Confirmed	Not directly testable	–
3	Confirmed	Confirmed	Not directly testable	Not directly testable	–
4	Confirmed	Confirmed	Confirmed	Confirmed	U.S. 10 out of 13 S.U. 9 out of 11
5	Confirmed	Confirmed	Not directly testable	Confirmed	U.S. 13 out of 18 S.U. 8 out of 14
6	Confirmed	Confirmed	Not directly testable	Confirmed	U.S. 14 out of 18 S.U. 8 out of 14
7	Confirmed	Confirmed	Confirmed	Disconfirmed except with U.S. tactical forces	U.S. 5 out of 13 (strategic) U.S. 8 out of 13 (tactical) S.U. 3 out of 11 (strategic) S.U. 3 out of 11 (tactical)
8	Confirmed	Confirmed	Confirmed (.02)	Confirmed U.S., Disconfirmed S.U.	U.S. 12 out of 22 S.U. 8 out of 26
9	Confirmed	Confirmed	Not directly testable	Disconfirmed	U.S. 10 out of 36 S.U. 10 out of 28
10	†	Disconfirmed	Not directly testable	Not directly testable	–

11	†	Disconfirmed	Disconfirmed	Disconfirmed	U.S. 0 out of 13 S.U. 0 out of 11
12	Confirmed	Disconfirmed	Disconfirmed	Disconfirmed	U.S. 0 out of 11 S.U. 1 out of 13
13	Confirmed	Disconfirmed	Not directly testable	Disconfirmed	U.S. 1 out of 18 S.U. 2 out of 14

* This column gives the proportion of the total number of observations in the historical crises that support each hypothesis. Results for the United States (U.S.) and the Soviet Union (S.U.) are reported separately. In the next-to-last column from the right a hypothesis is reported as confirmed if the majority of the observed changes were in the predicted direction. The procedure for determining the total number of observations in each case is as follows: Each historical crisis was divided into three time periods (see Table 1) and judges rated every variable in each period. To explore the nine Zinnes hypotheses that were testable with our historical data, the change in a variable from one period to another was examined (that is, the change from Initiation to Peak, and from Peak to Resolution). Theoretically, there were sixteen potential shifts or changes in value for each variable across the eight crises. However, if the first named variable in a Zinnes hypothesis showed no change in value from one crisis period to the next, that potential observation was deleted from the analysis. The result is that some entries in the last column have an *N* that is less than sixteen. With those hypotheses (5–9 and 13) in which the Zinnes variable of "expression of hostility" was operationalized by combining both "use of strategic forces" and "use of tactical forces," the total number of observations or shifts can exceed sixteen.

† The hypothesis was confirmed in the simulation before nuclear proliferation occurred, but not afterward.

– Not directly testable.

desire for and/or receptivity to communications. Hypothesis 10 asserts that communication is more likely among alliance partners. We could not directly test this proposition but we can say that the perceived friendliness of allies, the perceived ease of communicating with them, and the degree of alliance cohesion are all positively related ($p \leq .05$). Hypotheses 11, 12, and 13 state negative expected relationships between perceptions of threat, unfriendliness, and expressed hostility, on the one hand, and frequency of interaction. In general, they were confirmed in the Brody simulations but they were not supported in the other studies.

These last findings pose an important problem: perceptions of threat and unfriendliness are associated with expressions of hostility but not with decreased communications. In our simulation study, however, we found a negative relationship between the desire to communicate with potential enemies and the adoption or recommendation of escalation ($p = .01$). The more one wants to communicate, the less likely is one to escalate. If perceived threat or unfriendliness cannot account for the behavior (communicate or escalate), what can? One possible answer involves the decision makers' perceptions and attitudes toward alliance cohesion. This potential explanation will be one of the topics explored in the final section.

COMPARISON AND BEYOND

Comparison. The results indicate both the utility and the constraints of the kind of cross-project, cross-system, cross-method comparisons attempted in this chapter. The four studies contain considerable areas of agreement. Not counting situations in which a hypothesis was not testable in one of the studies, the Zinnes 1914 study and the author's simulation agreed on all seven hypotheses; the Brody and the author's simulations agreed on five hypotheses, partly agreed on a sixth, and disagreed on only one; the Zinnes–Schwartz cases comported with each other on five, partly comported on three more, and were in contradistinction to each other on only one finding; the Brody simulation and the author's historical analysis agreed, or partly agreed, on six of the nine comparable hypotheses.

As useful as replications and retests are, great utility can also be derived from research which is basically comparable, but designed differently from the preceding studies. By including both strategic and tactical expressions of hostility, for example, we were able not only to compare verbal with military expressions of hostility, but also to indicate limitations and refinements in the posited relationships.

This last section of the chapter introduces a few additional relationships from the author's simulation study which refine and extend the initial hypotheses with respect to two questions: (1) When do decision makers recognize a conflict as a crisis? (2) What effect do alliances have on the decision to either escalate or communicate with an enemy? These new findings themselves are, of course, in need of replication, refinement, and retesting. If their presentation encourages such additional research, we shall move nearer to a theory of crisis behavior.

Recognition of crisis. When do decision makers perceive a conflict to be a crisis? This is a crucial question because it is part of the definition of the situation, so basic to any decision analysis. In our simulation study, we sought to determine the perceptual set associated with the recognition of crises. We found that crisis recognition in the simulation was primarily a function of the overall international system and of alliance considerations. All of the following relations are significant at the .01 level or better unless otherwise noted.

1. A perception of world threat to the nation is positively related to the recognition or definition of a conflict situation as a crisis.
2. A perception that the conflict deals with important political issues is positively related to crisis recognition.
3. A perception that a world problem poses a threat to one's alliance is positively related to crisis recognition.
4. A sense of national efficacy to reduce world threats is negatively related to crisis recognition; the less efficacious one feels, the more conflicts are defined as crises.
5. A perception that the international political system (environment) is warlike is positively related to crisis recognition.
6. A perception that one's potential or actual enemies are hostile is positively related to crisis recognition.

As noted in the presentation of the research design, the simulation devoted considerable attention to the role of alliances. In a system where alliances play a major role in the foreign policy behavior of states, the simulation data supported the following hypotheses:

7. A perception of threat emanating from the alliance is positively related to crisis recognition.
8. When the threat from both one's alliance and the rest of the external world is high, national decision makers perceive a crisis. When world threat seems high but alliance threat is low, the situation is significantly less likely to be deemed critical. *Alliance conditions do importantly affect international conflict; they can be tension multipliers or conflict control agents.*
9. A perception of low alliance cohesion is positively related to the definition of a conflict as a crisis ($p = .05$).
10. A perception of the alliance as inefficacious to meet world threats also significantly correlates with crisis recognition.
11. When the best-perceived alternative alliance is also perceived to be ineffective, crisis recognition results. (This proposition is an example of the "switching matrix" problem mentioned earlier.)
12. If one's allies seem unpredictable, decision makers increasingly perceive world problems as crises ($p = .05$).

Alliances, cohesion, and escalation. Alliance variables do more than influence the perceived friendliness or threat posed by another nation (Zinnes' Hypotheses 1 and 2) and they do more than affect the decision makers' recognition of a conflict as a crisis (supplemental Hypotheses 7–12). The simulation study examined alliance cohesion—a variable which allows us to choose between several intuitively plausible, but mutually inconsistent, hypotheses. Consider the question—raised elsewhere[12]—as to whether alliances are instruments of national policy or become ends in themselves. If alliances were the ends and not the

12. Arnold Wolfers, *Discord and Collaboration* (Baltimore: Johns Hopkins Press, 1962).

means of policy, one might expect nations to escalate conflicts in order to increase a low perceived level of alliance cohesion. Such activity did not occur in our simulation, reinforcing the position that alliances remain instrumentalities. Another set of rival hypotheses results from the observation that low alliance cohesion often creates tension. Do nations pursue escalatory policies as a function of the tension created by low cohesion or do they escalate only when high alliance cohesion engenders confidence? Our data suggest an answer. *Nations may tend to perceive crises when cohesion is low but they tend to adopt or recommend escalation of those crises only when cohesion seems high. In the presence of sufficient world threat to make conflicts into crises, alliance cohesion and its determinants augur for escalation. If cohesion continues to appear low, nonescalatory behaviors are likely.*

These findings lead to the following additional hypotheses confirmed in the simulation:

13. The perception that an alliance is efficacious to reduce world threat is positively related to escalation ($p = .05$).

14. A perception that cohesion will be important in order that the alliance be efficacious to reduce world threat is positively related to escalation ($p = .05$).

15. Cohesive behavior is positively related to escalation ($p = .02$).

We now possess the information necessary to chart a plausible "perception-to-behavior" process, which may predict the decision to adopt escalatory or nonescalatory crisis policies in nations which are part of a system dominated by alliances. Given a situation in which sufficient perceived world threat and enemy hostility exist to generate the recognition of a crisis, one of the following relationships confirmed in the simulation study may account for the outcome.

When the alliance is perceived as efficacious by a nation's decision makers, who exhibit cohesive alliance behaviors, escalatory behavior is likely. When the alliance is seen as inefficacious, nonescalatory behaviors are likely, regardless of the attitude of the decision makers toward the necessity for a cohesive alliance. When the alliance is seen as cohesive and efficacious by the decision makers, who exhibit noncohesive behaviors toward the alliance, nonescalatory behaviors are likely.

In summary, this chapter has presented hypotheses that relate perceptions in crisis to expressions of hostility and escalation. Initially, the two studies of the author provided a further test of the thirteen hypotheses which Zinnes investigated with her own data and with that of Brody. In this final section additional data from the author's simulation research have been used to extend the inquiry. Specifically, we have sought to explain when conflicts are recognized as crises and the circumstances under which crises lead not only to hostile expressions but to escalation when the nations are part of an alliance system.

chapter nine

EDITOR'S INTRODUCTION

The second chapter in this section uses simulation for different purposes than those which guided the preceding study by Schwartz. As in the Schwartz chapter, data generated from repeated trials of a simulation provide evidence gathered to explore specific hypotheses. In this chapter, however, the investigation of the particular hypotheses serves as a means of addressing three larger questions concerning the study of crisis. How appropriate is simulation as a research method for the study of international crises? Of what empirical and theoretical utility is the concept of crisis when it is defined in terms of high threat, short decision time, and surprise? And, finally, if crisis is defined as in the previous sentence, does it make much difference whether the components of crisis are ascertained by the individuals or groups experiencing the crisis rather than by knowledgeable observers?

When one encounters simulation techniques for the first time, one may ask whether simulations tell us anything about the "real world." As natural as this question may be, it offers a blunt and imprecise form of inquiry for making sound evaluations. In some areas simulations have proven of value to their users, as in training astronauts and airline pilots or in allowing television networks to project the outcomes of elections from quite incomplete returns. In some other areas the utility of simulation is open to serious doubt. Therefore, the initial broad inquiry might be more appropriately formulated in terms of such questions as: Are any existing simulations "valuable" (defined according to some specific criteria) for the particular problem in which one is interested? Regardless of the existence of a usable simulation, are there properties of the problem that make unlikely the applicability of some—or all—kinds of simulation and gaming techniques? Questions like these should be addressed to those games and simulations used to explore crises. Aside from simulations of voting behavior, political scientists probably have employed simulations and games more frequently to represent aspects of crisis behavior than for any other purpose. Frequently, one either has had to reject the findings of such simulations out of hand or accept their relevance to actual crises on faith. We need to begin the systematic evaluation of these techniques specifically for crisis research.

In addition to exploring the relevance of simulation techniques, this chapter makes an initial effort to investigate one definition of crisis. By now the reader should be familiar with the definition of crisis advanced by the editor and James A. Robinson (see Chapter 2). For scientific purposes the value of a definition rests on whether phenomena organized in terms of the definition are discovered to participate in law-like relationships with other phenomena. The proposed definition of crisis suggests that certain relationships should be different when a situation is characterized by high threat, short decision time, and surprise than when a situation has less than all three of these properties. Simulation allows us to vary the presence of these traits to see if the results are different between situations with, for example, only high threat and short time (but no surprise) and situations having all three properties. The author investigates five hypotheses, using different combinations of the stipulated crisis traits.

The third question addressed in the chapter inquires about the relationship between crises as defined by actors in the simulation and crises defined by observers of the simulation. This aspect of the research returns to a major issue for the contributors of Part III of the volume (Chapters 6 and 7). Wolfers once wrote that the need to know the perspective of the policy maker in a situation varied according to the circumstances under consideration. As an illustration of conditions in which knowledge of the individual policy maker would not be required, he cited the case of a number of individuals who find themselves inside of a house on fire. "It would be perfectly realistic to expect that these individuals, with rare exception, would feel compelled to run for the exits. General fear of losing the cherished possession of life, coupled with the stark external threat to life, would produce the same reaction, whatever the psychological peculiarities of the actors."[1] That particular analogy invites the inference that crises, in general, may be one type of situation in which one can dispense with data on the perceptions of the policy makers. This chapter explores this issue by comparing the results of crisis when *observers* determine that the three stipulated properties of crisis are present with the results when the simulation *participants* indicate that the crisis traits are present. If crises are situations in which the stimulus appears so overwhelming that the response depends little on the specific perceptions of the policy makers, then the fit between our simulation actors and observers should be reasonably high.

The book editor and author of this chapter is an Associate Professor of Political Science and Associate Director of the Mershon Center for Research and Education in Leadership and Public Policy at Ohio State University. He has authored several previous publications on crisis research, including *Crises in Foreign Policy* which draws on the same simulation experiment as the present chapter.[2] This chapter, however, reports for the first time the values of each of the three crisis properties as determined from the *a priori* estimates of the experimenters. These new data have a number of implications. First, they permit the more complex analysis of variance design for which the simulation was intended. Second, they allow the use of data from all 360 experimental situations and not just a sample of them. Third, they make possible the use of the interaction effect as the operational indicator of crisis. And, finally, they establish a method for determining the extent to which the runs were actually replications of one another and for determining the impact of the nation variable.

1. Arnold Wolfers, "The Actors in International Politics," in William T. R. Fox, ed., *Theoretical Aspects of International Relations* (Notre Dame, Ind.: University of Notre Dame Press, 1959), p. 94.

2. In addition to Charles F. Hermann's *Crises in Foreign Policy* (Indianapolis: Bobbs-Merrill, 1969), see his "Some Consequences of Crisis Which Limit the Viability of Organizations," *Administrative Science Quarterly*, 8 (June 1963), 61–82; "An Attempt to Simulate the Outbreak of World War I" (with Margaret G. Hermann), *American Political Science Review*, 61 (June 1967), 400–416; "International Crisis as a Situational Variable," in James N. Rosenau, ed., *International Politics and Foreign Policy* (New York: The Free Press, 1969), rev. ed., pp. 409–421; and "Search Under Crisis in Political Gaming and Simulation" (with James A. Robinson and Margaret G. Hermann) in Dean G. Pruitt and Richard C. Snyder, eds., *Theory and Research on the Causes of War* (Englewood Cliffs, N.J.: Prentice-Hall, 1969), pp. 80–94.

chapter nine

THREAT, TIME, AND SURPRISE: A SIMULATION OF INTERNATIONAL CRISIS*

Charles F. Hermann

DEFINITION OF CRISIS

The Introduction to this volume noted the absence of agreement on the definition of crisis among policy makers, journalists, and scholars. An even greater problem than the divergent definitions of crisis is created by those who use the term and leave to their audience the task of assigning it a meaning. A vague and loosely applied concept has no real value for identifying a class of situations about which useful knowledge can be accumulated. To have utility for scientific theories, crisis must be rigorously defined so that any competent individual can reliably determine whether or not a particular occurrence constitutes a crisis. Not only must the class of phenomena be readily identifiable, but as a set they must enter into theoretical relationships with other concepts. Simply put, the selection of certain events as crises must lead to some knowledge about the entire class of situations.

This research stipulates a definition of crisis.[1] Because of the absence of consensus on the meaning of the term, the definition will deviate from what many people assume to be a crisis. As noted, the utility of the definition depends upon our ability to incorporate the concept in empirically verifiable generalizations or hypotheses which are subsequently confirmed.

For this study a situation is said to be a crisis if, and only if, it (1) threatens one or more important goals of a state, that is, the group of authoritative policy makers who constitute the state, (2) allows only a short time for decision before the situation is significantly transformed, and (3) occurs as a surprise to the policy makers. Not all international situations commonly cited as crises conform to this definition, but a number of such situations do have these characteristics. For example, from the perspective of American policy makers, both the 1950 invasion of South Korea and the 1962 Soviet emplacement of offensive missiles

* In addition to the other contributors to this volume, who commented on this paper at our symposium on international crisis, the author wishes to acknowledge the participants on a panel at the 1967 annual meetings of the American Political Science Association. At that time a version of the paper was presented under the title, "International Crises: Theoretical Implications of Current Research." The panelists were Morton Kaplan, Robert Keohane, Charles McClelland, Linda Miller, and Oran Young. Harold Guetzkow also offered a number of useful comments on that paper.

1. The larger research project which provides the basis for this additional analysis was conducted under Contract N123 (60530) 32779A from Project Michelson at the U.S. Naval Ordnance Test Station, China Lake, Calif. A report of the research findings appears in Charles F. Hermann, *Crises in Foreign Policy* (Indianapolis: Bobbs-Merrill, 1969).

in Cuba were consistent with this definition of crisis. Both occasions constituted major threats to American objectives. With respect to Korea, the policy makers feared that unless they acted within a period of twenty-four to forty-eight hours that country would be overrun. Intelligence supplied President Kennedy and his advisers in the Cuban missile crisis indicated that medium-range ballistic missiles would be operational within a week of their discovery. Although intelligence sources recognized both situations as possibilities prior to their occurrence, the American government in each case had concluded that they were extremely unlikely. Each event came as a surprise.

It is the premise of this research that situations like the Korean and the Cuban crises usually involve certain kinds of processes and decisions unlikely to occur in other situations. More specifically, in situations involving high threat, short time, and surprise, certain behaviors are more likely than when none of these three attributes is present or when only one or two of them exists. Positive evaluation of the proposed definition of crisis depends upon confirmation of this macro hypothesis. Simulation served as the means for the systematic comparison of illustrative decision processes in situations differing in the amount of threat, decision time, and surprise.

USING SIMULATION TO STUDY CRISES

Games and simulations offer the increasing number of interested social scientists a type of model that can represent nonlinear changes in an evolving system. As appreciation of the simulation-gaming technique has grown so have its applications to the study of international crises. Members of the RAND Corporation, early users of gaming in the United States, viewed the analysis of crises as one of the principal reasons for developing the technique. In the RAND-type political games, teams of individuals assume the roles of national leaders to devise policies in response to a particular crisis described in a scenario. Such political gaming of crises has been conducted by governments, research groups, and teaching institutions.[2] Although the greatest number of studies have been conducted with exercises of the RAND variety, the examination of crisis has not been limited to all-man political games. For example, an all-computer simulation has been constructed to replicate the process of information selection and retention that decision makers are assumed to experience in handling crisis communications.[3] The author has been associated with crisis experiments that use still another kind of simulation—a hybrid involving both human participants and highly structured programs.[4]

2. For examples of the RAND Corporation studies see Herbert Goldhamer and Hans Speier, "Some Observations on Political Gaming," *World Politics*, 6 (October 1959), 71–83; Harvey Averch and Marvin M. Lavin, *Simulation of Decisionmaking in Crises*, RAND Memorandum RM-4202-PR, August 1964. For variations and extensions of the RAND type of gaming see Sidney F. Griffin, *The Crisis Game* (Garden City, N.Y.: Doubleday, 1965); Lincoln P. Bloomfield and Barton Whaley, "The Political-Military Exercise," *Orbis*, 8 (Winter 1965), 854–870. See also the previous chapter by David C. Schwartz.

3. Ithiel de Sola Pool and Allen Kessler, "The Kaiser, the Tsar and the Computer," *American Behavioral Scientist*, 8 (May 1965), 31–38.

4. Charles F. Hermann, *Crises in Foreign Policy*; Charles F. Hermann and Margaret G. Hermann, "An Attempt to Simulate the Outbreak of World War I,"

Given the considerable use of political games and simulations to study crises, it is noteworthy that the applicability of these techniques has been sharply questioned. One commentator has stated that "the emotional overtones which always characterize international crises can seldom—if ever—be simulated in the laboratory."[5] Another has observed: "Many simulations of hazardous military performance and missions, judged by experienced officers to be stressful, failed to yield behavior meeting these criteria."[6] Even a user of experimental gaming contends that "if a model of warfare ignores the pain, the fear, and the cost of war it cannot encompass the bargaining process. . . . Without explicit uncertainty it is hard to generate the phenomenon of brinksmanship—of competitive risk-taking, of the game of chicken."[7] If crises are extreme situations with risks of severe punishment and deprivation to those persons and social organizations involved, how can such circumstances be represented in an artificial, simulated system?

No one experiment can determine the appropriateness of the simulation-gaming technique for studying crises. Nevertheless, in this chapter we will make a conscious effort to consider the problem. First, we will direct particular attention to the amount of threat and other affect experienced by the participants; second, we will investigate selected propositions about crisis for which information is available from other sources. To some extent the applicability of the technique depends on the relationship between the manner in which crisis is defined and the kind of simulation employed. The proposed definition of crisis has been advanced. The specific type of simulation used for studying the concept was the Inter-Nation Simulation which will be described in general and then in the particular form used in the research.

Inter-Nation Simulation

This operating model, developed by Guetzkow and his associates,[8] combines the activity of human participants with a set of machine computations. In short, it is a mixed, man–machine simulation. The relationships between variables in the programmed calculations are the established part of the model that remain constant from one simulation trial or run to another. The participants, assigned in groups of two or more to one of several nations, assume roles in the foreign policy organization of their nation.

American Political Science Review, 61 (June 1967), 400–416; and James A. Robinson, Charles F. Hermann, and Margaret G. Hermann, "Search Under Crisis in Political Gaming and Simulation," in Dean Pruitt and Richard C. Snyder, eds., *Theory and Research on the Causes of War* (Englewood Cliffs, N.J.: Prentice-Hall, 1969), pp. 80–94.

5. Robert H. Davis, "The International Influence Process," *American Psychologist*, 21 (March 1966), 240.

6. Meredith P. Crawford, "Dimensions of Simulation," *American Psychologist*, 21 (August 1966), 794.

7. Thomas C. Schelling, "War Without Pain," *World Politics*, 15 (April 1963), 465–485.

8. More detailed descriptions of the Inter-Nation Simulation can be found in Harold Guetzkow, "A Use of Simulation in the Study of Inter-Nation Relations," *Behavioral Science*, 4 (July 1959), 183–191; and in Harold Guetzkow, Chadwick F. Alger, Richard A. Brody, Robert C. Noel, and Richard C. Snyder, *Simulation in International Relations* (Englewood Cliffs, N.J.: Prentice-Hall, 1963).

Nations in the simulation are not intended to correspond to any particular country that existed in the past or exists in the present. Accordingly, the participants do not assume identifiable offices, such as the Prime Minister of England or the Premier of the Soviet Union. Both the roles and the nations are abstractions that represent generalized properties, rather than replications that attempt to portray the details of a specific individual or political system. In a similar fashion, the crises introduced are hypothetical situations containing the designated crisis characteristics rather than representations of historical events.

The Inter-Nation Simulation operates in cycles or periods each sixty to seventy minutes long. In every period at least one exchange occurs between the machine and the human elements of the model. This exchange begins when the decision makers allocate the original resources of their nation in an effort to achieve their selected objectives. To remain in office, every government must successfully pursue at least one objective. Unless the national elites (military juntas, political parties, or other politically active sectors of society) are satisfied by the actions of the decision makers, the calculated programs will eventually indicate that these groups have established a new government. The elites or "validators" are symbolically represented in the programmed calculations. Their level of satisfaction with the government, reported each period to the decision makers, depends primarily on the amount of consumers' goods allocated to them and the relative military standing of their nation.

Nations have four kinds of resources: (1) *basic capabilities* represent the natural, human, and industrial resources of a nation required for the production of the other three kinds of resources as well as additional basic capabilities; (2) *consumption satisfaction* units portray the totality of goods and services available to the populace and reflect the nation's standard of living; (3) *nuclear force capabilities* symbolize nuclear weapon systems; and (4) *conventional force capabilities* constitute all non-nuclear military components. Allocations of these resources to remain in office, as well as for other policies, may involve internal development and a variety of interactions with other nations (for example, trades, alliances, wars).

Once each period, every nation summarizes the decisions they have made on a form submitted to the simulation's calculation staff. On the basis of the programmed assumptions, the consequences of a nation's decisions are computed (1) to determine whether the government continues in office, and (2) to fix the amount of resources (net gain or loss) now available to the decision makers. The results of these calculations are returned to the nation, and the cycle is repeated as the participants engage in a new round of interactions and decisions. A modification of this general simulation model provided the method for studying crisis.

Simulation of Crises

The crisis project involved ten replications or separate "worlds" of the Inter-Nation Simulation conducted at the Great Lakes Naval Training Center. Petty Officers in the United States Navy served as the simulation decision makers. The thirty men in each run were assigned one of five roles in any of six nations. Within each nation the experimenters appointed one individual as head of government, or Central Decision Maker (CDM), with ultimate authority for all governmental policies. Three other men assumed roles in the government as subordinates responsible to the CDM. The Internal Decision Maker (IDM) handled budgetary allocations; the External Decision Maker (EDM) conducted most foreign affairs; and the Force Decision Maker (FDM) controlled military matters. The occupant of a fifth role in the nation, the Aspiring Decision Maker (ADM), was not a member of the government. As the representative of rival elites within the country, the ADM attempted to replace the CDM as head of state.

The basic Inter-Nation Simulation model contains some organizational characteristics. The representation of organizational features required special attention, however, because the present research focused on the internal process by which nations handled foreign policy crises. To more fully incorporate organizational properties in the simulation, each nation contained (1) a detailed specification of roles, (2) an increase in bureaucratic complexity resulting from the construction of subgroups and mediated communication, and (3) an extended hierarchy of authority.[9]

Each of the six simulated nations operated by Navy men received a series of experimentally introduced situations. The situations varied in the amount of threat, time, and anticipation they offered the participants. Every effort was made to present each situation similarly through all ten runs in order that they might be treated as replications of one another.[10] To increase the comparability of the crises in each of the ten runs, a group of staff members posed as participants and initiated all the experimental situations. A ploy, to the effect that an insufficient number of men had appeared to participate, was used to explain the involvement of non-Navy personnel. Every situation was introduced as a prepared message from one of these confederates. The messages remained identical in all runs. The distinction between actor and observer perspectives arises with the question: Who determined the amount of threat, time, and surprise contained in the situation created by an experimental message?

ACTOR AND OBSERVER MEASUREMENTS OF CRISIS

Measures by Experimenters

The analysis involved two alternative measures of the dimensions of crisis to ascertain what differences exist between the actor and observer perspectives. For the observer measures, the experimenters[11] determined the amount of threat, time, and surprise contained in each specially induced message. They rated the threat present in each situation as high, moderate, or low according to four

9. For a review of the organizational literature on these properties and a fuller description of their incorporation in the Inter-Nation Simulation, see Charles F. Hermann, *Crises in Foreign Policy*, pp. 45–54.

10. A preliminary two-way analysis of variance using "nation" and "run" as independent variables was performed with each of the dependent variables reported in this study. Between runs a significant difference ($p \leq .05$) resulted with only one of the five variables (external communication). The analysis of differences between nations proved significant for three dependent variables and, therefore, the present research includes nation as one of the examined variables. With regard to replication, however, the important finding is the absence of any significant variation between the runs on four of the five variables.

11. In addition to the author, the experimenters in the project were James A. Robinson and Margaret G. Hermann.

criteria: (1) Was it likely that the source proposing the threat could execute it without external assistance? (2) If carried out, would the threat have blocked all means of reaching the goal? (3) Was the threat accompanied by some action, that is, physical commitment as opposed to merely a verbal warning? (4) If carried out, would the threat have involved violence, that is, military action? These criteria include elements of the nature of threat as mentioned by a number of writers.[12] When the experimenters agreed that the four questions representing the criteria could be answered affirmatively, then the situation involved high threat. Low threat resulted when none or only one of the criteria received affirmative ratings. If the experimenters gave positive ratings to two or three of the criteria, a moderate threat classification was assigned to the situation.

For any threat to be effective, it must obstruct some objective that motivates an individual or group. Therefore, the simulated nations had to be assigned goals and the participants had to be motivated to obtain them before the occurrence of an obstructing act would create a threat. Each of the six nations received three goals. Both positive and negative incentives were incorporated into the simulation to encourage goal achievement. A participants' manual, distributed several days before the exercise, stressed the importance of working toward the assigned goals to excel as a decision maker. Also before the simulation, the participants selected those goals they regarded as most important and received positions in a government having these goals. Calculations regularly estimated each nation's goal progress. Governments that advanced toward any given goal received a bonus in basic capabilities during the following period. In addition, they obtained an increase in their validator satisfaction scale indicating the pleasure of their elites with the progress. Nations experiencing a move away from any goal suffered a loss in validator satisfaction, thus increasing the probability that the existing government would lose office.

To measure the amount of decision time, the experimenters specified that all situations would be significantly altered after the lapse of either fifteen or fifty minutes. Those messages permitting fifteen minutes for response by the participants were designated short decision time situations, whereas those which changed after fifty minutes represented extended decision time situations. The experimenters based their judgment for estimating decision time on previous experience with the time required to make important decisions in the simulation. The fifteen minutes allocated for decision time attempted to rush the participants without physically preventing certain minimal activity that might be coded by observers as dependent variables.

The third component of crisis—surprise—occurred when the experimenters provided the participants with no advance warning of a situation that was subsequently thrust upon them. As indicated earlier, the confederates created an experimental situation at a given time by addressing a message to the target nation. In those cases to be defined as anticipated (i.e., nonsurprise), one of the confederates provided an indication of the event about to happen approximately thirty minutes in advance. These anticipative notices consisted of rumors

12. For discussions of threat that influenced the construction of these criteria, see Arthur Gladstone, "Threat and Responses to Threats," *Bulletin of Research Exchanged to Prevent War*, 3 (1955), 23–31; Thomas C. Schelling, *The Strategy of Conflict* (Cambridge: Harvard University Press, 1960); and Stephen B. Withey, "Reaction to Uncertain Threat," in George W. Baker and Dwight W. Chapman, eds., *Man and Society in Disaster* (New York: Basic Books, 1962), pp. 93–123.

reported by the newspaper or vague references communicated by one of the confederate nations. In each instance the advance notice suggested the general behavior that might occur, but it did not provide details. Interventions designated as surprises appeared without warning.

If each simulated nation had experienced the entire set of situations possible by combining the different levels of threat, time, and surprise, the nation's decision makers would have received twelve experimental interventions ($3 \times 2 \times 2 = 12$). The time available for the simulation did not permit such an elaborate design. Instead, each of the six nations led by Navy personnel experienced situations involving all three levels of threat (high, moderate, and low) and both short and extended decision time. In the even-numbered runs, half of the experimental situations directed at a given nation appeared as surprises. The three other situations (to be anticipated) occurred after an advance warning. The odd-numbered runs interchanged anticipated situations with those previously introduced as surprises. By combining the situations experienced in two runs, each of the six nations encountered the following set of situations:

Odd-Numbered Runs	Even-Numbered Runs
surprise/high threat/short time (crisis)	anticipated/high threat/ short time
anticipated/moderate threat/ short time	surprise/moderate threat/ short time
surprise/low threat/short time	anticipated/low threat/short time
anticipated/high threat/ extended time	surprise/high threat/extended time
surprise/moderate threat/extended time	anticipated/moderate threat/ extended time
anticipated/low threat/extended time	surprise/low threat/extended time

When some values of a variable or factor (in this case, surprise) occur in only one level of another factor (in this case, every other run), the two variables are said to be "nested." Described in statistical parlance, this experimental arrangement becomes a nested-factorial design.[13] For ease of comprehension, the list given above presents the situations in the same order for both odd- and even-numbered runs. In the actual simulation experiment, a randomizing process (an incomplete Latin Square) determined the order in which the situations occurred, thus ensuring that the sequence in which the situations appeared was different in each of the ten runs. Among other benefits, this procedure prevented an "experience effect" from being an important element in the overall results. Any pattern of decision that emerges from the accumulated findings of all the runs cannot be attributed to the constant appearance of the crisis situation at the end of the simulation after the decision makers have gained considerable experience; nor can the pattern be explained as a function of the early appearance of crisis in every run. The ten runs involved a total of 360 experimental situations with each nation receiving six induced situations in every run.

Using the experimenters' estimate of the crisis dimensions affords certain advantages. First, the efficiency and control of the experiment can be improved

13. B. J. Winer, *Statistical Principles in Experimental Design* (New York: McGraw-Hill, 1962), p. 184.

substantially because the experimenters' ratings can be obtained in advance of the simulation. We can be assured that each nation will receive every type of situation required by the design and these events will occur in the predetermined order. Second, and equally important, a participant may not be fully conscious of the relative degree of threat, time, or surprise present in a situation with which he is coping. Although his behavior may be affected by these elements, the participant may be unable to supply a reliable report.[14]

Measures by Participants

Whatever the merits of defining crisis from the perspective of the observer, strong arguments can also be made for the actors' perspective. If one chooses the decision-making approach, as we have done in this study, then the actors' perspective becomes extremely important. "What matters in policy-making," the Sprouts assert, "is how the milieu appears to the policy-maker, not how it appears to some sideline analyst or how it might appear to a hypothetical omniscient observer."[15] No situation, no matter how grave or foreboding, will influence a decision maker unless he perceives it. For this reason the participants —the actors in the simulation—provided measures of each crisis characteristic. Immediately after the deadline for responding to an experimental situation, the participants completed a questionnaire. This instrument included scales asking the decision makers to rate the amount of threat, decision time, and surprise that they had experienced. The mean scores of the participants in a simulated nation furnished a composite estimate of each crisis dimension for every experimental situation.

Using the participants' estimates of the amount of each of the three crisis characteristics, samples were drawn from the 360 experimental situations. The crisis sample consisted of the twenty-four situations the decision makers perceived to have had the highest threat, the shortest decision time, and the greatest surprise of all those introduced in the ten simulation runs. A noncrisis sample of equal size contained the situations perceived as involving the least threat, the most time, and the greatest anticipation. Together, the crisis and noncrisis situations constituted a pair of samples. To check the merits of the proposed definition, we also drew six other paired samples. These additional samples controlled for one or two of the crisis traits. For example, to control for threat, the experimenters divided all 360 experimental situations into equal thirds according to the amount of threat perceived by each of the participants. We drew eight cases from the third of the distribution containing the highest threat situa-

14. In a series of interviews conducted by the author, a number of former officials with high-level responsibilities for American foreign policy described several crises in which they had been intimately involved. At the end of the interview, each person rated on a ten-point scale the degree of threat, time, and surprise present in the situation he had discussed. On several occasions the respondent located his problem at one extreme of the scale. When reminded of another problem even more extreme—say, in restricted decision time—he would agree that his own situation had not been as severe as his rating implied. More than once, the individual went on to observe that when he experienced the problem, decision time looked as limited as he could imagine.

15. Harold Sprout and Margaret Sprout, "Environmental Factors in the Study of International Politics," in James N. Rosenau, ed., *International Politics and Foreign Policy* (New York: The Free Press, 1961), p. 113.

tions. An equal number were drawn from the middle and bottom thirds of the threat distribution. Thus the twenty-four situations in this sample ranged over the entire distribution with respect to the controlled dimension of threat, but these situations were selected only if they also contained extreme values for the uncontrolled dimensions (for example, extended time and surprise). We chose the following six additional paired samples in this manner:

high vs. low threat (time and surprise controlled)
short vs. extended time (threat and surprise controlled)
surprise vs. anticipation (threat and time controlled)
high threat–short time vs. low threat–extended time (surprise controlled)
high threat–surprise vs. low threat–anticipation (time controlled)
short time–surprise vs. extended time–anticipation (threat controlled)

Let us review the reason for these additional six paired samples that involve the control of one or two dimensions. Recall the macro hypothesis of this research states that when a situation contains high threat, short time, and surprise (that is, a crisis), the decision processes will be different from those in situations with none, one, or two of these characteristics. An investigation of the validity of this proposition requires that we compare the decision processes in crisis with the processes in situations having less than the full contingent of crisis traits. For the actors' measurement of crisis characteristics, these less-than-crisis situations appear as the controlled paired samples. With the experimenter ratings of the crisis characteristics, we can determine the influence of one or two dimensions alone through the use of analysis of variance, thus eliminating the need for situations that have some controlled characteristics.

In general, the participants' ratings of the crisis traits agreed with those of the experimenters. A *t*-test based on the data from all runs established a significant difference in the degree of surprise perceived by the participants between situations the experimenters classified as surprise and those they classified as anticipated ($p = .04$). The participants' ratings revealed a similar difference between the experimenters' definitions of short and extended time ($p = .007$). An analysis of variance on the levels of threat indicated that the participants perceived a significant difference between the three levels defined by the experimenters ($p = .001$). Tests on the individual components of variance confirmed significant differences between high and moderate threat ($p = .01$) and high and low threat ($p = .01$), but not between moderate and low threat. These tests indicate that the participants could distinguish between the categories devised by the experimenters. Whether the perspectives correspond sufficiently to identify situations that have similar decision processes remains to be determined.

EFFECTS OF CRISIS ON DECISION PROCESSES

This section reports the effects of crisis and other situations on five selected decision processes: authority structure, alternative proposals, internal communication, external communication, and frequency of action. An investigation of these working or micro hypotheses furthers the three major concerns of this chapter. First, the composite results provide an initial check on the theoretical and empirical utility of the proposed definition of crisis by furnishing evidence on the macro hypothesis of the study. Specifically, the effects of crisis on each decision process can be compared with those of situations having less than the three specified characteristics. Second, actual international crises supply some evidence for the validity of the five selected propositions. Therefore, the degree of consistency between findings from "real world" crises and those generated in the simulation offer insight into the applicability of simulation for crisis research. Third, some consequences of using the actor rather than the observer definition of the situation result by interchanging in every hypothesis the experimenter and participant ratings of the situation. Although the findings on the five working hypotheses may be of some intrinsic interest, they function primarily as means to these three objectives.

Contraction of Authority

In crises the number of decision makers assuming a major role in the decision will be reduced; that is, there will be a contraction in the number of individuals exercising authority.

Both the 1962 Cuban missile crisis and the 1950 decision to intervene in Korea support this hypothesis. Instead of using the complex organizational machinery designed for handling foreign affairs, both Presidents made their decisions with the aid of approximately a dozen advisers. Other crises also illustrate the contraction of authority.[16] To estimate the number of participants active in a given decision, each person indicated on a questionnaire, administered immediately after the deadline for responding to an experimental situation, whether he had written or talked with his associates about the problem. The number of individuals in a nation who claimed that they participated constituted an indicator of involvement. Decision makers completed the questionnaire periodically throughout the simulation under the guise of providing material for a history of the simulated world.

As with the other four hypotheses, a four-way analysis of variance served as the method to interpret data involving the experimenter ratings of the crisis characteristics. The statistical procedure allowed us to determine the effect on participation of four independent variables—surprise, threat, time, and nation. The impact of each variable was calculated separately and in various combinations. In other words, the analysis of variance permitted us to identify the main effect of each of these variables independently of the other three. In addition, we examined the interaction effect of the variables taken two, three, or four at a time. Interactions determine whether some systematic effects are attributable not to a single independent variable, but to a particular combination of two or more independent variables. With interactions, the question asked is: Are there unique effects resulting from the combination of variables? We were particularly interested in interactions among threat, time, and surprise because that combination constitutes the measure of crisis. The main effects and interactions provided information similar to that we obtained by creating six additional paired samples with the participants' ratings. The analysis of variance also gives information on the effect of the nation variable—data unavailable from the participants' ratings.

To confirm the hypothesis with data from the observer perspective, the interaction of threat, time, and surprise should produce a significant downward

16. Additional examples are discussed in Charles F. Hermann, "Some Consequences of Crisis Which Limit the Viability of Organizations," *Administrative Science Quarterly*, 8 (June 1963), 70.

change in the amount of participation. No such relationship occurred. However, relationships between the level of participation and several other kinds of situations occurred with a far greater frequency than one would expect by chance alone ($p \leq .05$). Situations having only one or the other of two crisis traits—threat or time—yielded significant main effects. As threat increased, the number of participants increased. This finding reversed the direction of the initial hypothesis. On the other hand, the relationship involving time ran in the predicted direction. As time decreased, the number of participants decreased. The amount of participation also varied from nation to nation, with larger nations tending to have fewer decision makers engaged in all situations. All but two of the possible interactions involving the nation variable significantly affected the amount of participation. The various interactions of nation with the situational characteristics require further investigation, but this task is beyond the bounds of a paper focused on the three assumed attributes of crisis. A summary of the analysis of variance results for contraction of authority appears in the first column of Table 1.

TABLE 1. CONTRACTION OF AUTHORITY VARIABLE WITH EXPERIMENTER AND PARTICIPANT RATINGS OF THE CRISIS DIMENSIONS

	Analysis of Variance (Experimenter Ratings) F Values	*Chi Square (Participant Ratings) X^2 Values*
Crisis (threat × time × surprise)	0.74	2.22*
Threat	17.00***	0.08
Time	6.08**	0.36
Surprise	2.46	0.78
Nation	7.36***	—
Threat × time	1.94	0.58
Threat × surprise	2.21	0.08
Threat × nation	3.14***	—
Time × surprise	1.81	0.44
Time × nation	3.31***	—
Surprise × nation	2.79**	—
Threat × time × nation	3.40**	—
Threat × surprise × nation	1.93**	—
Surprise × time × nation	1.61	—
Threat × time × surprise × nation	0.71	—

* $p \leq .10$.
** $p \leq .05$.
*** $p \leq .01$.
NOTE: F and X^2 values cannot be compared directly

To explore the same hypothesis with crisis defined by the participants' ratings, the situations in each sample were assigned to one of two categories. If four or more of the decision makers indicated they had participated in the decision, that situation then received a "noncontraction" designation. The other category, "contraction," consisted of situations involving less than four participants. Chi squares determined if the number of contractions differed between crisis-noncrisis and the other paired samples. Table 1 displays the results in the second column. (Notice that because the nation variable was not possible in this analysis, rows of the table concerned with that variable remain blank.) For crisis-noncrisis, the results run counter to the hypothesis. Crisis decisions engaged more individuals than noncrisis decisions. Using the participants' ratings, no one or two of the crisis traits identify situations that alter the amount of participation. In short, although the actor and observer perspectives lead to different results, neither supports the contraction-of-authority hypothesis.

Number of Alternatives

In crises the number of alternative solutions to the situation that will be identified by the national decision makers will be reduced.

Based on the Cuban missile crisis, the Wohlstetters and Schelling suggest that the number of alternatives increase in crisis.[17] We postulate the opposite relationship in this research, however, on the basis of a somewhat broader range of evidence. For example, a content analysis of diplomatic messages exchanged prior to the outbreak of World War I supports the proposition that "as stress increases decision makers will perceive the range of alternatives open to themselves to become narrower."[18] In addition, a study of the decision to intervene in Korea confirms the proposition and a substantial number of psychological studies conclude that severe stress reduces alternatives.[19]

A content analysis of all messages and conference transcripts determined the number of distinctive alternatives considered by the participants in each different type of experimental situation. The frequency count obtained from that analysis served as the basis for a proportion consisting of the number of alternatives advanced in a standard unit of time. This proportion controlled for the potential fluency differences between short and extended time. After a period of training, coders attained a high degree of reliability in identifying when decision makers advanced new alternatives.[20]

The first column of Table 2 summarizes the findings for the linkage between the number of alternatives and the experimenters' ratings of situations. The interaction of threat, time, and surprise with the number of alternatives produces no statistically significant relationship. Thus, from the observers' perspective, the hypothesis between crisis and alternatives fails to receive confirmation. Separately, however, two of the three components of crisis constitute situations that significantly affect the number of alternatives. As time increases, fewer alternatives are considered; as threat increases, more alternatives are considered. In addition, two significant interactions occur among the three crisis variables. One

17. Albert Wohlstetter and Roberta Wohlstetter, *Controlling the Risks in Cuba*, Adelphi Paper No. 17, Institute for Strategic Studies (London), April 1965, p. 18; Thomas C. Schelling, *Arms and Influence* (New Haven: Yale University Press, 1966), p. 96.

18. Ole R. Holsti, "The 1914 Case," *American Political Science Review*, 59 (June 1965), 365.

19. Richard C. Snyder and Glenn D. Paige, "The United States Decision to Resist Aggression in Korea," *Administrative Science Quarterly*, 3 (December 1958), 362. For a review of psychological studies on this point see Richard S. Lazarus, *Psychological Stress and the Coping Process* (New York: McGraw-Hill, 1966).

20. Intercoder reliabilities for the content analysis of alternative proposals was .93 using a Pearson product moment correlation.

TABLE 2. NUMBER OF ALTERNATIVES VARIABLE WITH EXPERIMENTER AND PARTICIPANT RATINGS OF THE CRISIS DIMENSIONS

	Analysis of Variance (Experimenter Ratings) F Values	*Mann-Whitney U (Participant Ratings) Normalized U's*
Crisis (threat × time × surprise)	0.87	0.74
Threat	37.37***	0.02
Time	13.58***	0.88
Surprise	0.48	0.94
Nation	4.52***	—
Threat × time	6.49***	2.95***
Threat × surprise	0.06	1.19
Threat × nation	1.43	—
Time × surprise	4.69**	0.24
Time × nation	8.20***	—
Surprise × nation	2.56**	—
Threat × time × nation	1.95**	—
Threat × surprise × nation	1.38	—
Surprise × time × nation	0.91	—
Threat × time × surprise × nation	0.84	—

* $p \leq .10$.
** $p \leq .05$.
***$p \leq .01$.
NOTE: *F* and *U* values cannot be compared directly.

is between threat and time; the other is between surprise and time. As indicated in Figure 1, when threat remains minimal, the amount of available time makes little difference in the number of alternatives discussed. As threat increases, decision time becomes steadily more important in determining how many alternatives will be considered. Under high threat in the simulation, a very limited amount of time encourages relatively more attention to enumerating alternatives than if time is extended. At the upper levels of threat, if participants possess more time, they use it for some other aspects of the decision process than generating alternatives. Another explanation might be that under high threat and limited time, participants become too pressured to discriminate between alternatives. Thus they mention courses of action which they would otherwise privately reject.

Figure 2 shows a reversal in the effect of anticipation on the number of alternatives depending upon the amount of time available for decision. When considerable decision time exists, the participants enumerate slightly more alternative proposals in situations that occur as a surprise than in situations that emerge after a warning. Under conditions of short decision time, however, an anticipated situation leads to more alternative proposals. Participants, who receive a warning of a forthcoming situation involving no urgency (i.e., extended time), may postpone consideration of the problem including the identification of solutions. On the other hand, should a fast decision be required, anticipation provides more precious time to consider alternative solutions. As displayed in the first column of Table 2, a significant main effect also results with the nation variable. Significant interactions occur between nation and anticipation as well

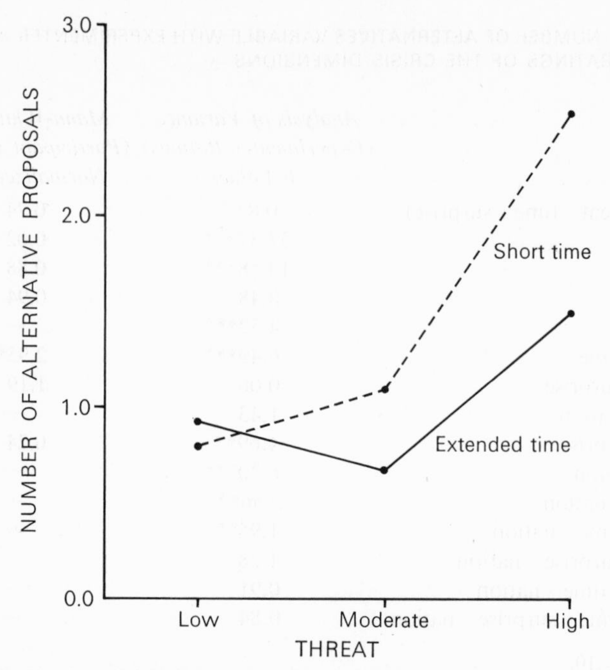

FIGURE 1. Number of alternative proposals per unit of time in six situations with different combinations of threat and time.

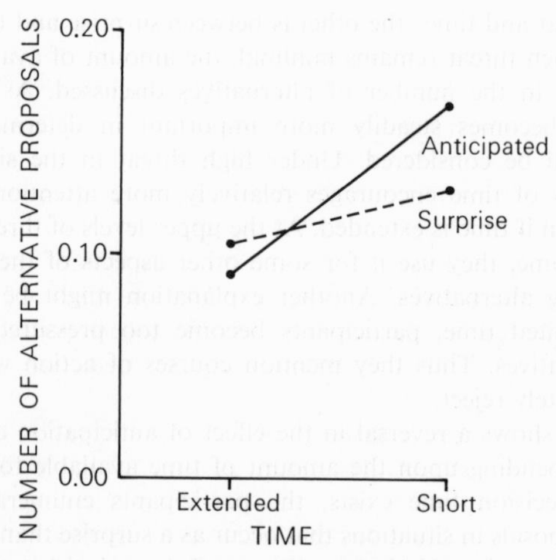

FIGURE 2. Number of alternative proposals per unit of time in four situations with different combinations of surprise and time.

as between nation and time. Three variables (nation, threat, and time) constitute a significant three-way interaction with the dependent variable, number of alternatives.

In moving from the experimenter to the participant measures of crisis, we shift from analysis of variance to the use of Mann-Whitney *U*'s. With this statistic, the researcher arranges situations in order according to rank with that situation having the most alternatives assigned the first rank; the situation with the next largest number of alternatives receives the second rank, and so on. The more situations from one sample which rank ahead of those from the other, the smaller the U and the greater the assumed difference between the categories represented by the two samples. (However, after converting U's to z scores to correct for tied ranks, the larger the resulting normalized U, the greater the difference between samples.) To examine data on the remaining hypotheses from the actor perspective, this statistic will compare each set of paired samples. As shown in the second column of Table 2, the data fail to support the present hypothesis that crisis reduces alternatives. The one significant difference reveals that situations perceived by the participants as high threat and short time result in more alternatives than occur in low threat–extended time situations. This result conforms to the finding obtained from the observer perspective.

Internal Communication

In crises the rate of communication within the foreign policy agencies of a nation will increase.

Statements of policy makers with experience managing crises support this hypothesis on increased communication within a government (internal communication). For example, a high-ranking member of the United States embassy in Beirut during the Lebanon crisis of 1958 related: "In a normal month the code room handled between 100,000 and 150,000 words but after the rebellion broke out the traffic quintupled to 700,000 words."[21]

Additional evidence comes from a study of the cable traffic between the Department of State and its Latin American embassies and consulates during the Cuban missile crisis.[22] That research shows a remarkable increase in communication even though officials urged that telegraphic communications during the crisis be confined to critical messages. In the simulation internal communication consisted of the number of sentences (both written and oral) exchanged between members of the same simulated nation. The total volume of communication in any situation was divided by the duration of that event to establish a rate of communication per minute.

The analysis of variance of crisis traits, as defined by the experimenters, yielded four significant interactions between various combinations of the independent variables and the volume of internal communication. Again, the critical threat/time/surprise interaction was not among them. All four significant findings, shown in Table 3, included the nation as one of the interacting variables. The recurrent combination between nation and one or more of the crisis traits suggests that national characteristics together with situational characteristics interact in some way to create different kinds of decision processes. The first column in Table 3 reveals that only time, among the separate components of crisis, significantly altered the rate of internal communication independent of the

21. Charles W. Thayer, *Diplomat* (New York: Harper & Row, 1959), p. 21.

22. William A. Runge, *Analysis of the Department of State Communications Traffic During a Politico-Military Crisis*, Research Memorandum OAD RM 109, Stanford Research Institute, Menlo Park, Calif., 1963.

TABLE 3. INTERNAL COMMUNICATION VARIABLE WITH EXPERIMENTER AND PARTICIPANT RATINGS OF THE CRISIS DIMENSIONS

	Analysis of Variance (Experimenter Ratings) F Values	*Mann-Whitney U (Participant Ratings) Normalized U's*
Crisis (threat × time × surprise)	1.18	2.52***
Threat	0.16	0.96
Time	9.90***	1.27*
Surprise	0.07	1.79**
Nation	1.48	—
Threat × time	1.38	3.09***
Threat × surprise	0.44	1.08
Threat × nation	3.00***	—
Time × surprise	0.33	0.49
Time × nation	3.56***	—
Surprise × nation	0.53	—
Threat × time × nation	4.31***	—
Threat × surprise × nation	1.13	—
Surprise × time × nation	0.20	—
Threat × time × surprise × nation	1.80*	—

* $p \leq .10$.
** $p \leq .05$.
*** $p \leq .01$.
NOTE: *F* and *U* values cannot be compared directly.

effects of nation. The rate of communication in short time situations exceeded that in extended time situations.

In contrast to the results with the experimenters' ratings, internal communication increased in crisis when the component traits of crisis were rated by the participants. As indicated in the second column of Table 3, significantly more internal communication occurred in crisis than in noncrisis. The table also shows that several of the traits, separately and in combination, produced significant effects on communication. The rate of communication in short time situations surpassed that in extended time situations. Furthermore, anticipated situations yielded more communication than those characterized by surprise. High threat–short time situations involved more internal communication than their opposite (low threat–extended time). The threat by time interaction for the experimenter ratings was not significant; but when "nation" was added to those two variables, the interaction was significant. The relationships concerning time alone and threat-time are the only ones relevant to internal communication in which the actor and observer viewpoints produced somewhat parallel findings.

External Communication

In crises, the rate of communication by a nation's decision makers to international actors outside their country will increase.

This hypothesis is a companion of the previous one; they differ as to the party to whom messages are addressed. The 1914 crisis before the outbreak of war illustrates this proposition. "As the crisis developed, decision makers in various capitals received rapidly increasing volumes of messages from various parts of Europe."[23] To study this relationship in the simulation, the experimenters followed a procedure similar to that used in the internal communication hypothesis. They examined all written messages and conference transcripts addressed to individuals outside the sender's nation and counted the number of sentences. Again, rates of communication were established by dividing the total number of sentences communicated during a situation by the length in minutes of that event.

The results of the analysis of variance using the experimenters' ratings of crisis appear in the first column of Table 4. The five statistically significant relationships with external communication exclude the predicted crisis interaction. Nation and time yield significant main effects—that is, they both independently affect the rate of external communications. Regardless of the kind of

TABLE 4. EXTERNAL COMMUNICATION WITH EXPERIMENTER AND PARTICIPANT RATINGS OF THE CRISIS DIMENSIONS

	Analysis of Variance (Experimenter Ratings) F Values	*Mann-Whitney U (Participant Ratings) Normalized U's*
Crisis (threat × time × surprise)	0.60	1.32*
Threat	0.91	1.39*
Time	24.38***	0.76
Surprise	0.10	0.28
Nation	3.34***	—
Threat × time	6.14***	1.47*
Threat × surprise	0.92	0.72
Threat × nation	0.72	—
Time × surprise	0.01	1.73**
Time × nation	4.15***	—
Surprise × nation	0.24	—
Threat × time × nation	2.40***	—
Threat × surprise × nation	0.30	—
Surprise × time × nation	0.18	—
Threat × time × surprise × nation	0.89	—

* $p \leq .10$.
** $p \leq .05$.
*** $p \leq .01$
NOTE: F and U values cannot be compared directly.

situation, nations with large amounts of resources tend to engage in more external communication than small nations. Moreover, as decision time decreases, the rate of external communication increases. Among the significant interactions, two involve the nation variable (nation/threat; nation/threat/time). The third interaction, diagrammed in Figure 3, combines the crisis traits of threat and time. The diagram indicates that the less severe the threat, the greater

23. Robert C. North, "Propositions from the 1914 Crisis," in Robert C. North, Ole R. Holsti, M. George Zaninovich, and Dina A. Zinnes, *Content Analysis* (Evanston, Ill.: Northwestern University Press, 1963), p. 164.

the importance of decision time in determining the rate of communication. Although in short time situations the rate of communication always surpasses the rate in extended time situations, the variation in time changes the amount of communication much more in the low-threat condition than in either the moderate- or high-threat condition. It may be that as threat increases, in short time situations the decision makers conclude that other tasks have priority over interacting with international actors.

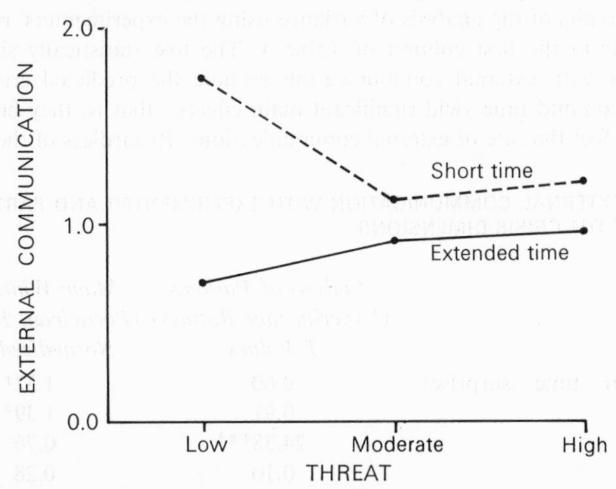

FIGURE 3. Rate of external communication per unit of time in six situations with different combinations of threat and time.

Unlike the results with the experimenter measure of crisis, the participants' ratings of the three characteristics support the hypothesis ($p \leq .10$) that crises influence external communication. (See the second column of Table 4.) Simulation decision makers communicated with actors outside their nation more frequently in crisis than noncrisis. When the threat characteristic is isolated, low threat produced more communication than high threat. In a finding similar to the threat by time interaction found with the experimenters' ratings, high threat–short time situations as perceived by the participants involved more external communication than did low threat–extended time situations. The combination of short time with surprise also led to more external communication than did situations with the opposite characteristics.

Frequency of Action

> In crises the frequency with which a nation's decision makers are likely to take action in response to the situation increases.

The American government undertook strong actions in both the 1950 Korean and the 1962 Cuban crises. The need for action which decision makers experience in a crisis receives documentation in the description of specific events —such as the 1914 crisis—and more general characterizations of crisis.[24] Action

24. For an account of the felt need for action in the 1914 crisis, see Robert C. North, "Perceptions and Action in the 1914 Crisis," *Journal of International Affairs*,

in the simulation consisted of any forms completed in response to a situation that allocated or deployed part of the nation's resources (for example, trades, blockades, military attacks, defense spending) or any external communication that indicated what the nation had done or would do about the situation. The total number of such activities constituted the frequency of action for each experimental situation.

Using the experimenters' ratings, more statistically significant relationships appeared between the various situational variables and the frequency of action than with any of the previous four dependent variables. Nevertheless, as displayed in the first column of Table 5, situations formed by the interaction of the

TABLE 5. FREQUENCY OF ACTION VARIABLE WITH EXPERIMENTER AND PARTICIPANT RATINGS OF THE CRISIS DIMENSIONS

	Analysis of Variance (Experimenter Ratings) F Values	*Mann-Whitney U (Participant Ratings) Normalized U's*
Crisis (threat × time × surprise)	0.14	1.80**
Threat	31.70***	0.35
Time	33.50***	1.67**
Surprise	0.00	1.93**
Nation	2.84**	—
Threat × time	4.75***	2.71***
Threat × surprise	0.19	1.33*
Threat × nation	4.15***	—
Time × surprise	0.05	1.72**
Time × nation	4.83***	—
Surprise × nation	1.14	—
Threat × time × nation	4.98***	—
Threat × surprise × nation	2.04**	—
Surprise × time × nation	0.42	—
Threat × time × surprise × nation	2.58***	—

* $p \leq .10$.
** $p \leq .05$.
*** $p \leq .01$.
NOTE: *F* and *U* values cannot be compared directly.

three crisis traits produced no significant increase in action. By contrast, threat and time—both as separate main effects and in combination with each other—altered the frequency of action. Taken in isolation, more situational threat increased the frequency of action. The consequence of time as a main effect was also direct; as time decreased, the frequency of action decreased. Figure 4 pictures the interaction of these two crisis components as they relate to action. In both conditions of time, increases in the threat component produced increases in the frequency of action, but the impact of threat in extended time situations exceeded that for short time situations. Moreover, the difference in the number

21 (1967), 103–122. A more general analysis of crises that reaches the same conclusion is Anthony J. Wiener and Herman Kahn, *Crisis and Arms Control*, Hudson Institute, 1962, p. 9.

of actions between the two time conditions became greater as threat increased. In summary, although action increased with threat, that increase took a more gradual course when decision time remained limited.

The first column of Table 5 indicates that once again variations in the nations influenced the value of the dependent variable. As a main effect, differences among nations related to differences in the frequency of action; specifically, the data suggest a slight trend toward more action by nations with more resources. Five significant interactions involving the nation variable appear in Table 5 or, put another way, only two possible combinations with the nation variable remained unrelated to the frequency of action.

As with several previous hypotheses, the substitution of the participants' definition of crisis for that of the experimenters' shifts the results from disconfirming to confirming. When defined by the participants, the combination of high threat, short time, and surprise increases the frequency of action. This

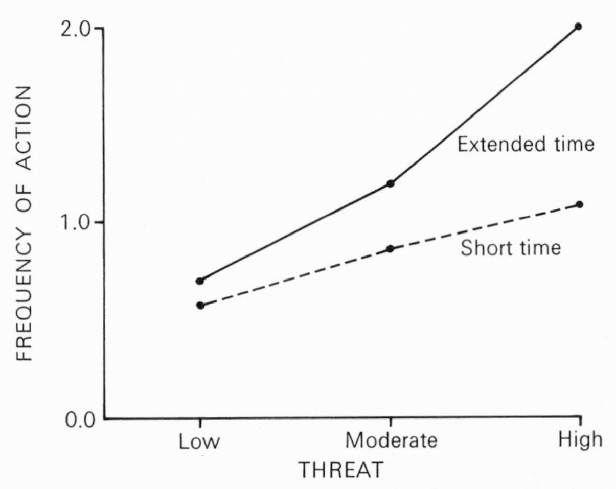

FIGURE 4. Frequency of action in six situations with different combinations of threat and time.

finding and the other results of the *U* tests appear in the second column of Table 5. As can be seen by comparing the pattern of significant results in the two columns of that table, the observer and actor measures of crisis produce similar results with two variables—time, and threat combined with time. More action occurs in situations that the participants perceive as involving short time than in situations they perceive as allowing extended time for decision. More action also follows in high threat–short time situations than in low threat–extended time situations. Three other types of situations, as defined by the participants, influenced action, but remained nonsignificant in the analysis of variance of the experimenters' ratings. The decision makers initiated more actions in situations they characterized as anticipated, low threat–anticipated, and short time–surprise than they did in situations with the opposite characteristics.

CONCLUSIONS

This chapter asked three questions relevant to a substantial portion of the research on crisis. They were (1) Of what empirical and theoretical utility is the concept of crisis when it is defined in terms of high threat, short time, and surprise? (2) Given the proposed definition of crisis, does it make much difference whether the components of crisis are ascertained by the individuals or groups experiencing the crisis rather than by knowledgeable observers? (3) How appropriate is simulation as a research method for the study of international crises? The conclusions address these questions using the results from the five hypotheses examined with simulation data.

Definition of Crisis

Regardless of the specific definition of crisis, it must permit the identification of a class of situations and participate in the development of theoretical assertions which yield empirically verifiable hypotheses. To that end this study involved a macro hypothesis that situations characterized by high threat to important goals, short time for decision, and surprise for the policy makers would increase the probability of certain decision processes not likely to occur in situations lacking one or more of the designated crisis traits. Five working hypotheses relating crisis, as defined, to selected decision processes served as an initial means of exploring the macro hypothesis. If situations characterized by the proposed crisis traits did alter most of the five decision process variables in a way that other situations did not, then these findings would offer initial support for the macro hypothesis. In turn, the substantiation of the macro hypothesis would suggest that the theoretical utility of the proposed definition of crisis warranted more extensive consideration.

Table 6 summarizes the relationships between the various combinations of situational variables and the five process variables that reached a certain confidence level ($p \leq .10$). If one compares the total number of relationships (column 3) in which each situational trait or combination of traits participates, then the proposed definition of crisis fares poorly. With the five process variables, more relationships result from situations distinguished only by the isolated trait of time or by the combination of time and threat than result from the integrated crisis definition. Furthermore, threat alone accounts for as many significant results as does crisis. This assessment of the proposed definition becomes less harsh if the analysis is confined to the participants' ratings of the crisis traits (Table 6, second column). Crisis and threat-time both enter into four of the possible five relationships, whereas no other trait or combination of traits produces more than two.

For a number of reasons, any conclusions drawn from this study must be quite tentative. The research involved an extremely small sample of process variables. The relationships between situation and process variables were explored in only one study by one method. Moreover, the data have been analyzed only for the existence of relationships, not for the strength or degree of relationship. Nevertheless, certain observations seem appropriate. The element of surprise entered into fewer relationships with the process variables than any of the other situational characteristics. Surprise may have been inadequately represented in the experimental situations; that is, the absence of significant results with surprise

TABLE 6. SUMMARY OF RESULTS BETWEEN EITHER EXPERIMENTER OR PARTICIPANT RATINGS OF CRISIS DIMENSIONS AND FIVE DEPENDENT VARIABLES

	Experimenter Ratings (Analysis of Variance)	*Participant Ratings (U or X^2)*	*Total Result with $p \leq .10$*
Crisis		_C_*, I, _E_, A	0 + 4
Threat	C*, N*, A	_E_*	3 + 1
Time	C, N*, I, E, A*	_I_, A	5 + 2
Surprise		I*, A*	0 + 2
Threat × time	N*, E, A	N*, I, _E_, A	3 + 4
Threat × surprise		_A_*	0 + 1
Time × surprise	N*	E, A	1 + 2
Nation	C, N, E, A		4
Threat × nation	C, I, A		3
Time × nation	C, N, I, E, A		5
Surprise × nation	C, N		2
Threat × time × nation	C, N, I, E, A		5
Threat × surprise × nation	C, A		2
Surprise × time × nation			0
Threat × time × surprise × nation	_I_, A		2

KEY: C = contraction of authority; N = number of alternatives; I = internal communication; E = external communication; A = action.

NOTE: Underlined letters represent relationships with *p* values between .10 and .05. An asterisk (*) indicates that the results with crisis or its components are in the reverse direction from that predicted in the hypothesis. For the analysis of variance interactions, conclusions on direction are based on only the two situations that correspond to the paired samples used in the *U* or X^2 tests. No determination on direction is made for results involving the nation variable.

could be a function of the research design. Alternatively, the situational quality of surprise may be relatively less important in the decision process than either threat or time. Consistent with this interpretation is a review of the crisis literature that found the property of surprise mentioned less frequently than the other two traits.[25] If the latter explanation is correct, then the concept of crisis might be recast to include only high threat and short time—the combination of situational traits that performed well with either the participant or experimenter ratings. The author, however, considers such a reformulation premature without further investigation of the initial definition.[26]

25. Charles F. Hermann, "Some Consequences of Crisis," pp. 63–65.

26. The treatment of surprise differed from that for threat and time in both the experimenter and participant ratings. As noted in this chapter, all combinations of surprise with the other two variables were achieved only by aggregating the results from two consecutive runs. Furthermore, participants, who frequently had more than they could readily manage, may have failed to read the warning messages. With respect to the participants' ratings, the questionnaire format for surprise varied from that used for the other traits and it may have been less effective. Until these possible explanations for the poor performance of surprise are corrected in subsequent experiments, the characteristic should not be discarded.

Actor and Observer Perspectives

The evidence from this study on the actor and observer perspective can be stated briefly. Whether crisis traits were defined by the participants or by the experimenters made a considerable difference in the simulation. The results with the process variables indicate that the two sets of situations defined by either actors or observers have different effects on the procedures for choice-making. Of the twenty-eight results reported in Table 6 (excluding the nation variable), eighteen findings established by one perspective remained unconfirmed by the other. In one of the five relationships substantiated by both the actor and observer perspectives of crisis, the direction of the relationship found with one measure reversed that discovered with the other. (With participant ratings, as contrasted with observer measures, short time involved more action.) Nowhere were the effects of the alternative perspectives more evident than with the proposed definition of crisis (Table 6, first row). None of the hypotheses received support from the experimenters' ratings. By contrast, three of the five hypotheses were confirmed with the participants' ratings of crisis and a fourth relationship was established in the opposite direction from that predicted. Of course, caution must be applied in interpreting these results; other observers might agree more closely with the perspectives of the actors. The alternative methods of analysis rather than the different perspectives could account for the results. Despite these reservations, the simulation findings suggest that the perspective from which crisis is defined—even when the same traits are used—is extremely important in comparing results from different crisis studies.

Appropriateness of Simulation

Some persons question the utility of the simulation-gaming technique for providing any useful insights about international politics. This chapter narrowed the issue to the applicability of the technique for research on a particular subject. No study based on a single type of simulation can offer definitive answers. Vast differences exist between the assets and liabilities of different types of games and simulations. The uses for which one simulation or game may prove valuable provide little evidence about the utility of another type. Nevertheless, the evidence acquired from various games and simulations contributes to the general assessment of the techniques as means of understanding crises.

All five hypotheses relating crisis to decision processes have been derived from studies of actual international crises. Given the present state of knowledge, one or more of the hypotheses may prove false, but initial examination suggests otherwise. If the simulation generated the important qualities of crisis and the context in which they occur, and if the hypotheses described actual conditions in coping with crises, then the simulation should confirm the hypotheses.[27] As previously noted, the data failed to confirm any of the hypotheses

27. This sentence should not be interpreted as an example of the *post hoc, ergo propter hoc* fallacy. The simulation could substantiate the hypotheses through operations that in no way matched those in actual crises. Hence the confirmation of the hypothesis in both the simulation and its referent system remains an incomplete validity check. However, failure to obtain similar results in simulated and actual crises might indicate the inadequacy of the model. For a discussion of this validity problem see Charles F. Hermann, "Validation Problems in Games and Simulations with Special Reference to Models of International Politics," *Behavioral Science*, 12 (May 1967), 216–231.

when the analysis involved the experimenters' ratings of the crisis traits. On the other hand, with the participants' definition of the situations, three of the five hypotheses received support.

The two unconfirmed hypotheses warrant brief examination. Despite considerable evidence that contraction occurs in crises,[28] the simulation findings (using participants' ratings) indicated more contraction in noncrisis than in crisis. For the contraction hypothesis, the representation of foreign policy organizations by five individuals may have proven unsatisfactory. One study of the American decision to assist Korea suggests that "the principal national crisis decision-making group will tend to vary in size from twelve to fifteen officials."[29] Thus, when faced with a crisis, a five-man simulated nation should strain to engage every possible man. This appears to have happened in the simulation with the result that contraction occurred more frequently in noncrises.

The second unconfirmed hypothesis contends that crises lead to the consideration of fewer alternatives. It is noteworthy that the actual crises reviewed for this hypothesis contained some contradictions regarding the number of alternatives. However, the measurement procedures used in the simulation offer another possible explanation for the absence of support for the hypothesis. The simulation involved experimental situations of strikingly different duration (fifteen as opposed to fifty minutes). Obviously, with sufficient restrictions on available time, the decision makers would examine fewer alternatives. To avoid confirming only this rather trite observation, the measure of alternatives was standardized for time by computing the number of alternatives per unit of time. In retrospect, this measure may have created new difficulties because it seems reasonable to suggest that at some point decision makers will elect to spend further increments of time on some other activity than enumeration of alternatives. This explanation is consistent with the data, under conditions of moderate and high threat, diagrammed in Figure 1. Although the absolute number of alternatives may be less in crisis, that type of situation may have a higher proportion of alternatives per minute than situations with extensive amounts of time. In summary, the discrepancies between the simulation data and the evidence on actual crises may be attributable not to the simulation technique, but to shortcomings in this particular experiment.

Although the participants experienced various amounts of threat, time, and surprise in the simulation, the question remains as to whether the values of the variables approached those of equivalent variables during actual international crises. The present study offers little systematic evidence on the problem but, in general, laboratory experiments appear to have more success in creating a wide range of values for some kinds of variables than for others. Using the three proposed components of crisis as an example, the author suspects that substantial variations in the time available for certain simulation decisions was more readily manipulated than either threat or surprise. The greater range of values for time may explain why that variable was the only one manipulated by the experimenters which resulted in changes in all five decision processes. Even though some variables may be subjected to greater variation in a simulation than others, crises in such models undoubtedly create less change in variables like

28. Bernard Berelson and Gary A. Steiner, *Human Behavior* (New York: Harcourt, Brace, & World, 1964), p. 370.

29. Glenn D. Paige, *The Korean Decision* (New York: The Free Press, 1968), p. 286.

affective perceptions than do actual crises. This limitation becomes severe if the variable to be manipulated is curvilinear so that its effects at lower levels cannot be easily projected to higher levels. However, if these difficulties temporarily drive the researcher out of the simulation laboratory, other problems in the study of crisis may encourage him to reenter. A rigorous effort to determine the effects of various situational variables separately and in a wide number of combinations, as undertaken in this analysis, would have been extraordinarily difficult to execute using actual international situations. The study of crisis may best be served by the analysis of both simulation and real world situations.

Nation as a Variable

In addition to the three questions that formed the core of this chapter, some concluding remarks must be addressed to the influence of the nation variable. As shown in the eighth row of Table 6, differences between nations resulted in changes in four of the five decision process variables. Of equal interest are the twenty-two relationships between process variables and some combination of situational traits and the nation variable. What differences among the six simulation nations might account for these relationships? Because each of the six nations was replicated ten times with different participants in each run, certain elements such as personality traits or organizational arrangements seem unlikely to explain the discrepancies. Across all ten runs, a given nation always began with the same number of resources, but no two nations within a run had the same capabilities. Thus differences in the amount of national resources could account for the effect on decision processes. Other possible attributes which differed from nation to nation throughout all the replications included alliance membership, national goals, and status in the international system. Whether one or a combination of these qualities, or some others, constitute the important difference between nations cannot be established with these data. Students of international policies would expect that different nations would use different decision processes. The significance of the present study lies in the recurrent influence of the interaction between the situation and the nation on decision processes.

part five

COPING WITH CRISIS

chapter ten

EDITOR'S INTRODUCTION

It is probable that scholars have devoted more attention to the escalation and intensification of crises than to deescalation or reduction of crises. If this contention is true, it is remarkable because the actions required for crisis deescalation are not necessarily the reverse of those used to make the situation more acute. Illustrating this point is the metaphor that Khrushchev related to Kennedy during the Cuban missile crisis about two men pulling on the opposite ends of a knotted rope until it could no longer be undone except by the sword. The analogy can be carried a step further. Providing slack on the rope must be followed by other positive acts if the knot is to be untied. Glenn Snyder's analysis of the role of bargaining in crisis offers one kind of perspective necessary for addressing the problem of deescalation. As such, it makes an important contribution to the study of crisis management.

As the earlier chapter by Glenn Paige and the following one by Thomas Milburn, the present chapter is rich in hypotheses. Unlike Paige's, Snyder's propositions are drawn not from an intensive examination of one or two case studies, but from a much wider survey. This broader base allows the present author to note contradictions or negative consequences associated with various generalizations. For example, he identifies conditions that can invalidate the maxim "He who commits first, wins"; and he describes some circumstances under which negotiating power can be lost when one applies the dictum, "Keep your options open in a crisis." As Milburn emphasizes in the chapter following this one, critical inputs for the study of crisis management include knowledge of the conditions under which a generalization may not hold and recognition of little-noticed side effects of a hypothesis.

Snyder's definition of crisis differs from that found in a number of the other contributions to this volume. It does not necessarily contradict definitions such as that based on the traits of threat, time, and surprise, but it does highlight different aspects of crisis. Considerable overlap probably exists between those situations in international politics which would be identified as crises using both the threat-time-surprise definition and Snyder's definition of crises as situations presenting a real possibility of war. Snyder's consideration of situations which risk war together with his emphasis on bargaining bring into prominence the critical issue concerning the role of force in crises. Because crises are defined as conflict situations that are less than war, the role of force is not that of destruction but rather that of demonstration or threat.

The strategic bargaining orientation permits Snyder to begin the development of a typology of moves or actions in a crisis. In this effort he, together with Charles McClelland (see Chapter 5), venture into unexplored terrain in crisis studies. What kind of outputs are generated by the parties to a crisis? To date, most research dealing at all with the moves taken in a crisis has described action as being simply more or less hostile. Although McClelland and Snyder's conceptualizations are different, one possibility for future research is to regroup the World Event/Interaction Survey data collected by McClelland and his associates into the categories (coercive, accommodative, basic, communicative, etc.) proposed by Snyder. This entirely feasible effort would allow the utility of Snyder's typology to be investigated in a large number of cases.

Finally, the reader should recognize the game theoretic perspective evident in this chapter. Even without extensive use of game matrices or attempts to apply or solve a particular type of game, the influence is evident. Bargaining in a crisis is seen as a mixed-motive game in which the outcome is dependent upon the choices of both parties. The introduction of game theory recalls the assessment by James Robinson of the minimal linkage between crisis research and the theory of games as well as the considerable debate that his position generated in the Symposium of the contributors to this volume (Editor's Introduction to Chapter 2). In some ways the bargaining-game theoretic perspective bridges the distinction between the decision-making and systemic approaches discussed throughout this book. Like an analyst who uses decision making, the student of bargaining is concerned with such matters as choices, motives, perceptions, and so on, but he also deals with interaction effects, with moves and counter moves, and with the consequences of moves on third parties.

Glenn H. Snyder is Professor of Political Science and Chairman of the Center for International Conflict Studies at the State University of New York at Buffalo. With others at the Center, he is currently doing research on the theory and practice of crisis diplomacy, applying various sorts of social science theory to case studies of crises in the nineteenth and twentieth centuries. He is the author of *Deterrence and Defense* (Princeton: Princeton University Press, 1961); *Strategy, Politics and Defense Budgets*, with Warner Schilling and Paul Hammond (New York: Columbia University Press, 1962); and *Stockpiling Strategic Materials: Politics and National Defense* (San Francisco: Chandler, 1967).

chapter ten

CRISIS BARGAINING*

Glenn H. Snyder

An international crisis is international politics in microcosm. That is to say, a crisis tends to highlight or force to the surface a wide range of factors and processes which are central to international politics in general. Such elements as power configurations, interests, values, risks, perceptions, degrees of resolve, bargaining, and decision making lie at the core of international politics; in a crisis they tend to leap out at the observer, to be combined and related in a revealing way, and to be sharply focused on a single, well-defined issue. International politics is pervasively conditioned by the "expectation of potential war."[1] In relatively placid periods this expectation is only in the background of the statesman's consciousness and its effects are rather muted and diffuse. But in a crisis the element of potential war is elevated from an underlying to a central and imminent position, and its behavioral consequences tend to be starkly revealed. Thus a crisis is a concentrated distillation of most of the elements which make up the essence of politics in the international system. It is a "moment of truth" when the latent product of these interacting elements becomes manifest in action and events.

It follows from this conception that a crisis can serve as a laboratory for the study of a great variety of processes and variables, and for the application of a number of different theoretical approaches. Effects of different system structures (e.g., multipolar vs. bipolar), alliance behavior, bargaining, decision making, the role of law and norms, and the interaction between domestic and international politics (to name the most obvious) can all be studied fruitfully in the crisis context. Moreover, the illuminating way in which all these processes interact in a crisis make this context an excellent one for the *integration* of theory.

However, this paper will focus on the process of *bargaining* in crises. The choice is not arbitrary since I believe that the central process in most crises is that of bargaining, subsuming within that concept the subprocesses of coercion and negotiation. Most crises are generated out of an attempt to coerce which is resisted, and the playing out of the crisis is strongly characterized by such factors as threats, warnings, demonstrations, concessions, and various other types of communications and "moves" which are generally considered aspects of bargaining and bargaining theory. The other processes mentioned above impinge upon

* This chapter is a product of research on "Negotiation and Bargaining in International Relations," a project under way at the Center for International Conflict Studies, State University of New York at Buffalo. It is supported by the National Science Foundation, Grant GS-2270.

1. I prefer this phrase to Stanley Hoffmann's "state of war" which is a bit too hyperbolic, although it nicely dramatizes the essential consequence of structural anarchy. Stanley Hoffmann, *The State of War: Essays in the Theory and Practice of International Politics* (New York: Praeger, 1965).

and affect the bargaining process and a full study of "crisis behavior" would have to deal with all of them. But I shall make only a few glancing references to the nonbargaining aspects; the reader will find treatments of some of them elsewhere in this volume.

We begin, conventionally, with a definition. For our present purpose an international crisis may be defined simply as a situation of severe conflict between adversary governments generated by the attempt of one side to change the status quo which is resisted by the other giving rise to the perception of a significant probability of war but not actual war. Other characteristics often present are surprise, shortness of decision time, unpredictability, and fears of losing control of events. But the element of a perceived real possibility of war is central and essential and the common denominator of all crises.

As a corollary of this, it is useful to conceive of a crisis as a "transition zone" between peace and war. Almost all wars are preceded by a crisis of some sort although, of course, not all crises eventuate in war. Theorizing about international relations has tended to assume either a condition of *peace* or a condition of *war*, with relatively little attention to the hybrid condition lying between and the process of transformation from peace to war.[2] A conception of crisis as a transition zone brings out one of the most significant and interesting characteristics of crisis: crisis behavior tends to be a mixture of behavioral elements typical of war and other elements typical of "peacetime diplomacy." A crisis is a sort of nexus where the coming together of these two different behavioral types creates a meld with unique characteristics of its own. Specifically, in bargaining terms, crisis behavior tends to be a mixture of *coercion* and *accommodation*. War in its most extreme forms is the pure, ultimate form of coercion—the raw, physical clash of armed forces—in a context where the pursuit of objectives in conflict greatly predominates over the pursuit of common interests. Peacetime diplomacy is typified by accommodative negotiation: the exchange of values or trading of concessions in order to realize some common interest or settle a dispute peacefully. In a crisis these two ideal types are modified in a converging direction. Coercion becomes coercion by potential or threatened force, or perhaps sometimes by small doses of actual force, usually administered for political effect rather than for physical compulsion. Negotiation is characterized by a sharp rise in the element of conflict over the element of common interest; the parties' aims shift from "trading for mutual advantage" toward "winning"; techniques change from the accommodative mode toward tactics of threat and pressure; and the emotional climate shifts from amity to hostility and fear. The convergence may or may not be complete. When it is, we may speak of the resulting interaction as "coercive negotiation." Often, however, we find that one or the other type tends to predominate in different *stages* of a crisis. A "stage model"

2. Studies of deterrence and the role of force in peacetime diplomacy have often implicitly assumed such an intermediate condition but, with a few exceptions, without attempting to clearly delineate it and explore systematically its structure and behavioral dynamics. Among the exceptions are Herman Kahn, *On Escalation: Metaphors and Scenarios* (New York: Praeger, 1965); Oran Young, *The Politics of Force* (Princeton: Princeton University Press, 1968); Charles F. Hermann, *Crises in Foreign Policy* (Indianapolis: Bobbs-Merrill, 1969); and Charles A. McClelland, "The Acute International Crisis," *World Politics*, 14 (October 1961), 182–205. Young's excellent volume is conceptually closest to the present paper; it is the first attempt to apply and test bargaining theory in crisis case studies.

of a crisis might appear as follows. Out of "peace" there develops a precrisis period of *active conflict*, in which one side indicates dissatisfaction with the status quo, plus an inclination to do something about it, and the parties engage in mild recriminations and warnings, but war is not yet perceived as a distinct possibility. This is followed by a *challenge*, either verbal or physical, which is *resisted*, and the possibility of war moves into consciousness. Then there is a period of *confrontation*, characterized by rising tension and the increasing predominance of coercive tactics, with each side standing firm and attempting to prevail, either offensively or defensively. This phase, of course, may move into *war* or, alternatively, if one side clearly establishes its dominance of credibility and resolve, or both decide they must retreat from the brink to avoid mutual disaster, it deescalates to a *negotiation* phase in which accommodative tactics come to the fore, although some coercive activity may still continue. Accommodation may range from creating a face-saving rationale for the loser to back down to both sides making genuine concessions to reach a settlement. The cycle then moves back again to "peaceful diplomacy," perhaps conditioned by modifications of perception and power following from the crisis outcome.[3]

We must admit that in this bit of conceptualization we have been constructing an ideal type which hopefully captures some essential elements but to which the real world, perversely as usual, refuses to conform in detail. The most superficial survey of historical crises reveals a great variety. Some are protracted, others are short-lived. Some involve demands and resistance with both sides hoping to get their way short of war; others are merely preludes to war or pretexts for war manufactured by a state bent on violence. Some are thrust upon the actors by a semi-autonomous "course of events"; others are deliberately created. Some, such as the "war scare of 1875," are "illusory" crises created by an emotional press and public opinion; others involve a real clash of state interests. Some, such as the Sarajevo crisis of 1914, are characterized by a high degree of loss of control over events by statesmen; others are more calculated and controlled. Some, such as the Franco-Prussian crisis of 1870, are essentially dyadic; others include participation by several states. Some involve the great powers; others do not. Some generate only a moderate danger of war, others a very high danger; and some, of course, actually result in war. Some, such as the present simmering crisis between Israel and the Arab states, include a considerable amount of short-of-war violence as bargaining moves; others are limited to nonviolent coercion. Some, such as the Lebanon crisis of 1958, are touched off by internal war or revolutionary situations; others are essentially inter-state affairs. The kinds of initiating challenges and issues at stake in crises are extremely varied. The list of variables and variations seems almost endless. Naturally, this heterogeneity makes generalization difficult. It means that empirical findings of across-the-board regularities are likely to be rather general in character and that more specific generalizations have to be tied to particular classes of crisis contexts.

SYSTEMIC ENVIRONMENT AND BARGAINING SETTING

The crisis context can be described in terms of two sets of variables: systemic environment and bargaining setting. The major variables in the *systemic*

3. I am indebted to Charles Lockhart for this phase model. Charles Lockhart, "A Bargaining Conceptualization of International Crises," Center for International Conflict Studies, State University of New York at Buffalo (mimeographed), April 1970.

environment are the general structure of the system (number of major actors and distribution of power among them), existing alliances and alignments, and the nature of military technology. These are not just passive factors to be sketched in as "background"; they may very strongly influence the nature, course, and outcome of the crisis.

For example, there are obvious differences between prenuclear crises and nuclear age crises (along with some similarities as well). Nuclear weapons have raised the costs of war by several orders of magnitude, although the behavioral effects of this are limited by the inability of the human mind to fully comprehend the horrors of nuclear war. Nevertheless, statesmen probably fear war a good deal more now than in the nineteenth century, and this induces a considerable measure of caution into crisis behavior. It has raised the threshold of challenge or provocation above which statesmen feel themselves willing or bound to fight. Consequently, it has released, below this threshold, for coercive purposes, a wide variety of moves which in former times might have triggered war. In the nineteenth century there was not much room for maneuver between verbal communication and full-scale violence. But, since World War II, states have been extremely inventive in developing a varied ensemble of physical maneuvers and "uses of force short of war" to communicate and test resolve in crises. Military force, in general, has been somewhat transformed from an instrument of direct physical coercion to one of psychological or political influence. Tests of will on such matters as the buzzing of aircraft, the lowering or nonlowering of truck tailgates, or the boarding or nonboarding of a vessel are preliminary psychological "battles," the outcome of which registers the probable "balance of resolve" on the main issue. Limited violence is now permissible as a means of crisis coercion so that in some cases "crisis" may merge imperceptibly into "limited war." In fact, much of the theory of limited war—ideas such as limited objectives, restrained application of means, symbolic action, escalation, and tacit bargaining—has close parallels in the developing theory of crisis behavior.

A hypothesis which presently enjoys considerable support is that crises perform a surrogate function in the nuclear age—they take the place of war in the resolution of conflict, between great powers at least, when war has become too costly and risky. This notion casts crises in a role somewhat similar to the eighteenth-century quadrilles of marching and maneuver which produced settlements from superiority of position rather than brute superiority in violence. From this point of view, nuclear age crises are functional rather than dysfunctional, but for obvious reasons, mainly the uncertainty about where the "threshold" lies, the hypothesis should not be pushed too far in policy.

There are other probable differences following from differences in system structure—the familiar multipolar-bipolar distinction. In the multipolar system of the nineteenth century, the security of the leading states was critically dependent on having reliable allies, but at the same time the defection and realignment of allies was an ever-present possibility. Consequently, the preservation of alliances was an important stake in crises, and the support or non-support of allies was a crucial determinant of their outcomes. Bargaining options were restricted by the differing interests of allies and the need to coordinate policy and tactics with the partner. Restraint of a too-intransigent ally was sometimes as important as defeating the opponent, but also difficult because of dependence on the ally's power. The shift to bipolarity after World War II considerably reduced in crises the role of alliance relations between the superpowers. The

United States and the Soviet Union, being much less dependent on allies for their power in crises and war, had a wider range and greater flexibility in their choice of bargaining tactics. Since their allies needed them much more than they needed their allies, and since realignment was not a realistic option for the lesser allies in any case, the superpowers could much more effectively restrain and even discipline their partners than was possible in the earlier multipolar system. The preservation of alliances became less important as a stake or constraint in the crisis when compared to other values and constraints involved in the conflicts between the superpowers themselves.[4]

The crisis preceding World War I, for instance, was very heavily influenced by the power structure of the international system in 1914, a structure of decentralized multipolarity organized in a two-alliance confrontation. The virtual equilibrium between the two alliances, and the substantial power contribution of the lesser alliance members, meant that the lesser and least responsible allies were able to call the tune; the alliance leaders (Germany and France) were unable to exert enough leverage on the lesser allies (Austria and Russia) to prevent them from carrying the crisis into war because they needed the lesser allies too much and, therefore, were unable to make the ultimate threat of withdrawal of support. The eruption of this crisis into war was largely determined by systemic factors—system structure and military technology—as well as rigid military plans over which the statesmen could exercise only limited control. Alliance relations in this crisis can be instructively compared with the high degree of control which the United States was able to exercise over its allies in the Suez and Formosa Straits crises, or Soviet control over its subordinate ally in the successive Berlin crises.

The *bargaining setting* includes a wide range of background factors which are more immediate and directly related to the bargaining process than those in the systemic environment. These include the conflict of interest which underlies the crisis, the recent relations between the parties, the parties' comparative valuation of the stakes at issue, their relative military capabilities and subjective fears of war, and precrisis commitments. Also a part of the bargaining setting are various other asymmetries between the parties such as geographical distance from the crisis area, who is the "aggressor" and who the "defender," conceptions of the "legitimacy" of the status quo or the demand to change it, and, most important, the parties' precrisis "images" of all these things, including, consequently, their reciprocal perceptions of each other's "resolve."

THE BARGAINING PROCESS

The systemic environment and bargaining setting establish the fundamental *structure* of the crisis. They produce an *incentive structure* and a *set of alternatives* for each actor, and a set of *initial images* held by each actor about the other's incentive structure and alternatives. The incentive structure is a set of values (payoffs) for each possible crisis outcome, of which the most prominent components are the parties' "interests" in the objects at stake, their "bargaining reputation," and their estimated costs of war. (Relative capabilities are reflected in their predictions about war outcomes, which in turn are reflected in subjective "war costs.") Images about the other party's incentive structure will have been

4. A similar point is made by Kenneth N. Waltz, "International Structure, National Force, and the Balance of World Power," *Journal of International Affairs*, 21 (1967), 218–219.

built up over time through observation of the party's past behavior, his verbal declarations, his geographical position, his political and social system, his military capabilities, and perhaps to some degree through "empathy."

Incentive structures and other parties' beliefs about them are the basic stuff of international politics and they are the basic determinants of behavior in, and the outcome of, a crisis. They are implicit in any situation even if no bargaining moves are made. They are the sources of "inherent" bargaining power. Bargaining "moves" or "tactics" are designed to manipulate and change alternatives, incentives, and the other's image of them so as to shift the outcome in a direction favorable to oneself.[5] In some cases bargaining moves are no more than a kind of veneer of dynamic activity which modifies only marginally the basic determinants; in other cases they may have a considerable effect. As a general rule, the greater the *uncertainty* in each party's image of the other's alternatives and incentives, the greater the possible effect on the outcome of the bargaining *process* and "tactical" bargaining power.

But what, exactly, is a bargaining move?[6] Rather than attempting a comprehensive definition, it seems more useful to distinguish some different kinds of moves. The first distinction is between *coercive* and *accommodative* moves. As the term implies, a coercive move puts pressure on the adversary to accept one's demand or bargaining "position," perhaps by threatening punishment if he fails to comply, or by a variety of other techniques. An accommodative move is one which moves a party's bargaining position closer to the opponent's, thus closer to a settlement. These two sorts of moves relate to the two principal dimensions of any bargaining process: the successive and possibly converging positions taken by the parties regarding the issues at stake (accommodative), and the pressures each brings to bear to persuade the adversary to accept its own current position (coercive). A typical coercive move is the "threat"; a typical accommodative move is the "concession."

A second and cross-cutting distinction is between *basic* moves and *communication* moves. Basic moves either (1) make an actual choice among action alternatives or (2) change the action options available to one or both sides or (3) both. In the coercive dimension, often, they also raise the level of shared ongoing cost and risk. A very simple crisis might have only two action options available to each party: "yield" completely or "fight" all out. To yield would be a basic accommodative move; to fight would be a basic coercive move. More complex situations may present a number of options in both the coercive and accommodative dimensions. On the coercive side, there may be a variety

5. Of course, the opponent's image of one's incentive structure may be modified during a crisis by information coming from many other sources than one's deliberate bargaining moves—for example, speeches made for domestic audiences, statements by Congressmen or the press, or evidence of support or opposition from general public opinion. Jervis calls these sources "indices," to be distinguished from deliberate bargaining "signals," which are equivalent to our "communication moves." See Robert Jervis, *The Logic of Images in International Relations* (Princeton: Princeton University Press, 1970).

6. Thomas C. Schelling defines a "strategic move" as "one that influences the other person's choice, in a manner favorable to oneself, by affecting the other person's expectations of how one's self will behave." As will be seen, this is a somewhat narrower definition than the totality of the classification given here. Thomas C. Schelling, *The Strategy of Conflict* (Cambridge: Harvard University Press, 1960), p. 160. The present essay owes much to Schelling's pioneer work on strategic bargaining.

of action moves between merely standing firm and an all-out "fight." And if the issue at stake is divisible or if side payments can be arranged, there will be a range of concession options available, short of full capitulation, on the accommodative side. Any actual choice among these various options we define as a basic move. The common denominator of all basic moves is that they change (reduce, increase, or modify) the basic alternatives available to the parties—that is, they create a *new situation* with a new problem or new choice facing one or both parties. Obviously, deciding to yield or to fight all out creates a radically different situation—either war or peaceful termination of the crisis. Choosing an intermediate option usually either forecloses alternatives or creates new alternatives (or transforms hypothetical ones to real ones) for either or both parties and thus changes the character of the ongoing crisis.

These intermediate basic moves may exercise coercion in several possible ways. An *escalatory* move is one which physically and visibly moves a party closer to an act of violence, or initiates a small amount of violence, or steps up the level of violence. The coercive effect comes from increasing the opponent's fears of an outbreak of violence or of intensified violence. A *committal* move eliminates the option of yielding for the committing party, usually by some physical or administrative act such as deploying troops on a boundary, blocking the opponent's access to the territory at stake, or handing over control of one's decision to an ally or subordinate officials who are known to prefer fighting to yielding.[7] Since the mover has eliminated his "yield" option, the adversary knows it is he who must yield if violence is to be avoided. A *circumventing* move is an end run around an opponent's committal move by inventing an option other than violence for preserving one's interests in the object at issue. As a committal move "passes the initiative," the burden of decision for starting violence, to the opponent, the circumventing move "reverses the initiative," passing back to the original committer the onerous burden of deciding whether to initiate war or greater violence. Finally, the *fait accompli* is a quick surprise transformation of the status quo; like the committal move, it forces upon the adversary the burden of deciding whether to initiate war or risk of war in order to undo the transformation. Other classes perhaps could be devised, and some moves may produce more than one of these effects.

Some examples of basic coercive moves would be the Russian mobilization in 1914 (escalatory), the German counter-mobilization and initiation of war (escalatory), the Soviet blockade of Berlin in 1948 (committal), the countermove of the airlift (circumventing), the Chinese artillery blockade of Quemoy island in 1958 (escalatory and committal), the U.S. convoying of supplies to Chiang's troops on the island (circumventing), the Soviet emplacement of missiles in Cuba (*fait accompli*), the establishment of the U.S. blockade in the Cuban crisis (escalatory and committal), the construction of the Berlin Wall (*fait accompli*), and so on. All these moves fundamentally changed the options of one or both parties in some way. Basic coercive moves are almost always physical acts of some kind, but not all physical acts are basic moves. For example, "shows of force," such as naval visits or troop maneuvers, are more properly considered "communication moves."

In the accommodative dimension an explicit concession can be considered a basic move, first, because it usually eliminates for the conceding party

7. We have in mind here Schelling's "irrevocable commitment" or "burning bridges." Schelling, *Strategy of Conflict*, chap. 2.

the option of retreating to his former position, and, second, because it creates for the other party the new option of accepting the concession as the basis for settlement. Thus, Khrushchev's offer to remove his missiles from Cuba if the United States would promise not to invade Cuba was a "basic accommodative move." In an earlier era, an example would be the French offer of Central African territory to Germany as a concession to end the Moroccan crisis of 1911.

Communication moves are not action choices, nor do they change the basic alternatives available to the parties. In game theory terminology, they are "preplay communication." The crisis may be conceived as a "game" with a set of action alternatives for each party.[8] The actual "play" of the game involves choices (basic moves) among these action alternatives, perhaps a sequence of choices and responses. The parties know that the outcome will depend not only on their own choices but on the adversary's choices as well. An outcome is usually a "bundle" of different sorts of consequences, and a party's "payoff" for each outcome is the sum of the utilities he attaches to the items in the bundle.

Within this context the purpose of coercive communications is to influence the other party's choice of basic moves in a direction favorable to oneself. They may accomplish this in two general ways: (1) by influencing the other's expectations of one's own basic choices, either by directly declaring one's intentions or by indirectly molding or changing his image of one's own incentive structure (payoffs), or (2) by changing his payoffs for the various possible outcomes.[9] If the crisis involves a sequence of basic moves and counter-moves, coercive communication can take place anywhere in the sequence and may attempt to influence any potential basic moves further on in the sequence.

An obvious example of a coercive communication move is the *threat*, which usually changes the threatener's own incentive structure by engaging new values (prestige, bargaining reputation), increases the probability that the threatener will choose the alternative threatened, changes the other party's *perception* of the threatener's incentive structure and probabilities of choice, and perhaps also modifies the other party's valuations of possible outcomes. But a threat is not a "basic move" because the action alternatives open to the parties are not changed. Its purpose is to influence the opponent's choice of a basic move at some future time. There are many other types of coercive communications which will be examined presently. In a crisis most coercive moves are communication moves. Basic moves are few, but more numerous in nuclear age crises than in prenuclear ones.

In the accommodative dimension a communication move may be described as a signal that one is willing to concede, perhaps contingent upon the other party's signaling a willingness to reciprocate. It may be a proposal for settlement based on mutual concession, possibly involving a "tie-in" with other issues in which one party concedes on one issue in return for the other's concession on another. It could also be a signal of willingness to deescalate violence or the risk of violence, to move down the "escalation ladder," again, perhaps, depending on receipt of a reciprocal signal.

The distinctions we have been discussing may appear clearer in Figure 1.

8. In an actual crisis, all the action alternatives may not be apparent at the outset; they may have to be searched for, discovered, or manufactured during its course.

9. Changing the adversary's payoffs usually involves changing his perception of the objective "bundles of consequences" for outcomes, not the subjective utilities by which he values the items in the bundles.

	Coercive	Accommodative
Basic	Choice of coercive action option (e.g., fight, escalate, physically commit)	Choice of accommodative option (e.g., yield, concede, accept other party's concession)
Communication	Signal intent to choose basic action option (e.g., threat, warning) Change adversary's payoffs or his perceptions of own payoffs	Signal willingness to choose accommodative option (hint of readiness to concede or deescalate; proposal for compromise settlement)

FIGURE 1. Types of bargaining moves.

A few clarifying and qualifying remarks may be in order. This matrix is merely designed to capsulize the preceding discussion and show how the coercive-accommodative and basic-communication dimensions intersect to produce four different classes of moves. As usual in classification schemes there is some overlap and fuzziness.

The distinction between basic and communication moves does not mean that basic moves do not also communicate something; in fact, that may be their most significant effect. For example, the coercive value of Thomas Schelling's "irrevocable commitment" or "burning bridges" lies in its being communicated to the adversary so that he realizes we have foreclosed our option of yielding and, therefore, he must yield to avoid high mutual costs. The essence of bargaining is in communication; the distinction being made here is that some moves *merely* communicate whereas others change the fundamental structure of the situation as well.

Some communication moves, like ultimata, are pretty basic in that they may irrevocably commit the communicator to carrying out the threatened act and foreclose other options. The point of difference, then, is only that the commitment is arranged by verbal rather than physical means. Conversely, certain physical "basic moves" may shade into the category of "threats." The U.S. blockade in the Cuban missile crisis, for example, would seem to be a clear basic move, since it apparently foreclosed for the United States the option of not firing on contraband ships which tried to force the blockade, and it created a new set of alternatives for the Soviets. But the U.S. Navy *could* have been ordered not to fire on a Soviet missile-carrying ship which refused to stop. From this perspective the blockade could be interpreted merely as a very strong threat by show of force—that is, a communication move. In terms of ability to commit, or coercive power, certain kinds of verbal communications may be stronger than certain kinds of physical basic moves. Or the committal quality of the latter, their apparent foreclosure or change in the parties' alternatives, may reside not so much in their physical irrevocability but, as in the case of threat, in the *costs* which would be incurred if they were retracted. Despite such ambiguities and grey areas at the boundary, it still appears that the distinctions we have made are analytically useful.

COERCIVE BARGAINING TACTICS AND THE "CREDIBILITY-CRITICAL RISK" MODEL

In actual crises one finds a great variety of coercive bargaining tactics or moves and at first glance they seem devoid of any regularity or pattern. However, it is possible to impose a pattern or classification in terms of coercive function by linking them to a game-type model which I shall call the "credibility-critical risk" model. It is adapted primarily from work by Ellsberg and Zeuthen.[10] Besides providing a means for classifying tactics (primarily coercive communication moves), it also models some of the dynamics of the crisis bargaining process.

Figure 2 portrays a rather simple crisis precipitated by an aggressor's demand that a defender yield something worth ten units under threat of war.[11] If the aggressor "stands firm" and the defender "complies," the payoffs are 10 and −10, respectively. If the defender is firm and the aggressor complies (fails to carry out his threat and lets the matter drop), the aggressor loses and the

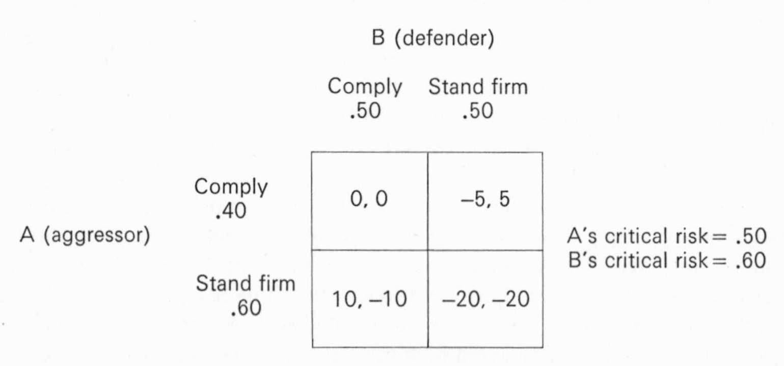

FIGURE 2. An illustration of the "credibility-critical risk" model.

defender gains bargaining reputation, prestige, and so on, worth 5 units. The consequence of both standing firm is war at a mutual cost of 20. The outcome comply-comply we assume, for convenience, is a compromise with no net gain or loss to either party. We assume further that each party is uncertain about the other's payoffs and that its own payoffs are subject to change.[12]

10. Daniel Ellsberg, "The Theory and Practice of Blackmail," a lecture delivered at Lowell Institute, Boston, March 1959, in a series entitled "The Art of Coercion: A Study of Threats in Economic Conflict and War." Frederick Zeuthen, *Problems of Monopoly and Economic Warfare* (London: George Routledge & Sons, 1930), chap. 4. A somewhat similar model is also presented in Richard E. Walton and Robert B. McKersie, *A Behavioral Theory of Labor Negotiations* (New York: McGraw-Hill, 1965), chap. 3.

11. The object at stake might conveniently be assumed to be a small third state which is allied to or protected by *B*. For *A*, to "stand firm" means, more explicitly, "attack if *B* does not comply." For *B*, standing firm means "defend if *A* attacks."

12. For the sophisticated game theorist, we should point out that this model drops certain standard game theory assumptions: that the preference schedules of the parties remain fixed during the bargaining and that each party knows or can find out the preference schedule of the other. Thus we have taken small steps toward "real life" in which, of course, values (or the objects valued) do change during interaction and there is always uncertainty about the other bargainer's values. As already indicated, coercion-by-communication in fact depends on the existence of these instabilities and

If either party can commit itself absolutely and irrevocably to "standing firm," and communicate this commitment, the outcome is clear—the other party must comply. However, this model assumes that commitments are not always (perhaps hardly ever) absolute; that there is always some uncertainty in the bargainers' minds as to whether the other party is "really" committed. The adversary's commitment is subjectively perceived as a probability estimate rather than a certainty one way or the other. In the vernacular, whether a party gives in or not depends on whether it feels the probability (credibility) of the other side's being committed is "too high to take a chance" or "worth risking."

The concept of "critical risk" as developed by Ellsberg expresses the notion that there is some threshold of risk representing the maximum risk a party can "stand" without capitulating. If the credibility of the other's threat or commitment is perceived as higher than this threshold, the party must give in; if it is lower, the party will continue to stand firm.

The critical risk for either side is derived from a comparison of its payoff from complying with its payoffs for standing firm. In our model, *B* loses 10 by complying with the demand. If he stands firm he either gains 5 or loses 20 depending upon *A*'s choice. If he estimates a .40 chance that *A* will comply and a .60 chance that *A* will be firm, *B*'s "expected value" for standing firm is -10, just equal to the cost of compliance. In other words, when *B* estimates the credibility of *A*'s threat at .60, *B* is indifferent between complying or standing firm. This is *B*'s "critical risk"—the credibility of *A*'s threat or commitment must be at least this high to force *B* to back down. A similar calculation will show that *A*'s critical risk is .50. If *A* estimates the probability of *B*'s firmness at higher than this, *A* must retreat (renege on his threat). If the probability seems lower than .50, *A* will firmly commit himself to attack.[13]

It is possible, of course, that *both* parties will feel that the credibility of the opponent's threat of firmness is lower than their own critical risk. In this situation both may firmly commit themselves and the outcome is war. It is war "by miscalculation," because if either side had perceived the other's firm commitment, then the other's threat credibility would have exceeded its own critical risk and it would have conceded. Conversely, if each party perceives that the credibility of the other's threat is higher than its own critical risk, neither can afford the risk of standing pat on its initial position and the stage is set for compromise.

Credibility is the *opponent's perception* of the probability that the threatened alternative will be chosen—that is, the probability that the party will "stand firm." In part, this is a function of the opponent's perception of the threatening

---

uncertainties. Also, contrary to pure game theory "in normal form," we assume the players move sequentially rather than simultaneously. We further assume that they predict the other's choices probabilistically, this being a consequence of their imperfect information about the other's utility schedules.

A 2×2 matrix is, of course, a considerable simplification of real cases. Many crises (though not all) present more than two basic alternatives to each party and these would require either an extended form "game tree" model or an "expanded normal form" model. A further simplification is that there are only two parties so that alliance phenomena are left out.

13. The formula for critical risk is $\frac{uF_1 - uC_1}{uF_1 - uW}$ when uF_1 is the utility of *successful* firmness, uC_1 is the (negative) utility of compliance, and uW is the (negative) utility of war.

party's payoffs for alternative outcomes. If *B*, for example, had confident and accurate knowledge of *A*'s payoffs, *B* might place little credence in *A*'s threat since *A*'s war costs are so much larger than his compliance cost and his valuation of the object at stake. Or, vice-versa, if *B* (mistakenly) believed that *A*'s cost of compliance was greater than his cost of war, he might attach 100 per cent credibility to *A*'s threat of firmness. But *B* does not have this kind of confident knowledge about *A*'s preference system; he has only vague impressions, which may suggest some general likelihood of *A* standing firm, but nothing more. So his estimate of *A*'s threat credibility must be probabilistic rather than absolute. A further complication is that *A*'s resolve to stand firm will also depend on his perception of *B*'s degree of resolve,[14] so *B* must also try to estimate this highly uncertain factor in judging the credibility of *A*'s threat.[15] (Of course, the same considerations apply to *A*'s assessment of the credibility of *B*'s threat.) Credibility estimates may also be made partly from more "direct" indices which do not involve estimating the threatener's payoffs and perceptions—for example, items such as his behavior in previous crises, his domestic political situation, his apparent freedom of choice, or his apparent degree of rationality.

For our present purpose the main point of interest is that a party can manipulate both his own threat credibility and his opponent's critical risk by a variety of bargaining tactics. This is possible largely because of the parties' uncertainties about each other's payoffs, perceptions, and intentions, and also because of uncertainties and instabilities in their estimates of their own payoffs. The "bargaining problem" for each side is to modify the other's perceptions and utilities so that the perceived credibility of its own threat of firmness is higher than the other's critical risk. Then the other must give way. Thus there are two broad classes of coercive bargaining tactics for each side—those which attempt to increase one's own threat credibility and those which seek to reduce the adversary's critical risk. The class of "increasing threat credibility" has two sub-

14. It is perhaps worth noting that "resolve" and "credibility" are close to being two sides of the same coin. Resolve is the party's own degree of determination to carry out the threatened alternative; credibility is the opponent's perception of that degree of determination. Theoretically, resolve is likely to be more absolute (less probabilistic) than credibility because, presumably, a party knows more about his own incentive structure than his opponent does. Cf. George Kent, "The Effects of Threats," Mershon Center for Education in National Security, The Ohio State University Pamphlet Series, no. 6, September 1967, pp. 84–86.

15. This last sentence deserves a little elaboration. In estimating the credibility of *A*'s threat, *B* must try to estimate not only *A*'s payoffs and other direct indicators of intent, but also *A*'s belief about *B*'s resolve, which is a function of *A*'s perceptions of *B*'s payoffs. In short, *A*'s resolve to stand firm will depend in part on his perception of *B*'s resolve, which in turn depends on *B*'s perception of *A*'s resolve, and so on. We enter here the familiar thicket of "infinite regress of expectations." We may cut through the thicket simply by saying that, given a party's set of payoffs for winning, yielding, or fighting, his resolve will further vary inversely with his perception of the probability that the opponent will stand firm; and the opponent must attempt to estimate this perception in making *his* estimate of the credibility of the party's threat. This is probably about as far as the infinite regress is ever carried in crisis diplomacy. Robert Jervis has discussed this regressive phenomenon in "Aspects of Security and Bargaining," Center for International Affairs, Harvard University, January 1970 (mimeographed), pp. 33–34. Jervis' essay has been published in revised form in J. Roland Pennock and John W. Chapman, eds., *Coercion*, NOMOS 14 (Chicago: Aldine, 1972).

classes: (1) changing the opponent's perceptions of one's own payoffs, and (2) changing the opponent's estimate of the probability of one's choices without modifying one's apparent payoffs. Reducing the adversary's critical risk involves only one general type of activity: changing the adversary's payoffs. What follows is an attempt to list and classify, in terms of these functional categories, a variety of coercive bargaining tactics. The list is far from exhaustive and the classification could undoubtedly be further refined.

I. TACTICS TO INCREASE CREDIBILITY

A. *Change one's apparent utilities* (payoffs)

Here the primary objectives are to minimize the adversary's perception of one's own net costs of war (initially, in the model, −20 for both sides), to maximize one's apparent valuation of winning the confrontation (10 for A and 5 for B), and to maximize one's apparent cost of compliance (initially, −5 for A and −10 for B). Some of these tactics may actually change one's payoffs; others merely change the opponent's perceptions of them. For bargaining effect it is, of course, the adversary's perceptions that count.

Reduce one's apparent net cost of war

1. Increase capabilities.
2. Increase readiness of capabilities.
3. Various verbal statements.
   a. "We don't fear war"
   b. "We will win"
   c. "Your ally will not support you"
   d. "Our ally will support us"
   e. "We believe the war will be limited"

Increase one's apparent valuation of the stakes (increase apparent costs of backing down, increase the apparent value of winning)

1. Make threats which engage prestige, honor, and future bargaining reputation.
2. Couple the present issue with other issues; make it appear as only one aspect of a larger confrontation.
   a. "If I give in here, you'll expect me to give in on X"
   b. "If I give in to this demand, this will only embolden you to make further demands"
   c. "I know that your ultimate aims are unlimited"
3. Cite the legitimacy or "fairness" of one's position.
   a. Inviolability of the status quo
   b. The "right" of compensation
4. Tie one's position to moral principles.
5. Invoke legal rights.
6. Invoke alliance obligations (moral principle as well as political value of alliance preservation and cohesion).
7. Cite need to "preserve the balance of power" or "redress the balance."
8. Cite danger of internal revolution if one capitulates.
9. Invoke historical tradition (e.g., Monroe Doctrine in the Cuban missile crisis).

B. *Increase apparent probability of firmness without changing payoffs*

Although some of the following tactics may carry indirect implications about one's payoffs, their primary intent or effect is to modify the opponents' direct perceptions of the probabilities of one's choices.

1. Irrevocable commitment (physically or administratively eliminate the alternative of compliance, or make compliance physically or administratively difficult; "relinquish the initiative").
2. Loss of control over subordinates (actually give up control, threaten to give up control, or claim lack of control, e.g., warn that "volunteers" will act).
3. Devolve decision-making authority to lower levels in the command hierarchy to persons whose incentive structure is more favorable to firmness than that of the governmental leadership (or threaten to do so).
4. Devolve decision-making authority to a proxy state or ally whose incentive structure is different than one's own (or threaten to do so).
5. Claim that one's constituency will not allow compliance or compromise (the constituency may be "the cabinet," "Congress," "public opinion," "allies," etc.).
6. Parliamentary votes and resolutions supporting one's position.
7. Pretend irrationality.
8. Express confidence in the adversary's rationality and good sense ("since you are reasonable and I am not, you must be the one to concede").
9. Express disbelief in the opponent's commitment or skepticism about his resolve ("my resolve is high because I think yours is low").
10. Emphasize uncertainties in the situation or the unpredictability of one's own behavior.
11. Show of force; minor use of force.
12. Represent oneself as a "force of nature," totally immune to argument and persuasion.

II. TACTICS TO REDUCE THE ADVERSARY'S CRITICAL RISK

The adversary's critical risk is a function of *his* payoffs—his cost of war and his valuation of the stakes. These utilities can be manipulated, although perhaps to a lesser degree than the adversary's perception of one's own utilities.

A. *Increase the adversary's estimate of his net costs of war*

1. Increase one's own capabilities and readiness.
2. Verbally exaggerate one's capabilities.
3. Emphasize the loyalty of one's own allies and the unreliability of the adversary's allies.
4. Stress the danger of escalation.
5. Indicate that one's objectives will expand after the war starts.

B. *Devalue the stakes for the adversary* (decrease his cost of compliance, reduce his estimate of the value of winning)

1. Provide a loophole or rationale which permits the adversary to back down or decommit himself with minimum humiliation.
2. Invoke community values (e.g., "peace") which he would serve by backing down.

3. Mobilize support of international community institutions for one's own position.
4. Undermine the legitimacy of the opponent's position (e.g., the status of West Berlin is "abnormal").
5. Challenge the legality of the opponent's position.
6. Minimize the element of duress or provocation in one's demands and threats.
   a. Pretend the crisis has arisen "autonomously" rather than by deliberate challenge (a Soviet tactic in the Berlin confrontations of 1958–1960 and 1961–1962)
   b. Give a noncoercive rationale for coercive moves (e.g., citing "technical reasons" for closing the Autobahn)
   c. Use ambiguous language or diplomatic "code language"
7. "Salami tactics."
8. Stress limited nature of aims ("this is my last demand").
9. Decouple the present issue from other or future issues ("This issue is special. I will not draw any conclusions about your general resolve if you concede on this issue").
10. Help the adversary undo his commitment by arguing that the situation does not meet the conditions specified in his threat or commitment.
11. Stress the common interests in settling the dispute and avoiding war.
12. Suggest plaudits to be gained from third parties or neutrals by giving in.
13. Use proxy state to present the challenge (devalues the stakes for the adversary because it is not a test of resolve with his primary opponent).

A distinction can be made between *direct* coercive communications, such as threats and warnings, which explicitly state or strongly imply an intent, and *indirect* tactics which attempt to manipulate underlying values or perceptions of them without explicitly stating an intent, although they may give support to direct statements of intent. Direct tactics have been rather thoroughly analyzed in the existing literature, so the discussion here will be limited to the indirect variety.

Typically, in crisis bargaining the parties try to impress each other with their high valuation of the object at stake and the dire consequences for themselves of backing down by invoking various kinds of values. A good example would be the reaction of the Western powers, principally the United States, to Soviet demands and threats during the successive Berlin crises of 1958 to 1962. We first invoked our legal rights under certain wartime and postwar agreements to remain in Berlin. Then we stressed our moral duty to protect the freedom of the West Berliners. We further expanded our apparent stake by citing the strategic and political values to us of standing firm. It was said that capitulating to the Russian demands would destroy West German confidence in their allies' will to defend them, seriously weaken the cohesion of NATO, and, most important, undermine the credibility in Soviet eyes of all our other commitments and thus seriously weaken our bargaining strength in future confrontations.

This latter tactic deserves closer examination. Jervis calls it "coupling" and Schelling refers to it as the "interdependence of commitments."[16] It was frequently invoked by Secretary of State Rusk and others during the Vietnam

16. Jervis, *Logic of Images*; and Thomas C. Schelling, *Arms and Influence* (New Haven: Yale University Press, 1966), pp. 55–59.

conflict under the label of the "integrity of American commitments." The party invoking these symbols is, in effect, drawing attention to the fact that the antagonists are involved in an infinite "supergame" with ultimately very high stakes, in which specific crises are recurrent "subgames." How a party comes out in a particular crisis—especially how the outcome affects the opponents' image of his resolve—will affect his bargaining power in future crises and ultimately the outcome of the supergame. In more conventional language, statesmen using this tactic are referring to a particular component of the balance of power which we might label the "balance of resolve," the other major component being the "balance of capabilities."

An analysis of the balance of resolve should deal with at least three questions: (1) To what extent do statesmen *actually* draw inferences about another state's probable future behavior from its firmness or weakness in a present crisis? (2) To what extent do statesmen *believe* such inferences are drawn by others and how does this belief affect their crisis behavior? (3) How frequently, and to what effect, do statesmen attempt to *communicate* such a belief as a bargaining tactic in crises? Only brief and tentative answers can be attempted here.

Logically, when a state reveals weakness in a crisis, the long-term balance of resolve shifts against it. The opponent, expecting future weakness, becomes more willing to challenge and stand firm in the next crisis. The first state finds it harder to communicate determination the next time, and, recognizing the other's increased resolve, may be forced to back down again with further damage to its resolve image, and so on through a sequence of losses. Or, if the disadvantaged state at some point *is* determined to fight, the over-confident opponent may precipitate a war by "miscalculation." There is an important truth in this simple logic which no statesman can afford to ignore. However, certain qualifications must be made. The theory of "interdependence of commitments," as usually stated, tends to ignore that a nation's degree of commitment in a particular crisis will depend on the value of its "interests" at stake, and that the intensity of these interests will vary across issues.[17] Statesmen probably perceive other nations as having a hierarchy of interests, some vital, some moderately important, some peripheral, and so on. If these perceptions are held with confidence (an important proviso), then the logic becomes more complex. A state which yielded on one issue would be expected to yield again when confronted with a similar level of risk on issues at the same level or lower in its interest hierarchy. But no reliable inferences could be drawn about its probable resolve on interests which are perceived as more important to it. Conversely, a *firm* stand on a particular issue probably would imply firmness on other interests at the same level or higher in the hierarchy, but not necessarily for lesser interests. If (as may very well be the case) the opponent is *uncertain* about the ranking and intensity of the state's interests, he may feel it is too risky to draw *any* confident inferences from one case to another. On the other hand, it could be argued that states consider their general reputations for resolve to be both much more important than, and relatively independent of, the more tangible stakes in a crisis—that is, that the game of "balance of resolve" is largely an autonomous game. If so, then "weakness is weakness"; yielding on any issue will strengthen the opponent's expectation that one will yield on other issues whatever the degree of intrinsic interest involved.

17. This point is made by Stephen Maxwell in "Rationality in Deterrence," Adelphi Paper no. 50, Institute of Strategic Studies (London), 1968, p. 19.

Images of resolve, and the balance of resolve, are likely to be less important in a multipolar system than a bipolar one because of the greater fluidity and uncertainty in the identification of other states as friends or foes. A show of weakness toward the antagonist of the moment may not necessarily be taken as a sign of weakness toward all possible opponents. Concessions in a crisis may not indicate general weakness, for they may be intended as a prelude to realignment with the opponent transformed into an ally. A state's resolve in a crisis will depend greatly on the degree of support it receives from its allies; hence its own past demonstrations of weakness or toughness are less reliable predictors. In a bipolar system, by contrast, enemy and ally identifications are relatively permanent; the superpowers are in conflict over a wide range of issues over a long period of time; their resolve is less dependent on the vagaries of allied support; and crises are likely to be viewed as linked episodes in a general global confrontation. In this system, it is more plausible that commitments and images of resolve will be "interdependent," that the parties will extrapolate demonstrated weakness or toughness from one situation to another. Also, with nuclear weapons super-imposed on a bipolar structure, the balance of resolve has increased in significance relative to the balance of capabilities. Since nuclear capabilities are essentially "unusable" by deliberate choice, physical comparisons of nuclear arsenals are less determining than reciprocal perceptions of resolve to take risks.

Even in bipolarity, however, there are further qualifications to be made. With the passage of time and shifts in the climate of public opinion, a nation's behavior in a past crisis may seem an increasingly unreliable indicator of future behavior. Regimes change, and it is at least problematical whether one government's reputation for resolve carries over to its successor. Finally, a government's degree of resolve is likely to be influenced considerably by the peculiar circumstances and context of each crisis (apart from differences in the interests engaged). Since crises tend to be diverse in structure, background, emotional content, and so on, predictions of a state's behavior from one case to another may seem too risky.

Considering questions (2) and (3), it can be asserted confidently that statesmen in a crisis often do express concern for their resolve reputations and a belief in the theory of "interdependence of commitments." Whether such expressions reflect an actual belief, or are intended merely as bargaining tactics, or as rationalizations to domestic publics for tough stances taken for other reasons, or perhaps all three, is often hard to discern in actual cases. The concern is expressed often enough in private intra-governmental discussion to indicate that it is genuine. Judging from the public record, it is more important to United States decision makers than to Soviet leaders, although it is not absent from Soviet crisis communications. For the United States, the concern is probably linked to a defensive self-image, and an image of the Soviets and Communist Chinese as persistently expansionist powers who are constantly probing for signs of our weakness.

As a bargaining tactic, invoking the interdependence of one's commitments or a need to protect one's resolve image is designed to magnify one's apparent values at stake in a crisis, and thus to convince the adversary that one must stand firm. The bargaining effectiveness of such statements does not depend directly on whether the opponent actually does predict our future toughness or softness from our behavior in the present instance, but on whether he perceives that *we believe* he does. If we can instill this perception, we have then increased his appreciation of *our* values at stake, and that is what counts for bargaining purposes.[18] However, the adversary's actual predicting processes probably will have an indirect influence on the credibility of this tactic. Our assertion of concern for our long-term reputation for firmness is likely to seem more plausible to him if he in fact does predict our future resolve from our behavior in the present instance. It will seem even more plausible if he believes we make similar inferences about him—if he believes in the interdependence of his own commitments.

The obverse of "coupling" is "de-coupling," to use Jervis' terminology.[19] Whereas coupling is a device to enhance the credibility of one's own threats and firmness, decoupling is used to lower the adversary's threshold of "critical risk" by reducing his perception of the values *he* would lose by complying. In general, the coercing party tries to convince his adversary that he will not draw any inferences about the opponent's future firmness on other issues if he capitulates on the present one. In one way or another, the party tries to communicate that the opponent should not think of the present dispute as a test of his general determination. One technique is to assert that the present case is "special" or unique, that other or future issues will be totally different in character, so that the opponent's resolve in those cases will be expected to reflect their particular circumstances. Another is to declare a belief that the present issue is not intrinsically important for the opponent; this implies, of course, that one will not expect him to back down later on other issues in which he has a greater interest. Finally, the coercer can promise that "this is my last demand." For example, in claiming that the Sudetenland was his "last demand," Hitler implied that his adversaries need not worry about the effects of concession on their future bargaining power because there would be no further occasions when their resolve would be tested. Rather similar was Khrushchev's speaking of West Berlin as the "bone in my throat": when this particular irritation was removed he would be satisfied. A general point to be made here is that a real concern about the interdependence of one's commitments depends on the assumption that one is facing an inherently aggressive and persistently adventuresome opponent, one whose aims are potentially unlimited.

Another tactic for reducing the opponent's critical risk is to invoke the common interest of all humanity in avoiding war, especially nuclear war, and to impress the opponent with his opportunity to render a great "service to mankind" and earn universal plaudits by stepping back from the brink. Thus in the Cuban missile crisis, President Kennedy called upon Chairman Khrushchev to "join in an historic effort to end the perilous arms race and to transform the history of man. He has an opportunity now to move the world back from the abyss of destruction—by returning to his government's own words that it had no need to station missiles outside its own territory, and withdrawing these weapons from Cuba."[20]

By such statements, Kennedy helped Khrushchev rationalize away the Soviet Union's political defeat in a postcrisis speech:

> *Which side triumphed, who won? In this respect one may say that it was sanity, the cause of peace and security of peoples, that won. Both sides*

18. Robert Jervis has stressed this point in *Logic of Images.*
19. *Ibid.*
20. Quoted in Elie Abel, *The Missile Crisis* (New York: Lippincott, 1966), p. 123.

displayed a sober approach and took into account that unless such steps are taken as could help to overcome the dangerous development of events, a World War III might break out.

As a result of mutual concessions and compromise, an understanding was reached which made it possible to remove dangerous tension, to normalize the situation.[21]

Inviting the opponent to capitulate or make concessions to avoid war as a "service to humanity" has the effect of diverting attention from the involvement of the conceding party's national honor and prestige, thus minimizing losses to these values. The focus is shifted from the conflict to the common interest and the defeated side thus appears not so much to be backing down under pressure from the opponent, because of his own fear of punishment from the opponent, but because of a concern for world community values. Humiliation and weakening of bargaining reputation may therefore be minimized.

A tactic which focuses more on the intrinsic value of the stakes is to claim that the existing status quo is in some way illegitimate. Khrushchev stated repeatedly during the Berlin crisis that the existence of a democratic and capitalist West Berlin in the middle of Communist East Germany was "abnormal," an anomalous tag end of World War II and a danger to international peace and security which should be liquidated. The argument apparently impressed President Eisenhower and others in the United States and Great Britain and contributed to dissension among the Western allies as to the extent of concessions which could be made on the Berlin issue. The effect of the "abnormality" tactic is to sow doubts in the defenders' minds about the legitimacy of their bargaining position. These doubts tend to devalue the defenders' appreciation of the value of the stakes. And when the abnormality can be portrayed as in itself a threat to international peace, the common interest in peace is mobilized as an offset to whatever values in the conflict dimension might be lost to the defenders in giving way.

Hitler made use of this gambit, in the form of the principle of national self-determination, with great success in the 1930s. It was abnormal or illegitimate, he said, for German minorities to be under the control of Czechoslovakia and for Austrian Germans to be separated from their fatherland. This argument struck a sympathetic chord in the Western democracies, especially England, because of their own commitment to the ideal of national self-determination. As long as Hitler could justify his demands by this slogan, they seemed in large measure legitimate, and his adversaries felt little loss in giving way to them.

Conversely, the defending side in a crisis may invoke the sanctity and legitimacy of the status quo. The established state of affairs (boundaries, spheres of influence, regularized procedures, etc.) gains legitimacy through general acceptance over time and this constitutes an important asymmetry favoring the bargaining power of the defender. The advantage is particularly marked in conflicts occurring within the generally recognized "sphere of influence" of a great power. The United States did not challenge the Soviet Union in Hungary in 1956, or in Czechoslovakia in 1968, basically because it realized that Soviet resolve would be extremely high in a crisis in its own backyard. In the Cuban missile case, President Kennedy emphasized that the Soviet intrusion "in an area well known to have a special and historical relationship to the United

21. *Ibid.*, p. 214.

States and the nations of the Western Hemisphere . . . is a deliberately provocative and unjustified change in the status quo which cannot be accepted by this country." The fundamental mistake of the Russians in this crisis was their failure to realize, until too late, that Cuba was for us like Hungary was for them.

Richardson has drawn attention to a technique which he calls "blurring the issues."[22] Here the aggressive side attempts to induce a belief among the defenders that the crisis has arisen "autonomously," as a result of factors in the situation which neither side controls. This tends to blur the fact that the crisis has been precipitated by the coercive behavior of one side. The Russians tried to explain the 1958–1960 Berlin crisis in these terms, arguing that tension had risen dangerously out of the facts of the situation itself and thus obscuring the fact that the responsibility lay in their own provocative behavior. The West was to "do its part," along with the Soviets, in liquidating a dangerous situation. If this tactic is successful, the victim of coercion can feel that his own prestige is not so pointedly engaged; concessions can be interpreted as simply cooperating in rectifying a mutually undesirable state of affairs, not as yielding to another state's coercion.

We have presented our list of tactics as if they were usable either for "aggression" or "defense," "compellence" or "resistance." Most of them *are* interchangeable, but some are not. For example, minimizing the element of duress, using "salami tactics," and stressing the limited nature of one's aims are usually aggressive moves. Engaging bargaining reputation by invoking the interdependence of one's commitments is more clearly a defensive tactic and so is the invoking of alliance obligations.

Some tactics, used defensively, are obvious counters to other tactics, used aggressively. For example, linking up the present issue with other or future issues is clearly the appropriate counter to an aggressor's attempt to use salami tactics or to decouple the present issue from future ones. Demonstrating the cohesion of one's alliance is a defensive counter to the adversary's attempt to divide the alliance or throw doubt on its solidarity. Making clear that the crisis has been caused by the opponent's challenge is a defensive counter to the opponent's attempt to portray the crisis as "autonomous."

Finally, our model should not be taken to imply that statesmen actually make precise numerical calculations of "payoffs," "credibility," and "critical risk." Obviously, they do not. The model is only an analytical tool and the utility and probability numbers are useful for clarifying logical relationships which probably occur in statesmen's thinking only as qualitative "considerations." There is some evidence, it must be admitted, that crisis decision makers may deviate considerably from the model's logic even in their qualitative thinking. In the Cuban missile crisis, for example, there does not seem to have been any attempt by the U.S. decision-making group to consciously or deliberately weigh the "value of the stake" against the "cost of war" discounted by some rough idea of the "likelihood" of war.[23] Getting the missiles out of Cuba was seen simply as an absolute imperative which had to be accomplished whatever the cost. Nuclear war was perceived as a definite possibility, but it was highly

22. James L. Richardson, *Germany and the Atlantic Alliance* (Cambridge: Harvard University Press, 1966), pp. 252–254.

23. President Kennedy, after the crisis, did say he thought the chances of nuclear war had been "between one out of three and 50–50," but this estimate does not seem to have entered into the deliberations during the crisis.

uncertain as compared to the certainty of the strong U.S. interest involved. In general, the decision makers acted upon the certainty of the interest and more or less gambled with, or resigned themselves to, the uncertain possibility of war, even though this possibility did induce a good deal of caution and prudence into their behavior. This case may not be representative, but it suggests that much empirical work remains to be done to uncover other sorts of "deviations," and, of course, it may turn out that the deviations overwhelm the logic. Still, the model is useful as an initial benchmark and as a device for clarifying the bargaining functions of coercive tactics.

OTHER VARIABLES IN COERCIVE BARGAINING

Publicity versus secrecy. In crisis bargaining the parties have a choice between communicating privately or publicly. In general, the public communication of threats and demands enhances their credibility, for the threatener is then more likely to be committed by maximum engagement of his prestige and bargaining reputation. Also, public opinion will expect the government to stand on a position publicly taken, and the bargainer can then cite public expectations as barring any concessions. There is, of course, the danger that if both parties become too committed to publicized positions their mutual inability to retreat will force them into a process of escalating moves as the only alternative.

There is much to be said for public bargaining if the prime objective is to become and appear committed, preferably before the opponent does, as is suggested in the writings of Thomas Schelling. However, this maxim contradicts a prominent theme in the more conventional treatment of diplomatic practice, to the effect that public diplomacy is bad because it commits the parties to uncompromisable positions and thus makes a settlement difficult. Essentially, the choice between the two approaches depends on what the objective is—whether it is to "win" the conflict, that is, to prevail over the opponent, or to reach a compromise settlement. The "public commitment" maxim focuses on the dimension of conflict and prescribes the best tactic for getting one's way in this dimension, while the "private diplomacy" norm focuses on the common interest in obtaining some kind of settlement regardless of who "wins." In practice, prudence may counsel a mixture of the two: perhaps a public but ambiguous statement of implied demands and hinted sanctions, combined with a more specific spelling out of one's position through private channels. The public communication then leaves room for some movement at the private level while preserving some of the pressure value of the public position.

Who communicates to whom. Another variable in the bargaining process is the choice of personnel to do the communicating—the actual voicing of demands, threats, offers, and so on. A communication carries greater weight, the more authoritative the source. Declarations of intent made by the President will be most readily believed, those by the Secretary of State will carry almost as much credibility, statements by the Secretary of Defense, members of the Joint Chiefs of Staff, and lesser officials will have somewhat lesser impact, and so on down the line. In theory, if the government is really committed to a position and wants to ensure its credible communication, the most authoritative spokesman should be chosen. Nevertheless, the available evidence does suggest a pattern of choosing lower level decision makers to issue the most severe threats. Since subordinate officials embody the national prestige to a lesser degree than the President and his top foreign policy advisers, and since statements by such officials can be disavowed with minimum embarrassment, they may be used to make pointed, explicit threats which would be too provocative or too committing when made at the topmost level.

For example, in the Quemoy crisis of 1958, the severest U.S. threat was made by the Secretary of the Air Force, James H. Douglas. He said, with State Department approval, that U.S. aircraft in the Formosa area "are capable of using high-explosive bombs or more powerful weapons, if necessary," a statement which was widely interpreted as a threat to use nuclear weapons, if necessary to protect Formosa.[24]

In the Cuban missile crisis, the stiffest Russian threats were uttered by subordinate officials. The press officer to the Soviet United Nations delegation declared to his American opposite number that "New York will be blown up tomorrow by Soviet nuclear weapons." A Soviet military officer, Lieutenant General Vladimir A. Dubovik, stated at a Soviet Embassy cocktail party that Soviet ship captains were under orders to defy the blockade around Cuba. "Our ships will sail through," he said. "And if it is decreed that these men must die, they will obey their orders and stay on course, or be sunk." Soviet Ambassador Dobrynin, at the same party, supplemented Dubovik's outburst with another bargaining tactic—that of feigning lack of control over subordinates in the crisis area—when he told his guests: "He is a military man; I am not. He is the one who knows what the Navy is going to do, not I."[25]

Certain specific persons and certain types of personnel may carry important symbolic significance as communicators during a crisis. The visit of Vice President Johnson to West Berlin at the height of the Berlin crisis in 1961 was important in demonstrating U.S. resolve, as was the appointment of General Lucius Clay as the President's special representative in Berlin. Clay's symbolic value lay in his former role as Commander of U.S. forces in West Germany, in the firm resolve he had demonstrated during the Berlin blockade of 1948–1949, and in the general knowledge that he was a "hard-liner." On the Soviet side, the appointment of Marshal Ivan S. Konev, a major Soviet war hero and Deputy Minister of Defense and also known as a hard-liner, as commander of the Soviet Army in East Germany had a similar significance.

An interesting example of the symbolic use of military personnel for intimidation purposes occurred at Hitler's famous confrontation with Chancellor Schuschnigg of Austria prior to the Austrian *Anschluss*. When Hitler met Schuschnigg at his mountain retreat, he was flanked by three high-ranking military officers, one of them the commander of German forces on the Austrian border. These officers were present during much of the conversation, or were called in by Hitler at strategic moments, especially when Schuschnigg balked at some demand. The presence and manipulation of these officers, plus the fact that Hitler himself was dressed in military tunic, probably had some psychological effect on the Austrian.

Private individuals may be usefully co-opted for bargaining purposes during a crisis. The most threatening words uttered by Khrushchev during the Cuban missile crisis were spoken to William Knox, president of Westinghouse

24. *New York Times*, September 27, 1958, p. 1.
25. Abel, *Missile Crisis*, pp. 133–134.

International, who happened to be in Moscow at the time on a private business mission. Knox was summoned suddenly to the Kremlin and told by Khrushchev that if the U.S. Navy began stopping Soviet ships at sea, Soviet submarines would start sinking American ships and this would mean World War III.

The essence of the final settlement of the Cuban crisis was proposed by a minor Soviet Embassy official to John Scali, diplomatic correspondent of the American Broadcasting Company. The message was that the Soviets would dismantle the missiles and ship them back to the Soviet Union if the United States would promise not to invade Cuba. Scali passed the proposal on to Secretary of State Rusk, who wrote out a note saying that it seemed to provide "real possibilities" for a settlement. Rusk also instructed Scali to stress that "time is very urgent"—a mild ultimatum.[26] This message, delivered orally by Scali to his Soviet contact, eventually produced a proposal from Khrushchev along similar lines which became the basis for the settlement.

Communicating to the other government through private persons serves the function of avoiding the full engagement of the government's prestige behind demands, offers, and threats. It communicates something to the other government about what is wanted, offered, or threatened, with some degree of credibility, but the statement can easily be disavowed later with little or no loss. More severe and provocative threats can be made to private persons than to governments because, when made to governments, such threats may so engage the recipient's *amour-propre* as to stiffen rather than weaken its resolve, and also because it is easier for the threatening government to renege on its threat when it is communicated to a private person.

Careful selection of the individual to issue a threat can also communicate to the opponent that the balance between "hard-liners" and "soft-liners" in the government may be shifting in the hard direction. Thus when Lloyd-George, well known as a pacifist, made a very bellicose speech at the height of the Moroccan crisis of 1911, it had a considerable impact on German perceptions of British support of France.

The role of allies. The role of alliance relations in crisis bargaining is too large a subject to be treated here beyond passing reference. It should be noted, however, that the primarily bilateral orientation of most discussions of strategic bargaining has tended to obscure the fact that international politics is an "*n*-person game" and that alliance factors may be influential in coercive situations. This was particularly true in the multipolar world prior to 1945, but has also been true since then. Many crises involve several state participants. One pattern is an "aggressor" attempting to coerce a smaller "victim" with allies either supporting the victim or urging a compromise upon him. The aggressor may try to exploit differences in the valuation of the stakes between the victim and the allies, modulating his demands to make them acceptable to the ally, even though unacceptable to the victim. The lower intrinsic valuation of the stakes by the supporting ally may, however, be offset by the ally's interest in preserving his own image of resolve vis-à-vis the aggressor and by his interest in maintaining cohesion of the alliance. For example, the strong British support of France during the two Moroccan crises of 1905–1906 and 1911 was motivated largely

26. Roger Hilsman, *To Move a Nation* (Garden City, N.Y.: Doubleday, 1967), p. 218.

by a desire to preserve the integrity of the Dual Entente, rather than by any strong intrinsic interest in the outcome.

When a challenge is to interests shared by alliance members, but in different degree, the alliance may face a problem in concerting upon a bargaining position, as in the Berlin crisis of 1958–1962. The alliance leader's bargaining flexibility may be limited by the interests of the lesser allies.

Some of the axioms of bilateral bargaining theory may have to be qualified when alliance considerations are introduced. For example, the principle that "he who commits first, wins" makes eminent sense in a bilateral situation, but too early a commitment to a threatened ally may reduce the supporting ally's power to influence his partner's moves and may stimulate excessive intransigence in the partner. In general, a firm commitment strengthens bargaining power vis-à-vis the adversary but weakens bargaining power vis-à-vis the ally. British leaders probably had this in mind when they refused to make an explicit commitment to France and Russia before World War I. Germany, on the other hand, in giving a "blank check" to Austria, paid for the possible gain in adversary bargaining by sacrificing her ability to control her ally.

DIMENSIONS OF "CRISIS MANAGEMENT"

We have been discussing processes of coercion. Coercion and coercion resistance are undoubtedly the predominant activities in most crises, but there are other dimensions as well. The parties' primary objective is to get their way, but usually they want to do this without precipitating war. Hence an important constraint on the use of coercive tactics is "disaster avoidance." Furthermore, some crises include a dimension of "accommodation": genuine attempts by the parties to reach a mutually satisfactory settlement by negotiation and concession. In this dimension their primary aim is to serve their common interest in peaceful settlement; the constraint is to do this while minimizing sacrifice to their self-interest. Thus, in theory, the "mixed motive" character of any bargaining situation—the coexistence of conflict and common interest—appears in a crisis as a complex interaction between two sets of goals and constraints: coercion versus disaster avoidance, and accommodation versus loss avoidance. Achieving an optimum mix among these four elements may be conceived as the ideal goal of "crisis management."[27]

Coercion versus disaster avoidance. Coercion is obviously conflict-oriented. The common interest is involved chiefly as an instrumental factor, as something

27. The term *crisis management* has been used rather vaguely in the literature, with a variety of meanings and emphases. The most precise formulation is in Alexander L. George, David K. Hall, and William R. Simons, *The Limits of Coercive Diplomacy* (Boston: Little Brown, 1971), pp. 8–11. The tension between the requirements of "crisis management" and "coercive diplomacy" is a central theme of this work, which develops in considerable detail the ways in which crisis management considerations act as constraints on coercion. These authors use the term crisis management more or less for what I am calling "disaster avoidance." Although this usage has merit in that the word *management* carries overtones of "prudence" and "control," I prefer to apply the term to the totality of the crisis decision maker's problem. Presumably, he wants to "manage" his strategy so as to "coerce prudently," or "accommodate cheaply," or some combination of both.

to be manipulated, typically via a threat to destroy it (e.g., a threat of war), as a means of exerting influence. Most contemporary theorizing about strategic bargaining tends to emphasize the coercive aim, more or less abstracting from or minimizing the common interest as something to be *realized* rather than manipulated.

Yet it is clear that in actual crises the parties are often at least as much concerned about their common interest in avoiding war as they are about getting their way. Statesmen are likely to have prominently in mind that they are in a dangerous, unpredictable situation, from which could easily erupt a war which neither side wants. This awareness introduces a set of considerations which tend to temper and modify their coercive efforts. That is, it creates a number of tensions or antinomies between tactics useful for coercion and other behaviors which are more appropriate for disaster avoidance.

Disaster-avoidance considerations fall into two broad categories. One is controlling or minimizing "autonomous" risks, the danger that the parties will "lose control of events." These risks are analytically separable from the bargaining process, if the latter is conceived as a deliberate, controlled affair, although they do impinge on the bargaining in various ways. What, precisely, people have in mind when they refer to the danger of "events getting out of control" is somewhat obscure, but there is no doubt that in many crises it is a prominent consideration in statesmen's minds, usually focused on the possibility of some violent accident or incident which would touch off uncontrollable escalation. The available evidence (plus a little imagination) seems to indicate at least four possible sources of "uncontrollability." Khrushchev alluded to one during the Cuban missile crisis when he told Kennedy that "if indeed war should break out, then it would not be in our power to stop it, for such is the logic of war."[28] The idea here seems to be that once violence breaks out, a whole new set of forces takes over, a new pattern of interaction, with an inner "logic" of its own which tends to develop to its fullest extent more or less autonomously. Or, second and more specifically, "events out of control" could mean "subordinates out of control," especially military subordinates. When violence begins there is at least the possibility that military commanders will react more or less automatically and independently according to preset plans, the "inherent right of self-defense," and so on. However, there appear to be very few if any cases in modern history of a war directly attributable to unauthorized military action. A third and more plausible possibility is the existence of rigid military plans which create a "necessity" for action in certain contingencies. Here, technically, the statesman still has control but cannot resist the imperatives built into the plans, or the pressures from military commanders to implement them. A good example would be the Russian and German mobilization and war plans prior to World War I. Finally, and probably the most likely, there may be "psychological compulsions" toward action or reaction—feelings of "requiredness" or "no choice" —based, essentially, on emotional or irrational factors such as pride, "face," rage, or even "duty."[29] The statesman "loses control" here in the sense that he stops calculating rationally; his emotions replace reason; he can only be "provoked," not coerced.

28. Robert F. Kennedy, *Thirteen Days* (New York: Signet, 1969), p. 87.

29. In many primitive social systems, with no strong central authority, it is considered a "duty" to exact reprisal in kind for injury done to oneself or one's kinsman. The international system is, of course, a "primitive social system."

The second category involves risks inherent in the bargaining process itself, conceived as controlled behavior based on reasoned calculation. The key risk here is that of *miscalculation*. The parties calculate, but for a variety of possible reasons, including misperception of the adversary's interests and intentions, they calculate badly. Moves intended for coercion or bargaining fail in their intended purpose and the parties become committed to a dangerous or disastrous course which they would have wished to avoid.

Manipulate versus minimize autonomous risk. One of the more dramatic coercive tactics suggested by Schelling is to raise the level of shared risk so that the opponent prefers to back down rather than accept continuation of the risk.[30] The risks Schelling has in mind are what I have called "autonomous" risks—essentially, the risk of inadvertent war through loss of control. Pressure is exerted on the adversary not by threatening deliberate violence but by raising the danger that war will occur through autonomous processes beyond the control of either party. The device can be considered a probabilistic substitute for coercion either by actual violence or by an "irrevocable commitment" to violence.

In theory, such "risk manipulation" might be an effective coercive tactic. Actual examples might include the U.S. convoying of supply ships to Quemoy island in 1958, creating a risk that a U.S. vessel might be hit by Chinese Communist artillery fire; or Soviet buzzing of transport aircraft in the air corridors to Berlin during the 1961–1962 Berlin crisis, creating a risk of accidental collision. However, certain doubts come to mind about the effectiveness of this maneuver as a coercive tactic. First, the risk created is a *shared* one, and it is not clearly apparent why the other party should be less willing to tolerate the risk than the party initiating it. Perhaps the reasoning is that the act of creating the risk demonstrates the risk tolerance of the initiating party and his determination to continue it; then, if the adversary feels the risk is intolerable, he also believes that only he can terminate the risk by complying with whatever is being demanded of him. But against this is the consideration that the adversary is being asked to give up something of substance as the price of ending the danger, and this is likely to seem more costly to him than stopping the risky behavior will seem to the risk initiator. He may feel compelled to start some risky behavior of his own to maintain his position in the balance of resolve. The coercive value of this tactic would seem to depend on a known asymmetry in the parties' tolerances for risk—that is, the tactic will be used only by the party who is confident that the risk will be more burdensome to the opponent than to himself. This confidence, in turn, would depend on a belief that the object at stake is worth considerably more to him than to the adversary,[31] or that the subjective cost of war looms greater to the adversary, or some combination of these two asymmetries. In terms of the model presented earlier in this paper, the tactic is useful and rational only for the party with the higher threshold of "critical risk" and, incidentally, the degree of risk created must lie somewhere in the "gap" between the two thresholds.

However, even if escalation of risk is conceded to have some coercive value, it is obviously inconsistent with the objective of disaster avoidance. A survey of historical crisis cases clearly indicates that statesmen are usually more

30. Schelling, *Arms and Influence*, chap. 3.
31. This is argued by Maxwell in "Rationality in Deterrence," p. 15.

concerned with avoiding or minimizing autonomous risks than deliberately heightening them. They are aware of and fearful of the possibility of "losing control" and a good deal of their behavior is aimed at reducing this risk, often at the cost of reducing the effectiveness of their coercive efforts.

As usual, the Cuban missile crisis is rich in examples. President Kennedy and other U.S. decision makers were extremely fearful of triggering some emotional, irrational "spasm response" by the Soviets which might send the crisis out of control, and they did everything they could to minimize this danger. The blockade option was chosen over the air strike largely for this reason, although moral considerations also carried some weight. Implementation of the blockade was heavily influenced by disaster-avoidance considerations. Thus the first Soviet ship to approach the blockade line, a tanker, was allowed to pass. The President decided that Khrushchev needed more time to consider his response, against the advice of coercion-minded advisers who argued that the ship should be stopped to demonstrate U.S. resolve. The President ordered the blockade perimeter pulled back by three hundred miles to give the Soviet premier more time for reflection. The first ship actually boarded was carefully selected as a vessel of non-Soviet registry.[32] Kennedy further ordered that interception of Soviet ships be delayed until the last possible moment and this order was sent "in the clear" so the Soviets would hear it.

The implementation of the blockade provides an excellent example of the potential conflict between coercion and disaster avoidance. George has written that the coercive aim tends to favor creation of a sense of urgency in the opponent's mind, a feeling that he must concede soon in order to avoid punishment or disaster; but this runs the risk that he will be stampeded into rash behavior by panic or lack of sufficient time to absorb information and make considered decisions. Disaster avoidance counsels slowing up the momentum of events both to reduce the chances of unauthorized or accidental violence and to maximize the time available to the adversary to reflect calmly about the options available to him. But this carries the danger that he will use this time to prepare effective counter-coercive measures. George notes that in choosing to emphasize risk minimization in carrying out the blockade, by delaying the confrontation with Soviet ships, Kennedy paid a price in terms of giving the Russians time to bring their missiles closer to operational readiness and time to develop their optimum counter-coercive strategy.[33]

Even though risk reduction usually seems to take priority over coercive risk manipulation in physical crisis moves, it is still possible to verbally play upon latent autonomous risks as a pressure tactic. These tactics may be defined as "warnings." The opponent is warned of autonomous risks inherent in the situation, or in his behavior, with the implication that only by terminating his undesirable behavior can these risks be avoided. Thus Khrushchev, for example, warned that the presence of U.S. Marines in Lebanon in 1958 might lead to an incident, precipitating a "chain reaction" which no one could control. In the summer of 1914, both sides reiterated many times that once a party instituted mobilization, war would automatically follow. During the Cold War era, both sides occasionally asserted that "a war in Europe could not be limited."

The coercive value of such warnings seems obscure at first glance, since

32. Robert F. Kennedy, *Thirteen Days*, p. 82.
33. George *et al.*, *Coercive Diplomacy*, pp. 233–234.

presumably both sides in a crisis are aware that they are in a dangerous, unpredictable situation. Their main function may be to communicate to the opponent that one believes these autonomous processes are real and that *one's own deliberate behavior may be affected by this belief.* In short, the warning implies a self-fulfilling hypothesis. If Khrushchev really believed in an autonomous "logic of war" once violence erupted, he might react so as to make this supposed logic a reality. If the parties to a crisis in Europe really believe "a war cannot be limited" they are less likely to try to limit it.

The simple informative value of such statements should not be ignored. If a party believes that a certain type of event, or a certain level of escalation, will subject him to "compulsions" beyond his control, communicating this credibly to the adversary may serve both a coercive and a disaster-avoidance function.

Finally, warnings of this kind can be used to camouflage and take some of the provocativeness out of a threat. If a party is told that if he doesn't change his behavior "things will get out of control" or "the consequences will be unpredictable," he is likely to get the point without feeling too affronted or challenged and, therefore, will be less likely to react emotionally or irrationally.

Centralized versus decentralized control. Another coercive tactic sometimes suggested is to delegate control to subordinates (e.g., military commanders) who can be expected to be tougher, more unpredictable, or more reckless than the top decision makers. The adversary faces more risk in challenging or standing up to such a decentralized decision-making apparatus and hence is more easily coerced or deterred. But here again there is conflict between the aim of coercion and the avoidance of inadvertent war. The latter goal requires a tightly centralized decision process which minimizes the chances of subordinates getting out of line and behaving dangerously. Ideally, the top decision maker himself should have precise, sensitive control of all the levers of action and channels of communication. If this is the case with both national actors, the chances of inadvertent disaster are minimized. The tension between the two aims arises not only because central control foregoes what might be an effective means of coercion but also because a decision maker in control is more *subject* to coercion than one who is not. The adversary knows, at least, that he has the option of conceding; he cannot plead inability to concede because control is effectively in someone else's hands.

Similarly, shifting effective control of events to an irresponsible small ally or "proxy" state may yield bargaining advantage but it jeopardizes the common interest of the alliance leaders in settling a crisis short of war. Germany's "blank check" to Austria increased the coercive power and reduced the coercibility of the Dual Alliance but at the price of setting in motion autonomous processes which produced an unwanted war. Firm control by the leading allies is the prescription for disaster avoidance.

In actual crises devolution of control as a coercive tactic is seldom practiced; the instinct of statesmen, especially in the nuclear era, is in the other direction. Thus Kennedy in the Cuban crisis ordered the atomic weapons in Europe defused so that they could be fired only by his personal command,[34] and in many other ways sought to gather as much control as possible in his own hands.

34. Robert F. Kennedy, *Thirteen Days*, p. 98.

Again, however, the threat or suggestion of either delegation of control or possible loss of control to subordinates may be exploited verbally. A good example was the Soviet threat in the second Berlin crisis to turn over control of the access routes to the East Germans. After the U-2 incident of May 1960, Marshal Malinovsky, the Soviet defense minister, announced that orders had been given to Marshal Nedelin, commander of the Soviet missile forces, to fire at any Western air base that allowed itself to be used as a base for future U-2 flights. The implication was that no further command needed to be given; Marshal Nedelin would act under predelegated authority. An example of pleading "lack of control" (as opposed to deliberate delegation) is provided by Hitler in the Austrian *Anschluss* crisis. In the course of intimidating the Austrian Chancellor Schuschnigg, he pretended inability to control the actions of his military forces if an invasion of Austria became necessary. "After the troops will follow the S.A. and the Legion. No one will be able to hinder the vengeance, not even myself."[35]

There are some good reasons, however, why even these verbal suggestions of impending "loss of control" may be counter-productive from the point of view of disaster avoidance. Particularly during the high-tension phase of a crisis, when war is perceived as a real and imminent possibility, the parties are likely to feel most strongly the need for mutual collaboration in moving back from the brink. Then they may wish to project an image of control, both of the actions of their military subordinates and of their own passions. Each wants the other to perceive him as not only a willing and trustworthy collaborator but also a capable one, as being effectively able to take and reciprocate tension-dampening moves. If, however, one party appears to be irresponsibly unpredictable or ineffective, the other may be reluctant to initiate such moves for fear they will be exploited or not reciprocated. Or, worse, fears that the other's subordinate commanders are about to undertake an unauthorized escalation may precipitate pre-emptive attack. There is some evidence that assertions of lack of control or pretenses of irrationality tend to be used, if at all, in the early phase of a crisis when the danger of war is moderate to low, but that exactly opposite signals predominate in the high-tension phase. In the early stages of the Cuban missile crisis, for example, at least two Soviet spokesmen suggested that the Russian navy or individual ship commanders would act "on their own" as they approached the blockade, and at least said nothing to dispel U.S. fears that the missiles might be placed under the control of Cubans.[36] But later on, when the crisis reached its peak, Khrushchev was at pains to assure Kennedy that the Soviet leadership was rational ("You can be calm in this regard, that we are of sound mind") and that the missile sites were fully controlled by Soviet officers.[37]

Commit versus preserve options. This category points to certain tensions between coercion and disaster avoidance in the bargaining process itself, strictly conceived as the interplay of rationally calculated moves—that is, abstracting from the nonrational "autonomous" elements. A "commitment" is a well-known coercive bargaining tactic and, theoretically at least, a powerful one. But for a

35. Winston S. Churchill, *The Gathering Storm* (Boston: Houghton Mifflin, 1948), pp. 262–263. Quoted by Herman Kahn in *On Thermonuclear War* (Princeton: Princeton University Press, 1960), p. 397.

36. Abel, *Missile Crisis*, pp. 133–134.

37. Robert F. Kennedy, *Thirteen Days*, pp. 87, 168.

variety of reasons it may jeopardize the common interest in settling a crisis short of war.

First, there are many ways in which a commitment can fail to coerce the adversary as intended. A successful commitment has three elements: (1) the act of commital, (2) communicating to the adversary that one is committed, and (3) a decision by the adversary to behave in the way you desire, as a result of the communication. Between each of these steps many things can go awry. The enemy may not perceive that your alternatives or incentives have been altered so that you are now committed, especially if the committal act is not physical and highly visible (e.g., like the troops in Berlin). Efforts to communicate this to him have to be processed by his perhaps unreliable intelligence system, and may be distorted by his pre-existing image, expectations, and emotional state. Even if the commitment is successfully communicated, there is still no guarantee that he will then behave in the manner you expect or demand of him. You may have misestimated his incentives, and his decision-making system will be subject to vagaries and rigidities of various kinds. Thus a commitment is inherently risky. It fully determines *your* subsequent behavior but by no means determines his. If the commitment fails to "work," the outcome could be disastrous or at least more costly than if freedom of action had been preserved.

Second, a commitment, especially a provocative one, may trigger a counter-commitment by the opponent, who either feels he must respond to preserve his prestige or thinks the only way he can force us to back down on *our* commitment is to make one even more firm and less revocable. There can be dangerous escalation in the making of threats and commitments just as there can be escalation in violence. This may produce the familiar situation of becoming "locked in," each side hoping and believing that its commitment will effectively intimidate the other and each failing to realize until too late that the other party has become committed too. This is what Khrushchev was referring to in the Cuban missile crisis when he used the metaphor of both sides pulling on the ends of a rope, gradually tightening the "knot of war" until it became so tight the parties would be powerless to untie it.

However, a commitment need not always be in tension with the constraint of disaster avoidance. If a party *is* determined to fight but is not sure the opponent realizes this, a clear and firm commitment, made early in the crisis, may avert war by miscalculation. George has pointed out another interesting way in which a highly coercive commitment may contribute positively to the avoidance of accidental disaster. If you think the crisis is about to get out of control as a result of some autonomous event, this may be the time for the strongest possible coercive pressure, in the hope of terminating the crisis before events slip away from the decision makers' control. In other words, action is taken, despite its risks, in the dimension which one *does* control in order to pre-empt the onset of disaster from noncontrollable elements. Thus the oral ultimatum which Robert Kennedy delivered to Soviet Ambassador Dobrynin at the height of the Cuban missile crisis came immediately after a U-2 plane was downed over Cuba; President Kennedy feared that another such incident might set in motion an uncontrollable train of events leading to war.[38] Another example would be the

38. George, *et al.*, *Coercive Diplomacy*, chap. 3, p. 59. Also Robert F. Kennedy, *Thirteen Days*, pp. 105–109. Another precipitating motive for the ultimatum may have been furnished by the fact that the missiles were fast approaching operational readiness, which would have greatly improved Soviet bargaining power.

German ultimatum to Russia in the Bosnia–Herzegovina crisis of 1908–1909. The ultimatum forced the Russians to withdraw their support for Serbia in its confrontation with Austria; in issuing it, the Germans were considerably motivated by the fear that the Serbians, counting on Russian support, might "provoke" an Austrian attack by their military posturing on the border.

The obvious alternative to a strategy of commitment is to preserve a maximum range of options so that one is free to react flexibly to the opponent's moves at minimum cost and risk. But option preservation may detract from coercive potency: the adversary can be fairly confident that if he misbehaves or fails to accede to our desires, our response will be the one which costs us least and does minimum damage to him. Moreover, we may be vulnerable to the opponent's coercion; *he* may be able to commit himself to precipitating mutual disaster unless we yield to him, safe in the knowledge that our flexibility gives us the option of yielding. In rather stark, abstract terms, this is the dilemma: commitment maximizes the chances of winning but flirts with disaster; option preservation maximizes the chances of avoiding war or extreme levels of destruction but risks being bested in the crisis contest of wills.[39] A large part of the crisis management problem is to resolve this dilemma optimally. In coercion-by-communication the dilemma appears mainly as the choice between clarity and ambiguity. In the domain of basic or action moves, it appears as the choice of where on the escalation ladder to begin action.

Clarity versus ambiguity. Maximum clarity in threats tends to produce maximum credibility. Values such as national prestige and bargaining reputation are then "engaged" to the highest degree and a failure to fulfill the threat would result in maximum losses to these values. Knowing this, the threat recipient will expect the threatener to fulfill the threat to avoid these losses. The threatener is most likely to be or seem "committed" as a result of having made the threat. On the other hand, an ambiguous threat leaves the threatener an out; he can reinterpret the threat, imply that it really didn't mean what it had seemed to mean, claim that the contingency or behavior of the other party is not that which was intended to activate the original threat, or even claim that he never really threatened at all. If, when making the threat, the threatener was not really clear about what he would do if his demand were resisted, ambiguity leaves him free to act as he wishes when the respondent's compliance, noncompliance, or degree of compliance is clear. In short, ambiguity "preserves options"; the threatener can avoid fulfillment with minimum value loss or can act at a lower level of mutual cost and risk than he had threatened.

But the threatenee, perceiving that the threatener has left himself an "out," may then believe that the threat is not intended to be executed—that it is a bluff. At least, in his eyes, it will have minimum "credibility." In these very general terms, then, ambiguity minimizes costs and risks in case the threat fails in its aim, thus contributing to the general objective of disaster avoidance, but at the price of sacrificing some coercive potency.

However, the difference is not all this clear cut. Ambiguity may have some positive value for coercion. For instance, an ambiguous threat may minimize

39. This dilemma is roughly analogous to the choice in preparedness policy between "deterrence by nuclear threat" and "defense by flexible response," an issue which was thoroughly debated in the late fifties and early sixties. Cf. Glenn H. Snyder, *Deterrence and Defense* (Princeton: Princeton University Press, 1961).

provocation; it engages the pride and self-respect of the opponent to a lesser degree than a direct, explicit one and, therefore, may make it easier for the opponent to comply with the demand.[40] Keeping threats ambiguous early in the crisis preserves the opportunity for escalating pressure on the opponent by gradually making them more explicit and moving closer to commitment. Feedback obtained from the adversary's reaction to earlier signals allows one to better judge the probable effectiveness of firmer commitment. There is some tendency for statesmen to want to preserve their verbal "big guns" for occasions in the crisis when the opponent makes, or seems about to make, some strongly coercive or dangerous move. Thus, in the Berlin crisis of 1961, Kennedy vetoed Acheson's suggestion of a declaration of "national emergency" because he wanted to save this for when the Soviets actually signed a peace treaty with the East Germans or made a move to block access to West Berlin.[41]

A threat may be ambiguous in either of its two components—*demand* and *sanction*—or both. In the demand component the threatener may do no more than indicate general dissatisfaction with the status quo, signaling that he is awaiting some acceptable offer from the other party.[42] A bit more explicit is the threat which demands only that certain broad arrangements or results be accomplished, leaving it up to the opponent just how this is to be done. He may be able to find a way which minimizes his prestige losses. Perhaps he can find a rationale which makes his compliance seem "legitimate" rather than craven capitulation. He is less likely to feel humiliated if he is allowed to formulate the details of compliance himself. For example, in the 1870 Franco-German crisis, the French at first demanded of King William only that the Hohenzollern candidacy to the throne of Spain be dropped; William was able to bring this about without damage to Prussian national honor by treating it as a "family matter."[43] Rather similar was the U.S. demand that the North Vietnamese undertake some reciprocal "deescalation" in return for a termination of the bombing of North Vietnam. Just what would constitute deescalation was left vague, and conceivably the North Vietnamese would be able to think of something which would save their dignity but which could be interpreted by the United States as compliance.[44] Ambiguity of this sort not only eases compliance for the victim of the threat, but also makes it easier for the threatener to interpret any particular behavior as compliance than if he had specified the details of compliance in advance.[45]

Governments are ingenious in inventing ways to make their threats am-

40. Schelling, *Arms and Influence*, p. 84.

41. Theodore C. Sorensen, *Kennedy* (New York: Bantam, 1966), p. 664.

42. James L. Richardson, "Pressure, Threat, Blackmail—the Political Use of Force," Harvard Center of International Affairs, Harvard University, 1962 (mimeographed), p. 21.

43. It was the later French demand that the Prussian state guarantee the renewal of the candidacy that eventually brought about the Franco-Prussian War.

44. Schelling, *Arms and Influence*, p. 85.

45. For a discussion of this point which reaches a different conclusion see Roger Fisher, *International Conflict for Beginners*, (New York: Harper & Row, 1970), pp. 80–81. Fisher argues that despite these advantages of ambiguity, on balance it is best for the threatener to present explicit demands. The other government's decision-making process will be simplified if it is clear what is being demanded of it; therefore, it is more likely to comply if it is presented with a specific "yes-able" proposition.

biguous. In fact, the language of diplomacy includes a kind of code system which allows governments to communicate rather severe threats with outwardly vague and innocuous language. A government may say, for example, that it cannot "remain indifferent" to certain events, as when the Soviet Union stated during the landing of U.S. forces in Lebanon in 1958 that it "could not remain indifferent to acts of unprovoked aggression in a region adjacent to its borders." In the nineteenth century a popular code symbol was the "disturbance" to "public opinion" which another government's action would provoke. One may say that if the opponent continues his undesirable behavior "events will take their due course," or one will "not be responsible for the consequences." The code system serves a common interest in preserving flexibility; since it is mutually understood, and since it is merely informal or conventional rather than authoritatively codified in a "diplomatic dictionary" which is kept on all foreign office desks, it is possible for statesmen both to threaten clearly and later to pretend that a threat was never issued. The code serves a further common interest in removing much of the emotional or provocative content from threatening communications. Although the symbols in the code change in both nature and meaning over time and today's code permits somewhat sharper and more explicit wording than the code of the nineteenth century, statesmen seem at all times to be tacitly agreed on the general meaning and amount of threatening content of the code phrases.[46]

Preserving action options. With respect to physical action or basic moves, the choice is whether to start high or low on the escalation ladder. It seems quite obvious that starting low keeps open a wide range of options and thus maximizes the chances of avoiding disaster. Action at a low level of damage or risk may be enough to persuade the adversary to comply and, if he does not, one can always move higher. Again, the Cuban missile crisis helps to make the point. If, as some U.S. decision makers advocated, we had dealt with the problem summarily by an air strike on the missile sites, the consequences could have been disastrous. The Russians would have been maximally provoked and probably would have felt impelled to take some physical counter-action, perhaps in Berlin or Turkey, or conceivably against the United States itself. Even a threat or warning of an air strike as the first move would have been problematical as to success and therefore dangerous. Despite attempts to draft such a warning in least offensive tones, Sorensen reports, "It still constituted the kind of ultimatum which no great power could accept."[47] It would have provided not only the stimulus, but also the time, for the Soviets to work themselves into a strong counter-commitment to violent reprisal. Even if they had remained cool and calm and calculated rationally, they would have faced a simple one-step calculation: was the United States really willing to take such a high risk of nuclear war? Lacking hard evidence about U.S. resolve (in fact, probably holding an image of weak U.S. resolve as a result of recent confrontations in Laos, the Bay of Pigs, and Berlin), they might have guessed wrong. And *we* could not have been at all sure just how they would guess. Starting with the blockade was minimally provocative, it communicated resolve, it gave the Russians time to deliberate, it kept risks down to a minimum, it was much more palatable to third parties than more drastic

46. For further analysis of diplomatic ambiguity and sign language reaching somewhat different conclusions, see Jervis, *Logic of Images*.

47. Sorensen, *Kennedy*, p. 772.

action, and it saved the most dangerous option (and intermediate ones as well) for later use if needed.

Furthermore, starting low in the escalation ladder has important information-gathering utility. It allows for "feedback"; how the adversary reacts to the first move provides valuable information about how he is likely to respond to moves higher up the ladder. Thus it protects the coercer against running excessive risks when the strength of the other's interests and resolve are uncertain. In setting up the Wall in the Berlin crisis of 1961, the Soviets began with barbed wire barriers, several gaps were left, and traffic through the barrier was not entirely cut off. After several days of no action from the West, the Russians were more confident that stronger action would not bring a violent response and proceeded to set up the full concrete barrier. The Cuban blockade performed a similar function for the United States: when the Russians chose not to run the blockade, this increased our confidence that higher options would also succeed and would not precipitate disaster.

Although it is not entirely clear, the weight of logic and empirical evidence seems to show that "starting low" is also the best strategy for coercion as well as for disaster avoidance. A low-level action involves *doing* something, not just saying something, and, as the old adage would have it, probably communicates resolve more clearly and credibly than merely verbal threats to act at a higher level. The Cuban blockade clearly demonstrated that we were resolved to sink or disable Russian ships. If we were willing to do this, the Soviet leadership probably reasoned, we were very likely willing to do more. The fund of apparent resolve yielded by the blockade "spilled over" into the Soviet assessment of our intent on higher rungs of the escalation ladder, including the air strike. Thus, when an ultimatum was actually issued later in the crisis, demanding removal of the missiles, it carried credibility because of the previous buildup of our resolve image.[48] Finally, as the blockade also exemplifies, the lower rungs on the escalation ladder may provide opportunities for shifting to the opponent the "last clear chance" to avoid violence.[49]

There is a contrary logic, however, which deserves mention. Starting low on the action ladder may seem timid, indecisive, indicating lack of "nerve." As used to be argued in the debate about deterrence by "massive retaliation," keeping options open might be interpreted as a lack of will to use the most costly or risky ones. Moreover, it prolongs the confrontation, providing time for the opponent to devise counter-tactics, demonstrate his resolve, and build up support for his case among third parties. It may start a process of escalation, not only of violence, but of deepening commitment and progressive magnification of the values at stake so that the adversary becomes less coercible and the ultimate disaster becomes more difficult to avoid. As argued by the air strike advocates in the Cuban case, the preferable course may be the *fait accompli*, which resolves the issue swiftly and summarily, provides no time for the opponent to mobilize counter-pressures, and in some cases (as the Cuban one) leaves him with no issue on which to focus counter-pressures, unless he wishes to create a new one. The game is over, he has lost, and if he is wise he will accept it. With similar logic, the Germans urged the Austrians to march quickly into Serbia in 1914 to pre-empt the mobilization of counter-pressures from the

48. This point is emphasized by George *et al.*, in *Coercive Diplomacy*, p. 135.
49. Schelling, *Strategy of Conflict*, chap. 2.

Entente powers. (For technical military reasons the Austrians rejected the advice.)

Accommodation versus loss avoidance. When we shift from the coercive dimension to the accommodative dimension the roles of the conflicting interests and the common interest tend to be reversed. Generally, in coercive bargaining the *purpose* of the parties is to make gains or minimize losses to their self-interests which are in conflict with the self-interests of the opponent; the *constraint* is to do this while still protecting the common interest in avoiding war or excessive risks of war. In accommodative bargaining the primary aim is to achieve a settlement and terminate the crisis, thus realizing the common interest in peace; the constraint for each party is to arrange this while at the same time avoiding or minimizing unilateral losses to self-interest.

The extreme accommodative move is "capitulation." This preserves the common interest but at the high price of sacrificing all of one's substantive interest concerning the issue in conflict. If the self-interests and inherent power of the parties are roughly symmetrical, they will each hope to do better than this. They will hope to get by with a minor or moderate "concession"; ideally, one which minimizes their losses in self-interest. A concession is a "proposal for settlement" which the other bargainer may or may not accept; the uncertainty about his willingness to accept is the essence of the conceder's problem just as uncertainty about the other's response to threats and commitments is the essence of the threatener's problem in coercive bargaining.

As a general rule, the greater the concession offered, the more likely the adversary will accept, but this runs counter to the conceder's interest in minimizing his loss. Therefore, he offers an "optimum" concession, one which seems to strike the best balance between three factors: probability of the other's acceptance, unilateral loss if he does accept, and unilateral loss if he does not. This third factor includes at least two items: the inability or difficulty for the conceding party to move back to his previous position, and the possibility that the adversary will interpret the concession as a "sign of weakness," encouraging him to stand firm on his own position in the expectation of further concessions.

There are really two different logics operating here. The conceder hopes that once his concession is made, the adversary will expect him to stand even firmer on the new position, so that he (the adversary) will prefer to accept the concession rather than run the higher risk of war. This hope is based partly on the logic of diminishing marginal utility. Some items around the periphery of the issue are valued lower by the conceding party than other items closer to the core of the issue. Presumably, the closer to the core a party moves the firmer he will stand. Thus his outstanding threats to "stand firm" acquire greater credibility. Also, and supporting this reasoning, the opponent's threshold of critical risk (with respect to continued confrontation) is lowered because the concession grants him a portion of his objective, and he is less willing to risk war in hopes of obtaining the remaining portion. If the effect of these two opposite movements is to place the conceder's new threat credibility higher than the other's new critical risk, the other party will accept the concession rather than continue the conflict. Logically, of course, the conceder wants to limit his offer to just that amount of concession which will bring about this result.

The reverse logic is that when the party offers a concession, the other may interpret it as a sign that the party's resolve is weakening and that more will be forthcoming if he just stands firm and waits. He may reason that if the other party wants to settle, he will first offer only a small concession, hoping to get by with that, but that he is really willing to offer more. Whether he is right or wrong depends, theoretically, on whether he has correctly calculated the new credibility–critical risk relation for further confrontation. If he is wrong, he has "miscalculated" in the accommodative dimension. This is similar to miscalculation in the coercive dimension in that the other party's degree of interest or resolve is misestimated, and if the misperception is not corrected the consequence could be an unwanted war. It differs in the *kind of move* whose meaning is misperceived. The underlying common denominator is a misperception of the other's changed incentive structure after the move is made.

Some of the antinomies discussed previously under coercive bargaining can now be considered in relation to accommodation. Take, for example, clarity versus ambiguity. A clear explicit concession cannot be readily retracted. One suffers special "bargaining reputation" costs if he does—not "reputation for resolve," as on the coercive side, but "reputation for trustworthiness." His future offers or hints of concession will not be believed or reciprocated. A clear offer is more likely to *succeed* in moving the bargaining toward a settlement (1) because the other, knowing it is costly to retract, is more likely to believe it is really meant, (2) because it is more likely to penetrate "noise" and the other's perhaps contradictory image of oneself as intransigent, or (3) because it presents a clear option which can be readily analyzed and evaluated by the other's decision-making system.[50]

An ambiguous offer, or mere hint that one is ready to concede, protects a party's self-interest in the issue at stake, because it can easily be disavowed if the other indicates he will not accept it or concede anything in return, or that he will consider it a sign of weakness. In other words, the party can then retreat to his former position with little or no cost in bargaining reputation.[51] But such an ambiguous move is less likely to succeed in the objective of reaching a settlement (1) because the other may not pick up the signal through the "noise" or it may be blocked out by his contradictory "image," (2) because he thinks the party does not really mean it and is trying to trick *him* into making a concession, or (3) because the offer does not present a clear-cut option to his decision-making system.

In sum, clarity in offers and concessions tends to maximally promote the primary aim of accommodation but works against the constraint of protecting self-interest. Note the parallelism with coercion where clarity in threats usually enhances their prospect of success but runs counter to the constraint of preserving flexibility in the interest of disaster avoidance.

There is also a certain parallelism with the disaster-avoidance policy in the coercive dimension of starting action lower on the escalation ladder than one is ultimately willing to go in order to preserve options. One reason this is done in coercion is the possibility that a minimum level of damage and risk may be enough to induce the opponent to capitulate, thus relieving the coercer of the need to move to higher levels. Likewise, in accommodation a party may start

50. Roger Fisher has emphasized the accommodative value of presenting clear, detailed propositions to the opposing decision makers. Fisher, *International Conflict for Beginners*, p. 81.

51. Edward Peters, *Strategy and Tactics in Labor Negotiations* (New London, Conn.: National Foremen's Institute, 1955), p. 154.

out with an offer much smaller than he is really willing to concede in the hope of buying a settlement cheaply. If the first offer is not accepted, he can always concede more, step by step, up to the limit to which he is willing to go. Second, initiating coercive action at a low damage-risk level also pays dividends in demonstrating resolve which can be "banked" and then drawn upon if and when a high-level threat has to be made. In a somewhat parallel fashion, making a series of minor "sham" concessions can create the impression that one has moved closer to one's "non-negotiable" core values than one actually has. Then when the accommodator does approach the limit of concession which he is prepared to make, this impression may enhance the credibility of his "last offer" and hence the likelihood that it will be accepted; it may also permit him to make a believable last offer well short of his maximum concession. In sum, preserving options or starting low in the accommodative process can make a settlement more likely with minimal or acceptable costs to the constraint of self-interest, just as the analogous policy in coercive bargaining improves the chances of successful coercion short of excessive strain on the constraint of disaster avoidance.

Combining coercion and accommodation. The optimum blend between coercion and accommodation is not easy to find. Too large a dose of coercive pressure may lead the adversary to believe that one is not willing to accommodate at all and that, therefore, the only way he can achieve his ends is through coercive means of his own. Too much intransigence may breed intransigence in the other, for both calculated and emotional reasons, leading to mutual escalation of commitments and possible disaster. Too obvious a willingness to accommodate may inflate the opponent's estimate of how much he can obtain, undermine one's coercive tactics, enhance the enemy's confidence in his coercive moves, and lead to dangerous miscalculation concerning the extent and valuation of one's core interests and where one firmly intends to draw the line.

To complicate matters, these divergent lines of reasoning are likely to be reflected in the decision-making process of one's own government or alliance. In a crisis the decision-making group will probably include both "hard-liners" and "soft-liners." The hard-liners will tend to view the situation as predominantly one of conflict, with coercion or counter-coercion the most appropriate strategy. Their image of the adversary will hold that he is aggressive, tough, and not to be trusted. His aims are seen as unlimited; the present challenge as merely the first in a series. Thus we must be absolutely firm to preserve our resolve image for future occasions. Even an offer to negotiate, let alone an offer of concessions, will be interpreted as weakness. Soft-liners, on the other hand, will see a considerable element of common interest in the situation. They will perceive materials for possible accommodation and will urge an attempt at accommodation, at least on issues not absolutely vital. Coercive moves, they will argue, will frustrate the chances of a settlement in the common interest and will also be provocative. Their image of the opponent will see him as having limited aims, thus minimizing the importance of considerations of future reputation for resolve, and his demands may be seen as being at least partly legitimate. He will be seen as trustworthy—at least if we give evidence that we trust him. These hard and soft positions competed within the U.S. government in both the Berlin and Cuban crises, and probably in the Soviet government as well. They are also to be found in turn-of-the-century crises—for instance, the Morocco crisis in

1905 when a German challenge to French policy split the French government, leading to the resignation of the hard-line foreign minister, Delcasse, so that French acceptance of the German demand for a conference became possible. The split between the "soft" Chamberlain government and the "hard-line" Churchill–Eden–Cooper faction in Britain during the Munich crisis is well known.

It falls to the central decision maker (e.g., the President and his immediate staff in the United States) to weigh these contrary views in search of the optimum mix between coercion and accommodation. Several kinds of objective factors in the situation itself may enter into this choice. A statesman who is sure of asymmetries favoring his country, chiefly in relative power and degree of interest, who is also sure that these asymmetries are perceived by the other side, is likely to come down on the side of coercion and intransigence. Examples would be Lord Salisbury's tough uncompromising stand against the French in the Fashoda crisis of 1898 or German bargaining tactics vis-à-vis Russia in the Bosnian crisis of 1908–1909. More recently, Kennedy's posture in the Cuban missile crisis makes the point, and may be compared instructively with U.S. behavior in the Berlin crisis of 1961–1962 when the asymmetries were not nearly so clear. Another important factor is the degree of "legitimacy" attributed to the opponent's challenge, demand, or position. In the Cuban case, the Russian challenge was seen as completely illegitimate by the United States; thus any substantial move toward accommodation would have violated our clear conception of what was "right" and, therefore, was "unthinkable." In the Berlin crisis, on the other hand, the Soviet position and interests were seen to have some degree of legitimacy: the status of West Berlin *was* abnormal, the whole German situation was awkward, ambiguous, and autonomously productive of conflict, and so on, so that there did appear to be a good deal of shared interest between us and the Communist side in tidying it up by negotiation. Hence an accommodative strategy appeared more appropriate. In this case the President faced a much more difficult choice between his hard- and soft-liners than he did later in Cuba and the actual behavior of the United States in Berlin was an interesting and somewhat uneasy mix between coercive and accommodating tactics, as was the behavior of the Soviet Union as well.

These mixed situations present the obviously difficult problem of how to appear firm and flexible at the same time; and the problem may appear in many different forms at successive decision points. In Berlin, for example, President Kennedy genuinely feared, consistent with the hard-line De Gaulle–Adenauer–Acheson view, that entering into negotiations would be interpreted by the Soviet Union as American loss of nerve. Nevertheless, he also felt that complete intransigence was inappropriate, that the Soviet Union had some legitimate grievances, that the United States could afford to sacrifice something, and that the United States had a "duty to mankind" to seek a solution.[52] Therefore, he directed preparation of a negotiating position, made speeches emphasizing U.S. willingness to negotiate, while still, however, stressing those vital interests over which we would fight, and issuing warnings against reckless or excessively coercive Soviet behavior. Later, at specific points during the crisis, coercive moves collided with accommodative aims. For example, General Lucius Clay

52. Arthur M. Schlesinger, Jr., *A Thousand Days* (New York: Fawcett Crest, 1967), p. 364.

was appointed as the President's personal representative in Berlin, more or less in charge of U.S. moves on the spot. This was probably intended as a coercive move, both because Clay was known as a hard-liner and because his mandate created the possibility that he might take tough or risky actions not specifically authorized by Washington. But Washington was alarmed by some of his initiatives, and his "compulsion to force issues" tended to create a climate uncongenial to negotiation.[53] Conversely, no really significant accommodative moves were made by the Western side, partly because it was hard to devise "significant" offers which would not compromise the core interests of the West, but also because of the hard-liners' insistence that serious larger concessions would be interpreted as weakness. In short, coercive considerations acted as a powerful constraint on accommodation.

Nevertheless, coercion and accommodation are not always or necessarily incompatible. Accommodative sacrifices are likely to be minimized if negotiations have been preceded by a clear demonstration of firmness via coercive moves.[54] Accommodating gestures made concurrently with coercive tactics may defuse a confrontation of much of its emotional overtones of hostility, duress, and engagements of "face." During the 1961–1962 Berlin crisis, the Western powers' show of willingness to negotiate provided the necessary pretext for Khrushchev to retreat. Since the West was "inclined to seek a solution," he declared he would withdraw his threat to sign a peace treaty with East Germany.[55] Conversely, couching an offer of concession in a context of threatening language and action tends to communicate the urgency of settling for that offer and to protect the conceder against an interpretation of his offer as weakness. Thus Khrushchev's settlement proposals in the Cuban missile crisis were accompanied by threats and denunciations and were quickly followed by two physical coercive actions: sending a single ship moving toward the blockade line and shooting down a U-2 plane.[56]

CONCLUSION

We have, in a sense, come around full circle from our opening remarks which emphasized that an international crisis is "international politics distilled," and bottled in a small container of time. Of course, factors such as time pressure, urgency of decision, and momentousness of possible outcomes lend special characteristics to crises which are not found in "ordinary" diplomacy. It is still valid to say, however, that crises tend to galvanize, concentrate, and bring out in high relief most of the central forces and elements in international politics, revealing their relationships in their starkest and most explicit forms. The dilemmas of crisis management—the use of coercive power while avoiding excessive costs and risks, accommodating to the interests of other states at minimum sacrifice to one's own interests—are also the central dilemmas of "statesmanship" in general.

In conceptualizing our analysis as "crisis bargaining," we have matched

53. *Ibid.*, p. 375.

54. Alexander George emphasizes the wisdom of waiting until one's resolve has been thoroughly established in coercive skirmishing before initiating negotiations. George *et al.*, *Coercive Diplomacy*, pp. 241–243.

55. Schlesinger, *A Thousand Days*, p. 372.

56. Hilsman, *To Move a Nation*, pp. 220–221.

up a *situation* and a *process*. If crisis, as a particular kind of situation, reveals many of the essential *elements* in international politics, bargaining, as a process broadly conceived as the employment of power and conciliation to resolve conflicts of interest, lies close to the core of political and strategic *interaction*.

We do not claim that bargaining analysis can describe and explain all crisis behavior. It directs attention to interaction *between* governments and deemphasizes processes of decision making within governments as well as broad systemic determinants of crisis outcomes. It captures much, but not all, of the interaction, and more of it in some crises than others. It could be argued, however, that the bargaining approach is the most fruitful central focus or starting point for the study of crisis behavior in all its aspects. Systemic "givens" such as power configuration and military technology then appear as external parameters of the bargaining process, and domestic factors such as statesmen's personalities and perspectives, decision-making procedures, power distribution between bureaucracies, "national styles," and so on furnish the internal parameters. Overall behavior and outcome can best be understood by pointing the analytical lens first at the central processes of coercion, resistance, and accommodation between governments, and then gradually widening the field of vision to include aspects of the external and internal parameters as factors conditioning and influencing the bargaining, even though in some cases their effects may be greater than the bargaining activity itself.

Bargaining theory relies fairly heavily on the assumption of rationality and logical analysis based on this assumption. It is possible to explain a good deal with this sort of analysis for human beings are, after all, rational and logical to a considerable degree. Of course, it is undeniable that they are also subject to many vagaries of emotion, error, misperception, and so on, which produce "deviations" from rational-logical patterns. Fortunately, bargaining theory can be linked to other disciplines such as social psychology, theories of communication and perception, and organization theory which are less tied to the notion of rationality and capable of explaining much of the deviation. Hopefully, future work in the integration of these theories, and their empirical application in historical case studies, will eventually yield a deeper understanding of actual crisis behavior and more reliable guidelines for effective crisis management.

chapter eleven

EDITOR'S INTRODUCTION

This chapter summarizes much of the research reported in earlier chapters and at the same time departs radically from all the other contributions. It is a summary in that many of the hypotheses on crisis investigated elsewhere in this volume appear again in this chapter. It is a radical departure in that the author addresses the tricky and often neglected question of how scientific knowledge can be made relevant to the needs of the policy maker confronted with a crisis. He also offers some unconventional ways of thinking about crises. (A sample of the novel ideas expressed in this chapter might include: the physiological effects of stress, the role of psychotherapy in crisis, the use of drugs to curb stress effects, and the positive functions of crisis.)

At the Princeton Symposium on International Crises that provided the common basis for all the contributions to this volume, the participants spent an evening with Ambassador Charles W. Yost, formerly the United States Representative to the United Nations. Drawing upon his extensive diplomatic experience, Yost stressed that crises were undesirable; that they should be avoided whenever possible, and quickly terminated when unavoidable. For the most part, Milburn does not disagree with that assessment and he does devote attention to crisis avoidance. As the title of the chapter suggests, however, he emphasizes crisis management and even gives some consideration to the use of crises as opportunities.

Managing crises, to say nothing of examining their positive values, is not always recognized as a proper task for research or training. Some argue that it may tend to overemphasize crises or to make men lose their healthy fear of the grave dangers inherent in any international crisis in the nuclear age. This view appears similar to the criticism rendered against Herman Kahn's "thinking about the unthinkable." Kahn's defense of studying thermonuclear war is also pertinent to the study of crisis management.

> *Social inhibitions which reinforce natural tendencies to avoid thinking about unpleasant subjects are hardly uncommon. The psychological factors involved in ostrich-like behavior have parallels in communities and nations.... If thinking about something bad will not improve it, it is often better not to think about it. Perhaps some evils can be avoided or reduced if people do not think or talk about them. But when our reluctance to consider danger brings danger nearer, repression has gone too far.... In our times, thermonuclear war may seem unlikely, but it is not impossible. To act intelligently we must learn as much as we can about the risks. We may thereby be able better to avoid nuclear war. We may even be able to avoid the crises that bring us to the brink of war.*[1]

In emphasizing the value of advanced preparation for crisis, Milburn makes an assumption which underlies this chapter. He assumes that some of the undesirable behaviors likely under extreme stress can be mitigated by (1) the

1. Herman Kahn, *Thinking about the Unthinkable* (New York: Horizon Press, 1962), pp. 19–21.

policy makers' awareness of the effects, and (2) the selection of crisis managers who are less likely to be severely affected by stress.

The references to stress introduce another significant feature of Milburn's contribution. At the Princeton Symposium the participants noted the confusion that exists between crisis and a number of seemingly related terms such as conflict, tension, emergency, disaster, threat, anxiety, panic, and stress. The present chapter deals explicitly with the relationship between crisis and stress and draws extensively on the psychological literature about stress. Given the focus on crisis managers and the psychological effects of stress upon individuals, it is not surprising that the perspective is more that of decision-making than of systemic analysis. However, a number of the hypotheses deal with the likely consequences in crises of certain actions on the adversaries. These propositions return us to some of the systemic bargaining issues discussed by Snyder in the preceding chapter.

Finally, particular attention should be given to the effort Milburn makes to distinguish between scientific findings and practical guidance for crisis managers. Others have called attention to the lack of applicability of many social science findings to the immediate problems faced by policy makers. The despair of those in government upon reviewing current scholarship can often be summarized in statements such as: "So what?" "What does all the jargon mean?" or "That's just common sense!" The distinctive contribution of this chapter is the attempt to translate research hypotheses into what Milburn calls decision rules.

Thomas W. Milburn is well qualified to address the task of relating research to policy. Currently Mershon Professor of Psychology and Public Policy at Ohio State University, he is the former head of the Navy's Project Michelson which was located at the U.S. Naval Ordnance Test Station, China Lake, California. This cross-disciplinary research program sought to bring behavioral science knowledge to bear on some of the larger issues of national security. Rather than a narrow "how-can-the-Navy-do-a-specific-mission-better" orientation, Project Michelson attempted to raise fundamental questions about the nature and consequences of deterrence, influence, and communication.[2] The concern with the application of social science knowledge to public policy is reflected in Milburn's previous writings,[3] and in his various current interests which include the assessment of the personality characteristics of decision makers at a distance.

2. For an introduction to Project Michelson see Thomas W. Milburn, "Intellectual History of a Research Project," in Dean G. Pruitt and Richard C. Snyder, eds., *Theory and Research on the Causes of War* (Englewood Cliffs, N.J.: Prentice-Hall, 1969), pp. 263–283.

3. For example, Thomas W. Milburn, "What Constitutes Effective U.S. Deterrence," in Dale J. Hekhuis, Charles G. McClintock, and Arthur L. Burns, eds., *International Stability* (New York: Wiley, 1964), pp. 174–187.

chapter eleven

THE MANAGEMENT OF CRISES*

Thomas W. Milburn

INTRODUCTION

Crises and their management or mismanagement are omnipresent in human society. They occur on many levels other than national and international, and in many realms other than financial, political, and military. Universities, business organizations, political parties, families, and even individuals face periodic crises created by a variety of situations. For example, business crises may include those produced by a threatened loss of present markets to newer products, the threat of lost profits, the threat of diminution of management prerogatives, a potentially costly strike in some labor-management dispute, or the threatened loss of control by experienced decision makers or top management. Universities, another type of formal organization, have lately confronted not only financial shortages, but crises concerning groups who wish to be heard, including students who feel threatened or frustrated by their sense of being ineffective and by their not being in the locus of power to make and implement decisions within the university. How effectively the crisis managers on both sides deal with the situation will determine the extent and intensity of each such confrontation.

Because crises at any level involve risks with potential for substantial loss, the importance of skill in handling crises is evident. The need for ability to cope with crises may be most unmistakable, however, when they involve nations and may precipitate international war. The events of the six weeks leading to World War I illustrate what may be one of the most costly examples of a mismanaged international crisis. The events constituted a series of critical incidents that may well be a lesson, for all decision makers in crisis situations, in how *not* to perform. The cost of these errors—in lives, property, and other values—was fantastically high. Though this was a war that none of the participants wanted in that precise form and at that time,[1] faulty communications concerning their intentions contributed to perceptions of threat. The policy makers in all the countries attended quite inadequately to the various contingencies and to the motives of others. The resulting war was dreadful and costly; and it changed the world.

There have been other examples of dire mismanagement of international crises in our time. One might argue, for example, that World War II resulted from a whole series of mismanaged crises including Munich, the Italian attack on Ethiopia, and Hitler's continuing preparations to invade Poland even after he realized that this act might lead the United Kingdom and France to oppose him. Similarly, the Japanese attack on Pearl Harbor derived, in part, from a

* The author of this chapter is indebted to Charles Hermann for a wealth of constructive suggestions, both substantive and editorial.

1. For an opposing view see Fritz Fischer, *Germany's Aim in the First World War* (New York: Norton, 1967).

failure of Japanese decision makers to evaluate properly the responses of the United States.

Although crises do occur at various levels of societal complexity and pose grave problems for their avoidance or management, can anything be learned by treating crises as general phenomena irrespective of level? If so, can general rules be formed to aid in crisis decision making? Before responding to these questions, it must be acknowledged that, despite occasional superficial likenesses, each crisis is unique; and thus there can be no clear and certain, always applicable, procedures for dealing with all of them. Even though it is apparent that industrial crises are in some ways very different from those that affect individuals—just as both are quite different from those of national or international scope—interestingly enough, hypotheses derived from studies of such crises may appear relevant to the international arena. Conversely, findings about crises at more complex levels of human activity may enhance the understanding of crises in simpler situations. Consider one simple example: one major consequence of even a few days of crisis at any level is that the persons involved grow very tired. Men have learned to question the judgments they make under the influence of fatigue. We could state the crisis management hypotheses about fatigue in the form of imperatives: (1) avoid fatigue, (2) avoid making decisions while fatigued, and (3) be aware of biases which may occur because of deciding while in a state of fatigue.

Though international crises involve more persons and, frequently, considerably higher stakes (even the fate of mankind) than individual or business crises, they all tend to involve drastic, if temporary, changes in priorities and perceptions and a considerable increase in communications and other stimuli directed toward the principal parties. A vast growth in demands is made on the participants, and is perceived by them. Knowledge of the nature of crises and their frequent effect on individuals, together with some preparation, could make a difference in performance in a crisis at any level. In short, information about the general impact of any crisis can be useful.

For example, although the bankers and economists on the Federal Reserve Board in 1929 were scarcely ignorant or unintelligent, their insufficient knowledge of economic theory and their lack of understanding of crises and correlated phenomena contributed to the exacerbation of the difficulties they inadvertently produced. They *happened to believe* that the speculation on the stock market reflected, or indexed, the fact of a dangerously inflationary economy. They *preferred* deflation to inflation. The members of the Board would have benefited not only from a more sophisticated economic theory, but also from an additional understanding of crisis phenomena. Their actions continued to show evidence of rigidity. For example, they continued to administer powerful contractions to the supply of money and credit in spite of information concerning the results of this course. The shocks they administered to an already contracting and slowing economy (housing and food prices were down, and the rate of circulation of money was already declining) served to slow the economy further, contributing to the Great Depression. If we could make crisis queries and decision rules explicit and relate these to systematic empirical studies of effective and less effective crisis behavior, we would be able to equip men to deal more effectively with other crises like those that confronted the Federal Reserve Board in 1929 or the leaders of Europe in 1914.

Assuming for the moment that there is a literature of confirmed scientific hypotheses about the effects of crises, a major and often overlooked problem arises in transforming scientific findings to information relevant to the policy maker. Scientific knowledge is general knowledge, and general knowledge is always limited in its application to specific situations. This limitation occurs because scientific statements are based on the abstracted common elements from many specific situations, each one in some ways different from the rest. In other words, scientific theories, including those concerned with political phenomena, deal with abstractions a step or so removed from concrete event-processes embedded in contexts of time and related situations. Theories describe relations between classes of events and omit nonsignificant details—a characteristic of all abstractions. The scientific quest for propositions general enough to describe phenomena largely invariant across transformations of time and situations—that is, the nature of scientific predictions—makes forecasts about a specific occurrence difficult.

Scientific explanations and predictions differ significantly from prophecies. Scientific predictions take the form of the assertion "If p, then q," where both p and q concern general classes of events. For example: "If positive reinforcement for acting independently occurs, the frequency of independent behavior will increase." Or, "If crises occur, the tension felt by participants will increase."

Scientific *explanation* consists of descriptions of the nature of the causal mechanisms hypothesized to account for the conditional "then q" statement. By contrast, prophecies ordinarily assert that a particular event, or series of events, will happen, *but without statement of a contingent relation*, that is, without mention of any necessary causal conditions. For example: "World War III will start in 1993, following a severe crisis."

A policy maker, dealing with specific problems, needs to know as much as he can about factors unique to the situation he faces. He needs information relevant to a specific problem within its own particular historical, social, political, and economic or military settings. He is less interested at a moment of crisis in a prediction that can be applied with a fairly high degree of probability across a range of situations than he is in rules for handling the immediate problem. He validates these rules when he employs them successfully, assuming criteria for success can be given. For these reasons prophecies may appear more useful for policy problems than verified scientific hypotheses. The trouble with prophecy is the prophet—or, more appropriately in this case, the experienced political leader or his wise advisers. Although unable to make fully explicit the reasons for their judgments, some statesmen may be gifted at dealing with crises on purely intuitive bases. In the past little more than intuition has been available. But we cannot count on the presence of political genius for the future; therefore, we must also prepare more ordinary men to act effectively.

Both predictions and prophecies are descriptive statements. Decision rules, on the other hand, are statements in imperative rather than descriptive form. Decision rules also presume values. They contain implicit value statements. For example: "If you smell smoke and your bedroom door is hot to the touch; keep the door closed." This imperative implies you will avoid harm from a fire by keeping smoke and fire shut out and reducing the likelihood of a draft which might expand the blaze. But it might happen that you will ignore the decision rule in a *real* fire in order to save your children. In that case you are observing a different value (harm to children over harm to self) as more salient or important than that implicit in the decision rule as stated.

Judgmental criteria, it may be noted, can be stated in decision rule form. For example, a college which admits no one of average intelligence or below has the policy: "Admit no one with College Board scores below 500." Such a decision rule may be based on a number of interrelated values and beliefs, including other decisions to restrict the size of the university.

This chapter attempts to move from descriptive and empirical hypotheses about crises in general to prescriptive hypotheses—that is, to decision rules. It should be recognized that many of the descriptive hypotheses used here as a basis for decision rules lack the confirmation by repeated investigation of crises at different levels that would be required if this chapter were to be more than an initial exploration. Before continuing, it will be useful to make some values underlying this chapter more explicit by stating them as assertions. Crises involve danger, which should be avoided or resolved, and unusual behavior by persons or groups, which ought to be understood. Attention to training and personnel selection should be considered helpful adjuncts to handling crises. Some crises may prove unavoidable, in which case we should try to become aware of their positive aspects, that is, of the ways in which they are opportunities.

THE NATURE OF CRISIS

Situations become crises when (1) they concern values identified by the threatened policy makers as significant; (2) they are unexpected so that there is no set of plans or any existing program to handle them; and (3) they involve a relatively short time in which to decide to act before loss to values will occur. Many of the effects of crisis reported in this chapter result from any individual's experience of stress. From this perspective a crisis may be regarded as a type of stress-producing stimulus—that is, as a form of complex stressor—involving three simple stressors: (1) threat of value loss, (2) pressure to decide relatively quickly, and (3) pressure to innovate in problem solving since no programmed decision, or relevant contingency plan, exists. Typically, crises may also involve correlated stressors such as information overload, restriction of performance by audience evaluation, ambiguous threat and situation, increased number and importance of demands, conflict with others within the group or organization, and, eventually, considerable fatigue.

The definition of crisis applies to a wide range of situations at many different levels and under different circumstances. Yet, in examining the nature of crisis, it is important to recognize different kinds of crises. One way of distinguishing crises is according to their dominant aspect. Effective behavior in a crisis may depend upon the proper identification of its most prominent characteristic. For example, it is the most salient aspect of a crisis that determines whether deception or open and redundant frankness is likely to prove more advantageous to both a single and a mutual "win." The salient theme determines the strategy; strategy should dictate the tactics.

Both the eminent historian of strategy, Liddell Hart, and that theorist of strategy, Thomas C. Schelling, emphasize the virtues of deception and controlling the paths of behavior available to adversaries in battle situations. Sometimes such deception and control are exercised by making apparent to an opponent that we lack freedom of choice. Schelling[2] suggests that for strategic reasons a

2. Thomas C. Schelling, *Arms and Influence* (New Haven: Yale University Press, 1966).

decision maker might wish to give the impression that he is behaving irrationally—if by that deception he could be assured that his opponent will behave rationally.

The appropriateness of such behavior would appear to depend upon the dominant aspect of the particular crisis. For example, some military crises are so nearly pure conflict in nature that they contain characteristics of actual battle. Under such circumstances, strategy of position or movement may be of utmost importance; deception concerning intentions may be vital. Deception concerning physical position, vulnerabilities, and capacities is also essential. If a battle is likely to occur, then mobilization of all available resources as quickly as possible appears exceedingly important. Exactly such a crisis was faced by the Israelis in June of 1967. The unexpected swiftness of their response generated considerable surprise, which they utilized to effective advantage.

On the other hand, some crises, such as that between the United States and the Soviet Union in the same June 1967, involve deterring each other through openness and a reassuring flow of information. At that crisis point the hot line between Moscow and Washington served to reduce ambiguity concerning intentions between the superpowers. The ambiguity and deception which would have been so important in a battle situation would have served only to dangerously increase tension in a mutual deterrent situation. In other words, some crises, among them the 1962 Cuban missile crisis, are pervaded by the need for *really effective* communication. In the missile crisis more than twenty different methods of communication were employed.

Some crises may have competition for resources or allies as their main aspect. If it is allies for which the crisis opponents are competing, then the main assets of either participant include persuasion and what he has to offer in relation to what his prospective allies fear. Thus, before precipitating the 1967 Egypt–Israeli crisis, Premier Nasser sought to win more allies to his side—for example, Hussein of Jordan. Competing for resources and allies may also be characteristic of intra-organizational struggles in which different coalitions strive to control a political system, as in the recent struggle for control of the values to be emphasized in Maoist China. *What* is threatened may determine the essential nature of a crisis. Mao Tse-tung has feared a loss of revolutionary *élan*, which he perceived as infecting various societal institutions. His solution was the cultural revolution.

We can offer no full typology of crises such as has been implied by this brief discussion of the importance of differentiating crises by their dominant aspects. We can do no more than indicate the need for such a classification. But, even without that differentiation, we are able to say things about crises in general as complex stressors and the effects of stress on the individuals involved.

STRESS AND CRISIS

Stress is generally considered as a response; and a stressor is looked upon as a stimulus. Stimulus events are usually considered to be stressors if they result in the following reactions: (1) physiological arousal, or activation, as measured by heart rate, skin resistance, EEG, and the like; (2) subjective reports of distress and anxiety; and (3) objective indications of aversiveness based on escape from or avoidance of the stressor.

Ordinarily, various stressors are studied one, two, or three at a time in experimental settings—that is, in molecular as well as molar ways. Typically, in real world crises it is not feasible to isolate one stressor or even a few at a time. Nor is it possible, as a rule, to collect blood and urine samples at different stages in the crisis to obtain a clearer picture of physiological correlates. Also, in real crises fewer opportunities arise for interviews, questionnaires, or behavioral observations. These separate measures can be taken only in laboratory settings where, in experiments, relatively unambiguous interpretations of causal relations and of functionally homogeneous processes may be made. In addition to increased access and replicability, the low costs of laboratory experiments and simulations compared with studies conducted in the real world further explain why much of the systematic knowledge about the effects of stress comes from laboratory research. Under the simplified and often artificial conditions of the experimental setting, however, it is difficult to generate acute stress.

Although the effects of severe stress may be difficult to study in the laboratory, or to simulate formally, actual crises may lead to the presence of extreme stress and its associated effects. Despite the difficulties with field studies of crises, careful examination of these situations contributes an important dimension to our understanding of the effects of stress on individuals and organizations. Therefore, laboratory experiments, simulations, and field studies each deserve emphasis—though not exclusively.

Chief among the effects of stress that have been reported from both laboratory and field studies are tiredness and sheer physical fatigue resulting from depletion of the adrenals. If continued long enough, fatigue leads to increased irritability, to subclinical paranoid reactions, to heightened suspiciousness, hostility, and increased defensiveness. A detailed summary of the effects of stress on human performance is beyond the intended scope of this paper.[3] However, what follows is a summary of the more general and better known effects.

The effect of psychological stressors on performance depends, in large part, on the intensity of the stress reaction and the complexity of the response to be performed. Although stress is often referred to simply by the fact of its presence or absence, most investigators regard it in terms of a continuum which ranges from none to very intense. Mild stress often facilitates performance, especially if the response is uncomplicated or well learned. As stress increases, performance generally worsens; and, with very intense stress, complete disintegration of performance can occur. The more complex the task, the more likely will stress disrupt performance.

3. More detailed reviews are available. See Harold Basowitz, H. Persky, Sheldon J. Korchin, and Roy Grinker, *Anxiety and Stress* (New York: McGraw-Hill, 1955); Charles Cofer and Mortimer Appley, *Motivation: Theory and Research* (New York: Wiley, 1964); William Harris, Robert R. Mackie, and Clark L. Wilson, *Performance Under Stress: A Review and Critique of Recent Studies*, Human Factors Research, Inc., Technical Report 6 (AD 103779), Contract NONR-[24], 1956; Fred E. Horvath, "Psychological Stress: A Review of Definitions and Experimental Research," in Ludwig Von Bertalanffy and Anatol Rapoport, eds., *General Systems: Yearbook of the Society for General Systems Research*, v. 4, 1959; Richard Lazarus, "A Laboratory Approach to the Dynamics of Psychological Stress," *Administrative Science Quarterly*, 8 (September 1963), 192–213; and Richard Lazarus, James Deese, and Sonia Osler, "The Effects of Psychological Stress Upon Performance," *Psychological Bulletin*, 49 (July 1952), 293–317.

In addition to the intensity of stress, and the tension it creates both in individuals and organizations, improved performance under stress depends upon the nature of the persons involved. Some individuals are so relaxed that rarely does any kind of situation they face place them on the descending-performance part of the stress curve. Most of the stresses they confront merely facilitate their performance. They may be shame-motivated,[4] that is, afraid of letting their colleagues down, but they are almost never frozen with terror. On the other hand, for the already anxious or for the oversocialized individual, stress may have a disruptive effect. For a person who has already internalized a good deal of stress or for an organization which has already absorbed much stress, additional stress may disorganize rather than organize the quality of performance, particularly when complex behavior is required.

Likewise, learning under stress conditions appears to depend on the complexity of the task. Simple learning, such as classical defense conditioning, is usually facilitated by stress; more complex types of learning, such as concept learning, appear to be disrupted by stress. One reason for slower learning under stress is that response perseveration—that is, resistance to extinction—is often enhanced by stress; and the response thus facilitated may happen to be maladaptive or incorrect.

If stress is intense and if it persists, there is a tendency for more recent, and usually more complex, behavior to disappear and simpler and more basic forms of behavior to reappear. Usually, such regression involves simplification of perceptual and motivational processes. Subjects under stress usually show a restricted spatial and temporal focus and, generally, a decreased ability to make fine discriminations. In the case of motivation, stress has usually been found to activate the more basic survival needs and to minimize those motives located high in the hierarchy of needs.

Bovard[5] has argued that stress acts to reduce the number of cues of which an individual is aware. For a time increasing stress requires that attention be given only to the more relevant cues and allows a person to ignore those which are irrelevant. After a while, however, even relevant cues tend to be bypassed. When external cues are not recognized, previously established conceptual sets take on greater importance. Men's expectations and beliefs—that is, their conceptual sets—may handicap, as well as facilitate, performance under stress. The rigidity of conceptual sets under severe stress means that responses to prior situations which were regarded as successful are likely to be repeated, even if the present situation is quite different.

Personality traits shift as crises produce caricatures of day-to-day motivational structures. Energetic, active people tend to behave even more energetically and actively under pressure.[6] Anxious people are more anxious; repressors repress more—especially if they consider it important to operate that way. Sometimes individuals find themselves in situations so untenable that they may experience a sense of panic and wish to withdraw as quickly as is feasible. Yet neither of these

4. Silvan S. Tomkins, *Affect, Imagery and Consciousness* (New York: Springer, 1963).

5. Everett W. Bovard, "A Note on the Threshold for Emotional Stress," *Psychological Review*, 68 (May 1961), 216–218.

6. Personal Communication from Starke Hathaway, May 27, 1966. See also Harold M. Schroder, Michael J. Driver, and Siegfried Streufert, *Human Information Processing* (New York: Holt, Rinehart & Winston, 1967).

reactions amounts to a conscious decision to surrender passively to circumstances rather than accept the challenge represented by the crisis.

Stress also affects the way individuals relate to others. For example, Fiedler[7] has repeatedly found that people operating in leader roles who are more task-oriented than human relations-oriented will become much more so under pressure, until they finally neglect human relations altogether. On the other hand, people who are primarily human relations-oriented will, under sufficient stress, pay less and less attention to the task and attend more to the human relations involved. Another example of interaction effects is the tendency in crises affecting organizations for the highest executives and their immediate staffs to become immersed in these crises because of the importance of the values being threatened. Since, typically, crisis decision making is by face-to-face groups, middle-management groups in the organization tend to be shunted out of the primary crisis decision-making process, except for a role in implementing decisions made at higher levels. As crises last longer or become more intense, those at the top of the organizational hierarchy draw more and more decision-making responsibilities to themselves—decisions that would normally be delegated to others. Typically, this tends to shorten communication lines to operational personnel even further.

SELECTING PERSONNEL FOR CRISIS MANAGEMENT

We identify three areas where decision rules are required as we turn from a summary of the effects of crisis as a stressor to the problems of coping with stress and crisis. First, some general qualifications should be specified for the personnel who must manage a crisis. Because men imperfectly control the forces that can create a crisis, it is unlikely that a crisis-free environment can be permanently devised for any individual, organization, or nation. Thus we have to evaluate the types of individuals who are most likely to perform well in crisis situations. Second, we should consider what steps can be taken to minimize or deescalate a crisis. If taken in advance of a potential crisis, these measures can sometimes prevent it from occurring. Third, we should not overlook the opportunities to use crises. This often neglected perspective leads to the generation of procedures for the utilization of crises.

Crises are sometimes inevitable, and crisis management is important because crisis mismanagement can be so costly. Any management problem can be considered a problem in decision making which typically includes several steps: (1) recognizing the existence of problems, (2) gathering adequate information about them, (3) formulating, constructing, and discovering alternative solutions, and exploring their probable consequences, (4) choosing among them, and (5) implementing a chosen solution which may involve subsets of the four previously indicated steps.[8]

Decision making grows harder when problems are strategic rather than puzzle-like. Problem solving with puzzles is analogous to decisions in games with nature as in most disasters. Strategic decision making—which includes most crises—concerns situations involving human interactions and, therefore, is

7. Fred E. Fiedler, *A Theory of Leadership Effectiveness* (New York: McGraw-Hill, 1967).

8. For pioneering work on some of these stages see Herbert A. Simon, *Models of Man* (New York: Wiley, 1957).

more susceptible to error and mismanagement. Our "solutions" become "problems" for our adversaries, and their "solutions" become "problems" for us. Another characteristic of crisis decision making, which makes the steps followed in simpler decision problems more difficult to apply, is the absence of anything equivalent to an algorithm. An algorithm is a "recipe" for the solution of a problem which, if carefully and accurately followed, assures a solution. By contrast, heuristic approaches, more applicable to real world situations, merely increase the probability of a solution if one exists. They provide no guarantees. Heuristic rather than algorithmic approaches are more appropriate to strategic problems, whereas the reverse holds true for puzzles. This uncertainty in crisis decision making emphasizes the importance of selecting and training crisis managers.

Anyone involved in a crisis needs and wants experienced, compatible, and effective colleagues—that is, intelligent people with considerable drive and staying power who will remain sensitive both to the demands of the situation and the feelings of those with whom they must negotiate. It is also preferable that these colleagues be articulate as well as dependable. They should remain organized and unflappable regardless of pressures. Though all of these characteristics are general attributes, they can be refined down to one specific requirement—crisis management teams should include several people who know how to get things done in situations like the one they face. This would indicate that each member must, or should, have very specialized talents as, for example, being a specialist on an involved country, understanding the nuances implicit in a useful foreign language, or being a skilled negotiator.

Only in extremely rare circumstances do crises fail to benefit from the presence of articulate people who write, speak, and think clearly and quickly. Therefore, people who have more than their share of anxiety should be avoided; so, also, should impulsive people or those who lack ability to imagine in some detail the consequences of choosing one line of action over another. Since crises may arouse defensiveness in those who must take risks on the basis of incomplete or otherwise inadequate information, it is preferable to work with people who ordinarily are free from defensiveness and are fairly open and direct.

When a choice is possible, it is better to work with people who have had broad experience on the social firing line and who have known a variety of cultures and situations, rather than with those whose lives have been more circumscribed and whose thinking has been in narrow or parochial areas. Although the obvious and optimum preference is for people who have intimately known several past crises—so that they do not over-generalize from experiences in a particular one—it may matter less whether they were principal actors or assistants who merely observed the proceedings. One significant guideline is to select people who are cognitively complex and who think in terms of fairly long time spans.

Since it is sometimes difficult to find colleagues with actual crisis experience, the next best procedure is to train them. Effective channels for such training include reading about as many varieties of past crises as possible, studying scenarios for possible future crises, joining crisis teams as an observer, and becoming a participant in a political exercise or in a man-computer simulation. If, by these means, a trainee can familiarize himself with some crisis problems and begin to intuit something about the way the world looks in a crisis, he will be that much ahead when faced with an actual situation.

Reviewing the prior experience of individuals in coping with crises and their responses to various crisis training techniques should aid in the selection of any crisis management group. As we have noted, people manage the tension or stress created by a crisis in widely divergent ways. Ideally, on any ad hoc team for dealing with crises, it would be best to include stress-resistant people whose quality of performance would improve with stress. For example, we have reported that stress intensifies the usual tendency of some people to be more task-oriented, while intensifying the usual disposition of others to devote their energy almost entirely to the human relations problems existing among members of the decision-making group. These latter types may perform well as clinicians but they would scarcely be effective in a crisis situation; nor would we want them as managers of important enterprises in a time of heightened tension. Crisis managers are so integral an element in all solutions that their decision making may well determine the duration and intensity of the situation.

Finally, we should emphasize that training not only serves as a screening device for selecting crisis managers, but also calls attention to the range of phenomena about which information is desirable in a crisis. For the most efficacious handling of crises, a manager should know many things. For example, he should know the resources available to him (directly and potentially) together with the costs of mobilizing them at different rates of speed; he should know what bottlenecks could develop during such mobilization and how these might be avoided. Likewise, he should be familiar with the problem of the substitutability of resources—what the economist calls elasticity of supply.

MINIMIZING CRISES

Ordinarily, the least expensive means of managing crises is to deescalate them—ideally without unilateral, or even mutual, loss. To minimize crises, a crisis-managing team should have a good knowledge of crisis phenomena and of how men behave under varying degrees and extents of stress and disaster. For example, in disasters or battles a good many people—perhaps 20 percent—act in an extremely disorganized fashion, whereas roughly an equal number are hyper-effective under such circumstances.[9] Therefore, it is extremely helpful to know an opponent as well as possible, in terms of culture, personality, *and in terms of the situations in which he sees himself.* It is equally essential that we have in mind a clear picture of *the positions in which we see ourselves.*

Another prime requirement is a number of detailed contingency plans which spell out many concrete details of the crisis. No crisis is likely to turn out in precisely the manner planned, but many of the considerations can be similar. Such a detailed listing minimizes the possibility of omitting or neglecting important provisions and reduces the likelihood of over-streamlining, or over-simplifying, relevant thought.

Crisis managers would find it very useful to know what cues lead to the more accurate prediction of crises so that they might be anticipated. A prevalent belief is that it is necessary to respond quickly in order to abort crises. Hence the policy maker would somehow like to ensure that he recognizes a crisis early and before it has an opportunity to expand. Some crises never reach public knowledge because they have been handled so swiftly and so discreetly.

9. See the discussion in Donald A. Hebb, *A Textbook of Psychology* (Philadelphia: Saunders, 1958).

It may be worthwhile to employ rapid-acting feedback loops to help discover when a crisis is inadvertently being precipitated. Rapid, accurate feedback concerning the effects of actions may prove a most useful substitute for limited abilities to forecast future events. The National Aeronautics and Space Administration (NASA) has been particularly effective in exploiting their prior predictions of possible crises in dealing with those which have actually developed. They have also utilized feedback well in situations where accurate forecasting was not feasible.[10]

It could also be of considerable advantage to defend against certain aspects of crises by empirically "defining" them out of existence. For example, if a crisis manager can increase his capacity to delay response—yet still be able to respond with the resources at his command—he gains more time and, therefore, is under less pressure to move precipitately. Thus he has acquired bargaining power he would not otherwise have. Bargaining power is more important in some kinds of crises than in others; but, in any event, having more time may alleviate one major source of pressure.

Decreasing the number of audiences a crisis team must face and communicate with in time of contention will often prove efficacious. During the Cuban missile crisis, members of the Kennedy team considered themselves to have had a very considerable advantage during the first several days of the confrontation before various publics were made privy to what was happening. (Once the U.S. government decided upon a course of action and the public was informed, the audience provided the government with much support.) Each audience adds stress and, because enough stress to motivate effective operation is already inherent in the situation, it is often preferable not to add to it before the crisis manager has committed himself to a strategy and articulated a plan for implementing it. Increased motivation such as may come from the attention of several audiences is more likely to produce more—and possibly superior—effort to carry out a quantitative production task. But, as we have noted, increases in stress are inclined to reduce the quality of the performance in crises where complex problem solving or innovation is required.

For a manager of a team which must deal with crises, improved performance can be expected from anything that serves to decrease his defensiveness, decreases the extent of his anxiety that he might have made a wrong decision, or serves to increase his willingness to admit he made a mistake. Such developments decrease the extent to which his prestige or face appear to him to be at stake and should lead to a less rigid, more flexible, and possibly more adaptive posture and performance. Regardless of the impression he might wish to give to his opponent, the crisis manager gains if he can retain flexibility, zest, and adaptiveness in crisis situations.

There is a kind of crisis therapy in which therapists *avoid* attempts to provide insight (frequently a goal of therapy), but instead help the "patient" to inventory resources, to deal with feelings through lengthening time spans so that the range of alternatives being considered becomes enlarged, and to direct commitments to reasonably achievable goals through readily available means. Such crisis therapy is usually supportive of any effort to decrease defensiveness and to increase self-assurance. It may deal with premises or point out consequences;

10. See Albert D. Biderman, "Anticipatory Studies and Stand-by Research Capabilities," in Raymond A. Bauer, ed., *Social Indicators* (Cambridge: MIT Press, 1966), pp. 272–301; see also other contributions to that volume.

and, above all, it involves quick energy and action directed toward defusing danger. Although policy makers seldom have an opportunity to interact with a trained therapist in our present organizational arrangements, the idea should not be too quickly dismissed—and certainly not the kind of knowledge and assistance that therapist-type roles might offer.

A last aid for minimizing crisis and the accompanying stress may, at first glance, seem equally strange, but in this day of psychic energizers and tranquilizers they deserve consideration. Psychopharmacological aids can be useful to improve the quality of personal performance by keeping the general level of attention closer to optimum than might otherwise be possible, in spite of outside stresses.

UTILIZING CRISES

The Chinese word for crisis means both threat and opportunity. Perhaps we should make an effort to see the opportunity side of our crises. The positive values or opportunities presented by crises can be viewed in several different ways. A distinction can be drawn between opportunities to do things *during* the crisis itself and opportunities *after* a crisis. Sometimes, for example, actions previously delayed by internal disputes can be implemented during a crisis. In the wake of a crisis, leaders may have the chance to reevaluate programs and machinery or institute new steps to reduce the possibility of future threats to the goals that had been endangered in the crisis. A distinction should also be made between the deliberate precipitation of a crisis and the use of a crisis when it occurs even if it was unsought and undesired. It is clear in an era characterized by the "politics of confrontation" that some leaders consciously initiate crises in an attempt to obtain their objectives. Furthermore, managers or executives occasionally like to use stress or crisis to increase their own motivation or that of their personnel up to the point—the plateau—of maximum effectiveness, but not beyond. The high costs associated with certain outcomes in any crisis—particularly in international politics—should serve as a caution for those who consider this course.

However, crises may prove less dangerous when seized and exploited as opportunities once they occur. It is generally recognized that crises can be opportunities to move forward values that have been of interest for some time; and they often present chances to change widely held definitions of the situation. Through his handling of the Cuban missile crisis and its aftermath, President Kennedy did much to help create improved relations with the Soviet Union. The hot line was an innovation more readily accepted after, and because of, the Cuban crisis.

Coser has restated a number of Simmel's propositions regarding conflict.[11] Among them are points concerned with positive functions of crisis-like conflicts. Crises bring conflicts out into the open; they clarify value positions; and they serve to clarify alternatives. They are also opportunities for action. At times crises may be used to motivate, to mobilize, to unify, or to organize interest groups, organizations, and parties. Crises can crystallize the attitudes and values of groups; they can provide opportunities for decisions that cannot be implemented in quite ordinary times. For instance, much of the thrust to improve

11. Lewis A. Coser, *The Functions of Social Conflict* (London: Routledge & Paul, 1956).

scientific education even at the elementary level in the United States got under way because of exploitation by educators of the Soviet initiative in hurling the first pieces of hardware beyond the atmosphere. That crisis *became* one for the United States *only after we defined it as such*; and it was an opportunity for education only after educators *accepted* the definition and used it to move forward values they regarded as important, such as the reconstruction of the teaching of elementary mathematics.

A useful tool would be to list a great many possible crises, together with possible gains, or values to be maximized, for each in turn. NASA early prepared a list of likely crises they might have to face, one of which occurred even before their book *Social Indicators*,[12] containing the list, appeared in print. This experience serves as an indicator that contingency plans can be coordinated with such listings. The idea is to list all *possible* crises that can be conceived and employ social science propositions as a basis for deriving *probable* consequences, good as well as bad, in the eventuality of each. Notice may be taken of the values to which these probable consequences are relevant, so that, if necessary, society-wide contingency plans can be developed for the exploitation of possible crises.

In a crisis everything seems more nearly related to everything else than otherwise. The psychologist would say that generalization gradients are flat. Without some application of Whitehead's assertion that to some extent all is related to all, it becomes difficult to imagine beforehand how the fact of Sputnik could have led to the New Math being introduced into the second grade—perhaps in itself an even more important development than the impetus and vigor Sputnik gave the U.S. space and missile programs. The possibility of drawing connections between previously unrelated issues during a crisis provides a means of discovering opportunities in crises.

CRISIS QUERIES, HYPOTHESES, DECISION RULES

At the outset of this chapter we referred to the gap between research findings relevant to scientific theory and specific knowledge applicable to policy problems. This important distinction bears repeating. In the world of the scientist, descriptive hypotheses help to approximate certain theoretical variables in concrete operational terms which the scientist may observe in the laboratory or field to note what happens. On the other hand, a decision maker employs prescriptive hypotheses as guides to his actions, as recipes for success or failure. Often he can employ particular guidelines only once; and he does not frequently deal with the abstractions from reality which the scientist *qua* scientist prefers. Scientific hypotheses resulting from operationally defined and empirically valid concepts usually occur in descriptive form. Hypotheses concerning crisis management are not like conventional scientific statements; rather, they are imperatives—recipes for action. They are prescriptive and often hortatory as well. Although they are based, in part, on descriptions of real world events—*what happens in a crisis*—they are also based on value premises: for example, the belief that crises are largely bad and those which are mismanaged, worse.

In this final section a more explicit attempt will be made to relate some still tentative abstract relationships about crises to assertions for policy. Throughout the chapter we have been examining crises from the perspective of the potential

12. Bauer, ed., *Social Indicators*.

manager with an implied decision-making approach. Using a decision-making focus to everything that follows the onset of a crisis entails a discipline for crisis management that involves queries and hypotheses; and, because decision making is an applied discipline, it also suggests decision rules.

Below are some queries which an experienced crisis manager might reasonably and legitimately seek to answer before, or at the start of, a crisis. Each question is followed by a statement of the relevant hypothesis or hypotheses from empirical research. Assuming that the hypotheses are accurate—that is, empirically valid—then decision rules would follow. Even though some hypotheses have not been rigorously investigated, they are followed by possible decision rules.

1. *Question:* What is the nature of the problem? Should its scope be enlarged? What parties are involved? What values are threatened, with what certainty, and how soon?

Hypothesis: The more well defined the crisis, the more likely it is to have dominant aspects.

Decision Rule: Perform according to the kind of crisis that is faced.

2. *Question:* In what short-term and long-term historical context does the crisis exist? What events led to it?

Hypothesis: A decision maker's felt understanding of a crisis increases as his awareness of prior and related events is increased.

Decision Rule: Consider a wide and detailed range of contextual factors.

3. *Question*: What resources are available? How quickly and in what quantities can they be used?

Hypothesis: In a crisis the more likely is a wide range of inventoried resources (human skills, material, and energy) to increase the scope and effectiveness of any response.

Decision Rule: Inventory available resources in terms of how readily available they are and what substitutes exist. Check rapidly with allies and others to survey what potential resources they might contribute.

4. *Question:* What else is going on, or might soon occur, which could compete for the attention, energy, and resources that are likely to be absorbed by the crisis? Will the crisis hold off the other events?

Hypothesis: The more acute the crisis, the more energy, attention, and resources are likely to be consumed.

Decision Rule: Face only one crisis at a time whenever possible. Delegate responsible personnel with necessary authority to prepare for problems that may arise in the wake of the crisis as a result of the postponement of other issues.

5. *Question:* Can incoming information about the crisis be trusted?

Hypothesis: The greater the dependency on one method or channel of information in a crisis, the greater the distortion in information available to the decision makers as a result of error variance in that channel.

Decision Rule: Do not rely on any *single* method or channel of information, nor upon a single point of observation. Use several techniques for evaluating the situation and conduct checks on the fidelity of information sources.

6. *Question:* Are communication channels becoming overloaded?

Hypothesis: Crises increase the tendency to reduce the number of communication channels and to increase the traffic or volume of communication transmitted through any channel which is used.

Decision Rule: Avoid channel overload by reducing the communication traffic concerned with noncrisis issues and by increasing the number of channels used.

7. *Question:* What subsystem crises—that is, bottlenecks within the organization—are likely to occur while the crisis is being met?

Hypothesis: The less available are substitutes or replacements for critical personnel or materials, the more likely are those persons or resources to become the source of delay and/or breakdown.

Decision Rule: Explore as many alternative sources of key materials or key personnel as possible. Do not expend such critical resources for any tasks that can be performed by substitutes. Systems analysis can be useful for making determinations as to the best use of scarce resources in a crisis.

8. *Question:* What allies and other friendly actors exist or might be generated with respect to the crisis?

Hypothesis: In crisis the tendency increases to seek the support of allies and other friendly actors without providing them with an opportunity to participate in defining the problem or the subsequent decisions.

Decision Rule: If the support of others is critical, communicate with them at an early stage in the decision process. After supplying them with your information about the nature of the crisis, listen carefully to see if they perceive the situation in a manner similar to your own. (NOTE: This need must be reconciled with the audience problem raised in Question 9.)

9. *Question:* Who is likely to be watching our action in the crisis? How are our communications, or our actions, likely to be restricted by the presence of various audiences in addition to the primary targets of our messages? Shall we restrict knowledge of the crisis? Can the presence of an audience be turned to our advantage?

Hypothesis: (a) The greater the number of audiences observing actions and statements in a crisis, the more restricted is the freedom of action of the negotiators and the decision makers.

(b) The greater the degree to which commitments are fully disclosed in public, the firmer the commitment.

Decision Rule: To the extent feasible, keep audiences restricted during a crisis until audience support is needed or until public announcement is desirable to add to the credibility of a commitment.

10. *Question:* Are we considering too few possibilities? Can we construct a range of alternative "solutions" to the crisis?

Hypothesis: The more severe the crisis, the fewer the number of alternatives that are likely to be considered.

Decision Rule: Undertake deliberate efforts to expand the range and differences among the alternatives. Consider the crisis as an opportunity for gain and look for the opportunities even in areas that do not seem immediately related to the crisis problem.

11. *Question:* What are some of the costs likely to be associated with each of the alternative solutions? What benefits might accrue from each? What are minor, as well as major, effects of the actions we contemplate? Are there side effects we are neglecting to see?

Hypothesis: As the stress in crisis increases, various costs and side effects of a "preferred" option tend to be neglected.

Decision Rule: Use simulation and imagination to explore possible costs and dangerous side effects. It is essential that value not be restricted to one kind of benefit or cost. For example, to restrict ourselves to economic, technical, or material costs and benefits may irrationally exclude important human values we also treasure. Quite apart from knowing the costs-benefits of alternative potential "solutions" to the crisis, we may also want to consider costs and benefits associated with the crisis itself. Costs of the existence of a crisis may include those associated with the centralization of command—that is, costs involving the shortening of command and communication lines. Costs could also include the creation of intense feelings of bitterness among opponents, which could prove exceedingly difficult to eradicate.

12. *Question:* Are our problem-solving efforts likely to be susceptible to *set*, that is, to rigid expectations?

Hypothesis: Increases in *set*—which are likely in a crisis—decrease the probability of adaptive solution through the overemphasis of similarities between the present and past situations.

Decision Rule: Be skeptical of "solutions" transferred from other situations exclusively for the reason that they "worked" in the prior cases. Be careful of "facts" in the present situation which seem to suggest that the previous situation is exactly like the present one. If there are no basic similarities, screen out that reference.[13]

13. *Question:* Are our perceptions of the situation highly definite and fixed?

Hypothesis: Crises increase a tendency toward rigidity of perception and thought.

Decision Rule: Avoid simplistic renditions of the problem, such as those cast in terms of the capacity of the other side without reference to their attitudes or intentions.

14. *Question:* Are our present decisions likely to commit us to paths with few branches within the foreseeable future? Is there a danger of taking irreversible action that could commit us unalterably to a particular position?

Hypothesis: The more irrevocable an action taken at one point in a crisis, the fewer opportunities one has for control and adaptation in the future.

Decision Rule: Attach greater utility value to those alternatives which appear not to limit the degrees of freedom of choice in the future. Irrevocable action may be desirable, but ordinarily only *after* the most profound deliberation and the most minute examination of alternatives.

15. *Question:* Are we considering only the period of time immediately preceding the crisis and during the crisis?

Hypothesis: The more severe the crisis, the more foreshortened become the decision makers' perceptions of time.

Decision Rule: Attempt to look beyond the crisis. Anticipate future relations and long-term consequences. Avoid contractions of time perspective and overemphasis on those things likely to occur in the immediate future.

16. *Question:* How quickly must we respond? How quickly can we act to implement whatever actions are decided upon? How quickly is a response possible compared to the rapidity with which a response is *needed*?

Hypothesis: Increased capacity to delay response tends to deescalate a crisis.

13. See Norman R. F. Maier, *Problem-Solving Discussions and Conferences: Leadership Methods and Skills* (New York: McGraw-Hill, 1963).

Decision Rule: Investigate routines and resources which could be used to increase the capacity to delay response.

17. *Question:* Does the crisis appear to give the other side more flexibility and alternatives, while restricting our own? As compared to the other side, do we seem to be losing our ability to control events?

Hypothesis: In a crisis one's own alternatives appear to contract while the other side's options seem to grow.

Decision Rule: Recognize that the other side is probably experiencing similar feelings of relative loss of control and limited alternatives. By your own action give the other side a range of choices; do not force them into a corner. Attempt to think through or simulate what the opponents may regard as limitations on their behavior. In order that the other side may seek and review alternatives, do not demand responses in substantially less time than they normally require for processing decisions.

18. *Question:* Do almost any losses by our opponent appear to be gains for us and, conversely, do any losses for us appear to be gains for him? What stakes does our opponent have in the crisis? To what extent are these similar or dissimilar to our own?

Hypothesis: Thought processes which are overly simplistic and concrete (as opposed to abstract) tend to occur among individuals experiencing crisis, and lead to thinking about the outcome of the situation in zero-sum terms (either I-win-you-lose, or I-lose-you-win).

Decision Rule: Avoid constructions of the possible outcome cast exclusively in zero-sum terms. Look for outcomes to the crisis which would amount to mutual losses (occurrences which both sides have an incentive to avoid) and for those which would amount to mutual gains.

19. *Question:* What steps can be taken to ensure that the other side in a crisis reads our messages as we intend them?

Hypothesis: In a crisis as opposed to a noncrisis, tacit bargaining and communication are less likely to be perceived as the initiator had intended.

Decision Rule: Make all communications in a crisis explicit, consistent, and transmitted through redundant channels to reduce chance of being misunderstood. Remember that perceiving him correctly is not the same as ensuring that he perceives your moves correctly.[14]

20. *Question:* Are the demands we make as part of our threats too vague?

Hypothesis: If threats are communicated as noncontingent—that is, if it is not clear what the other side must do to avoid punishment—then it is likely that the threats will be perceived as extremely provocative or the equivalent to announcements of intention to attack.

Decision Rule: Make punishment contingent on failure of the other side to comply with demands that are explicitly stated in ways the opponents can

14. One major problem in crises is the tendency of overgeneralizing "solution," that is, thinking that a favorite solution from the past will work in the present, that Vietnam, say, is "like Korea." To no avail, Lord Edward Grey, Foreign Secretary of Great Britain in 1914, kept trying to persuade parties to the 1914 crisis to meet in conference, a successful solution he had proposed to an earlier crisis. A second major problem is the failure to use known facts. For two different types of studies on these problems see Morton H. Halperin, "Nuclear Weapons and Limited War," *Journal of Conflict Resolution*, 5 (June 1961), 146–166; and Thomas Scheff, "A Theory of Social Coordination Applicable to Mixed-Motive Games," *Sociometry*, 30 (1967), 215–234.

understand. Devise tests for establishing that the demands have been received and understood.

21. *Question:* Are our threats credible?

Hypothesis: The credibility of threats increases when (a) there is consistency between verbal statements and actions, (b) there is consistency between threats and the capabilities of those making the threats, and (c) there is redundancy in the communication of the threats.

Decision Rule: Seek to make your threats credible and appropriate with respect to costs and your own goals. Keep all communication to the other side about threats consistent and redundant.

22. *Question:* Do we demand what is beyond the control of our opponent to supply?

Hypothesis: Demands to the other side in a crisis which they cannot produce (a) increase their feelings of helplessness, (b) increase their expectations of still further demands or of being attacked, and (c) are likely to provoke an attack as a response.

Decision Rule: Avoid demanding what opponents cannot deliver or can surrender only at extreme cost to themselves. Ask if your side could meet the demands being made on the opponents, if the situation were reversed.

23. *Question:* Do we wish to pay the price associated with the humiliation of the other side?

Hypothesis: The more the humiliation of the other side, the more likely are (a) increased costs of any solution to the crisis, (b) increased rigidity by the other side, and (c) increased time required to obtain a solution to the crisis.

Decision Rule: Avoid demands whose compliance requires the humiliation of the other side. Allow them a nonhumiliating way out of the crisis.

24. *Question:* Are we increasing the demands required of our opponents after they indicated a willingness to comply with our earlier demands?

Hypothesis: Increasing demands on the other side after they have complied with an initial set of demands is likely to be perceived by them as a signal that those making demands do not wish to be satisfied by compliance and prefer to continue the crisis; such behavior tends to provoke escalation and possible attack.

Decision Rule: Except to intensify the crisis avoid adding demands to those already imposed after initial compliance.

We have already cautioned the reader about the tentative nature of the hypotheses enumerated above—although he will recognize that many have been explored in previous chapters in this volume. In addition to further explorations into the validity of these and many other crisis-relevant hypotheses, more must be done with respect to the development of useful decision rules. Our examples indicate how prescriptive statements can be derived from scientific hypotheses and how values can be introduced. One needed area of expansion is the explication of alternative value premises leading to alternative decision rules using the same hypotheses. Another necessary development is to list the empirical conditions (kinds of crises, types of decision structures, etc.) under which a decision rule would, or would not, be applicable. In other words, our decision rules remain at a higher level of generality than would be desirable to aid a policy maker facing a specific crisis. Nevertheless, this section does illustrate one approach for linking scientific research with policy problems.

SOME FINAL THOUGHTS

Even aside from its scientific status—which at this point is not yet high—crisis management, though well regarded in certain circles, does not always have a good reputation. To some it connotes a Machiavellian approach; to others a "1984" flavor. Some scholars feel that international crisis management is too closely associated with the concept of strategic deterrence—that is, influencing another nation's leaders to turn aside from an act because they fear the consequences inherent in the other side's strategic nuclear weapons. These men contend that too often deterrence typifies—and incorrectly gets too much attention as—an effective epitome of crisis management. It seems most unlikely that control of crises by means of a delicate balance of nuclear terror will long remain effective because mutual threats antagonize, particularly if tension is high. To precipitate crises in the hope of managing them successfully seems a little like riding a tiger: "unable to stay on, and afraid to get off." Crises can be dangerous as conscious tools of policy, because the fatigue of crises may lead to inadequate judgment or may lead to ignoring the capabilities of others in light of the threats they actually pose.

Crises will come, however, posing threats to important values and demanding quick and unplanned-for actions. They will come even though we may find ourselves unable to forecast exactly which crisis will catch us unaware or what will be the date of its occurrence. We are more likely to cope adequately if we can systematically prepare for crises as general phenomena, attempt to avoid them, turn them aside, and even upon occasion exploit their presence. Research on crisis which develops empirical support for hypotheses on the subject, coupled with deliberate efforts to put these results into prescriptive form as action rules (decision rules) for national leaders, would appear to be an important aid to survival.

part six

CONCLUSIONS

chapter twelve

ALTERNATIVE MODELS OF INTERNATIONAL CRISIS BEHAVIOR*

Charles F. Hermann and Linda P. Brady

The Editor's Introduction to Chapter 2 reproduced a brief segment of the exchange that occurred at the Princeton Symposium on International Crises over whether the concept of crisis participated in any theories relevant to the social and behavioral sciences. In this concluding chapter we take a somewhat different approach to the important issue of the theoretical relevance of crisis. Rather than examine existing theories to determine if they can be extended to include crisis, we have attempted to develop models dealing specifically with behavior in crisis.[1] The assumption is that such interrelated generalizations about the patterns of crisis activity—if confirmed—improve our ability to discover relationships between crisis and other areas of theoretical interest to students of human behavior.

As a basis for model building, we have abstracted 311 propositions concerning crisis from the ten research efforts in Chapters 2–11. The entire collection of propositions appears in an Appendix to this chapter. For the most part, the authors advanced these hypotheses as discrete relationships rather than as components of some larger theoretical network. Furthermore, most of their hypotheses are bivariate, stating the relationship between only two variables. From these studies we attempt to construct chains of propositions that can be associated with some broader or meta-hypotheses which characterize one of several alternative perspectives on crisis behavior.

In some cases the original authors formed explicit hypotheses; in others we have recast into propositional form relationships between variables that we found in the author's research. Particularly in the latter cases, we may have interpreted the contributors in ways they did not intend. Therefore, it is important to acknowledge at the outset that although the propositional inventory draws exclusively from the contributions to this volume we are responsible for the specific construction and interpretation of the propositions. (To help the reader make his own evaluation, the Appendix provides the page from which each proposition was abstracted.)

If one examines the 311 propositions as we have stated them in the

* An earlier version of this chapter was prepared by the first author for a conference, "Political Theory and Social Education," at Michigan State University under a grant directed by Cleo H. Cherryholmes from the U.S. Office of Education, OEG-0-70-2028(725). The second author, Linda P. Brady, is a graduate student at the Ohio State University. In addition to contributing to the revision of the earlier paper, she abstracted the propositions upon which this chapter is based.

1. As used throughout this chapter, the term *model* refers to a set of interrelated and empirically testable propositions or hypotheses. By *interrelated* we mean that the dependent variable of one proposition serves as an independent or intervening variable for some other proposition.

Appendix, one encounters a number of apparent contradictions about crises. For example, one author claims that the response of a party in a crisis is a function of the amount and intensity of hostility he perceives in the communications directed at him. Another holds that the response is a function of his ability to cope with stress. In one study the author concludes that crises reduce the predictability of opponents, whereas another suggests that a party's behavior in a crisis can be reliably determined from the nature of the stimuli. Some propositions claim that more alternatives will be considered in a crisis whereas others advance the exact opposite. Some relationships indicate that organizational effectiveness will increase in a crisis, whereas others contend that the organization may manifest symptoms of extreme disorder. Another contradiction critical for the study of international politics concerns the opposing relationships postulated between crisis and war. At least one author suggests that crises have increasingly become surrogates for war; others suggest that crises increase the probability of war.

How are we to account for these apparent contradictions? Various competing explanations warrant examination. For one thing it is by no means certain that the same variable mentioned in two different studies is conceptualized in identical fashion, and even when the conceptualizations are the same the operationalizations can differ. With no term is this point clearer than with the basic term of crisis. In general, the authors of the ten studies employ one of two different definitions of crisis. On the one hand, crises are conflict situations between two or more parties in which the likelihood of war, or the level of violent interaction, abruptly increases. On the other hand, crises are defined as situations characterized by high threat to major national values, short time for decision, and surprise to the policy makers. When one selects actual situations in international politics that are consistent with each alternative definition, a considerable number of the same events appear in both groups. Nevertheless, the differences in definition may account for some contradictory hypotheses. This same definitional difference could apply to other variables as well.

Another explanation assumes that one of the competing hypotheses is actually false and can be disconfirmed. Using empirical data for final selection between competing hypotheses found in this volume would be premature because the type of evidence presented in these ten studies varies widely. In some instances the author advances the proposition as the product of his intuition and general understanding of crises. In other words, we have the act of hypothesis creation, but no evidence. Some propositions are illustrated with one or two case studies. Support for other hypotheses comes from such diverse sources as systematic interviews or questionnaires with crisis participants, various observer-based measures such as events data or content analysis, or the operation of simulations and games. To summarize, the hypotheses differ sharply in the nature and degree of investigation that has been performed to determine their validity. These variations could account for apparent contradictions.

An alternative explanation supposes that competing hypotheses can be true under certain circumstances and that the task is to identify these conditions or intervening variables that have not been made explicit in the original formulations. For example, what may hold in an international system such as existed in the summer of 1914 may not be valid in a system of nuclear powers. As another illustration, consider the possibility that within the situations identified by one of the definitions of crisis mentioned above, there exist other critical properties each with different consequences. Variables such as geographical distance or relative capability might consistently differentiate crises. As a result, instead of one type of crisis, we have a "family" of crises.

Considerations such as these serve as mine fields that are likely to explode beneath those who uncritically accept propositions that have been abstracted (perhaps one should say "yanked") from unknown and often quite different contexts. The growing number of propositional inventories—as valuable a resource as they are—can be badly misused unless one is aware of more than the simple assertion of the relationship between two or more variables.

The authors of this chapter have attempted to maintain a sensitivity to these various sources of explanation that might account for the competing hypotheses about crisis. The thrust of our work, however, rests on the assumption that different students of crisis make reference to alternative models of crisis. A substantial number of the discrete propositions can be associated with (if not specifically derived from) one or another of these theoretical perspectives. The four models considered in this chapter can be described as (1) individual stress, (2) organizational response, (3) hostile interaction, and (4) cost calculation. After examining the models and the individual hypotheses associated with each one, we will be able to address more general questions about the differences between the models.

INDIVIDUAL STRESS MODEL

Like the other three models, the one based on individual stress can be stated in terms of several assumptions and propositions—many of which have received empirical support in studies of crisis. The basic statements for the individual stress model are as follows:

1. *Assumption.* International crises involve a threat to one or more major national goals of the nation experiencing the crisis.
2. *Proposition.* Individual national policy makers tend to internalize national goals and to treat them as personal objectives toward which they are motivated.
3. *Proposition.* Threat to personal objectives increases stress within that individual.
4. *Proposition.* Therefore, national policy makers experience stress in international crises.

By *national policy makers* we mean those individuals who have de facto or de jure authority to structure, select, and execute the policies of the nation. International crises can threaten harm to any national goal, but almost always include goals associated with the nation's foreign policy or national security. This consideration has implications for the particular subset of policy makers most affected by the crisis.

5. *Proposition.* The national policy makers likely to experience the most stress in an international crisis are those charged with the conduct of the nation's foreign affairs.

Stress is defined as the activation of the individual's coping mechanisms including the capability for "reality" appraisal and evaluation (perception, memory, learning, and calculation).[2] As previously noted, two primary definitions of *crisis* appear in the basic studies upon which this work is based. Threat to national goals is a component in each. In one definition the threat is specified as an increase in the risk of war which is normally a danger to the basic goal of the nation's continued existence. The other definition does not specify the goal, but requires that it be of major significance for the government. Thus the relationship between crisis and stress should occur with either definition.

Both definitions of crisis support the following further specification of the relationship between crisis and individual stress.

6. *Proposition.* International crises increase the probability of disruptive stress.

Disruptive stress refers to the defective operation of a person's coping mechanisms—such as misperception or rigidity in cognitive processing. Not all stress stimuli produce defective coping—in fact, the degree of stress and the nature of the individual experiencing it appear to be important determinants. In general, evidence suggests that the relationship between stress and various indicators of performance conforms to an inverse "U-shaped" curve.[3] Threats that create only mild stress result in improved performance. Increases in threat produce increases in performance (but in gradually decreasing increments) up to some point beyond which performance begins to decline. Beyond that threshold we can refer to stress as disruptive. As might be expected, the kind of performance or task involved makes a difference in the point at which the threshold is reached. The threshold point also varies considerably with individual differences; that is, some people can experience much more threat to their goals than can other individuals before the defective operation of their coping mechanisms begins to depreciate their performance.

Why are international crises likely to produce defective coping mechanisms in the policy makers experiencing them? The specific answer depends on the selected definition of crisis, but with both conceptualizations the effect is the same—to create threat of such magnitude and problems of such complexity that they almost always exceed the critical threshold of most individuals. When a crisis is viewed as a sudden increase in the risk of war, the threat by itself will be enough to surpass the beneficial side of the stress curve. When crisis is defined in terms of threat, time, and surprise, the latter two components serve to compound or intensify the threat to any of a number of basic values. "Temporal nearness of the confrontation with harm increases the threat."[4] Similarly, situations that occur as a complete surprise contain more threat than those for which some anticipation has led to planning and preparation.

Some of the propositions in the ten crisis studies deal specifically with elements of the individual stress model as we have described it. In his interviews with State Department officers, Lentner found that in crisis they did not dis-

2. The definition of stress used in this chapter has been strongly influenced by Margaret G. Hermann, "Testing a Model of Psychological Stress," *Journal of Personality*, 34, no. 3 (September 1966), 381–396; and Richard S. Lazarus, *Psychological Stress and the Coping Process* (New York: McGraw-Hill, 1966).

3. The nature of the relationship between stress and performance has been established in a number of diverse studies. For example, see C. N. Cofer and M. H. Appley, *Motivation: Theory and Research* (New York: Wiley, 1964).

4. Lazarus, *Psychological Stress and Coping Process*, p. 119.

tinguish between threats to the nation, their bureaucratic organization, and themselves (67).[5] This finding suggests the internalization of national and organizational goals. The State Department officers also reported that they experienced stress and anxiety in times of crisis (82). A comparative study of the 1950 Korean crisis and the 1962 Cuban crisis led Paige to advance several hypotheses about the confounding or multiple effects of international crises (40, 42) and the increases in threat that result when national values of the highest priority are threatened (41). From his knowledge of the psychological literature, Milburn includes several hypotheses about the curvilinear relationship between stressand performance (262, 263, 264) and about the differences that task comp-lexity (265) and personality (266, 267) make in determining disruptive stress.

In addition to hypotheses relevant to the basic relationship between international crises and disruptive stress, the selected studies of crises contain propositions detailing the defective nature of coping mechanisms. Disruptive stress reduces the number of cues or bits of information of which one is aware and induces a rigidity in perception (271, 294). Such stress also increases rigidity in cognitive processes and reduces one's ability to engage in complex learning (268, 269). Two studies report that the individual's time perspective collapses under stress so that he becomes almost exclusively concerned with what happens in the present or very immediate future (47, 296). Consequences of defective coping not mentioned in this volume could be described, but those included provide sufficient basis for other hypotheses about the effects of stress on behavior.

In his hypothesis the author of one of our studies may simply report a direct relationship between crisis (or stress) and some observed behavior. Although we will cite the more general hypothesis, the particular defective coping mechanisms triggered by the crisis suggest more specific reasons for the behavior. For example, Paige notes that in an international crisis less attention is paid to the domestic political consequences of any intended action (18). This neglect can now be interpreted as a result of collapsed time perspectives. After the public learns of actions taken in a crisis, it usually takes some time for politically relevant groups to make the prior crisis behavior a political issue that could affect the public life of the policy maker. The stress theory suggests that policy makers are unlikely to have futuristic orientations during a crisis that would make them sensitive to such long range political considerations.

Now consider some other reported crisis behaviors that can be understood as consequences of disruptive stress. The threat that is an integral part of any crisis may be sufficient to lead policy makers to a restructuring of their priorities in terms of tasks and objectives to be given first consideration (259). The reduction in the policy maker's time frame which we already mentioned as an effect of disruptive stress also tends to reorganize an individual's priorities.

Several studies indicate that policy makers recognize fewer alternatives in a crisis than they do in a noncrisis, or that they perceive that their side has relatively fewer options available to it than do their opponents (49, 50, 51, 298). A reduction in alternatives can be explained in terms of rigidity in cognitive processes and the inability to engage in the complex learning tasks required to create additional options. Cognitive rigidity also might account for the

5. Numbers in parentheses in the text refer to one of the numbered propositions in the Appendix.

return to simpler forms of behavior which Milburn reported (270) and the tendency to see any outcome of the crisis in terms of absolute victory or defeat (299). With stereotyped communications and increased difficulties with complex cognitive tasks, it can be expected that tacit bargaining will be difficult for policy makers in an international crisis to comprehend (300). Tacit communication by its very nature involves a degree of ambiguity and uncertainty. Detecting such signaling under conditions of reduced cognitive processing would certainly reduce the probability of their successful use. Finally, the restriction on cues and the limitations on cognitive processing can be expected to result in the increased tendency to make inadequate analogies to past situations (15) and to repeat actions taken in prior situations that were regarded as successful (272, 273). The difficulty in being innovative and creative in the construction of new alternatives tailored to the present crisis has already been noted. Moreover, the inability to identify aspects of the existing situation that would differentiate it from prior occurrences increases the tendency to believe that old successful actions will work again.

Figure 1 summarizes the relationships described in the individual stress model of crisis behavior. The general implication of this perspective on crises is clear. If the threat present in the international crisis is sufficiently severe, the policy makers' normal abilities necessary to handle the situation will be impaired —perhaps critically.

ORGANIZATIONAL RESPONSE MODEL

Another theoretical perspective on crisis behavior rests not upon the effects of such situations on individuals but, rather, on the changes the situations bring in the organizations that conduct the nation's foreign affairs. At its core this model contains statements about the number and location of the policy makers who will cope with the crisis.

1. *Proposition.* Participation in the decisions regarding the treatment of an international crisis is limited to a small group of individuals.

2. *Assumption.* Individuals charged with the formation and conduct of foreign policy in contemporary nations are embedded in large, hierarchically structured organizations.

3. *Proposition.* The more important to the nation a foreign policy problem is perceived to be by those in the government who detect it, the higher in the organizational hierarchies will be the individuals who consider the problem.

4. *Assumption.* International crises are defined by those in foreign policy organizations as extremely important problems.

5. *Proposition.* Therefore, in an international crisis, participation in the decision as to the treatment of the situation will primarily be limited to a small group of individuals from the highest levels of the government's foreign policy organizations.

In brief, the organizational response model holds that crisis decisions are concentrated in the hands of a small number of the government's foreign policy leaders. Thus crisis decision making can be contrasted with "normal" decision making in which a much larger number of individuals at various levels throughout the foreign policy bureaucracies become involved. Notice that the statements do not assert that all of the highest level foreign policy makers will be involved. The head of state will most likely select persons who enjoy his personal trust,

FIGURE 1. Relationships associated with the individual stress model of crisis behavior. The number in parentheses after each variable refers to the number of the appropriate proposition in the Appendix. Plus and minus signs indicate positive and negative relationships, respectively.

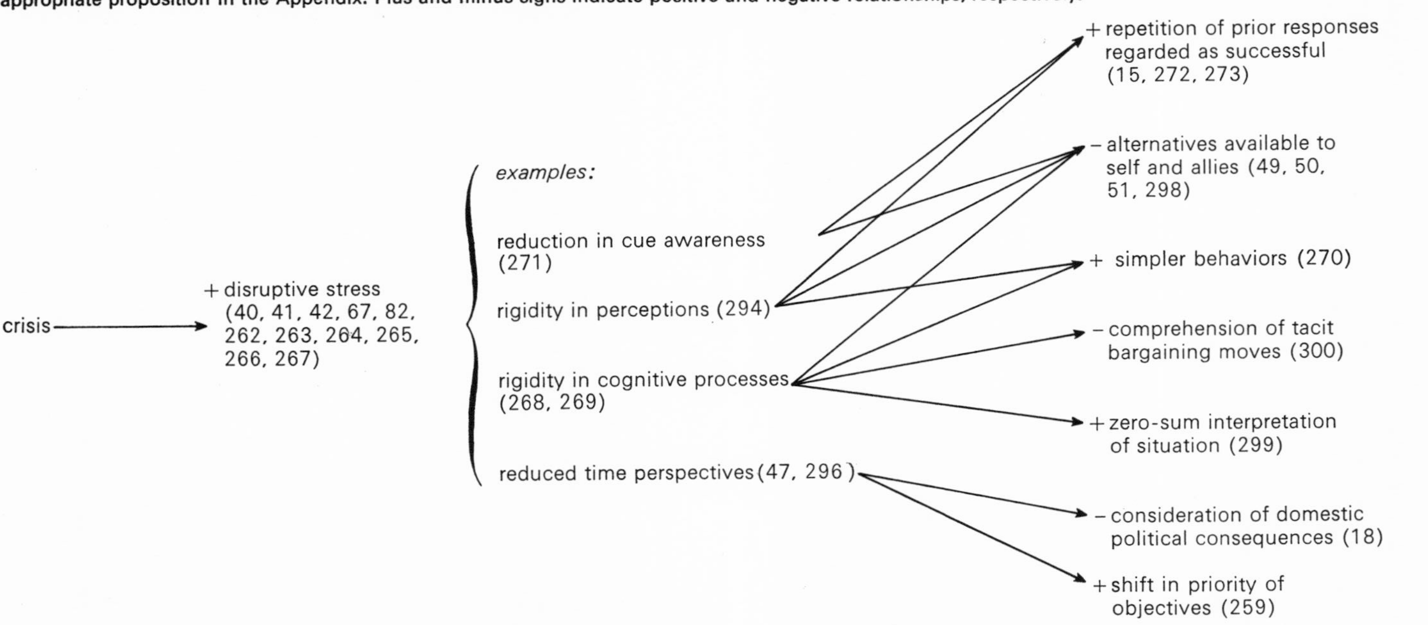

whose judgment he respects, and whom he feels have special knowledge of the substance of the issue. He may also include one or more individuals strictly on the basis of his appreciation of their advice even though they presently hold no high position in any foreign policy bureaucracies. This personal selection of participants often makes the decision units ad hoc rather than a permanent and formally constituted organ of government. The occasional inclusion of trusted persons from outside the foreign policy bureacracies explains the qualification in point five that the decision unit consists *primarily* of high-level foreign policy office-holders. Therefore, the following additional statement appears appropriate:

6. *Proposition.* High-level office-holders in governmental foreign policy organizations are more likely to be included in the crisis policy-making group if they enjoy the strong personal confidence of the head of state; individuals who do not hold high-level office in one of the governmental foreign policy organizations will not be included unless the head of state has extremely high personal confidence in them.

Several important definitional problems in these six statements demand attention. The concept of a *small group* figures prominently in this model. Although an appropriate definition cannot be established by specifying a precise maximum number of individuals, limits on group size can be indicated in terms of functions to be performed. The group must be small enough to permit face-to-face interactions in which each participant will have an adequate opportunity to express his views without elaborate, formalized procedural rules. Some crude indicators might be that the group be able to gather around an available table and that the members share a sense of "intimacy" so that if each is not familiar with all the others at the outset of their deliberations, he can become so in a very brief time.

As always, the dual definitions of crisis in the studies must be considered. Are the six organizational response statements appropriate characterizations of crisis activity regardless of which way crisis is defined? It seems reasonable to assume that the events classified as crises by either definition will be perceived as extremely important problems by members of foreign policy organizations and, therefore, will be referred to the highest level decision makers. When crises are defined in terms of threat, time, and surprise, the short decision-time dimension serves to keep limited the number of participants in the decision process. Time is insufficient for widespread discussion throughout the government. Similarly in the other definition of crisis, a relatively brief period may elapse between the initiation of events that sharply increase the perceived likelihood of war and the occurrence either of conflict or the psychological dissipation of the threat. Besides physical time limitations, other factors act to keep the group small. When major goals are threatened, policy makers often feel a need for secrecy during the deliberative stage which can best be achieved by limiting the number of individuals involved. The high stakes associated with major threats generate a concern for careful coordination and surveillance of actions taken during the crisis. Policy makers often feel they can best perform these tasks if direction stems from and feedback returns to a small, coherent group. Thus there is reason to expect either definition of crisis will identify situations that activate the basic triggering features described in the organizational response model.

The proposition that decision making in crises is conducted by a small group of the highest authorities received support from a number of the ten basic studies. Evidence supports both the small size of the decision unit (10, 84, 133, 135, 280) and its limitation to the highest level officials (9, 14, 74, 279). Of even greater interest is the large number of hypotheses in the studies that appear to follow directly or indirectly from this characterization of the decisional unit.

The magnitude of the crisis problem and the limited number of individuals participating in its management forces the policy makers to put aside most of the other matters that would normally come to their attention (6, 39, 71). (Incidentally, this deferral of other issues may lead to subsequent crises because matters of grave importance fail to receive the proper attention at the critical moment.) The near total commitment of the highest authorities to coping with the crisis means that they will demand more information from the governmental information network (13), and spend a considerable proportion of the time searching for alternative methods of treating the crisis (4). Here we have a potential conflict with the individual stress model of crisis which would imply less search because of defective cognitive processes. It is interesting to note that several hypotheses that contended search would be less in crisis were not confirmed (81, 138).[6] Without relinquishing any of the decision-making authority, these search procedures of high-level officials may generate extensive demands for information inputs from subordinates in their bureaucracies (11). As a result of these inquiries and—at a later stage—the instructions for action, the total volume of internal communication within the government increases (149, 150, 152, 259, 286). But, because the decision unit is small with physical limitations on the number of communication channels in which each individual can participate, the number of communication channels is less in crisis than noncrisis (286). The individual stress model suggests that psychological reasons as well as physical limitations minimize the number of channels used by the policy makers. If the number of channels becomes too restricted, the probability of distortion in the information increases because of the imperfect fidelity that exists in any channel (285). The heavy communication traffic and restricted number of communication channels result in a severe strain on the communication system that can be referred to as communication overload (53).[7]

Because most of the participants in the decision unit are high-ranking

6. It may be that stress reduces the effectiveness of search procedures, rather than the amount of effort devoted to it. There may be more search for information or alternatives, but less discovery of new inputs. Alternatively, if high-level officials devote their time and effort exclusively to the crisis, they may actually generate *more* alternatives than are obtained for noncrisis. The stress, however, may appear in the efficiency of this effort. In other words, it may take more time and energy to obtain a given number of options than would be required under less stress. The fewer number of alternatives in noncrisis (compared to crisis) may result from the absence of a strong incentive to search for them. Crisis provides the motivation for identifying the alternatives, but at the same time the stress that accompanies a crisis makes the acquisition more difficult and costly.

7. In the research for Chap. 6, Lentner asked officers in the State Department if information in a crisis was either overwhelming or inadequate. The officers did not associate an acute crisis with either of those characteristics (85, 86). His finding, however, is not surprising because his respondents did not include officials at sufficiently high levels of the organization to be likely candidates for inclusion in the crisis decision-making group. Therefore, they would be less likely to experience the information channel overload.

officials in the government's foreign policy organizations, they have the authority to bypass established procedures, authorize innovations in operations, and otherwise establish new and innovative procedures that seem appropriate in the immediate crisis situation (9). This ability to innovate and get things done fast as well as the almost exclusive attention that these men devote to the crisis may contribute to the increased frequency of action that occurs in crisis (60, 162, see also the explanation in the hostile interaction model) and certainly adds to the range or diversity of actions taken in a crisis (61). In turn, the volume and diversity of actions, together with the demands imposed on the government by the highest authorities dealing with what they regard as a major threat, contribute to the tendency for crises to consume energy and resources and to focus attention (284).

Because of the small size of the group, there is little slack in the decision unit. Each man's participation quickly becomes vital. The loss of a man or some occurrence that obstructs his continued participation becomes a serious disability to the group. When individuals assume such critical positions in the decision process, they serve as potential bottlenecks or points of breakdown (287). Unfortunately, crises often lead to fatigue and physical exhaustion (7, 258) that increase the probability of a critical man being slowed down or forced to withdraw from the group. The great stakes and the urgency imposed by time constraints are the brutal factors that induce fatigue by depriving men of rest and diversion.

Another characteristic of the small decision-making unit is its increased ability to control information about the details of the crisis and to keep it from various audiences—domestic and foreign. Such control has diverse consequences. The policy makers can deliberately and emphatically take a public position on aspects of the situation, thereby increasing their commitment to that position (290). Alternatively, they can, to a greater degree than in a large decision unit, attempt to minimize public knowledge of their current position, thus increasing their ability to shift at a subsequent point if it should be advantageous to do so (289).

Nongovernmental members of the small, high-level group also provide another means of transmitting commitment to allies and opponents. We have previously noted that one or more highly trusted citizens may be members of the decision unit. In crisis, the head of state may be increasingly tempted to use them for the communication of positions (199). By selecting private individuals more or less closely associated with the head of state, policy makers vary the credibility of the communication (196). Private emissaries prove valuable in crises not only for reasons of credibility but also to circumvent the previously noted tendency for overload of regular communication channels. Their use may partially account for the observation that crises give rise to improvised communication channels (57).

Several propositions we have reviewed—such as those concerning the control of information and the instituting of search routines—suggest a more general proposition. It might be stated as follows:

7. *Proposition.* A government in which action is directed by a small group of men, whose complete attention and energy is addressed to the crisis and who are able to command all the available resources of the government, is less likely to permit an unintended or uncoordinated response than a government whose

response is a product of bargaining between large bureaucratic organizations.

This hypothesis explains the statement in one study that a centralized decision process reduces the likelihood of inadvertent war (214).

When the organizational response model—which is summarized in Figure 2—is compared to the individual stress model with respect to behavior in crisis, major differences appear. In general, the stress model expects behaviors in crisis to be less "effective" than those in noncrisis. By contrast, the organizational response model suggests both positive and negative implications for effective behavior. On the one hand, dangers of inappropriate responses can result from too few communication channels, information distortion, breakdowns following fatigue, and so on. On the other hand, the small high-level group increases control over the decision process and over the information available to various audiences. It activates search procedures, it makes innovation more likely (or at least makes less likely bureaucratic obstacles to nonroutine actions), and it expands the array of attempted international behaviors.

HOSTILE INTERACTION MODEL

The third model relevant to some of the individual hypotheses about international crisis behavior asserts that the actions of a nation in crisis are a function of the hostility its government leaders perceive the nation to have previously received.[8] The basic elements of this model can be briefly summarized as follows:

1. *Proposition.* The expression of hostile behavior by governmental policy makers toward a target is a function of the previous hostility they perceived the target or its associates to have directed at their country and their own prior expression of hostility toward the target.
2. *Assumption.* International crises involve a sudden threatening action that will be perceived by the leaders of one or more nations as hostile behavior addressed at them.
3. *Proposition.* Therefore, the more threatening the policy makers perceive the act precipitating the crisis to be, the more hostile their response and, conversely, the less threatening the act is perceived to be, the less hostile their response.

The critical terms in these three statements are hostility, expression, perception, and of course, crisis. As used here, *hostility* can be defined as opposition to some nation, its government, or actions (either initiated or anticipated) by representatives of that government or nongovernmental groups within that nation. Hostility ranges from mild statements of displeasure to physical acts of massive violence. *Expression* refers to the communication of that hostility by either verbal statements or physical deeds in a manner that *can* (but not necessarily will) be detected by the human targets of the hostility. Despite the highly technical use of the term *perception*, we stipulate that it is the interpretation by a

8. In contrast to the individual stress and organizational response models, the hostile interaction model and the final model to be considered in this chapter (cost calculation) apply to a broader range of behavior than that occurring in crisis. Recalling Robinson's concern (Chap. 2) with the participation of the crisis variable in theoretical formulations about other areas of human activity, these two models offer an explicit—if tentative and incomplete—bridge.

FIGURE 2. Relationships associated with the organizational response model of crisis behavior. The number in parentheses after each variable refers to the number of the appropriate proposition in the Appendix. Plus and minus signs indicate positive and negative relationships, respectively.

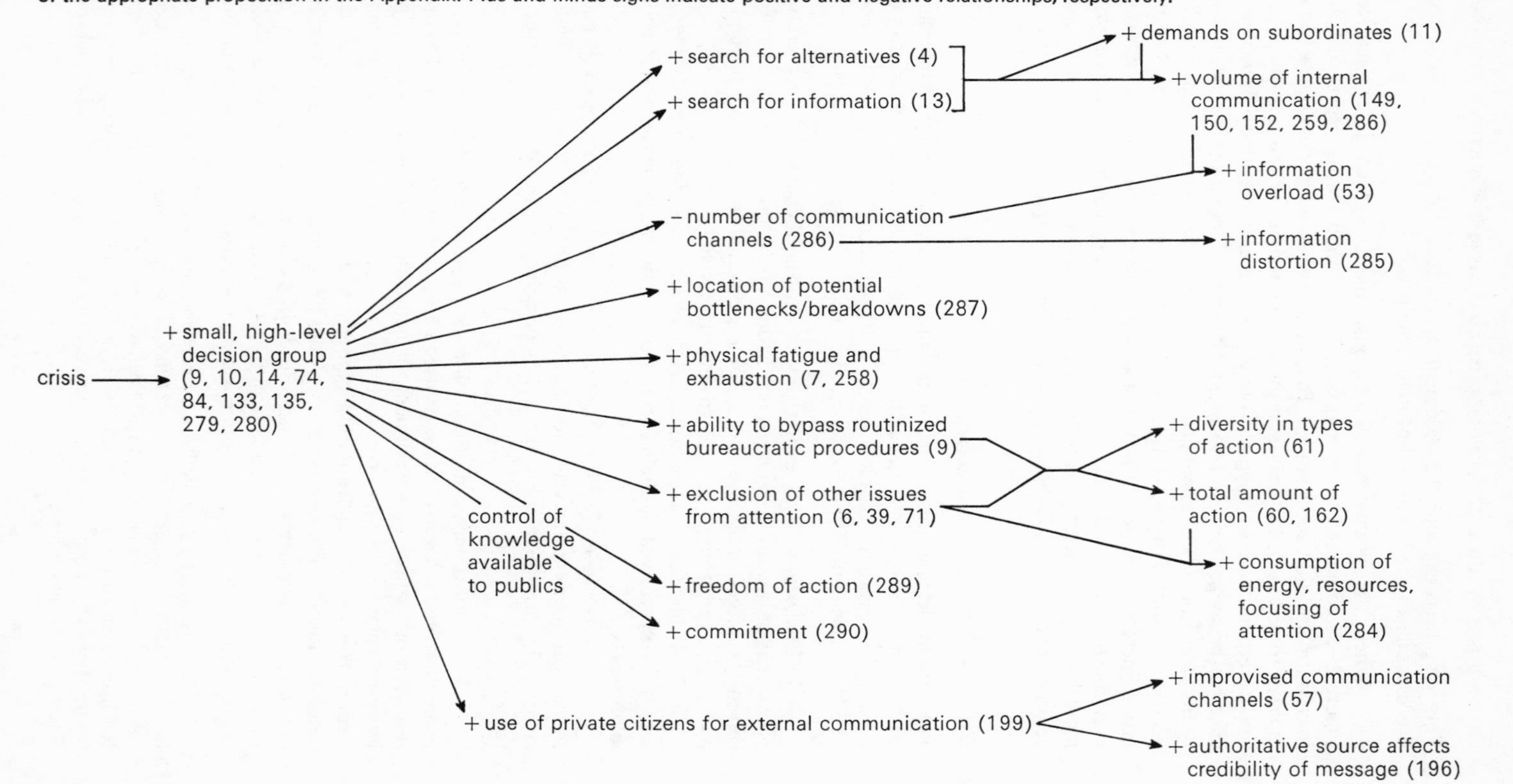

nation's policy makers that they or some part of their nation is the target of another nation's hostility. We have previously established that both definitions of crisis used in the ten studies involve threat. The initiation of a threat is one kind of hostile behavior; that is, it is behavior indicating the future intent to harm the values of the target if the target does not conform to the demands of the one making the threat. Thus international crises are occasions that precipitate substantial hostile behavior.

Considerable evidence for the basic relationships in the hostile interaction model appears in Chapter 7 by Zinnes, Zinnes, and McClure and in Chapter 8 by Schwartz. For example, they substantiate the relationship between crisis and hostility (87, 122) and between expression of hostility by one party (*A*) and the perception by the target (*B*) of that hostility (93, 94, 95, 106, 107). The research by the Zinnes' and Snyder (Chapters 7 and 10) confirms the impact of actor *B*'s previous expressions of hostility toward *A* on *B*'s current expression of hostility toward *A* (90, 255). In addition, these studies support the hypothesis that *B*'s perception of hostility from *A* influences *B*'s current expression of hostility toward *A* (89, 96, 97, 98, 99, 100, 101, 108, 109). One of the basic extensions of these initial statements stems from the severity of the threats associated with international crises—a point discussed earlier in connection with the individual stress model. The more severe the threat, the greater the probability of physical acts of force and violence (62).

4. *Proposition.* If hostility occurs in the context of an international crisis, then the likelihood of physical acts of force and violence increases.

Of course, one form of force and violence is war, but there are many such physical acts short of war. The introduction of violent physical acts into a conflict, even though they be on a much less massive scale than war, increases the possibility of even more violent acts of reprisal by the other party (204, 205), thus initiating an escalation cycle. Although the introduction of physical acts of force and violence makes escalation more likely, this progression of increasing reciprocal hostility can occur in a crisis even in the absence of violence.

Figure 3 displays the deadly sequence. *A* triggers the crisis for *B* which responds with stronger expressions of hostility toward *A*. In turn, *A* perceives the hostile expressions of *B* and initiates new and more intense hostile actions toward *B*. Figure 3 does not show a feedback line from *A*'s counter-expressions of hostility to new perceptions of hostility by *B*, but that loop is justified in terms of the hostile interaction model. None of the present studies offer evidence that the hostile expressions of the second party in a crisis lead to perceptions of hostility by the first, but such a link can be inferred given the hypotheses concerning additional hostile actions by the initiator of the crisis (223, 250, 251). The escalation spiral requires a fifth statement.

5. *Proposition.* Hostile expressions by the recipient (*B*) of the behaviors that precipitated the crisis will be perceived by the initiator *A* and will result in more intense expressions of hostility by *A* toward *B*.

In this unmodified form the hostile interaction model means that, inevitably, every crisis spirals to higher and higher levels of hostile expression and, presumably, ends in war and destruction. Because actual situations defined as international crises by either of our definitions do not always lead to war, researchers must consider amendments to this basic model that could alter the

FIGURE 3. Relationships associated with the hostile interaction model of crisis behavior. The number in parentheses after each variable refers to the number of the appropriate proposition in the Appendix. Plus and minus signs indicate positive and negative relationships, respectively. For example, a plus sign in front of an intervening variable means that the higher the value of that intervening variable, the higher will be the value of the dependent variable.

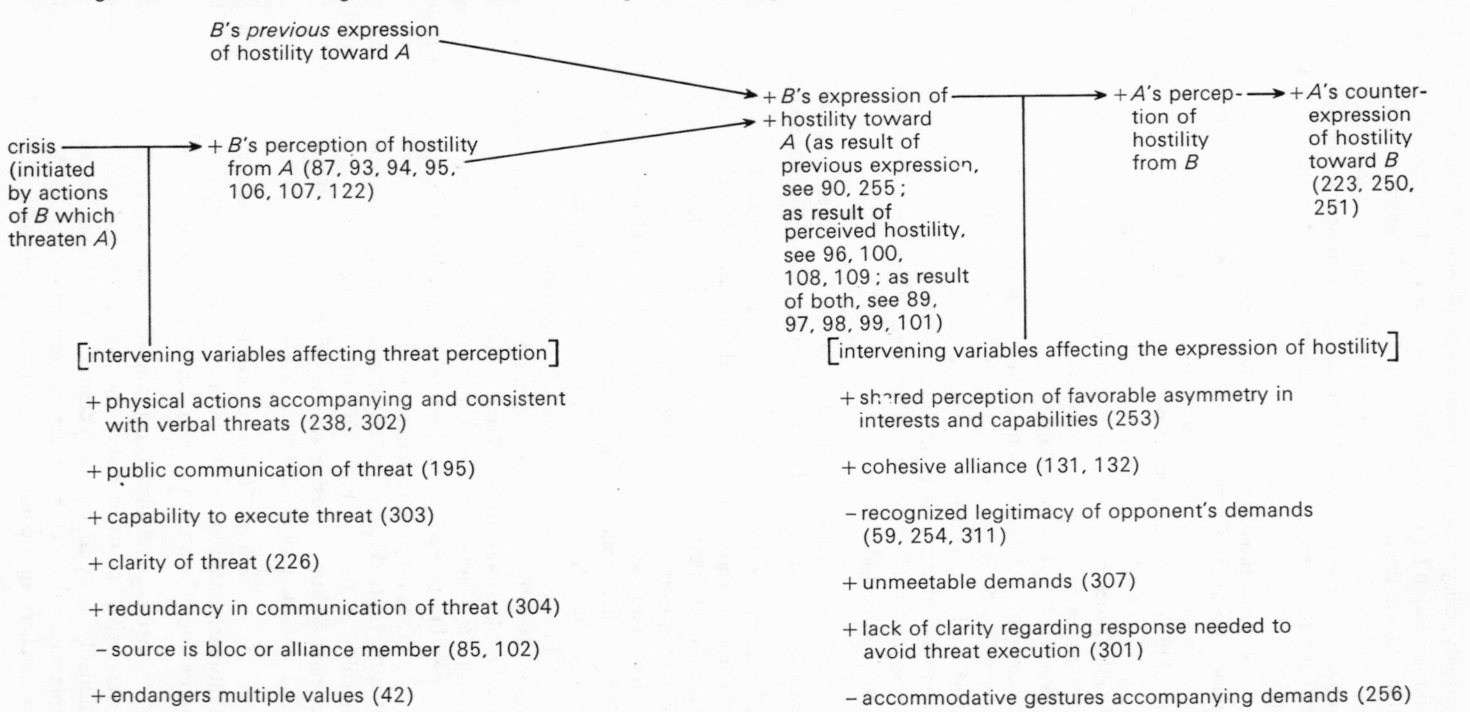

escalation cycle. Our studies yield hypotheses that can be seen as intervening at one of two points: (1) considerations that affect the intensity of the perceived threat (one kind of hostility), and (2) considerations that curb the expression of hostility.

Among the variables mentioned which alter the perception of threat and hostility are a number based on the general hypothesis that the more credible the threat, the greater the perceived degree of danger and hostility. Therefore, many of the relevant intervening variables are concerned with increasing or decreasing the credibility of threats. For example, several studies support the proposition that the credibility of threats increases if physical actions accompany, and are consistent with, verbal threats (238, 302). The credibility of a threat increases if it is publicly communicated (195), thereby making it more difficult for the policy makers to fail to execute the threat should their demands not be met. The existence and availability of the capability necessary to execute the threat also constitutes a necessary element of credibility (303). If the threat is well defined and specific, then this clarity will increase the threat's credibility (226). Redundant communication contributes to clarity as well as to the initiator's determination and commitment, and hence increases credibility (304).

The perceived intensity of a threat varies with the source. Thus the reaction of a nation's leaders to unfavorable actions by its allies are not likely to be seen as threatening as equivalent actions by nations with whom past relationships have been less friendly (85, 102). The scope of the issues involved in a threat also affects its intensity. Actions that policy makers perceive to endanger multiple major values or goals will be more threatening than actions affecting only one value or goal (42). The prospect of total war represents exactly that kind of multiple-value threat. Before considering the other type of intervening variables, we should emphasize that most of these propositions concern threats and may not be applicable to other forms of hostility. Crises, by definition, involve threats so the hypotheses apply to the first cycle of hostile interaction described by the model. If subsequent cycles involve other forms of hostility these qualifications may not be operative.

The policy makers of a nation may perceive hostility but may be constrained in expressing hostility in reply; or, alternatively, intervening conditions may make their expressions even more hostile than they might otherwise be. Some of these intervening variables appear in hypotheses advanced in the ten studies. If the policy makers perceive a favorable asymmetry between their nation and the opponents with respect to the relevant capabilities and investment in the issues involved, and if they believe the opponents perceive a similar asymmetry, then the policy makers' expression of hostility will be more severe (253). Membership in a cohesive alliance will increase the probability that such a favorable asymmetry will be perceived and, therefore, contribute to an escalation of hostile expression (131, 132).

When demands are involved, as they always are when the hostility is in the form of threats, then the assessment of the demands will affect the expression of hostility. The more legitimacy the policy makers attribute to the demands contained in their opponents' threats, the more curbed will be their own expressions of hostility (254). Conversely, the more unreasonable the policy makers regard the demands, the more likely is some escalatory hostile response (59, 311). Furthermore, if the demands are beyond the capabilities of the policy makers and their nation to fulfill, then this particular kind of unreasonable request will also precipitate an escalatory hostile response (307). Threats which are not clear as to the response required to avoid execution of the threat will be regarded as extremely provocative and will increase the likelihood of a very hostile behavior in reply (301). Accommodative gestures, however, which are undertaken simultaneously with coercive tactics (such as threats) may signal a desire to prevent an escalation spiral and will reduce the probability of an extremely hostile response (256).

The hostile interaction model, which is summarized in Figure 3, differs from the others we have considered in that the nature of the crisis behavior is clearly established in the basic statements of the model. It stipulates one and only one kind of crisis behavior—hostility—and the issue in the development of the model is essentially how much and under what conditions might the escalatory spiral be broken.

COST CALCULATION MODEL

The final model characterizes the policy makers as weighing the benefits of any given action—in crisis as well as noncrisis—against the costs it is likely to incur. In one sense this model can be viewed as identifying some of the properties which curb or prevent the endless cycle of hostility described in the hostile interaction model.

The basic statements for the cost calculation model of crisis behavior are as follows:

1. *Assumption.* The national goals that are most important to national policy makers concern the physical survival of the presently constituted nation and certain core values that define the society. The policy makers' commitment to the protection of these goals and values will be called their survival goals.
2. *Assumption.* The national goals initially endangered in an international crisis may or may not include danger to survival goals.
3. *Proposition.* In response to an international crisis, national policy makers will take actions designed to eliminate or minimize the danger presented by the crisis to major national goals.
4. *Proposition.* If the policy makers believe that the initiation or continuation of certain actions in the crisis substantially increases the danger of destroying survival goals, they will seek to negotiate a settlement of the crisis or, failing a successful negotiation, they will forfeit the threatened nonsurvival goal(s).
5. *Proposition.* If the crisis poses a direct threat to survival goals, the policy makers will seek to negotiate a settlement and will refrain from any deliberate actions that they believe will reduce the likelihood of a settlement.
6. *Proposition.* Therefore, the more an international crisis threatens a nation's survival goals, the more effort will be made to achieve a settlement; and, conversely, the less threat to survival goals, the more likely are hostile actions to be taken as part of the effort to protect the major goals that are endangered.

The basic statements could be interpreted as the guidelines for a national decision maker who calculates his costs. He has a preference ordering of goals that minimally distinguishes between those goals necessary for existence and those which are not. He will take such action (including hostile action) as he thinks necessary unless or until responses to his actions are likely to greatly endanger even more fundamental goals. As used in this paper, *survival goals* refer to the commitment of national policy makers to protect from externally directed attacks (1) their nation's territory, people, and institutions, and (2) the core values that are regarded by all politically relevant groups within the nation as essential for the definition of their society (e.g., the rights of the individual, the nature of government, etc.). The two definitions of crisis have slightly different implications in the calculation of cost model. If crises are defined as situations that suddenly increase the likelihood of war and if war is construed to involve heavy sustained attacks on the homeland (i.e., "central war"), then such crises *always* endanger survival goals. The threat-time-surprise definition of crisis, however, need not involve survival goals. The difference in definition will be important in establishing whether the onset of a crisis leads to hostile reactions and escalatory behavior (less likely, according to the model, if survival goals are immediately endangered).

Among the ten research chapters, the study by Snyder (Chapter 11) offers the most detailed consideration of hypotheses related to the cost calculation model of crisis behavior.[9] He uses the risk-of-war definition of crisis, therefore, we can assume that survival goals almost always are present in situations he analyzes as crises. For this reason he advances hypotheses about behavior in all crises that are consistent with those basic cost calculation statements concerning crises in which survival goals are endangered. For example, Snyder contends that in crises the policy makers will be increasingly concerned about avoiding war and reducing risks (203, 211). Snyder also introduces the concept of critical risk that can be interpreted as the maximum risk of war a party can stand without capitulating. He contends that when an opponent's threat credibility exceeds the policy makers' critical risk, they will then make concessions (245). If one treats an executable threat directed at survival goals as exceeding the critical risk threshold, then this proposition—like the two previous ones—supports the sixth basic statement. That statement holds that crises endangering survival goals will lead to increased efforts to obtain a settlement.

When crises are not defined so as to always involve survival goals from the outset, then the parties to the situation will behave in such a manner as to make increasingly hostile behaviors likely. McClelland (Chapter 5) refers to this as the "upswing phase" of a crisis and it is represented in the top portion of Figure 4.

The basic studies suggest four hypotheses regarding a crisis—or that stage of a crisis—in which survival goals are not involved. First, the policy makers are more likely to give the appearance of irrationality or inability to control events (70, 221).[10] This deliberate effort to appear unable to control the situation is used as a tactic to shift responsibility for modifying positions to the opponents. Second, because survival goals have not been endangered, policy makers have a tendency to perceive opportunities in the situation to increase their opponent's risk relative to their own. As a result policy makers will be willing to manipulate

9. Some of the work by Charles McClelland in Chap. 5 also bears on the cost calculation model.

10. Proposition no. 70 results from Lentner's interviews (Chap. 6) with State Department officials and does not indicate whether the loss of control is a ruse or an actual condition. Because his respondents were lower level officers who would not be involved in crisis decision making, according to the organizational response theory, they may actually feel that they have far less control in crises as compared to noncrises in which they exercise somewhat more influence in shaping the government's action.

FIGURE 4. Relationships associated with the cost calculation model of crisis behavior. The numbers in parentheses after each variable refer to the number of the appropriate propositions in the Appendix. Plus and minus signs indicate positive and negative relationships, respectively.

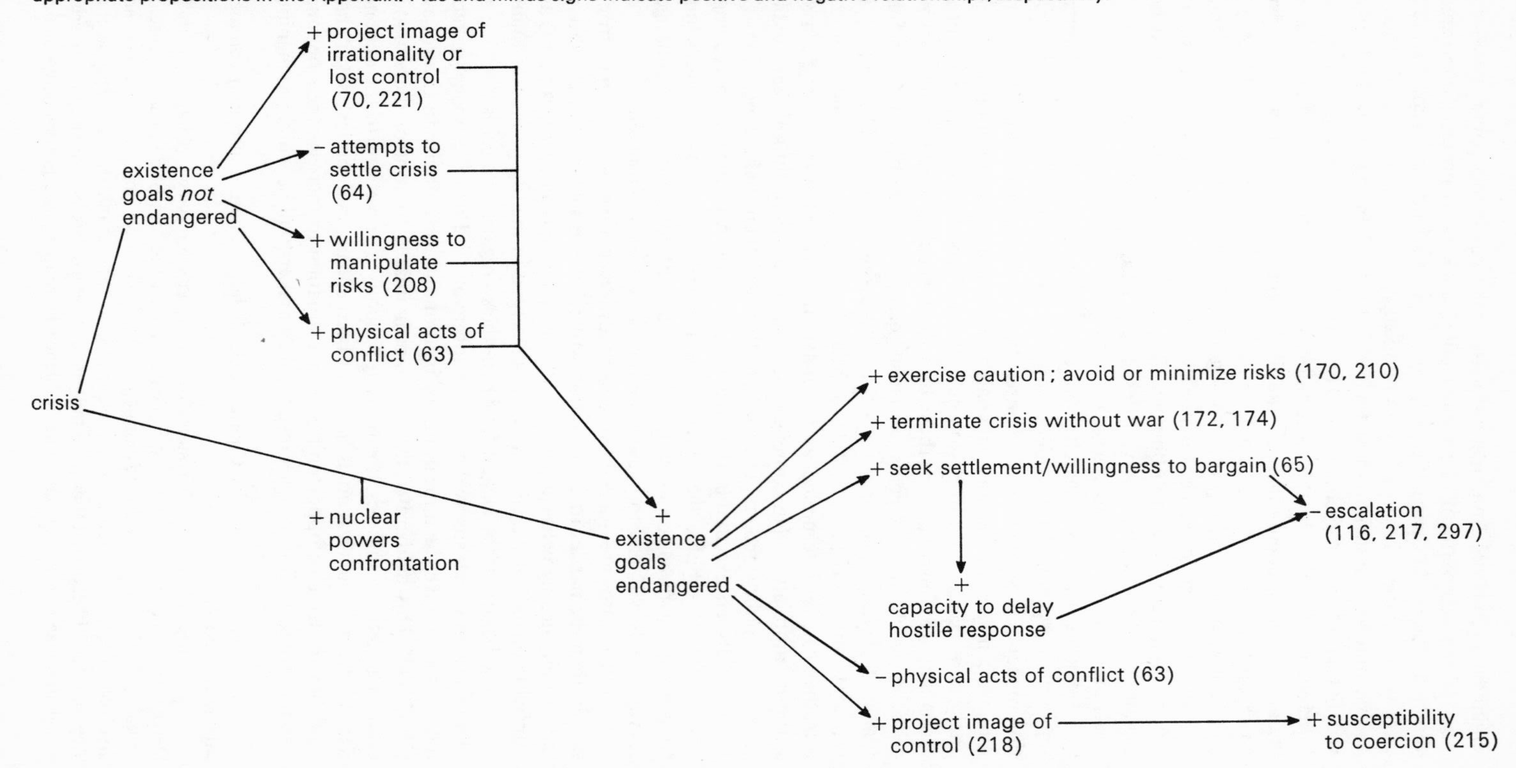

the amount of risk present in the crisis (208). The previously mentioned tendency to appear irrational to the opponents may be a specific manifestation of the tendency to increase risk. Third, when survival goals are not endangered, the policy makers will initiate fewer attempts to settle the crisis (64). Finally, they will initiate more conflictful, physical actions (63). All of these behaviors tend to increase the hostility between the parties to the crisis and make likely the expansion of the goals threatened, so that at some point survival goals are perceived to be endangered. This development—shown in Figure 4—represents a seventh basic statement in the cost calculation theory.

7. *Proposition.* International crises that do not initially involve existence goals will tend to result in increasingly hostile behavior until the policy makers perceive that their survival goals have become endangered.

At the point when policy makers believe that significant threat jeopardizes survival goals, the crisis enters a second stage in which different kinds of behavior occur. These behaviors will be like those associated with crises in which survival goals have been involved from the outset. Before proceeding to the examination of behaviors that occur when crises reach this stage, it should be emphasized that the capabilities of the parties to an international crisis can be decisive in establishing whether threat to survival goals is perceived at its beginning. If the threat explicitly calls for the use of military force in the event execution should become necessary, then a substantial differential in military capability will lead the lesser nation's policy makers to perceive a threat to their survival goals. Similarly, if both parties have the capability to inflict substantial damage on the other's homeland, both groups of policy makers are then more likely to perceive threat to their survival goals. A special case of this symmetrical situation involves a crisis between nuclear powers. Certainly, the prospect of nuclear war threatens destruction of survival goals. Thus in Figure 4 the nuclear power status of the parties to the crisis is an intervening variable that assures threat to survival goals. Some abstracted propositions concern crises in the nuclear age or among nuclear powers, but for our purposes these hypotheses can be regarded as applicable to any crisis in which the nation's most basic goals are threatened.

We can briefly identify the propositions in the basic studies that seem appropriate characterizations of crises involving such threats. In contrast to earlier behaviors, policy makers will exercise great caution and will engage in efforts to avoid or minimize the introduction of further risks in the situation (170, 210). They will seek to terminate the crisis without war (172, 174). To this end, the government will initiate fewer physical acts of conflict than during the earlier phase (63). Furthermore, more efforts will be made to seek a settlement and to enter into negotiations with their opponents (65). The resulting willingness to communicate with their opponents increases the probability of few actions that will expand the existing level of hostilities (116, 217). The attempts to seek a settlement can be interpreted as one form of the capacity to delay hostile responses, and as such decreases the probability of escalation (297). Finally, as shown in Figure 4, the policy makers will attempt to project to their adversaries an image of firm control over the actions taken by their country (218) in order to ensure that an accidental or irrational action will not precipitate the execution of threats. One consequence of seeming to be in control, however, is increased susceptibility to coercion from the opponents (215).

The last proposition raises an important question. What happens if one nation's policy makers perceive their survival goals to be severely threatened and their opponents do not? More specifically, if—because of this asymmetry or for some other reasons—attempts at settlement fail, what happens? This query moves beyond the insights offered by the cost calculation model, but two answers seem possible. Either the party that perceives threat to some survival goals redefines the necessities for survival to exclude those goals so that it can forfeit the goals in question or it engages in war.

CONCLUSIONS

We began with a number of discrete propositions, some of which appeared to be contradictory. A fairly large number of the propositions were related to one of the four models of crisis behavior. The association of individual hypotheses with one of the larger frameworks makes more evident that different levels and units of analysis are involved. The stress model concerns individual psychological and physiological behaviors. The organizational response model, as the name implies, deals with collectivities of individuals and suggests that small groups will replace formal organizations in the performance of certain decision activities during a crisis. Both of these models are largely indifferent to the external parties that normally participate in an international crisis. By contrast, the hostile interaction model achieves a dynamic quality by building on the effects each party to a crisis has on the other. Finally, the cost calculation model ignores the actual nature of the decision unit, but assumes that it will have a clear ordering of goals and will act in such a way as to give maximum protection to the most important goals. Thus the models deal with different aspects of crisis and are not in complete contradiction.

Contradictions do exist, however. These opposing perspectives can be seen by examining at a macro level the kinds of crisis behavior expected by each model. In general, the individual stress model suggests ineffective coping behavior—it may be total capitulation to the opponents or complete intransigence. Whatever the behavior, it will be based on an assessment of reality and the actor's relationship to that reality which is less accurate than would occur in a noncrisis. The behaviors predicted by the organizational response model are mixed, ranging from information distortion that produces ineffective coping similar to that encountered in the individual stress model to innovation and an increased array of kinds of actions. With some important qualifications, the hostile interaction model predicts cycles of increasingly hostile expressions. And, finally, the cost calculation model suggests that under certain conditions efforts will be undertaken to curb hostile behavior and seek a settlement.

The conflict may be sharpest between the individual stress and cost calculation models. The cost calculation model depends on the effective operation of certain cognitive processes which the stress model indicates will be defective. For example, the cost calculation model suggests the existence of a preference ordering of goals and that behavior depends on what goals in the preference ordering are threatened. The stress model, on the other hand, contends that priorities and time perspectives will be altered by the stress experience. It does not take much extrapolation from the stress model to contend that the goal which has been immediately and severely threatened will be treated as the highest priority objective regardless of its position prior to the crisis. In brief, the stability of the preference ordering is called into question.

Undoubtedly, multiple solutions to the points of contention between the four models can be advanced. In these conclusions we propose one means of integrating certain basic features of each model that allows a resolution of the differences between them. Although it does not account for all the individual propositions previously associated with each model, we believe this integrative model could be expanded to incorporate most of them.

According to the integrative model, any crisis contains critical branching points that have the effect of engaging, combining, or overriding the salient features of each of the four models. The actor's response to the crisis depends upon the route taken at these major branching points. To represent the model pictorially in Figure 5, we have used a flow chart like those used in computer programming. The flow chart provides an unambiguous sequence and highlights the branching points (represented as yes-no questions in the diamond-shaped boxes). For the present, it allows us to avoid the difficult problem of what factors determine the response to a given question. As indicated in Figure 5, the integrative model yields four alternative behaviors as the response to any crisis (represented as trapezoids).

One response—the expression of hostility to the opponent—involves the hostile interaction model supplemented by disruptive stress. The absence of threat to any survival goals releases the policy makers from the restraints that would likely result from danger to these most basic values. At the same time, the experience of disruptive stress blocks the positive effects of search and innovation that might otherwise occur from such organizational response features as high level decision group and bureaucratic bypass. Under such conditions the policy makers react in terms of the hostility they perceive in the crisis and the prior hostility they have expressed to that opponent. Thus the response constitutes a step in the escalation cycle postulated by the hostile interaction model.

If the policy makers experience neither a threat to survival goals nor disruptive stress, then the positive effects of the organizational response model combine with the rationality present in the cost calculation model. Innovative methods of tackling the situation and information generated from search routines —both consequences of the small, high level decision group and bureaucratic bypass—become inputs in the decision process. Should the policy group calculate that their position in the present situation is favorable relative to their opponent, then their response will be coercive and will put pressure on the opponents to yield. These calculations also increase the likelihood of behaviors allowing the enemy to withdraw with some grace or face-saving gesture.

The two columns on the right side of Figure 5 both result when policy makers perceive survival goals as threatened. When they remain free of disruptive stress, the policy makers calculate that their energy must be devoted to preserving the survival goals and, therefore, accommodative behavior occurs—proposals for settlement, offers to negotiate, partial withdrawals. Imaginative proposals for accommodation can occur from the search input that has not been minimized by disruptive stress. Also note that accommodative behavior results when the policy makers calculate that the balance of resources applicable to the present situation favors their opponents.

Perhaps the most troubling response appears in the extreme right column of Figure 5. The decision group experiences threat to their survival goals and the reduction in effective cognitive processing that follows from severe stress. Rational calculations that in the absence of stress would lead to accommodative

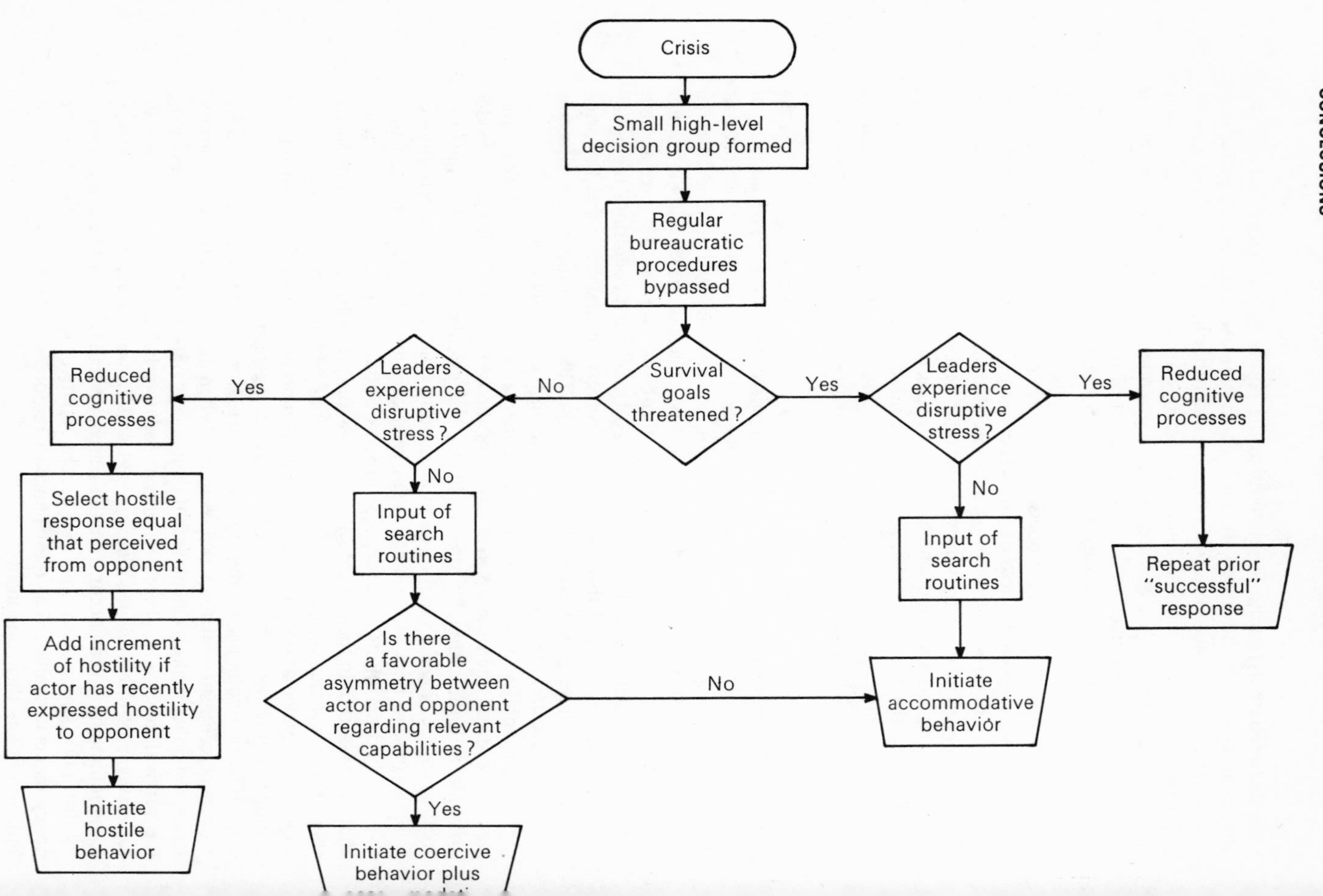
Crisis
Small high-level decision group formed
Regular bureaucratic procedures bypassed
Survival goals threatened?
Yes
No
Leaders experience disruptive stress?
Yes
No
Reduced cognitive processes
Repeat prior "successful" response
Input of search routines
Initiate accommodative behavior
Leaders experience disruptive stress?
No
Yes
Input of search routines
Is there a favorable asymmetry between actor and opponent regarding relevant capabilities?
No
Yes
Initiate coercive behavior plus
Reduced cognitive processes
Select hostile response equal that perceived from opponent
Add increment of hostility if actor has recently expressed hostility to opponent
Initiate hostile behavior

behavior become unlikely. Experiencing reductions in cue awareness, restricted time perspectives, and rigidity in perceptions and cognitive processing, the policy makers fall back on their prior experiences and equate the present situation with a previous one to which a successful response was made. In a "knee-jerk" reaction that may be quite inappropriate to the present crisis the policy makers may do nothing, escalate sharply, or suddenly capitulate. If the crisis continues through multiple cycles, responses that initially passed through the extreme left-hand path in Figure 5 will shift to the extreme right when the exchange of hostilities has increased to the point that threat to survival goals occurs.

The proposed integrative model remains incomplete. We noted that it does not account for all the propositions in the other models. Furthermore, the dynamic processes between parties that are necessary for systematic analysis have not been considered. To include the interaction would require determining the opponent's processes and responses to the initial reactions of the actor diagrammed in Figure 5 plus a means of introducing these further inputs into the present model. Such expansion exceeds the basic inventory of propositions abstracted from this book. What the integrative model does provide is one way of connecting the various models introduced in this chapter and a possible explanation for the diverse outcomes associated with actual crises. Its elaboration or replacement awaits the further study of international crises.

APPENDIX

The ten original studies of international crisis presented in this volume (Chapters 2–11) provide the source for the 311 empirically testable propositions presented in this Appendix. The propositions are listed by chapter and within each chapter according to the order in which they appear in the text. The parenthetical comment following the statement of each proposition indicates the type of evidence the author advanced for that relationship and—when statistical analysis is performed—whether the proposition is supported or not supported. Five categories of evidence are reported: (1) illustrations, (2) simulation, (3) events data, (4) content analysis, and (5) interviews/questionnaires. In many cases the abstractors restated the original hypotheses in order to establish good propositional form without reproduction of large sections of the author's work. Page references allow the reader to check each author's original formulation of the relationship.

JAMES A. ROBINSON, CHAPTER 2

1. The longer the period of time available for response, the greater the search for alternatives (p. 23; illustration: Korean War vs. Bay of Pigs).

2. As task complexity increases, perception of response time decreases (p. 25; illustration: Britain's first attempts to secure membership in the Common Market—1960–1962).

3. In a crisis as opposed to a noncrisis decision situation, alternatives are less likely to be given (p. 26).

4. In a crisis situation, the search for alternatives constitutes a substantial portion of decision-making time (p. 26).

5. The greater the efficiency of information processing within an organization, the more likely will warnings about impending events reach top-level decision makers (p. 28; illustration: Korean crisis).

6. In a crisis as opposed to noncrisis situation, decision makers tend to focus attention exclusively on the crisis, postponing action on other matters that may originally have had a higher priority on their scale of values (p. 33; illustration: Cuban missile crisis).

7. In a crisis as opposed to noncrisis situation, the probabilities of personal exhaustion and physical risk to decision makers increase (p. 33; illustration: Cuban missile crisis).

8. In a crisis as opposed to noncrisis situation, the predictability of an adversary's response is reduced (p. 34).

9. In a crisis as opposed to noncrisis situation, problems tend to be brought to the top of the organizational hierarchy for consideration (p. 34).

GLENN D. PAIGE, CHAPTER 3

10. In a crisis as opposed to a noncrisis situation, decisions tend to be made by small ad hoc decisional units (p. 45; illustration: Korean crisis, Cuban missile crisis).

11. As the level of crisis increases, leader solicitation of subordinate advice increases (p. 46; illustration: Korean crisis, Cuban missile crisis).

12. As the level of crisis increases, the clarity of differentiation between task leadership and emotional affect leadership roles increases (p. 46; illustration: Korean crisis, Cuban missile crisis).

13. In a crisis as opposed to noncrisis situation, search behaviors for new information about the threatening event increase (p. 47; illustration: Korean crisis, Cuban missile crisis).

14. The greater the crisis, the more information about it tends to be elevated to the top of the organizational hierarchy (p. 47; illustration: Korean crisis, Cuban missile crisis).

15. The greater the crisis, the greater the propensity to supplement information about the objective state of affairs with information drawn from past experience (p. 48; illustration: Korean crisis, Cuban missile crisis).

16. The more the flow of past unconfirmed warnings that the crisis precipitating event will occur, and the more face-to-face assurance by an opponent that the action is not contemplated, the greater the emotional shock when the event takes place (p. 48; illustration: Cuban missile crisis).

17. In a crisis as opposed to noncrisis situation, a dominant goal-means value complex is evoked that persists as an explicit or implicit guide to subsequent responses (p. 49; illustration: Korean crisis, Cuban missile crisis).

18. In international crisis as opposed to noncrisis decision making, explicit general discussion of the domestic political implications of the event or of intended action decreases (p. 49; illustration: Korean crisis, Cuban missile crisis).

19. The greater the reliance on group problem-solving processes, the greater the consideration of alternatives (p. 51; illustration: Cuban missile crisis).

20. The longer the decision time, the greater the conflict within decisional units (p. 52; illustration: Cuban missile crisis).

21. The longer the decision time, the greater the investment of emotional affect in policy and personal differences (p. 52; illustration: Cuban missile crisis).

22. The longer the decision time, the greater the needs for effective leadership within decisional units (p. 52; illustration: Cuban missile crisis).

23. The longer the decision time, the greater the achievement of decisional unit consensus through processes of changes in individual positions and withdrawal of dissenters (p. 52; illustration: Cuban missile crisis).

24. The longer the decision time, the greater the efforts to secure decisional reversals by proponents of different courses of action (p. 52; illustration: Cuban missile crisis).

25. The longer the decision time, the greater the consultation with persons outside the core decisional unit (p. 52; illustration: Cuban missile crisis).

26. The longer the decision time, the greater the proliferation of functionally specific subordinate organizations designed to provide the decision makers with premises for choices (p. 52; illustration: Cuban missile crisis).

27. The longer the decision time, the greater the probability that the dominant leader will seek confirmation of the soundness of his choices from trusted friends before public commitment (p. 52; illustration: Cuban missile crisis).

28. The longer the decision time, the greater inputs of written versus oral information and interpretation (p. 52; illustration: Cuban missile crisis).

29. The longer the decision time, the greater the probability of information disclosures that may facilitate unfavorab leopponent counter-action (p. 52; illustration: Cuban missile crisis).

30. As decision time increases, shifts in the value bases designed to legitimate the crisis responses will tend to occur (p. 52; illustration: Cuban missile crisis).

31. The longer the decision time, the greater efforts to communicate with allies on a face-to-face basis (p. 52; illustration: Cuban missile crisis).

32. The longer the decision time, the greater the frequency of public deception to conceal information about the way in which the crisis is perceived and about the probable costs of coping with it (p. 52; illustration: Cuban missile crisis).

33. The longer the decision time, the more alternative courses of action are considered (p. 52; illustration: Cuban missile crisis).

34. In a crisis situation, use of an ultimatum tends to create short decision time (p. 52; illustration: Korean crisis, Cuban missile crisis).

35. The higher the level of rapid deprivational action pursued, the shorter the decision time (p. 52; illustration: Korean crisis, Cuban missile crisis).

36. The greater the overloading of the problem-solving capacities of decision makers, the shorter the decision time (p. 52; illustration: Korean crisis, Cuban missile crisis).

37. In a crisis situation, avoidance of the use of an ultimatum tends to provide more extended time for decision (p. 52; illustration: Korean crisis, Cuban missile crisis).

38. The slower the action in relation to opponent values, the more extended time for crisis decision deliberations (p. 52; illustration: Korean crisis, Cuban missile crisis).

39. The greater the minimization of other problems thrust upon a decision maker's attention, the more extended time for crisis decision deliberations (p. 52; illustration: Korean crisis, Cuban missile crisis).

40. In a crisis as opposed to a noncrisis situation, there is a tendency to perceive one central value as severely threatened and then to distinguish many other important values related to it (p. 52; illustration: Korean crisis, Cuban missile crisis).

41. As targeting on values of high priority in the opponent's normative hierarchy increases, the sense of threat to values will also tend to increase (p. 53; illustration: Korean crisis, Cuban missile crisis).

42. As many values are threatened simultaneously, the sense of threat to values will tend to increase (p. 53; illustration: Korean crisis, Cuban missile crisis).

43. As past threats to values are increasingly evoked, the sense of threat to values will tend to increase (p. 53; illustration: Korean crisis).

44. The closer an adversary acts to one's psychological space, the greater the sense of threat to one's values (p. 53; illustration: Cuban missile crisis).

45. The greater the extent to which an event is anticipated, even specifically, while the opponent gives explicit reassurances that the action will not be taken, the stronger the emotional reaction when the event occurs (p. 53; illustration: Cuban missile crisis).

OLE R. HOLSTI, CHAPTER 4

46. As stress increases in a crisis situation, time will be perceived as an increasingly salient factor in decision making (p. 63; content analysis : not supported).

47. As stress increases in a crisis situation, decision makers will become increasingly concerned with the immediate rather than the distant future (p. 63; content analysis: supported).

48. The greater the perception of first-strike capabilities in the opponent, the greater the tendency for a nation to increase its own preparations for military action (p. 66; illustration: 1914 case).

49. In a crisis as opposed to a noncrisis situation, decision makers will tend to perceive their own range of alternatives to be more restricted than those of their adversaries (p. 67; content analysis: supported).

50. In a crisis as opposed to a noncrisis situation, decision makers will tend to perceive their allies' range of alternatives to be more restricted than those of their adversaries (p. 69; content analysis: supported).

51. As stress increases, decision makers will perceive the range of alternatives open to themselves to become narrower (p. 70; content analysis: supported).

52. As stress increases, decision makers will perceive the range of alternatives open to adversaries or potential adversaries to expand (p. 70; content analysis: not supported).

53. The higher the stress in a crisis situation, the heavier the overload of channels of communication (p. 73; content analysis : supported).

54. The higher the degree of participation in the early stages of crises, the less the increase in daily average message volume (p. 73 ; content analysis : supported).

55–56. The higher the stress in a crisis situation, the greater is the volume of messages from officials abroad to their central decision makers as compared with the message volume from (a) central decision makers to officials abroad, (b) the central decision makers of one nation to those of another, and (c) central decision makers to other decision makers in the same nation (p. 73; content analysis: supported).

57. The higher the stress in a crisis situation, the greater the tendency to rely upon extraordinary or improvised channels of communication (p. 75; content analysis: supported).

58. The higher the stress in a crisis situation, the higher the proportion of intra-coalition as against inter-coalition communication (p. 75; content analysis: supported).

59. As misperception of the level of violence in the action of the opponent increases, the probability of escalation of the conflict will tend to increase (p. 78; illustration: 1914 case, Cuban missile crisis).

CHARLES A. McCLELLAND, CHAPTER 5

60. In a crisis as opposed to a noncrisis situation, the simple volume of action between conflict parties will tend to increase (p. 90; events data: supported).

61. As change from noncrisis to crisis period occurs, a "fanning out" rather than "channeling in" movement takes place (p. 92; events data: supported).

62. In a crisis as opposed to a noncrisis situation, there is an increase in the prevalence of force and violence (p. 96; events data: supported).

63. Conflict deeds tend to increase slightly in the uptrend phase of a crisis and decrease more strongly in the downturn or abatement phase (p. 97; events data: supported).

64. As a shift across the turning point from crisis uptrend to crisis downtrend occurs, attempts to settle and settlement interactions will tend to increase (p. 97; events data: supported).

65. Abatement in a crisis situation increases the frequency of attempts to settle (p. 101; events data: supported).

66. Abatement in a noncrisis situation decreases the frequency of attempts to settle p. 101; events data: supported).

HOWARD H. LENTNER, CHAPTER 6

67. In a crisis as opposed to a noncrisis situation, decision makers tend not to make distinctions between the involvement of personal, organizational, and national threat (p. 117; interviews/questionnaires: supported).

68. In a crisis situation, neither instability nor military action necessarily tends to occur (p. 119; interviews/questionnaires: supported).

69. In a crisis as opposed to a noncrisis situation, uncertainties in formulating alternatives for dealing with a situation increase (p. 119; interviews/questionnaires: supported).

70. In a crisis as opposed to a noncrisis situation, control over events and their effects is reduced (p. 119 ; interviews/questionnaires: confirmed).

71. In a crisis as opposed to a noncrisis situation, unusual organizational behavior increases (p. 120; interviews/questionnaires: supported).

72. A crisis in general may be anticipated, but its particular form and dynamics will contain an element of surprise (p. 122; interviews/questionnaires).

73. Those decision makers who do not conceive of crisis as always acute are likely to believe that uncertainty is only occasionally an element in crisis (p. 125; interviews/questionnaires: supported).

74. If a decision maker views crises as always acute then he will also tend to think that a crisis always precipitates higher level concern and higher level decision making (p. 126; interviews/questionnaires: supported).

75. If a decision maker does not view crises as always acute, he will then be less likely to think that such situations always lead to higher level concern and higher level decision making (p. 126; interviews/questionnaires: supported).

76. If a decision maker views crises as always acute, he will then tend to maintain that decision time decreases and time pressures increase in a crisis situation (p. 126; interviews/questionnaires: supported).

77. If a decision maker does not view crises as always acute, then he will tend to think that a crisis does not raise tensions (p. 126; interviews/questionnaires: supported).

78. In a crisis situation, clarity as to which decision makers need information increases (p. 127; interviews/questionnaires: supported).

79. In a crisis as opposed to a noncrisis situation, the information available to participants is inadequate (p. 127; interviews/questionnaires: not supported).

80. In a crisis as opposed to a noncrisis situation, the information avail-

able to participants is overwhelming (p. 127; interviews/questionnaires: not supported).

81. In a crisis as opposed to a noncrisis situation, the number of alternatives for action by decision makers is reduced (p. 128; interviews/questionnaires: not supported).

82. In a crisis as opposed to a noncrisis situation, the sense of urgency which produces stress and anxiety among those alerted is increased (p. 129; interviews/questionnaires: supported).

83. In a crisis as opposed to a noncrisis situation, tension among the participants handling the situation increases (p. 129; interviews/questionnaires: supported).

84. In a crisis as opposed to a noncrisis situation, decision making becomes increasingly centralized (p. 130; interviews/questionnaires: supported).

85. In a crisis situation, an adversary country is somewhat more often involved than either an ally or neutral country (p. 132; interviews/questionnaires: supported).

86. U.S. involvement in a foreign policy crisis does not necessarily produce a crisis situation for the rest of the world (p. 132; interviews/questionnaires: not supported).

DINA A. ZINNES, JOSEPH L. ZINNES, AND ROBERT D. McCLURE CHAPTER 7

87. In a crisis as opposed to a noncrisis situation, the amount and intensity of hostile messages increases (p. 140).

88. If a decision maker perceives another state as extremely hostile and then receives a very mild message, he is likely to alter his perception, but he is not likely to do so drastically (p. 140; content analysis: supported).

89. A decision maker's expression of hostility on a given day is a consequence of both his perception on that day and his previous expression of hostility (p.141; content analysis: supported).

90. An alliance's perception of hostility on day $(n+1)$ is determined, in part, by whether or not it perceived hostility on the previous, nth, day (p. 152; content analysis: supported).

91. The probability of repeating "reinforced" response in learning situations is greater than the probability of changing responses following a nonreinforced response (p. 152; content analysis: supported).

92. In the absence of hostile messages and when there is no prior perception of hostility, decision makers should continue to perceive no hostility (p. 153; content analysis: supported).

93. If an expression of hostility by one alliance is received by a target alliance, then a hostility statement in which the perceiver and target belong to one alliance but the perceived belongs to the other alliance should follow (p. 155; content analysis: not supported).

94. In the absence of hostile messages when there is a prior perception of hostility, decision makers should then perceive no hostility (p. 157; content analysis: supported).

95. In the presence of hostile messages when there is no prior perception of hostility, decision makers should perceive hostility (p. 157; content analysis: supported).

96. When there are *no* hostile perceptions, there should be less tendency to express hostility than when there exist *some* hostile perceptions (p. 158; content analysis: supported).

97. In the absence of hostile perceptions, decision makers should express more hostility when there is a prior expression of hostility than when there is no prior expression of hostility (p. 159; content analysis: supported).

98. In the presence of hostile perceptions, decision makers should express less hostility when there is no prior expression of hostility than when there is a prior expression of hostility (p. 159; content analysis: supported).

99. In the absence of hostile perceptions and when there is no prior expression of hostility, decision makers should continue to express no hostility (p. 159; content analysis: supported).

100. If hostility is perceived, decision makers will then continue to express hostility (p. 159; content analysis: supported).

101. If no hostility is perceived, then decision makers will modify their prior expressions of hostility (p. 160; content analysis: supported).

DAVID C. SCHWARTZ, CHAPTER 8

102. Nations outside the bloc will be seen as more threatening than nations within the bloc (p. 169; simulation: supported).

103. Nations outside the bloc will be seen as more unfriendly than nations within the bloc (p. 169; simulation: supported).

104. There will be more hostility transmitted between blocs than within blocs (p. 169; simulation: supported).

105. There is a positive relationship between perceptions of threat and perceptions of unfriendliness (p. 169; simulation: supported).

106. There is a positive relationship between x's expression of hostility to y and y's perception of threat (p. 169; simulation: supported).

107. There is a positive relationship between x's expression of hostility to y and y's perception of unfriendliness (p. 169; simulation: supported).

108. There is a positive relationship between the perception of threat and the expression of hostility (p. 169; content analysis: supported).

109. There is a positive relationship between the perception of unfriendliness and the expression of hostility (p. 169; simulation: supported).

110. There is a positive relationship between x's expression of hostility to y and y's expression of hostility back to x (p. 169; simulation: supported).

111. Frequency of interaction within the bloc will be greater than frequency of interaction between blocs (p. 169; simulation: supported).

112. The greater the perceived threat, the less the frequency of interaction (p. 169; simulation: not supported).

113. The greater the perception of unfriendliness, the less the frequency of interaction (p. 169; simulation: supported).

114. There is a negative relationship between x's hostility to y and y's frequency of interaction with x (p. 169; simulation: supported).

115. The greater the perceived friendliness of allies and the greater the perceived ease of communication, the greater the degree of alliance cohesion (p. 182; simulation: supported).

116. The greater the desire to communicate with potential enemies, the

less likely the adoption or recommendation of escalation (p. 182; simulation: supported).

117. The greater the perception of world threat to a nation, the more likely the recognition or definition of a conflict situation as a crisis (p. 183; simulation: supported).

118. The greater the perception that a conflict deals with important political issues, the more likely will crisis recognition occur (p. 183; simulation: supported).

119. The greater the perception that a world problem poses a threat to one's alliance, the more likely will crisis recognition occur (p. 183; simulation: supported).

120. The greater the sense of national efficacy, the less likely will conflicts tend to be defined as crises (p. 183; simulation: supported).

121. The greater the perception that the international political system (environment) is warlike, the more likely will conflicts tend to be defined as crises (p. 183; simulation: supported).

122. The greater the perception that one's potential or actual enemies are hostile, the more likely will conflicts tend to be defined as crises (p. 183; simulation: supported).

123. The greater the perception of threat emanating from the alliance, the more likely will conflicts tend to be defined as crises (p. 183; simulation: supported).

124. When threat from the world is high but alliance threat is low, national decision makers are less likely to perceive a crisis (p. 183; simulation: supported).

125. When the threat from both the world and one's alliance is high, national decision makers perceive a crisis (p. 183; simulation: supported).

126. The greater the perception of low cohesion, the more likely will conflicts tend to be defined as crises (p. 183; simulation: supported).

127. The greater the perception of the alliance as inefficacious to meet world threats, the more likely will conflicts tend to be defined as crises (p. 183; simulation: supported).

128. When the best perceived alternative alliance is also perceived to be ineffective, crisis recognition results (p. 183; simulation: supported).

129. If one's allies seem unpredictable, decision makers then increasingly perceive world problems as crises (p. 183; simulation: supported).

130. The perception that an alliance is efficacious in reducing world threat is positively related to escalation (p. 184; simulation: supported).

131. A perception that cohesion will be important in order that the alliance be efficacious to reduce world threat is positively related to escalation (p. 184; simulation: supported).

132. Cohesive behavior is positively related to escalation (p. 184; simulation: supported).

CHARLES F. HERMANN, CHAPTER 9

133. In a crisis as opposed to a noncrisis situation, there will be a contraction in the number of individuals exercising authority (p. 196; simulation: not supported).

134. As threat increases, the number of participants in a decision tends to increase (p. 197; simulation: supported).

135. As time decreases, the number of participants in a decision tends to decrease (p. 197; simulation: supported).

136. The larger the nation, the fewer decision makers engaged in all situations (p. 197; simulation: supported).

137. Crisis decisions engage more individuals than noncrisis decisions (p. 198; simulation: supported).

138. In crisis the number of alternative solutions to the situation that will be identified by the national decision makers will be reduced (p. 198; simulation: not supported).

139. As time increases, fewer alternatives are considered (p. 198; simulation: supported).

140. As threat increases, more alternatives are considered (p. 198; simulation: supported).

141. When threat remains minimal, the amount of available time makes little difference in the number of alternatives discussed (p. 199; simulation: supported).

142. As threat increases, decision time becomes steadily more important in determining how many alternatives will be considered (p. 199; simulation: supported).

143. Under conditions of high threat, a very limited amount of time encourages relatively more attention to enumerating alternatives than if time is extended (p. 199; simulation: supported).

144. At the upper levels of threat, if decision makers possess more time, they use it for some other aspects of the decision process than generating alternatives (p. 199; simulation: supported).

145. Under conditions of high threat and limited time, decision makers become too pressured to discriminate between alternatives (p. 199; simulation: not directly testable).

146. When considerable decision time exists, decision makers tend to enumerate more alternative proposals in situations that occur as a surprise than in situations that emerge after a warning (p. 199; simulation: supported).

147. Under short decision time, an anticipated situation leads to more alternative proposals (p. 199; simulation: supported).

148. Situations perceived by decision makers as high threat and short time result in more alternatives than occur in low threat–extended time situations (p. 201; simulation: supported).

149. In crises the rate of communication within the foreign policy agencies of a nation will increase (p. 201; simulation: supported).

150. The rate of communication in short time situations exceeds that in extended time situations (p. 202; simulation: supported).

151. Anticipated situations yield more communication than those characterized by surprise (p. 202; simulation: supported).

152. High threat–short time situations involve more internal communication than their opposite (low threat–extended time) (p. 202; simulation: supported).

153. In crises the rate of communication by a nation's decision makers to international actors outside their country will increase (p. 202; simulation: supported).

154. Regardless of the kind of situation, nations with large amounts of

resources tend to engage in more external communication than small nations (p. 203; simulation: supported).

155. As decision time increases, the rate of external communication increases (p. 203; simulation: supported).

156. The less severe the threat, the greater the importance of decision time in determining the rate of communication (p. 203; simulation: supported).

157. In short time–low threat situations the rate of external communication is higher than in short time–high threat situations (p. 204; simulation: supported).

158. As threat increases in short time situations, the decision makers tend to conclude that other tasks have priority over interacting with international actors (p. 204).

159. Low threat tends to produce more communication than high threat (p. 204; simulation: supported).

160. Decision makers will tend to perceive high threat–short time situations as involving more external communication than low threat–extended time situations (p. 204; simulation: supported).

161. Short time–surprise situations tend to lead to more external communication than extended time–anticipated situations (p. 204; simulation: supported).

162. In crisis as opposed to noncrisis, the frequency with which a nation's decision makers are likely to take action in response to the situation increases (p. 204; simulation: supported).

163. As situational thieat increases, the frequency of action tends to increase (p. 205; simulation: supported).

164. As time decreases, the frequency of action tends to decrease (p. 205; simulation: supported).

165. In both conditions of short and extended time, increases in the threat component produce increases in the frequency of action, but the impact of threat in extended time situations exceeds that for short time situations (p. 205; simulation: supported).

166. As threat increases, the difference in the number of actions between short and extended time situations increases (p. 205; simulation: supported).

167. Nations with large amounts of resources tend to engage in more action than do small nations (p. 206; simulation: supported).

168. More action occurs in situations that the decision makers perceive as involving short time than in situations they perceive as allowing extended time for decision (p. 206; simulation: supported).

169. More action tends to follow in high threat–short time situations than in low threat–extended time situations (p. 206; simulation: supported).

GLENN H. SNYDER, CHAPTER 10

170. As fear of war increases in a nuclear age, a considerable measure of caution is introduced into crisis behavior (p. 220).

171. As fear of war increases in a nuclear age, the threshold of challenge or provocation above which statemen feel themselves willing or bound to fight is raised (p. 220).

172. As fear of war increases in a nuclear age, a wide variety of moves which in former times might have triggered war are released for coercive purposes (p. 220).

173. As fear of war increases in a nuclear age, military force in general tends to be transformed from an instrument of direct physical coercion to one of psychological or political influence (p. 220).

174. As war becomes too costly and risky, crises tend to take the place of war in the resolution of conflict, at least between great powers (p. 220).

175. In a multipolar system leading states have less flexibility in their choice of tactics because of the need to accommodate the wishes of lesser allies (p. 220; illustration: nineteenth-century Europe).

176. In a bipolar world great powers are less concerned about shaping tactics to suit allies because they are less dependent on them (p. 221; illustration: twentieth-century).

177. The greater the uncertainty in each party's image of the other's alternatives and incentives, the greater the possible effect on the outcome of the bargaining process and "tactical" bargaining power (p. 222).

178. If the credibility of the other's threat or commitment is perceived as higher than the critical risk threshold, then the party must give in; if it is lower, the party will continue to stand firm (p. 227).

179. If both parties feel that the credibility of the opponent's threat of firmness is lower than their own critical risk, both may then firmly commit themselves and the outcome is war (p. 227).

180. If each party perceives that the credibility of the other's threat is higher than its own criticial risk, neither can then afford the risk of standing pat on its critical position and the stage is set for compromise (p. 227).

181. As one nation reduces its apparent net cost of war, the credibility of that nation's threat increases (p. 229).

182. As one nation increases its apparent valuation of the stakes, the credibility of that nation's threat increases (p. 229).

183. As a nation increases its apparent probability of firmness without changing its payoffs, the credibility of that nation's threat increases (p. 230).

184. As the adversary's estimate of his net costs of war increases, his critical risk decreases (p. 230).

185. As the adversary's estimate of the stakes is devalued, his critical risk decreases (p. 230).

186. In a crisis, the parties try to impress each other with their high valuation of the object at stake and the dire consequences for themselves of backing down (p. 231; illustration: U.S. in the successive Berlin crises of 1958 to 1962).

187. As the adversary increasingly accepts the objective plausibility of the claim of interdependence of commitments, the effectiveness of the interdependence-of-commitments tactic increases (p. 234).

188. As the adversary increasingly perceives the actor's commitment to the interdependence-of-commitments tactic, the effectiveness of that tactic increases (p. 234).

189. Assertion that the present case is "special" or unique tends to produce decoupling in a crisis situation (p. 234).

190. Declaring that the present issue is not intrinsically important for the opponent tends to produce decoupling in a crisis situation (p. 234).

191. Claiming the finality of a demand tends to produce decoupling in a crisis situation (p. 234; illustration: Hitler and the Sudetenland).

192. If the actor invokes the common interest of all humanity in avoiding

war, the opponent's critical risk then decreases (p. 234; illustration: Cuban missile crisis).

193. If the actor claims the status quo is illegitimate, the opponent's critical risk then decreases (p. 235; illustration: Khrushchev's claims in the Berlin crisis).

194. In a crisis, the defending side tends to invoke the sanctity and legitimacy of the status quo to increase the credibility of its threat (p. 235; illustration: Cuban missile crisis).

195. The public communication of threats and demands tends to increase their credibility (p. 237).

196. A communication carries greater weight, the more authoritative the source (p. 237).

197. As the severity of threats increases, the use of lower level decision makers to issue these threats also increases (p. 237; illustration: Quemoy crisis of 1958, Cuban missile crisis).

198. In a crisis, certain specific persons and personnel tend to carry important symbolic significance as communicators (p. 238; illustration: Berlin crisis, 1961).

199. In a crisis situation, private individuals may be usefully co-opted for bargaining purposes (p. 238; illustration: Cuban missile crisis).

200. In a multipolar as opposed to a bipolar system, alliance factors tend to be influential in coercive situations (p. 238; illustration: nineteenth-century Europe).

201. When a challenge is to interests shared by alliance members, but in different degrees, the alliance may face a problem in concerting upon a bargaining position (p. 240; illustration: Berlin crisis, 1958–1962).

202. In general, a firm commitment strengthens bargaining power vis-à-vis the adversary but weakens bargaining power vis-à-vis the ally (p. 240; illustration: 1914 case).

203. In a crisis situation, the parties are often at least as much concerned about their common interest in avoiding war as they are about getting their way (p. 241; illustration: Cuban missile crisis).

204. If violence breaks out in a conflict, an uncontrollable pattern of interaction then tends to develop (p. 241; illustration: Cuban missile crisis).

205. If violence breaks out in a conflict, there is then at least the possibility that military commanders will react more or less automatically and independently according to preset plans (p. 241).

206. The existence of rigid military plans tends to lead to a sense of uncontrollability in a conflict situation (p. 241; illustration: Russian and German mobilization plans prior to World War I).

207. In a crisis situation, emotional or irrational factors tend to produce "psychological" compulsions toward action or reaction (p. 241).

208. Risk manipulation will be used only by the party who is confident that the risk will be more burdensome to the opponent than to himself (p. 242).

209. Confidence of risk as more burdensome to the opponent than to oneself depends on a belief that the object at stake is worth considerably more to him than to the adversary, or that the subjective cost of war is greater to the adversary (p. 242).

210. In a crisis situation, statesmen are usually more concerned with avoiding or minimizing autonomous risks than with deliberately heightening them (p. 242; illustration: Cuban missile crisis).

211. In physical crisis moves, risk reduction usually seems to take priority over coercive "risk manipulation" (p. 243).

212. If a party believes that a certain type of event or a certain level of escalation will subject him to "compulsions" beyond his control, communicating this credibly to the adversary may serve both a coercive and a disaster-avoidance function (p. 244).

213. If a party is warned that a change in his behavior is necessary to prevent things from getting out of control, he is then less likely to react emotionally or irrationally than if he is threatened (p 244).

214. The more centralized the decision process, the more likely the avoidance of inadvertent war (p. 244).

215. A decision maker in control is more subject to coercion than one who is not (p. 244).

216. If leading allies exercise firm control in a conflict situation, disaster is more likely to be avoided (p. 244; illustration: 1914 case).

217. During the high-tension phase of a crisis, the parties are likely to feel most strongly the need for mutual collaboration in moving back from the brink (p. 245).

218. During the high-tension phase of a crisis, the parties tend to project an image of control, both over the actions of their military subordinates and over their own passions (p. 245).

219. If one party appears irresponsibly unpredictable or ineffective, the other will be reluctant to initiate tension-dampening moves (p. 245).

220. If one party to a conflict fears unauthorized escalation by his opponent's military commander, he will then engage in a pre-emptive attack (p. 245).

221. Assertions of lack of control or pretenses of irrationality tend to be used in the low-tension as opposed to high-tension phase of a crisis, (p. 245; illustration: Cuban missile crisis).

222. If a committal act is not physical and highly visible, then the enemy may not perceive that alternatives or incentives have been altered so that the actor is, in fact, committed (p. 246; illustration: Berlin crisis, 1961).

223. A provocative commitment tends to trigger a counter-commitment by the opponent (p. 246; illustration: Cuban missile crisis).

224. If a party is determined to fight but is not sure the opponent realizes this, then a firm clear commitment made early in the crisis may avert war by miscalculation (p. 246).

225. Strong coercive action in the dimension which one does control tends to pre-empt escalation , from noncontrollable elements (p. 246; illustration: Cuban missile crisis).

226. Maximum clarity in threats tends to produce maximum credibility (p. 247).

227. In a conflict situation, ambiguity tends to preserve options (p. 247).

228. In a conflict situation, ambiguity minimizes costs and risks in the event a threat fails in its aim (p. 247).

229. In a conflict situation, an ambiguous threat tends to minimize provocation (p. 247).

230. If threats are ambiguous early in the crisis, then the opportunity to escalate pressure on the opponent increases (p. 248).

231. If feedback is obtained from the adversary's reaction to earlier signals,

the opportunity to better judge the probable effectiveness of firmer commitment is increased (p. 248; illustration: Berlin crisis, 1961).

232. Formulation of details of compliance by the capitulating party tends to reduce the degree of humiliation experienced by that party (p. 248; illustration: 1870 Franco-German crisis).

233. In a conflict situation, ambiguity of demands increases the ease with which the threatener can interpret any particular behavior as compliance (p. 248).

234. In a conflict situation, use of a code system tends to preserve flexibility (p. 249).

235. In a conflict situation, use of a code system tends to remove much of the emotional or provocative content from threatening communications (p. 249).

236. Starting low on the escalation ladder tends to keep open a wide range of options and maximizes the chances of avoiding disaster (p. 249).

237. Starting low on the escalation ladder tends to allow for feedback (p. 250; illustration: Berlin crisis, 1961).

238. A low-level action tends to communicate resolve more credibly than merely verbal threats to act at a higher level (p. 250; illustration: Cuban missile crisis).

239. Starting low on the escalation ladder tends to communicate a timid, indecisive attitude to one's opponent (p. 250).

240. Starting low on the escalation ladder tends to prolong the confrontation (p. 250; illustration: 1914 case).

241. If the self-interests and inherent power of the parties are roughly symmetrical, both parties will then tend to avoid capitulation (p. 251).

242. The greater the concession offered, the more likely the adversary will accept (p. 251).

243. The closer a party moves to the core of an issue, the firmer his stand on that issue (p. 251).

244. Concession tends to reduce the opponent's threshold of critical risk (p. 251).

245. If the conceder's threat credibility is higher than the other's critical risk, the other party will then accept the concession rather than continue the conflict (p. 251).

246. When the party offers a concession, it may be interpreted as a weakening of resolve (p. 251).

247. An ambiguous offer tends to protect a party's self-interest in the issue at stake (p. 252).

248. Clarity in offers and concessions tends to maximally promote the primary aim of accommodation but works against the constraint of protecting self-interest (p. 252).

249. "Preserving options" or "starting low" in the accommodative process tends to make a settlement more likely with minimal or acceptable costs to the constraint of self-interest (p. 253).

250. If an extreme amount of coercive pressure is applied to an adversary, the adversary will then tend to assume that the only way he can achieve his ends is through coercive means of his own (p. 253).

251. Extreme intransigence may breed intransigence in the other, leading to mutual escalation of commitments (p. 253).

252. If an actor appears too obviously willing to accommodate, he will

then tend to (1) inflate the opponent's estimation of what he can obtain, (2) undermine coercive moves, (3) enhance the enemy's confidence in his coercive moves, and (4) lead to miscalculation (p. 253).

253. If a statesman is confident of asymmetries favoring his country and believes these asymmetries are perceived by the opponent, he is then likely to employ coercion and intransigence (p. 254; illustration: Cuban missile crisis).

254. The greater the degree of "illegitimacy" attributed to the opponent's challenge, the greater the extent of coercion and intransigence employed (p. 254; illustration: Cuban missile crisis, Berlin crisis, 1961).

255. If negotiations are preceded by a clear demonstration of firmness via coercive moves, accommodative sacrifices are then likely to be minimized (p. 255).

256. The use of accommodating gestures in conjunction with coercive tactics tends to reduce the hostile character of a confrontation (p. 255; illustration: Berlin crisis, 1961).

257. Couching an offer of concession in a context of threatening language and action tends to decrease the probability of interpretation of the offer as weakness on the part of the conceder (p. 255; illustration: Cuban missile crisis).

THOMAS W. MILBURN, CHAPTER 11

258. In a crisis situation, fatigue increases as time increases (p. 260).

259. In a crisis as opposed to a noncrisis situation, variations in priorities and perceptions and an increased volume of communications occur (p. 260).

260. In a mutual deterrent as opposed to a hostile situation, ambiguity and deception tend to increase tension (p. 263; illustration: Cuban missile crisis).

261. If allies are the subject of competition in a crisis situation, persuasion and the allies' fear are then the opponents' main assets (p. 263; illustration: 1967 Egypt-Israeli crisis).

262. In a crisis situation, mild stress often facilitates performance (p. 264).

263. As stress increases in a crisis situation, performance generally worsens (p. 264).

264. In a situation of very intense stress, complete disintegration of performance tends to occur (p. 264).

265. The more complex the task, the more likely will stress disrupt performance (p. 264).

266. The more relaxed an individual decision maker, the greater the tendency for stress to facilitate performance (p. 265).

267. The more anxious an individual decision maker, the greater the tendency for stress to disrupt performance (p. 265).

268. Simple learning, such as classical defense conditioning, is usually facilitated by stress (p. 265).

269. The more complex the type of learning (e.g., concept learning), the more likely will stress disrupt the learning process (p. 265).

270. If stress is intense and if it persists, there is a tendency for more recent and usually more complex behavior to disappear and simpler and more basic forms of behavior to reappear (p. 265).

271. As stress increases, the number of cues of which an individual is aware decreases (p. 265).

272. When external cues are not recognized, previously established conceptual sets take on greater importance (p. 265).

273. Under conditions of severe stress, the rigidity of conceptual sets leads to the repetition of prior responses (p. 265).

274. In a crisis situation, energetic active people tend to behave even more energetically and actively (p. 265).

275. In a crisis situation, the anxiety expressed by anxious-prone individuals tends to increase (p. 265).

276. In a crisis situation, repressors tend to repress more (p. 265).

277. People operating in leader roles who are more task-oriented than human relations-oriented, will become much more so under pressure until, finally, they neglect human relations altogether (p. 266).

278. People who are primarily human relations-oriented will, under sufficient stress, pay less and less attention to the task and attend more to the human relations involved (p. 266).

279. In a crisis situation the highest executors and their immediate staffs tend to become involved because of the importance of the values being threatened (p. 266).

280. As crises last longer or become more intense, centralization of authority tends to occur in the decision-making process (p. 266).

281. The more well defined the crisis, the more likely it is to have dominant aspects (p. 272).

282. A decision maker's felt understanding of a crisis increases as his awareness of priority and related events is increased (p. 272).

283. In a crisis the more likely is a wide range of inventoried resources to increase the scope and effectiveness of any response (p. 272).

284. The more acute the crisis, the more energy, attention, and resources are likely to be consumed (p. 272).

285. The greater the dependency on one method or channel of information in a crisis, the more likely the distortion of information (p. 272).

286. Crises increase the tendency to reduce the number of communication channels and to increase the traffic or volume of communication transmitted through any channel which is used (p. 272).

287. The less available are substitutes or replacements for critical personnel or materials, the more likely are those persons or resources to become the source of delay and/or breakdown (p. 273).

288. In crises the tendency increases to seek the support of allies and other friendly actors without providing them with an opportunity to participate in defining the problem or the subsequent decisions (p. 273).

289. The greater the number of audiences observing actions and statements in a crisis, the more restricted is the freedom of action of the negotiator and the decision makers (p. 273).

290. The greater the degree to which commitments are fully disclosed in public, the firmer the commitment (p. 273).

291. The more severe the crisis, the fewer the number of alternatives that are likely to be considered (p. 273).

292. As stress increases in a crisis situation, various costs and side effects of a preferred option tend to be neglected (p. 273).

293. In a crisis situation, increases in set decrease the probability of adaptive solution (p. 274).

294. Crises increase a tendency toward rigidity of perception and thought (p. 274).

295. The more irrevocable an action taken at one point in a crisis, the fewer opportunities one has for control and adaptation in the future (p. 274).

296. The more severe the crisis, the more foreshortened become the decision makers' perceptions of time (p. 274).

297. Increased capacity to delay response tends to deescalate a crisis (p. 274).

298. In a crisis one's own alternatives appear to contract while the other side's options seem to grow (p. 275).

299. Thought processes which are overly simplistic and concrete tend to occur among individuals experiencing crisis, and lead to thinking about the outcome of one situation in zero-sum terms (p. 275).

300. In a crisis as opposed to noncrisis, tacit bargaining and communication is less likely to be perceived as the initiator had intended (p. 275).

301. If threats are communicated as noncontingent, it is then likely that they will be perceived as extremely provocative or the equivalent to announcements of intention to attack (p. 275).

302. The credibility of threats increases when there is consistency between verbal statements and actions (p. 276).

303. The credibility of threats increases when there is consistency between threats and the capabilities of those making the threats (p. 276).

304. The credibility of threats increases when there is redundancy in the communication of the threats (p. 276).

305. Demands to the other side in a crisis which he cannot produce increase their feelings of helplessness (p. 276).

306. Demands to the other side in a crisis which he cannot produce increase their expectations of still further demands or of being attacked (p. 276).

307. Demands to the other side in a crisis which he cannot produce are likely to provoke an attack as a response (p. 276).

308. The more the humiliation of the other side, the more likely are increased costs of any solution to the crisis (p. 276).

309. The more the humiliation of the other side, the more likely is increased rigidity by the other side (p. 276).

310. The more the humiliation of the other side, the more likely is increased time required to obtain a solution to the crisis (p. 276).

311. Increasing demands *after* compliance is positively related to escalatory behavior on the part of the nation complying (p. 276).

INDEX

A

B

C

D

E

F

G

H

I

J

K

L

M

Q

R

S

T

U

V

W

Y

Z